agpies □ murder of crows □ bouquet of pheasants □ kindle of kittens □ bevy of larks □ congregation of plove
of seals □ building of rooks □ sloth of bears □ malocclusion of beavers □ richness of martens □ rafter of turke
ounder of warthogs □ warren of rabbits □ bevy of quail □ mustering of storks □ gaug of elk □ fall of woodcoc
peep of chickens □ business of ferrets □ shrewdness of apes □ pitying of turtledoves □ route of wolves □ pric
flock of sheep □ gaggle of geese □ cete of badgers □ brood of hens □ deceit of lapwings □ string of ponies
□ tiding of magpies □ murder of crows □ bouquet of pheasants □ kindle of kittens □ bevy of larks □ congreg
f ravens □ pod of seals □ building of rooks □ sloth of bears □ malocclusion of beavers □ richness of martens
aw of whales □ sounder of warthogs □ warren of rabbits □ bevy of quail □ mustering of storks □ gaug of elk
n of nightingales □ peep of chickens □ business of ferrets □ shrewdness of apes □ pitying of turtledoves □ rou
□ litter of pups □ flock of sheep □ gaggle of geese □ cete of badgers □ brood of hens □ deceit of lapwings
rs □ colony of ants □ tiding of magpies □ murder of crows □ bouquet of pheasants □ kindle of kittens □ bev
ards □ unkindness of ravens □ pod of seals □ building of rooks □ sloth of bears □ malocclusion of beavers
nt of woodpeckers □ gaw of whales □ sounder of warthogs □ warren of rabbits □ bevy of quail □ mustering
clowder of cats □ watch of nightingales □ peep of chickens □ business of ferrets □ shrewdness of apes □ pityir
ts □ charm of finches □ litter of pups □ flock of sheep □ gaggle of geese □ cete of badgers □ brood of hens
ocusts □ singular of boars □ colony of ants □ tiding of magpies □ murder of crows □ bouquet of pheasants
angaroos □ spot of leopards □ unkindness of ravens □ pod of seals □ building of rooks □ sloth of bears □ ma
□ walk of snipe □ descent of woodpeckers □ gaw of whales □ sounder of warthogs □ warren of rabbits □ bev
oxes □ swarm of wasps □ clowder of cats □ watch of nightingales □ peep of chickens □ business of ferrets
f goats □ trunkful of elephants □ charm of finches □ litter of pups □ flock of sheep □ gaggle of geese □ cete
ove of cattle □ plague of locusts □ singular of boars □ colony of ants □ tiding of magpies □ murder of crows
orpoises □ pocketful of kangaroos □ spot of leopards □ unkindness of ravens □ pod of seals □ building of rook
f asses □ knot of toads □ walk of snipe □ descent of woodpeckers □ gaw of whales □ sounder of warthogs
aterpillars □ skulk of foxes □ swarm of wasps □ clowder of cats □ watch of nightingales □ peep of chickens
□ pride of lions □ trip of goats □ trunkful of elephants □ charm of finches □ litter of pups □ flock of sheep
ovey of partridges □ drove of cattle □ plague of locusts □ singular of boars □ colony of ants □ tiding of magpie
curs □ purpose of porpoises □ pocketful of kangaroos □ spot of leopards □ unkindness of ravens □ pod of sea
sparrows □ pace of asses □ knot of toads □ walk of snipe □ descent of woodpeckers □ gaw of whales □ sound
doves □ army of caterpillars □ skulk of foxes □ swarm of wasps □ clowder of cats □ watch of nightingales
□ school of fish □ pride of lions □ trip of goats □ trunkful of elephants □ charm of finches □ litter of pups
on of peacocks □ covey of partridges □ drove of cattle □ plague of locusts □ singular of boars □ colony of an
overs □ cowardice of curs □ purpose of porpoises □ pocketful of kangaroos □ spot of leopards □ unkindness o
turkeys □ nuisance of sparrows □ pace of asses □ knot of toads □ walk of snipe □ descent of woodpeckers
of woodcocks □ dule of doves □ army of caterpillars □ skulk of foxes □ swarm of wasps □ clowder of cats
of wolves □ bevy of larks □ school of fish □ pride of lions □ trip of goats □ trunkful of elephants □ charm o
ring of ponies □ ostentation of peacocks □ covey of partridges □ drove of cattle □ plague of locusts □ singula
arks □ congregation of plovers □ cowardice of curs □ purpose of porpoises □ pocketful of kangaroos □ spot o
ss of martens □ rafter of turkeys □ nuisance of sparrows □ pace of asses □ knot of toads □ walk of snipe □ de
s □ gaug of elk □ fall of woodcocks □ dule of doves □ army of caterpillars □ skulk of foxes □ swarm of wasp
turtledoves □ route of wolves □ bevy of larks □ school of fish □ pride of lions □ trip of goats □ trunkful of e
ceit of lapwings □ string of ponies □ ostentation of peacocks □ covey of partridges □ drove of cattle □ plagu
e of kittens □ bevy of larks □ congregation of plovers □ cowardice of curs □ purpose of porpoises □ pocketfu
sion of beavers □ richness of martens □ rafter of turkeys □ nuisance of sparrows □ pace of asses □ knot of toad
il □ mustering of storks □ gaug of elk □ fall of woodcocks □ dule of dove□ skulk o
ness of apes □ pitying of turtledoves □ route of wolves □ pride of lions □ s □ tri
rs □ brood of hens □ deceit of lapwings □ string of ponies □ ostentation o ges
et of pheasants □ kindle of kittens □ bevy of larks □ congregation of plover ose o
th of bears □ malocclusion of beavers □ richness of martens □ rafter of turk pac
of rabbits □ bevy of quail □ mustering of storks □ gaug of elk □ fall of woodcocks □ dule of doves □ army o
ss of ferrets □ shrewdness of apes □ bevy of quail □ mustering of storks □ gaug of elk □ fall of woodcocks
ep of chickens □ business of ferrets □ shrewdness of apes □ pitying of turtledoves □ route of wolves □ bevy
ale of turtles □ harras of horses □ hover of trout □ parliament of owls □ exaltation of larks □ labor of moles

ALSO BY GARY K. CLARKE

I'd Rather Be On Safari
The Adventures And Misadventures Of His First 100 Safaris To Africa.

HEY MISTER—
YOUR ALLIGATOR'S LOOSE!

*For the Silver Lake
Public Library —
READ BETWEEN THE LIONS!*

Gary K. Clarke

HEY MISTER— YOUR ALLIGATOR'S LOOSE!

A lifetime of intimate animal adventures

Gary K. Clarke

Director Emeritus
World Famous Topeka Zoo

BARANSKI PUBLISHING COMPANY

Baranski Publishing Company
214 North 2100 Road
Lecompton, Kansas USA 66050

ISBN 0-941974-23-3

Library of Congress Control Number: 2009906717

Draft Interpretation by Joyce and Becca Wells
Manuscript Editing by Dorothy Harvey
Manuscript Preparation by Mike LaRue
Editorial Advisor, Randy Austin
Original Art by Alice C. Sabatini
Photographic Composition by Joe Sutcliffe
Alligator Illustration by Sherry Best
Production Coordinator, Deb Potter
Design Coordinator, Sheri Siebert

FIRST EDITION

1 3 5 7 9 8 6 4 2

Printed in the United States of America

Dedications

Family —
> *To my wife and children, parents and siblings.*

Community —
> *To the wonderful support community of the*
> *World Famous Topeka Zoo.*
> *To the volunteers at the World Famous Topeka Zoo.*

Colleagues —
> *To the superb staffs who served as my teammates.*
> *To my professional colleagues in zoos across*
> *the nation and around the world.*

Intangibles —
> *To the spirit of the young people who attended the*
> *World Famous Topeka Zoo during my tenure.*
> *To the childlike nature in all zoo visitors.*

CONTENTS

Prologue

"Hey Mister—Your Alligator's Loose!"

"Hey mister—your alligator's loose!"

It was one of those crazy dreams that seemed *so-o-o-o* real. I was on an airplane flying to Des Moines, Iowa, to make a presentation. Schroeder, my live-at-home alligator (nearly 4 feet long) was with me, snug in a large leather satchel between my feet.

"*Mister!.* **MISTER!**" The voice in the dream was now shouting, and it felt like someone was actually shaking my shoulder.

"MISTER!" I awoke with a start to see a panic stricken passenger looking at my feet. OHMIGAWD! Schroeder was crawling out of the satchel (which I called my "alligator briefcase"). Nodding a "thank you," I reached down with both hands to shove Schroeder back in his satchel. No luck. When an alligator is pulled backward, its natural tendency is to crawl forward. I knew that.

Now Schroeder was on the floor, moving under the seat in front of me. I was on my knees holding him as tightly as I could, but his strength was greater than mine. His nose was about to touch the back of the shoes of the woman in the seat. Uh—oh! She heard the commotion and was peering back through the small space between seats.

My dream was now a nightmare. How did I ever get in this predicament? And how would I ever get out of it?

Obviously, this was in the days before stringent airport security. And my alligator friend was tractable despite his size. He had accompanied me on lecture tours for years and, while I knew there was no danger, his mere presence could cause pandemonium.

Schroeder was just a hatchling when he joined my home menagerie. Like most baby alligators he would hiss and snap if you got too close or tried to touch him. Later he outgrew his aquarium and we kept him in the bathtub. Occasionally we would forget to advise guests going to use our bathroom about Schroeder, and sometimes without warning he would start hissing while they were . . . doing their business. Then the question would arise on "how did I take a bath?" I wanted to respond that I had scars all over my derriere, but I refrained. Actually we took him out of the tub and let him run around the house while we bathed—so he wouldn't get soap in his eyes.

As he matured he became quite docile and was a perfect animal for lectures. Well known and extremely popular, he starred in hundreds of venues, from preschools to retirement communities, serving as a great ambassador for all wildlife. Certainly I did not want this airplane ordeal to reflect unfairly on his character.

Wrestling with Schroeder under the seat, I had barely gained control when a flight attendant happened down the aisle. She freaked out and ran to the cockpit. Just as I was getting Schroeder back into the satchel, the copilot loomed angrily above me. Word had spread among the passengers. I could hear the whispers up and down the rows: *"That guy has an alligator!"*

Assuring the copilot (and everyone else) that they were safe, I explained I was a zoo director and told about Schroeder in loving terms, while emphasizing that this entire incident was **my** fault, not his. When we traveled together I usually opened the top of the satchel to give him a little air. This time I had dozed off in flight and Schroeder got curious.

This satisfied the crew and calmed most of the passengers, except the woman in front of me. Her ferocious glare implied she wanted to throw me off the plane—NOW!

After completing my program in Des Moines, I dreaded the return flight to Kansas. Luckily, Schroeder's reputation had preceded him. Much to my relief he was greeted at the airport like a celebrity! I even presented a brief program with him in the departure lounge prior to the flight. Even so, Schroeder was not awarded any frequent flyer miles.

Preface

I Love Zoo (a confession)

I have a confession.

Although I ended up being the director of a zoo, I was perfectly happy as an animal keeper. I felt privileged to associate on a close personal basis with countless living creatures from all over the world—anteaters to zebras—and to learn directly from them about their habits, behaviors, individual characteristics, their little known secrets . . . all of the things *not* in the natural history books or on wildlife videos—knowledge you gain *only* from living with them day to day.

I feel so lucky that my central focus has always been empathy with animals. To understand animals from their perspective, to appreciate them in their context, to gain their confidence and trust, to be accepted on their terms, is for me a fascinating and meaningful dimension of life.

When as a youth I mapped out my zoo career, I thought I should be a keeper until I was at least 30 years old in order to gain that much firsthand experience from animals themselves. Then I might seek a curatorial level opportunity in the zoo field. By age 40 or so I hoped to have enough expertise, maturity and wisdom to be considered for a top administrative position.

Well, it did not turn out quite the way I planned: keeper at 18, curator at 23, zoo director at 24. HA! So much for my adolescent agenda. A bit ahead of schedule, but it all sorted out because of strong community support, dynamic volunteers, donors and sponsors, a dedicated staff, a sincere city parks and recreation department, and the advocacy of professional colleagues.

*****

Being zoo director is not a job—it's your entire life. You eat—sleep—drink—breathe—live ZOO, every moment!

You can never 'not be' the zoo director. The animals don't know when it's quitting time, or that Aunt Martha is in town, or the Super Bowl is on, or it's New Year's Eve. It is extremely demanding and totally consumes your energies. You lead a super-charged existence, but it's great!

Things that seem to be totally unrelated to the zoo are part of your continual thought process. You see someone cutting down a dead tree in their yard and you think what a great perch it would make in the aviary. Or you read an article about innovative construction techniques and materials and you wonder if they would work in the zoo.

The only drawback to this wonderful career is that it can be a hardship on your family. In my case I am blessed with a wonderful family: a patient and understanding wife, Margaret, and four children—two boys and two girls. For no particular reason all of their names start with the letter J: Janet, James, Joyce and John. They were born in 1961, 1962, 1963, and 1964. Then we bought a TV set.

My youngsters literally "grew up in a zoo." In the early days, when we had no nursery facilities at the zoo, our home was the substitute. Our household was occupied at times by baby pumas, Alaskan brown bears, and other assorted creatures that needed special care. Since the zoo was a part of the children's everyday existence the animals were accepted as routine. While other children were excited about a trip to the zoo, mine thought it was no big deal. (They'd rather go to the city water treatment plant.)

While I loved every minute as zoo director, I always tried to be careful not to force it upon others. Whenever I was invited to a social function I would talk about topics unrelated to the zoo. But sooner or later someone would ask, "Oh, you're the zoo guy, aren't you?" From then on all any of them wanted to hear were zoo stories—which actually was fine with me.

Being a zoo director follows you everywhere, even when you're outside your own community. Periodically I would travel out of town to professional meetings. Invariably I took along information on current projects or reading material to pass the time on the plane. I might be reviewing schematic designs for a new exhibit or reading an article on animal management. The person next to me would glance over, see this material, and their curiosity was piqued. They would ask what I did, and when I told them, they would (unsolicited) review all of their favorite zoo stories with me.

Sometimes people would not understand what I was doing. One time I was intently studying a technical paper on herpetology, the science of reptiles and amphibians. A nice elderly woman sitting next to me tapped me on the shoulder and said, "Excuse me, young man, are you studying to be a doctor?" "No ma'am," I replied, "I'm reading a paper on herpetology." At that she sat up straight, her eyes lit up, and she exclaimed, "My, that's wonderful. I've been growing roses for years."

Often I needed to be twins. Requests for speaking engagements and programs about the zoo kept me busy three to four times a week, and frequently on weekends. More than once I've had a presentation at a breakfast Optimist Club, a noon Kiwanis meeting, and an evening Rotary dinner

—a full day indeed! It was not a question of doing the same presentation three times. I thought it was important to tailor each program specifically to the group I was addressing. It was important to acknowledge the support and special projects of each organization in the past and to outline the role it played in the continuing development of the zoo. I was also motivated by the fact that many of the members were in more than one organization, and had already heard my jokes.

Speaking locations ranged from the grand ballroom of a downtown hotel, with an audience of several hundred, to a handful of enthusiastic listeners in someone's living room. I was always happy to speak about the zoo. I never really considered myself a public speaker, but I found that if you talk about something you know and love, it's easy. I could have spent much more time on speaking engagements, but I still had a zoo to run and a family to raise. Thank heavens for my great staff and wonderful family. Had I been twins, one of me could have been at home each evening with my wife and children.

Some zoo directors call the constant focus of attention by the news media "the fishbowl routine." No matter where you go, you are recognized. Or almost. I recall one time I was in a downtown high-rise office building, the only person on the elevator. Just before the doors closed an older woman got on. As we were going up I could feel her eyes sizing me up. Then she blurted out, "Has anyone ever told you that you look like Gary Clarke?" Since no one had, this caught me off guard and I said, "No, ma'am." She replied, "Well, I see him on TV a lot, but he's taller than you are." And she got off.

*****

I've always thought that a zoo director was like a symphony conductor. It fascinates me how a conductor can take a group of musicians with various talents and specialized instruments and lead them through a musical score to create a magnificent whole. Separately, each player and instrument has its own importance, but when brought together they create a memorable emotional experience.

And so it is with a zoo.

All of its many elements have to be in harmony: animals, keepers, exhibits, maintenance, landscaping, education, volunteers, visitors and tourists. And just as with an orchestra, each of these elements has to be in tune.

This book tells of my life with animals, from childhood to professional career. It is simply a personal account, together with a number of guest authors (who tell aspects of the story better than I), and supplemental material from various sources. Some sections or chapters were written at the time they occurred; others have been composed just for this tome. Titles of zoo staff members or volunteers reflect the time frame of events. While a large portion of the book is devoted to my tenure as zoo director in Topeka (1963-1989), it is not meant to be an "official" history of the zoo, nor a reflection of activities prior to my arrival or subsequent to my departure. It is, however, intended especially for those who visited and supported the World Famous Topeka Zoo during those years, and to the child in all of us who joyfully emerges with a visit to any zoo.

Over time my duties and responsibilities as zoo director changed. I became more involved with elected officials, various boards, architects and engineers. I was more active with community service, public relations and fund raising. An increasing amount of my time was taken with personnel matters, government regulations, professional organizations, while less of my time was available for the fun stuff of zoobiz: direct contact with animals, schmoozing with visitors, interacting with students.

One of the things I enjoyed the most, but got to do the least, was taking young children on tours of the zoo. We had a trained group of volunteer docents who did this, but now and then I would steal away from the mountain of paperwork on my desk and conduct a tour myself. Even with a zoo full of exotic animals, sometimes the kids were just as excited to see a squirrel run across the walk. Frequently they made comments during the tour that had nothing to do with what I was talking about, such as, "My brother threw up last night," or "Mommy dyed her hair."

One time I had a group of little people, about "this tall," and I was sharing with them all of my wisdom about polar bears. I explained how they have more fur on the bottom of their feet than other bears to give them better traction on ice and snow (and one youngster told me it helps keep their feet warm, too). About that time a bold little guy broke ranks, walked over and stood in front of me, intently looking up. Even if someone is only five or six years old, you feel the stare. So I paused in my lecture, looked down to acknowledge him and said, "Yes?" Abruptly he asked, "How come you don't have any hair on the top of your head?" I remembered something my father used to tell me and replied, "Grass doesn't grow on a busy street."

Without hesitation this little smarty-pants shot back, "Grass doesn't grow on *concrete*, either."

Kind of keeps you humble.

The zoo is like a secret garden.

As zoo director, I held the key.

What a joy each day

to share the allure and magic

in the enchanting lives of

wondrous and incredible animals

with children *and* adults—

to make it *their* secret garden as well.

—Gary K. Clarke

Introduction

Zoos Touch Our Lives

Zoo-going is America's favorite pastime. More people visit the zoos and aquariums in our nation each year than attend all the major spectator sports combined!

Why is this?

I think it is because animals are a universal language. They appeal to everyone from two to ninety-two. As our lives become more artificial and complex, we seem to have a greater need to associate with nature and other living things. What better place to do that than at the zoo?

Zoos touch our lives in ways that are accepted and taken for granted—yet they have a major impact and play an important role in our society, even though we don't always recognize it.

Zoos mean different things to different people. To the family, the zoo serves as an exciting, mutual experience. To the student, the zoo is a source of knowledge and wonder; to the tourist, a favorite attraction; to the artist, a place of beauty. To the handicapped, the zoo offers a sense of acceptance—animals make no judgment, and accept everyone for just being themselves; to the mentally ill, a feeling of security—animals ask no questions and make no demands; and to the terminal cancer patient, the zoo can serve as a daily revival for the spirit—a communication with life and nature. I know, because all of these types of encounters happened at my zoo.

Zoos are doing more—much more—than simply exhibiting animals for educational purposes, conserving wildlife around the world, or propagating endangered species for the future. Zoos are creating memories!

Visiting the zoo is a social experience and a prominent family activity in our society. Thousands of times I've seen three generations sharing a visit. It's an experience that can be enjoyed by all family members regardless of age. It bridges any generation gap. Zoo-going can also be a very one-on-one personal experience. If you do exit interviews with three generations you find that each person has his or her own perspective on the experience. It's fascinating to observe how often grandparents see the zoo through the eyes of their grandchildren.

The relationship between animals and people is exemplified in the zoo situation, including the misunderstandings and gross misconceptions that many people seem to have about animals—and about zoos.

Understanding animals leads to a better understanding of ourselves, and the zoo is the ideal place to gain this insight. Yet, most people really don't know how to visit a zoo.

Now wait a minute!

I would venture that most of you have probably visited a zoo somewhere at some time, and maybe even many zoos on various occasions. Who am I to tell you that you don't know how to visit a zoo?

During my many years in the zoo profession I learned as much about people as I did about animals, or at least about people's attitudes toward animals and about visitor behavior in the zoo. Every day I saw a passing parade of humanity—people from all walks of life, every educational background, and a variety of cultures. These people would cruise around the zoo, look at the animals, make such comments as, "Oh, he's ugly," or "Oh, she's pretty," and then say "Let's go home." They didn't get much out of their visit because they didn't put much into it.

If I could, I would like to take each of you reading this, assemble you together as a group, and ask the following question: before visiting the zoo, how many of you have gone to your local library and checked out just one book on your favorite animal? I doubt that more than five percent would answer yes. This should be your first indication that you really don't know how to visit a zoo.

That's like going to a football game and not knowing the rules of the sport, the teams involved, names of the players, records of the teams or how the points are scored. Reminds me of the story of the novice who went to the football game with his good friend, the expert. All during the game the expert was jumping and yelling and cheering while the novice just sat there. On the way home the expert asked his friend what he thought of the game. The novice said, "I thought it was an awful lot of trouble for 25 cents." The expert asked, "What do you mean?" The novice responded, "Everyone kept yelling, 'Get the quarterback, get the quarterback.' "

The novice completely misinterpreted his football experience because of his lack of understanding and inadequate preparation. Many of us do the same thing on a visit to the zoo.

We live in an instant society: instant fast food, instant money at ATMs, instant info via the internet, instant photos on digital cameras, instant communication by cell phone and email, instant television—we zap the remote to zip through a hundred different channels in seconds.

In our culture we do not like to stand in line, and become impatient if we have to wait—for anything. This is quite evident when we go to the zoo. We are conditioned for "instant nature." We expect every animal to be doing what we think it should be doing the very moment we are there to observe it. The lion should be roaring. The elephant should be trumpeting. The eagle should be flying. The rattlesnake should be rattling and the orangutan should be swinging through the exhibit. This is unrealistic but we have been so programmed by films and television to these spectacular behaviors that if the animals are not doing something exciting, we quickly lose interest and move on. Often animals will be in the resting phase of their daily behavior cycle or they are adapting to climatic conditions. Our attention span has been shortened to the point that we fail to appreciate the normal, routine behavior that leads to a better understanding of these magnificent creatures.

The same thing happens in Africa. On dozens of photo safaris since 1974, I have witnessed it time and again. The first animal people want to see is a lion. And the first lions they see are usually asleep, so they are disappointed. Lions in the zoo are frequently asleep as well. It is natural for lions to sleep from 18 to 20 hours every day—either in Africa or at the zoo. So they're not lazy, they're just "doin' their thing"—they're just being lions.

Yet, even as they sleep, there are some interesting things to learn about lions. One technique zoo visitors could use to enrich their experience would be to check the lions as soon as they arrive at the zoo, note their behavior, positions, and the weather conditions. Then check the lions again midway through their visit and once again just before they leave the zoo. They could then note the differences in the position of the sun and the postures and behaviors of the various individual lions. What are the weather conditions? What is the air temperature? Are they sleeping in the sun or in the shade? What is the proximity of other lions to them? Are the other lions asleep? Sleeping is an important part of an animal's daily cycle and the zoo is an ideal place to learn about it.

Everyone has a zoo story. Whenever I complete a speaking engagement, people from the audience come up afterwards to tell me about the time they were at a zoo or aquarium when a particular incident happened. They never forget.

During my many years as zoo director I saw countless students on their field trips to the zoo or in a classroom setting. It was always stimulating for me to see the wonder in their eyes and the expressions on their faces when they learned something new. Frequently I received additional reactions in the form of letters from students. They would write to share with me some of their new-found "facts." After that I usually did not hear from them again—nor did I expect to.

But as time passed I received some unexpected reactions to long past zoo encounters. In the late 1980's I trekked to the bottom of the Grand Canyon with a 55-lb. backpack. As I lay exhausted and grimy on the ground at my campsite, a National Park Service Ranger stopped by to check my permit. He looked down at me and said, "You're Gary Clarke from Topeka, aren't you?" I told him I'd rather not be at the moment. He explained to me that because of a zoo tour I conducted for his class when he was 12 years old he had decided to go into wildlife conservation.

In another instance I had written to the Association of Science Technology Centers in Washington, DC, requesting information on their publications. After answering my inquiry the lady wrote: "You probably do not remember me but I have fond memories of the summer of 1976 when I was a participant in Zoo School. I still remember a few Swahili phrases (specifically 'Jambo' and 'Pah hali pa wan y ma'—or something like that) and all the words to 'Gary Clarke he had a Zoo' (sung to the tune of 'Old McDonald had a Farm'). So good luck for the future and thank you for the part you played in making the summer of '76 a very happy one!"

These examples demonstrate to me the importance and value of the zoo experience in shaping the attitudes and perspectives of young people. I am less concerned about students remembering that giraffes have seven bones in their necks and more hopeful that they gain a greater understanding and appreciation of wildlife and nature. I want the zoo experience to be a positive influence for the responsible stewardship of living things.

I think it is terribly important for us as people to accept animals on their terms, for just being themselves. We should utilize the zoo as a resource to help us understand and appreciate animals.

Animals are fascinating, wonderful creatures. And with all due respect to books and videos, the animal itself is the greatest teacher in the world. The next time you visit a zoo, turn yourself into a sponge and soak up all the knowledge that is readily available. Come away over-flowing with new information.

The zoo is unique because it is **real**. The animals are not on film or the printed page, they are not cartoon characters or advertising gimmicks—they are themselves, alive in all their glory.

With the natural world rapidly disappearing, zoos serve as the last outpost for living fragments of shattered animal populations. With so much of humanity now living in urban areas, zoos provide a way to maintain a connection with the fascinating world of animals.

Zoos touch our lives in very special ways.

Foreword

Applause

By Phil Grecian
Television Personality
Internationally Published & Performed Playwright

I have known Gary Clarke for a long, long time, and here's something I've come to realize: Gary Clarke can do anything.

In the time I've known Gary, he's been a master photographer, a master of advertising and public relations, a master of television and radio performance and ad lib, a master raconteur, a master safari director, a master writer-of-books, and, oh yeah, a master zoo director. There's a legion of other skills he's mastered, a plethora of talents he possesses, but you get the picture here: Gary Clarke can do anything.

And do it well.

When Gary came to the Gage Park Zoo in Topeka it was a rag-tag collection of animalia, including too many spider monkeys surrounded by a moat, a handful of coyotes, quite a few bears (at least one of which was concrete), and three lions: two with cores of concrete, the other, Wonderful William, with a core of hardened arteries.

Employing wondrous magic, Gary Clarke made the Gage Park Zoo into The World Famous Topeka Zoo. He started by managing the career of a promising young painter who happened to be an orangutan, and providing an atmosphere in which a couple of eagles could astound the world. The ape was a hit and managed to earn an impressive national art prize; the eagles laid an egg but, in this case, that's not a bad thing.

Gary got things built—a rain forest, a "Discovering Apes" building, a Lions Pride, a . . . well, he expanded that little zoo beyond anyone's dreams.

Then he rode off into the sunset on the back of a gorilla, calling "Hiyo Silverback!" in his wake.

He had other things to do because, of course, Gary Clarke can do anything.

He named the place The World Famous Topeka Zoo, and he always referred to it that way. He never said, "The Zoo" or "The Topeka Zoo" or "The Gage Park Zoo" or "Knott's Berry Farm" (which would have been pretty silly, now that I think of it). He always referred to it by its full name—given, middle and surname: "The World Famous Topeka Zoo."

And, you know, if you tell a woman she's beautiful long enough, she *becomes* beautiful. And if you tell people it's "The World Famous Topeka Zoo" long enough—it *becomes* world famous, and the people take pride in it.

In the past, Gary has written . . . oh, five or six hundred books about African safaris, I guess (on reflection, maybe not quite that many, but maybe so; Gary Clarke can do anything). I know nothing about African safaris. Closest I've ever come to a safari through the jungle is walking through the Optimists' lot to pick out a Christmas tree.

But zoos, now that's something I know a little about, especially Gary Clarke's tenure at the World Famous Topeka Zoo. From 1981 through 1987 we did a television show for KTWU, the Northeast Kansas PBS affiliate. I'd visit Gary at the W.F.T.Z., we'd talk about animals; sometimes I'd ride them or handle them or carry them.

Or run from them.

I'd do my research, but I have an odd memory that harbors trivia and offers it up at the slightest provocation. Whether I was quoting Bible passages about coneys or waxing eloquent on elephants, Gary would reply, "That's an excellent observation, Phil." I would follow with a question and he would say, "A very good question, Phil," and provide a quick and accurate answer on the finer points of the featured fauna.

It's a rule of television hosting that you never ask a question for which you think the guest hasn't an answer; but Gary Clarke always had an answer, I knew he always would.

Gary Clarke, you see, can do anything.

We did that show for seven years, and it aired in reruns on KTWU for at least another seven before the master tapes wore out. It was fun. It was good television, and Gary was great. I miss the adventures I had doing that show. During one shoot an elephant came up behind me and held me in its trunk in fond and muddy embrace. Another time I sat in the grass with Gary and held a diapered baby orangutan in my arms. I looked down into its sweet and solemn-comic face and broke up. How could you not love a face like that?

Truth be told, I just miss my time with Gary at the zoo. Excuse me, I mean The World Famous Topeka Zoo.

And so I'm glad that we have this chance to visit again with Gary Clarke as our guide. The golden age of The World Famous Topeka Zoo lies here, between these covers. We'll not see its like again, but it's good to remember.

"That's an excellent observation, Phil."

How about you? Do you remember?

"That's a good question, Phil."

Come with me. Let us remember together.

"One of the mild surprises of advancing age
is to discover that part of one's lifetime
has turned into history,
a process which one generally assumes
had come to a halt about the time
that one was born."

—Elspeth Huxley

Part 1

Pink Porpoises and a

Misunderstood Octopus

Childhood menageries (snails and tarantulas) as well as real life encounters with wild animals at Kansas City Zoo, Midwest Research Institute (the infamous snakebite), and Fort Worth Zoo.

Animals are such agreeable friends—they ask no questions, they pass no criticisms.

—George Eliot

Art work by Alice C. Sabatini

Courtesy of the Topeka and Shawnee County Public Library

Part 1

Pink Porpoises and a

Misunderstood Octopus

It Started With a Snail
A Tarantula in the Closet
The Zoo I Never Knew
Final Score: Sea Lions 6, Zoo Keeper 2
A World of Animals
Snakes Alive
SNAKEBITE! The Day Big Red Lost His Temper
Those 16 Little Yellow Pills
Monkeyless Island and Polar Bear Parasites
Keeper Characters of the K. C. Zoo
Days on the African Veldt
Pink Porpoises and a Misunderstood Octopus
Skeletons in my Garage

It Started With a Snail

Being a "Zoo Director" at seven years of age developed a number of useful skills: how to deal with a lack of funding (my allowance was five cents a week); how to manipulate upper management (my parents were tolerant and eventually became supportive); how to operate with minimal staff (my brother was just a year old and in my opinion somewhat incompetent); how to utilize public relations (my grandmother couldn't wait to see my home zoo on each visit); and how to handle disappointment (it was bad enough when my goldfish died, but when my mother flushed it down the toilet that seemed less than a proper interment).

You've heard of the boy who goes around with a snake in his pocket and an orphaned squirrel perched on his shoulder? Guess who? Praise and glory to my long-suffering mother.

The first permanent resident of my menagerie was a rather large snail that I maintained for quite some time. I kept it in a fishbowl and loved to watch it slide up the inside of the glass with that giant foot and those marvelous mouth parts sucking in the algae. I was about six years old. My father liked to travel and we would frequently do weekend trips. While my snail would have been fine over the weekend, I really wanted to take her along. So I devised a traveling Mason jar half filled with water and she'd go wherever I went . . . and seemed to enjoy it. When my mother took me on my first flight on a DC-3, yes—I took my snail along (shades of things to come).

A native Kansan, I was born in Wichita on January 19, 1939. Although my formative years occurred in Alexandria, Virginia and Kansas City, Missouri, I recall visits to my paternal grandmother's house at 1231 South Main in Wichita, a storybook place. Even though it was in a residential neighborhood, there was a railroad crossing at the end of the block. When the crossing signal sounded and the red lights flashed, I would run to the corner and wave at the engineer of the slow moving train.

The first zoo I visited (I was told) was in Central Riverside Park in Wichita. The first zoo I remember visiting was the National Zoo in Washington, DC, at age seven. Little did I dream I would visit nearly 250 zoos around the world by my 50th birthday.

My father had a very strong influence in developing my interest in wildlife and the world in general. As soon as I could read, he presented me with my own membership in the National Geographic Society. He had been a member for years, so I was already familiar with the magazine. Because this was back in the days before they had Junior memberships in the NGS, mine was a full-fledged membership and I received my very own copy of the magazine. I felt very grown-up.

As a young man my father suffered from polio and as a result lost use of both legs. Rather than a wheelchair, he used crutches to get around and developed very powerful arm and shoulder muscles. He could lie flat on his back on the floor, throw me up in the air and catch me when I weighed as much as 30 or 40 pounds. He did not let his physical disability limit his intellectual curiosity and sense of adventure. He was intrigued with the world and read constantly. His automobile was modified with a hand throttle and stirrups on the brake and clutch pedals. He hooked his feet onto the pedals and pushed on his knee to use the brake or clutch.

My father had a great sense of humor and was one of those people who could visit with a beggar or a king, feel comfortable, and be accepted. He worked for the Department of Agriculture and when we lived in the Washington, DC, area in the late 1940's he frequently took me to meet with a variety of people. Some were from foreign countries and it was exciting to meet people of different nationalities. He spoke several languages and often took me to foreign language films. In the evenings he would turn on his shortwave radio and, through the static and wavering tones, I could hear crackly voices from all over the world. What a thrill! Once he identified a country on the radio, he would then point it out on a world map. What impressed me most was that I actually could hear Big Ben striking in London! No doubt these evenings were the genesis of my lifelong urge to travel.

I remember my first BIG trip and it was so typical of my father. He came home from work in Washington on a Friday afternoon and said to my mother, "Let's go to New York City." I was about eight at the time and my little brother Steve was two. My mother hurriedly prepared some sandwiches, put blankets and pillows in the back seat of our 1946 Ford and we were off. My father had the ability to stay awake and drive all night, and when I woke up we were in New York City. The streets were dark and deserted and I remember seeing garbage trucks making the rounds at dawn and sheets of newspaper blowing along the sidewalks, and pigeons everywhere. It was all tremendously exciting.

Back home in Washington we regularly attended the National Zoo and the Museums of the Smithsonian. A favorite activity with my father was visiting pet stores and aquarium shops. Washington had a lot of them. It always seemed so funny to me that you could carry a goldfish home in a little white carton with a wire handle, just like Chinese take-away.

I spent hours fixing up various aquariums. I not only wanted to make them look attractive (exhibit design), but also it was great fun to figure out things for fish to do. I created tunnels they could swim through, seaweed beds where they could hide, and even games they could play. Some people may question this, but you can try it yourself. I'd feed them in different corners of the aquarium and they'd swim back and forth in search of food. I'd put my hand in the water with my fingers extended and they'd swim between my fingers. The best was probably the little red rubber ball (about half the size of a golf ball) that I would float on the water and the fish would swim to the surface and push the ball around. Today in aquariums and zoos these structured activities are called "behavioral enrichment."

My parents divorced when I was ten years old and my mother struggled to support my brother Steve and me back in Kansas City. My father was living in Las Vegas with my uncle when he unexpectedly died of a heart attack at age 47. How he would have loved my zoo career and eventual adventures in Africa!

My mother remarried, giving us a loving stepfather, and eventually the joy of two half-sisters. Our house at 7717 Summit was so small that the attic—with a low, angled ceiling—was converted to a bedroom for Steve and me.

Our neighborhood had the usual assortment of pet dogs and cats and I was a friend of all of them. We owned a black cocker spaniel named Midnight. She was a wonderful dog and delivered her first litter of four puppies in that attic bedroom. What a gift!

Ever since I can remember I had a pet of some kind, usually not of the domestic variety. When you own a few animals considered unusual, you quickly develop a reputation. Some people view you as a curiosity while others turn to you for help (even if you are "just a kid"). They not only ask advice about their pets, but also bring you baby birds that have fallen from the nest, injured opossums, et al. And so your zoo grows . . . along with the rewards and hardships. As I was soon to find out.

A Tarantula in the Closet

Trying to Master Plan my home zoo in the Waldo area of Kansas City was an exercise in futility. Oh, I would spend hours drawing and redrawing the ideal design, only to face the reality that there was so little space available, and even that was disjointed. Hardy animals like raccoons and coyotes were housed in a small detached garage at night, with access to the fenced backyard during the day. Within the yard I partitioned an area with shade, grass, a shallow pool and loose soil that was devoted to box turtles. So many box turtles were brought to me that quite a colony developed . . . and thrived. The neat thing was that the turtles would dig deep in the soil in late fall and hibernate through the winter. What fun to anticipate their emergence in the spring!

In the summers I would ride my bicycle many miles to Swope Park (hard to imagine now) and spend the day in wooded areas looking for lizards and snakes. Reptiles were ideal to keep as they were locally available, did not shed hair or feathers, and did not bark at the postman. Snakes were the most fascinating and only ate once a week. Rat snakes, bull snakes, racers, ring-necks, even copperheads—WOW! At the end of the summer I would sack them in my mother's old pillowcases, tie them on my bicycle, ride out and release them where I found them so they could hibernate for the winter.

What few delicate creatures I maintained year-round were kept in the attic bedroom. One of the most notorious was a red-tailed boa, Victor the Constrictor. On cold winter evenings when I did my homework he was quite content to curl up inside my shirt where it was snug and warm.

And then there was Gertrude the tarantula, who spent her days in the closet, secure in the darkness. When I returned home from school I'd take her out and let her climb on my arms and hands while I did my homework. She was lovely.

My animal friends served as ambassadors for their species in the frequent programs I presented for scout troops, school assemblies, even science fairs. It was wonderful to share them with so many people, and help others gain understanding and appreciation of animal life.

Compared to my menagerie, school was dull. However, I took 7th and 8th grade in the same year and started high school (De La Salle Military Academy) at age 13. To help pay tuition, I worked as a janitor after school each day. When I was 15 I started working weekends at *The Kansas City Star* assembling the Sunday newspaper. *The Star* is a great paper, but this was the toughest job I've ever had! The pressroom was noisy, claustrophobic, and covered with grunge. I stood at a metal table, took advertising sections off the press, "stuffed" them into the Sunday comics (which had been printed elsewhere), shuffled the stack and placed it in overhead conveyor buckets. This was on Friday from 5:00 pm to 10:00 pm or so. Saturday morning I started at 9:00 am and did the same thing, this time with all of the just printed feature sections. Now each stuffed paper was bigger and heavier, so assembly took longer. The work was monotonous and time dragged slowly. Hopefully we finished by 5:00 pm or so, at which point I was very tired, stained with printer's ink on hands, arms, and face, desperate for a bath to get rid of the sweat and filth.

But the worst was yet to come. At 9:30 pm Saturday night the final press run spewed the main news and sports sections. Just when I was so exhausted I could barely move, I faced an eternity of a night stuffing, stacking and lifting bundles of the entire Sunday paper. Every week a certain percentage of the crew failed to show for this last shift, even though they knew they would be terminated with no pay. The rest of us had to do their work *and* ours, carrying on, hour after hour, paper by paper: 11 pm; midnight; the presses kept running; 2:00 am; the conveyor kept moving; 4:00 am; the papers got heavier; the night crept on and I felt like a zombie. With luck, the last paper would be out a little before 6:00 am Sunday morning, and with luck I'd catch the 6:00 am bus. Often I'd miss it by just a few minutes and have to wait an hour, sometimes in freezing weather, for the next bus. And after such agony my take-home pay was—get this—$11.29 for the total weekend. But the job and the pay were important to me, and there was a certain pride when I would see a Sunday Star, knowing I had been part of the process. I read *The Star* yet today.

Working every day after classes at De La Salle left me little time for extracurricular activities, such as sports. No problem; I was not athletically inclined anyway. But I was envious of the jocks. Whenever we had a dance with one of the all-girl schools (St. Theresa's or Loretta Academy), these guys were always the most popular. So, in my senior year, and as ridiculous as this was, I tried out for the *varsity* football team. Never had there been a cadet with so little talent and with less experience. But I made the team, probably because of a sympathetic head coach. A dedicated, inspirational, yet commanding individual, Godfrey Kobets was affectionately known as Coach Kobe.

With absolutely no chance of making the starting lineup, I was relegated to the role of a living tackle dummy for the A-team. Even with helmet and pads, never could I have imagined such punishment! Those guys were BIG and *tough* and **mean**!

But I suited up for every game, rode on the bus with the team, then sat on the bench in my unsoiled uniform and yelled (I was good at that). En route to the bus after each game, the team ran past the cute female cheerleaders from the girls' academies. In order to look like one of the jocks, I would roll around in available dirt or mud, splash water on my head to simulate perspiration, and act out of breath as I ran past them. Whether or not this façade ever impressed the girls, I'll never know. It did, however, boost my teenage ego and fulfill some macho fantasies. However, these were soon to be shattered.

Our team was never very good and our absurd schedule put us at a disadvantage. The first game of the season each year was with Boys Town! Yes—the famous one in Nebraska. Those guys were all tough and in their 20's. We would always lose by a score of 60-10 or so, and half of our team would be on crutches for the rest of the season. Why didn't we play them last? Well, that game was reserved for our anathema, Rockhurst High School. The winner of that game claimed a most coveted trophy: the Little Brown Jug.

The most significant football game of my high school career was in my senior year against Rockhurst. I was part of the team albeit on the sideline. We won the coin toss and elected to receive. To demonstrate utmost support for my team, I stood on the narrow wooden bench for the opening kick-off. Our star halfback received the ball and ran it back for a touchdown! Bedlam reigned, and in the ensuing excitement, I fell off the bench and fractured my elbow. No joke!

Yes, I felt asinine, like a buffoon in a farce. No one believed me initially, but it *was* a valid injury—and I was in pain. My teammates simply roared. When Coach Kobe finally realized the situation, he was exasperated. Not only was this a frivolous distraction from a crucial game, but also the most idiotic football injury he could ever envision.

The father of one of our players, a physician, was the unofficial team doctor, and tended to me. It was decades before Coach Kobe could laugh about the incident at the annual De La Salle Alumni banquets, but to this day I remain a "legend" among my classmates.

While working at *The Star* I dreamed of working at a zoo—not just my home zoo but a *real* zoo. On my 16th birthday (January 19, 1955) I applied for a summer job at the Swope Park Zoo in Kansas City. I was devastated to learn the minimum age was 18, but I recognized it was a sensible policy—wild animals are dangerous and a bit of maturity is advantageous. So, I vowed to apply again in two years.

Meanwhile, I graduated from De La Salle in 1956 with the rank of Cadet Captain, which had been a good learning and leadership experience. And I found another job. Doty Technical Laboratory conducted analyses for the baking industry and I prepared samples for the chemists. The pay was better and the people were great. The only problem was I lived in south Kansas City with no car and the Lab was in Kansas City North. This necessitated walking a mile to the end of the streetcar line, riding all the way downtown, transferring to a bus and finally walking several blocks to the Lab, a time of nearly two hours each way. When I started my freshman year at Rockhurst College that fall, I had to leave my house at 4:00 am each weekday to start work at 6:00 am, then get to class by mid-morning.

In addition to the required first year courses at Rockhurst, I enrolled in the Introductory Zoology course. I was excited at the prospect of some formal instruction, especially at the university level. That quickly turned to disillusionment, as the archaic professor was a disciple of the 18th Century botanist, Carolus Linnaeus, the father of scientific naming. His lectures consisted of writing the scientific classification of the entire animal kingdom on the chalkboard for us to copy and memorize. Ye Gods! I wanted to know about live animals, how they behaved, and where they lived. Zoology lab was just as dismal, with the usual dissection of deceased formaldehyded frogs. AAHHRRGGHH! I wanted to learn about *live* animals, not dead ones. So I spent every spare moment haunting the Swope Park Zoo where I was literally surrounded by life.

At last it was my 18th birthday and I applied for a summer job at the zoo. The first step involved a test by the City Personnel Department which had absolutely nothing to do with animals or zoos, but I passed anyway. Then to the zoo for an interview with the director, who explained the job would entail maintenance and groundskeeping, as well as a chance to work with animals. Out of numerous candidates, I was one of only 12 selected. My first official day would be June 1, 1957. I had waited a lifetime for that proud moment and rushed home with the good news.

The Zoo I Never Knew

So . . . at long last, the big day arrived, the fulfillment of a dream. My first day on the job at the Swope Park Zoo—a *real* zoo. Oh, such anticipation!

In my mind I had played over and over how this day should unfold. First, a special introduction to all the other keepers and, aware of the knowledge and practical experience I possessed, they would extend a warm welcome. Then an extensive behind the scenes tour of the zoo, together with a history of the animals as well as their individual personality traits. Next, a review of the zoo's records and animal inventory, and maybe some reading or research in the zoo library. After a safety briefing on how to work with the more dangerous species I would be provided with my own set of keys and assigned to a "mentor" keeper for detailed training. I couldn't wait!

It was so exciting. I took the bus to the end of the line in Swope Park, arrived early at the zoo, and proceeded downstairs to the keepers' locker room in the basement of the old Main Zoo Building. Built in 1909, the building housed big cats, primates and pachyderms in basic quarters.

After the keepers showed up and signed in (there was no time clock), they sat around the lunch table smoking cigarettes (not the image I had expected) and talked about their cars, their wives or girlfriends, baseball, the weather—everything except animals! How disappointing. Oh, well, I was *here* and *ready!* And wondering which animals I would work with first: lions? hippos? chimps? elephants? polar bears?

It made no difference to me as I had read about and studied them all. And I actually had watched for many hours the individual animals at *this very zoo*, so I knew them on a first name basis. I was READY!

The keepers ignored me so I stood off to one side with the other eleven newly hired summer help. They ignored me, too, as they complained about being tired from having been out late the night before.

Starting time—8 o'clock—came and the assistant director, who really served as the zoo foreman, simply barked out the order, "OK—let's bow and arrow it!" I had no idea what he meant, but soon learned that to bend forward to shovel dung and then stand up straight and toss it was to "bow and arrow it."

The assembled keepers, decked out in rubber boots and pith helmets, grabbed their buckets, rakes, and shovels and trudged up the narrow concrete steps, muttering profanities under their breath. The assistant director then turned to us, the new kids. We comprised what was known as the "chain gang," and our jobs consisted of unskilled labor—mostly grounds keeping and basic maintenance. I was given a large gunnysack (a used feed bag) and an old wooden stick with a sharp nail on one end (a paper picker) and told to go clean the zoo parking lot.

WHAT? No introductions? No orientation? No tour? No animals?

Clean the parking lot! ME? God's gift to the Zoo World! And on my very first day? This certainly was not what I had hoped for, but I wanted to work in the zoo so badly that I would do anything, and dutifully went to the parking lot.

Ohmigosh! Did I ever receive an education! I learned a lot about animal behavior that first day at the zoo, but it was illustrated by the human species. Everything imaginable must have taken place in that zoo parking lot during the previous 24 hours. Yes, there were the usual paper sacks, cups, plastic bags, boxes and garbage from picnics. And while numerous well-marked litter receptacles were present, many people evidently considered the parking lot a public trash dump, leaving everything from dirty diapers to emptied ash trays to beer and whiskey bottles, not to mention—well, I won't.

When visitors arrive at a zoo parking lot and it is neat and clean they take it for granted. If it is dirty, however, this immediately creates a negative first impression and sets the tone for their entire zoo visit. That first day enabled me to understand how important even the most mundane and menial job was, and to appreciate all the behind the scenes unsung heroes (staff and volunteers) who carry out these tasks at any institution. Besides, I was now actually working at the zoo, and decided to clean this parking lot better than anyone had previously!

Zoo Director William T. A. Cully was a wise man with a method. Certainly there was much "non-animal" work to be done around the zoo, but it was also a test to see who among the new recruits was serious. So, for the rest of the summer (and Kansas City summers are H-O-T) we swept sidewalks, painted fences and guard rails, cut grass and weeds, planted trees, unloaded and stacked hay, dug for broken sewer and water lines, cleaned restrooms, serviced vending machines and, yes, kept that parking lot spotless! And this was six days a week. I became very familiar with aspects of the zoo I had never known.

As Mr. Cully had expected, the hard realities of the job disillusioned those expecting glamour and excitement. Every week one of the twelve would simply quit, often without notice, and sometimes not returning for their final paycheck. In those days the main access road and end-of-the-line bus stop for the zoo was on a hill to the east. When someone quit the assistant director would say they went "over the hill." They were not replaced, however, and this increased the workload on the rest of us.

Our busiest times were weekends because of the increase in attendance. Zoo admittance was free and on Sundays we were open from 8:00 am to 8:00 pm, making a long day with thousands of visitors. We never scheduled major maintenance or animal moves on Sundays—too many people. It was a full time job just monitoring the crowd and picking up after them.

Since I had the gift of gab, Mr. Cully pressed me into service on patrol, which meant that on Sunday afternoons I would interact with visitors (many of the old grizzled keepers seemed to resent visitors and tried to ignore them) answering questions and giving directions. This I really enjoyed. I spent my lunch hours reading about animals and often stayed after work to study these wonderful creatures. I was eager for people to know more about them.

We had some of the most magnificent wildlife species on earth, alive and right here in Kansas City, for the wonderment of our visitors. So what was the most frequently asked question? "Where are the rest rooms?"

After being at the zoo for nearly 14 hours every Sunday, we then had to start an hour early on Mondays to "hose the zoo down." Feeding of the animals by visitors was permitted and the concession stands sold peanuts in the shell. On Monday mornings the broad public walkways were carpeted with peanut shells—millions of them—and way too many to sweep. But Mr. Cully had the solution. Using an oversized fire hose with a huge pointed brass nozzle, a two man team (I was the helper/puller) would hose down the walks. Pressure from the fire hydrants was powerful and the person handling the nozzle had to exert tremendous strength to keep it under control (eventually I achieved that status).

Tons—and I mean tons—of peanut shells were blasted to large mesh covered grates over drains, so many shells they would block the flow of water. Periodically we would stop (whew! it was tiring) and, with a strong rake and large coal shovel, I would fill giant baskets with wet peanut shells (they were *heavy)* and dump them in a truck bed to be hauled away. Monday morning crowds started slow, but we tried to be finished and out of visitors' way by 10:00 am. It was exhausting work but I always felt so proud as the golden sun filtered through the green trees onto the wet, black asphalt. The zoo simply sparkled!

Fresh and clean after a long hot Sunday, the zoo assumed renewed vigor. Even the animals seemed energized. Monday morning was the best time to visit.

I must admit that it looked like I never would get to work with animals. But this was all the grand scheme of Mr. Cully. In his long and distinguished career he had seen many aspiring young zoo people start out like a ball of fire and then quickly fade. He figured if a novice stuck with it and did a good job in a variety of grounds-keeping and maintenance chores, then they might have some potential as an animal keeper. Now that I look back I see how valuable it was for me to learn first hand about the operation of the zoo literally from the ground up.

By the end of that first summer I was the sole survivor of the summer help. In today's sports parlance, you might say I started with the untested twelve, made it to the elite eight, on to the final four, and ended with the championship. I was about to be rewarded for my perseverance. Mr. Cully called me to his office and explained, "One of our regular keepers is scheduled for his vacation. We're going to train you to fill in for him during those two weeks."

I was honored, excited, scared to death . . . and just 18 years old!

Final Score: Sea Lions 6, Zoo Keeper 2

Responsibility. That was my concern about the long-awaited opportunity to be a real zoo keeper: zoological responsibility to the animals and moral accountability to myself. The area for which I was to be trained was one of the oldest in the zoo and did not have a glamorous designation such as African Veldt or Peaceful Valley or Main Zoo Building. It was simply— the north end.

North end animals were not the best known to zoo visitors—no lions or tigers or bears, no elephants or giraffes or gorillas. Rather, they were a miscellaneous hodge-podge of species: peafowl, emu, kangaroo and wallaby; American bison and dromedary camel; a South American group with rhea, capybara, tapir, and the four species of New World camel—llama, guanaco, vicuna and alpaca. Other hoofed mammals included wild sheep and goat species—mouflon from Sardinia and Corsica, aoudad from North Africa, tahr from the Himalayas—plus a collection of deer consisting of white fallow, spotted fallow, Japanese sika, European red deer, American elk and Scandinavian reindeer. This exciting assortment totaled over 40 mammals and 25 birds for one keeper—a lot!

Willie, the longtime keeper, was a quiet, short, amiable man with a hunchback. The story was that, years ago, a fully loaded hay truck accidentally crushed him against the rock barn in the zoo's South American yard. After recovering he returned to work without hesitation. Willie was a bachelor and these animals were his life. He knew each individual and had excellent rapport with them. For me this was good and not so good. Good— in that I could learn so much from an experienced keeper. Not so good—as everything had to be done his way and I might not live up to his expectations.

Willie proved to be a good teacher. He never seemed to pass judgment or hold my youth and inexperience against me. Methodically he showed me the daily routine and profiled the behaviors and characteristics of each animal. This is what I had hoped for since day one, and to be honest, Willie was not the individual I would have expected to give me such a gift. Granted, he was not an academic zoologist and knew little about animal species outside of his area, but he took me into his confidence and shared his world. More importantly, he *entrusted* his animals to me, and that instilled confidence.

The first day on my own was a near disaster. Everything that could go wrong did! The animals knew I was not Willie and put me to the full test. Things that were so simple in training were now great imposing obstacles. The camels wouldn't transfer to the adjacent stall, the tapirs didn't respond to the whistle to come out of the pool, the guanacos spit all over me, and the normally docile reindeer became aggressive. Even the birds were a problem. Doing exactly as Willie had shown me, I stepped into the emu yard with arms extended to shoo the birds into the barn for the night— but they turned around and ran right over me!

Eventually the day ended with all animals safe and sound. I was physically exhausted, dirty and a bit beat up . . . but on an emotional high! I had **done it**, and walked to the bus stop that evening with a great sense of satisfaction and accomplishment.

Over the next few days I learned from the animals, and they accepted me to the point that together we settled into a comfortable routine. The two weeks of Willie's vacation flew by and I almost wished he would be away longer. Still, I was eager to "show-off" the north end to him. On his return we toured his area together and he was pleased . . . even impressed. He gave me high marks and Mr. Cully expressed his pride. I needed that as I still had some lingering embarrassment from the "sea lion incident" earlier in the summer when I was still on the chain gang.

The circular sea lion pool was one of the most popular exhibits in the zoo. Built in 1951 it was 90 feet in diameter with water from six to nine feet deep and several islands for the sea lions, one island containing a shelter. Visitors had 360 degree viewing from an elevated walkway around the pool. With ten California sea lions (one male and nine females) there was always activity. Their regular diet was herring and mackerel, which they swallowed whole, headfirst. (Incidentally, the male sea lion is called a "bull," the female a "cow," and the baby a "pup," rather than a calf.)

Every Wednesday the 311,700 gallon pool was drained and cleaned for the week. As the water level dropped, the sea lions came off the islands into the water and eventually settled on the floor. They would then obligingly move out of our way as we worked. Cleaning entailed scrubbing the build up of algae off the concrete floor and walls with a long handled stiff brush, a backbreaking task. Just to get to the bottom of the empty pool was hazardous. We had to walk over a high narrow bridge (with no handrails) to the main island (scary) and then down concrete steps (again with no handrails) slick with algae (tricky). And it was a balancing act as we had to carry all of our paraphernalia (buckets, algaecide, brushes, even a heavy power scrubber which would consistently give the operator convincing shocks) as well.

The public seemed to find this weekly spectacle intriguing. As I would look from the deep end of the pool up to the sky, I would see a complete circle of zoo visitors around the guard fence.

In the summer, with the sun beating down, it was a sweat box in the depths of that concrete hole! And slick! Manning the high pressure hose pushed us backward making it difficult to maintain balance. It took all afternoon to finish the job. And we knew we had to do it again in seven days.

Whenever a sea lion had to be caught for any reason (veterinary exam, transfer to another zoo, etc.), Wednesday was the day to do it, when the pool was drained. One week two specimens were scheduled to be caught, and guess who was assigned the duty?

While they would avoid you during the cleaning of the pool, sea lions could be dangerous when cornered. And to catch one, you had to corner it, risking serious injury. A shipping crate would be placed along the wall and your job was to encourage the sea lion into it with a 4x8 foot sheet of plywood as a barrier, all the while keeping a long handled scrub brush handy to fend off an attack.

The sea lions could easily out-maneuver us and were able to scoot over the wet concrete nearly as fast as they could swim through water. Chasing one was extremely frustrating. After slipping and sliding all over the pool in vain, when you finally did get one almost into the crate, it would charge the plywood and knock you flat on your back. A cheer would erupt from the crowd—they were rooting for the sea lion! And the sea lion's incessant bark—"arrf, arrf, arrf, arrf"—echoing around the empty pool sounded like a mocking laugh.

In the course of my endeavors that day, I was knocked down a half dozen times, but eventually got both sea lions in a crate.

When I went to the keepers' locker room to sign out that night, I noticed that someone had written on the chalkboard: Sea Lions 6, Zoo Keeper 2.

A World of Animals

Something happened . . . unexpected and quite significant . . . in the summer of 1958.

I had completed two years at Rockhurst College in Kansas City, but found academia dull and uninteresting. Hence, my grades were miserable. All I could think about was returning to the zoo for a second season. Even with some chain gang duties I would still be around animals.

Which animals were my favorites? Certainly reptiles were paramount in my mind, probably because I had been able to keep them in my home and observe them closely. Dan Watson had been the longtime reptile keeper at the Kansas City Zoo, and because of my interest and experience I was assigned at the beginning of the summer as his assistant and relief keeper. FANTASTIC!

Except—Mr. Cully, wise and perceptive zoo director that he was, confronted me one day and asked: "Gary, can you get *beyond* reptiles? We have a limited number here and you won't learn much new. I'm a good friend with the director of the St. Louis Zoo, which has one of the largest reptile collections in the country. I could try to get you on there. However, if you want to be a general zoo man, I'll give you as much practical experience as I can and let you work with all species in our zoo." His challenging question caught me off guard and I did not have a ready answer. To buy some time I said I'd like to think about it overnight.

What *did* I want to do with my life and my career?

The next morning I couldn't wait to tell Mr. Cully of my decision: I wanted to be a general zoo man. Yes, reptiles were my first love, but **all** animals were so wondrous that I did not want to limit myself.

And true to his word, he gave me a full range of zoo experiences.

Compared to school, the zoo was alive and brimming with excitement. Every day was a new adventure with so much to learn. *This* was *my* classroom, and I had the greatest teachers in the world—the animals themselves. I felt very much at home in the zoo. All I had to do was be aware, receptive, and patient.

The guttural snarl of a leopard.

The power of a boa constrictor.

The anatomy of an elephant's ear.

The mystery of a kangaroo's pouch.

The vivid colors of a mandrill baboon.

The hiss of a Galapagos tortoise.

The long sharp claws of a giant anteater.

One by one the fascinating secrets of the animal kingdom were being revealed to me—not by books or films or hearsay—but on a personal level by living individuals. What a wonderful resource, this zoo! A world of animals at my fingertips. And what a special privilege to be a part of it. How lucky can a person be?

The standard workweek was six days, and on the seventh (always a weekday) I rested—by going to the zoo! The everyday uniform was khaki pants and shirt, and I was awarded the official patch to proudly wear on my sleeve. The zoo logo was a circle surrounding the profile of a sea lion's head, which was enclosed in a larger circle with the words PARK DEPT— ZOOLOGICAL GARDENS. Headgear was a pith helmet (especially in summer) or a billed cap. On Sundays we added a touch of class with a khaki tie in the afternoon.

Now back to the question posed earlier: What were my favorite animals? Such a dilemma. Here was the situation: every new animal I would meet face to face resulted in a bond, a feeling that united me with the intrinsic nature, quality, and character of that species. If this sounds spiritual, I guess it is.

After my first encounter with a particular species I would urgently seek all the information I could about its life and behavior, in the wild or in a zoo. What I learned always proved to be so enchanting and spectacular that immediately *this* species became my favorite animal . . . *until* I worked with and researched the next one.

Such a quandary.

My days were filled with new animals, up close and personal, and my evenings were busy with reading, making notes, and reviewing what I had learned. Trained as a relief keeper in diverse areas of the zoo, I worked with sloths, otters and anteaters; pelicans, penguins and flamingos; agoutis and coatimundis; sun bears and lesser pandas; swans, geese and ducks; grizzly bears, black bears and polar bears, as well as all of the species at the north end. Later I would be introduced to the big cats, primates, Asian elephants and animals of the African Veldt.

In addition to all this involvement with mammals and birds, I still had my reptile responsibilities, which had expanded as Dan Watson moved to another zoo and I was now Keeper-in-Charge! Fortunately reptiles are not so demanding in their eating patterns as warm blooded creatures, and I could fit them in during early morning, late evening—even on my day off. Most snakes ate once a week and lizards ate every few days. Only the giant tortoises were fed daily. Incidentally, most animals had a fixed monetary value for inter-zoo exchanges, and in the 1950's giant tortoises were priced by weight—$2.50 per pound. Some weighed as much as 500 pounds.

Working behind the scenes with the reptile exhibits provided insight into visitors' attitudes toward them. Verbal comments were clearly audible and most were negative. Yet, people were fascinated, and they wanted to be frightened as long as they knew they were safe. Looking through the mesh top of the exhibit units and then at an angle through the front glass you could see visitors. A young couple on a date always provided predictable behavior: while she gazed intently at a snake, he would put his hand behind her back (or lower), grab her and yell, "Arragh!" She would jump and squeal, sometimes playfully slapping him while he laughed, then they would kiss and make up. Ah, the role of reptiles in romance!

My most bizarre happening with a snake at the K.C. Zoo was when, with the aid of several strong keepers, we were stretching a rather large boa constrictor to record its length. I was facing it and, with both hands, holding the neck just behind the head. Before I knew what happened the boa abruptly broke my grip and bit me with lightning speed on the inside of *both* wrists! Astonished, I saw blood flowing but felt no pain. The other keepers immediately dropped the riled constrictor and fled. I had to catch it on my own, which I did with a burlap bag and snake hook, safely returning it to the exhibit. After that no one offered to help, so we never did get a measurement. In the zoo records it was simply listed as "enormous."

Something else momentous happened that summer. Word had been going around that the zoo might acquire a spectacular new species—one usually found only in the most prominent zoos. It seemed unlikely to me and I wrote it off as a rumor. Then one day the maintenance crew began modifying facilities in the Main Zoo Building. WOW! Could it be true? It was!

July 26, 1958 marked the arrival of Big Man, the first gorilla in the history of the K.C. Zoo. Although weighing only 35 pounds and standing less than two feet tall at the time, he would frequently walk upright in a proud way, with his back straight and head up; hence, his name. I felt he was destined to become a charismatic personality like Bushman of the Lincoln Park Zoo in Chicago, Bamboo at Philadelphia Zoo, Gargantua of Ringling Brothers Circus and Phil at the St. Louis Zoo.

Never did I think I would see a gorilla in Kansas City! I was excited . . . Mr. Cully was excited . . . the whole town was excited.

Big Man was donated to the zoo by Dr. Deets Pickett, a Kansas City veterinarian, and his wife, Jeannie. They had been in the central African nation of Cameroon when a local villager showed them a sick baby gorilla. They obtained the orphan and Dr. Pickett treated him for pneumonia and a yeast infection. Mrs. Pickett cared for him until they returned to Kansas City.

Large crowds gathered daily to see Big Man, and I was lucky enough to be one of his keepers. In the afternoons we would take him outside on the lawn between the Main Zoo Building and the sea lion pool where he would play and cavort to the delight of visitors and keepers alike. Who could ask for a better summer?

One more reference to that critical question, "What is your favorite animal?" This plagued me when I became a zoo director and my official response was: "I have no favorites; I cherish and esteem *all* animals." Certainly a politically correct answer, albeit sincere with a bit of explanation. I *do* like all **species** of animals, but during my lifetime certain individuals emerged as favorites because of my association and experience with them. You have met some earlier and will make the acquaintance of others in the pages of this book.

Snakes Alive

While snakes had always held my interest, and while I had kept them at home and cared for them at the Kansas City Zoo, little did I dream that I would have an opportunity to make some significant contributions to herpetology at—of all places—Midwest Research Institute (MRI). Located not far from the famed Country Club Plaza, MRI is part of Kansas City's scientific and cultural community, a complex that includes Rockhurst College, the University of Missouri at Kansas City (UMKC) and the Linda Hall Library (LHL), which is the largest privately supported public library of science, engineering, and technology in North America. How I loved to lose myself in the miles of shelving at LHL and become absorbed until closing time with volumes on zoology I'd never seen anywhere else (such as *The Anatomy of the Gorilla* with life-size pull-out drawings of gorilla arms and legs).

MRI is another unique K.C. institution. As their newsletter says, "an independent, not-for-profit organization that conducts scientific research and technology development for government and private-sector clients."

However, I must back up for a moment. After graduating from De La Salle Military Academy in 1956 (at age17) I began my freshman year at Rockhurst College. By the fall of 1958 I had completed two years at Rockhurst and finished my second summer at the zoo, which did not have any permanent positions available. Not having enough funds to return to Rockhurst full-time I decided to seek a job and take a course or two in the evening at UMKC. MRI was advertising for a lab technician, and with experience at Doty Technical Laboratories on my resume, I was fortunate to be hired. And I could walk to class at UMKC after work.

Although my duties initially were somewhat routine (cleaning the labs and lab equipment), the daily association with so many dedicated professional scientists and engineers was educational and inspiring. Then the most fortuitous thing happened. Mr. Cully, the Kansas City Zoo Director and my former boss, called me and said the K.C. Zoo was discontinuing the reptile collection, and would I like to have it! Heck yes, but—where to keep it? AH-HA! It probably was a farfetched notion, but . . . MRI?

I met with my supervisor, Dr. William B. House (the best of mentors), and explained what a golden opportunity it would be for the institute to have all these snakes. And that the corner storage room in the basement would be a perfect reptile lab: out-of-the way, secure, climate controlled. Plus, there were some important studies that could be—no, needed to be— done on snakes, and I felt I could get funding. Dr. House became convinced (bless his heart) and carried the proposal to his superiors, who agreed. I will forever be indebted to MRI for encouraging and supporting me (then just a Lab Tech with no degree) in my efforts to secure grants and conduct research in such an offbeat and specialized field.

I knew that when the snakes were at the Kansas City Zoo they were infested with snake mites (*Ophionyssus natricis*). This was a common problem in zoos throughout the world, one that (in my opinion) needed to be addressed. The snake mite is a blood-sucking ectoparasite that can kill a snake from exsanguination within a few weeks if it is heavily parasitized. The snake mite will also attack many species of lizards and occasionally parasitize tortoises.

At MRI, we assembled a high powered (mostly) team to conduct an investigation to find an effective means of eradicating or controlling snake mites on captive reptiles. Team members were J.H. Caiman, Ph.D., Professor of Entomology, University of Kansas, Lawrence; L.H. Goodson, Ph.D., Head, Biochemistry Section, Midwest Research Institute; H.R. Shuyler, Ph.D., Entomologist, Conservation Industries, Inc., Kansas City, Kansas; and me.

I suggested we approach the New York Zoological Society (NYZS) for funding, and MRI asked me to draft a proposal. The NYZS agreed to sponsor the research program and the project began. Our goal was to find a method that would eradicate or control the mites without harming their reptilian hosts and without necessitating removal of the reptiles from exhibit. To do this properly we would have to conduct "field" tests under simulated zoo conditions. Since they were no longer in use at the K.C. Zoo, we were able to obtain a variety of the actual display units, and I arranged them in the reptile lab as though they were in a zoo.

Eighty-seven snakes were involved in a long and detailed process to test 45 materials. Dramatic results were obtained with two of the acaricides tested, and all our findings from the investigation were eventually published in *ZOOLOGICA* (Scientific Contributions of the New York Zoological Society), Vol. 49, Issue 2, Summer 1964. The paper is titled "Control of the Snake Mite, *Ophionyssus natricis,* in Captive Reptile Collections," and coauthored by the four team members.

Since the K.C. Zoo now had no reptiles, MRI became a community resource for information and education about snakes, lizards and the like. Regularly I responded to questions by phone or letter, presented programs, wrote public service pamphlets, identified dead snakes (most were harmless) for snake bite victims at hospitals and public safety agencies, and caught live snakes (some were poisonous) found in residential basements and garages.

Apparently word spread beyond the K.C. area that MRI was involved with reptiles. A medical doctor in South Dakota came to the Institute with an idea for a "snake repellent." He wanted a chemical that one could spray around an area to serve as a barrier snakes would not want to cross. Since snakes have a keen sense of smell we tested a variety of organic compounds with offensive aromas, but nothing was foolproof. Snakes do, however, have an innate fear of people, and the most effective odor—this is no joke—was from a dirty pair of socks ripe with human perspiration. Our conclusion was to advise outdoor enthusiasts to not wash their clothes during camping trips.

As a member of the American Society of Ichthyologists and Herpetologists (ASIH), I received their technical journal *Copeia*. One paper that intrigued me was by a well-known and respected researcher at the University of California in Los Angeles (UCLA). He had implanted electrodes in rattlesnakes to record their electrocardiograms. It seemed to me that the snake might not reach a true resting heart rate with the irritation of an implanted electrode. I wondered if noninvasive external electrodes might be devised to record a snake's basal heart rate.

In collaboration with MRI engineer Thomas I. Marx (who was afraid of snakes) we devised an external strap electrode to record snake electrocardiograms. And we achieved much lower resting heart rates in several species than had been reported in the *Copeia* paper. To confirm our results we had to replicate the exact same conditions and procedures as the UCLA researcher, even to the species of snake.

Enter Big Red.

A primary species used in the UCLA study was the red diamond rattlesnake (*Crotalus ruber ruber*), restricted in range to lower southwestern California and the northern and central part of the Baja California peninsula, and thus not commonly found in living collections.

Through the San Diego Zoo we had a specimen shipped to MRI. Large and handsome on arrival, he was 52 inches long and weighed nearly six pounds. Brick red in color with a white diamond pattern the length of his body (hence the common name), he was robust and magnificent. When I first saw him the nickname "Big Red" sprang to mind.

Big Red was an ideal research subject and, using our new technique, we recorded his cardiogram at various temperatures during resting condition, during excitement—even during a strike! Our data proved the external wrap-around technique superior to implanted electrodes, and jointly we prepared a paper. Nervously, I presented this at the 39th Annual Meeting of the ASIH on June 12, 1959 in—of all places—San Diego, CA, with the UCLA researcher in the audience! But it was well received and later published in *Copeia*, No.3, September 26, 1960 as "Heart Rates of Unanesthetized Snakes by Electrocardiography."

By now Big Red was a popular personality, the most well known snake in the reptile lab, and certainly my favorite.

Yet, the mingled destinies of rattlesnakes and men are sometimes curious. Big Red and I played major roles in an unscheduled scientific investigation at MRI.

He bit me. On my left leg. The fourth of November, 1959. It was my fault.

I was quite familiar with the literature on venomous snakebites but had never seen a case history involving a red diamond rattlesnake. So when this happened I was compelled by the scientist in me to keep a record, which turned out to be the first fully documented bite by this species. (The full story follows in the next chapter.)

From my notes and those of my fiancée (now wife) Margaret, I prepared a 26 page detailed report of the bite. This included specific data on Big Red, and on myself, variable factors as well as circumstances of the incident, first-aid and emergency room procedures, and then—as much as possible—a minute-by-minute account of my reactions and treatment. This was supplemented (with permission) from official records of the Menorah Medical Center in Kansas City. These included pulse, temperature, and respiration rates during hospitalization; laboratory results of hematology analysis and urinalysis; and white blood cell counts during hospitalization. Additionally, I included sixteen black-and-white photographs, with general views of the condition of my left leg as well as close-ups of the area of the bite.

All of this was submitted to and accepted by the ASIH, and I presented it as a paper at their 40th Annual Meeting at the Field Museum of Natural History in Chicago, IL, on June 17, 1960. Subsequently this was published as "Report on a Bite by a Red Diamond Rattlesnake, *Crotalus ruber ruber*" in *Copeia,* No.4, December 19, 1961. So the incident was properly documented in the technical literature.

However, it has always amazed me that my bite by Big Red generated so much interest in the popular press. This turned out to be a bit embarrassing for me. If you are a NASCAR Champion, then you should not have a serious wreck in the parking lot. The same is true with a professional herpetologist—you should have enough experience and skill to avoid being bitten by a poisonous snake.

But . . . herpetology happens.

Shortly after the bite the story was briefly told in local news coverage, I was interviewed on the NBC Monitor program over nationwide radio, and Big Red made the front cover of the Bulletin of the Philadelphia Herpetological Society. Later the story took on a life of its own.

Berton Roueche of *The New Yorker* flew to Kansas City and interviewed me. He reported in detail in an "Annals of Medicine" essay in the January 21, 1961 issue of the magazine. This account was characterized as "a classic adventure in medical research." It was published as "A Certain Contribution" in Berton Roueche's book *A Man Named Hoffman and other narratives of medical detection* (Little, Brown and Company, 1965). Incidentally, the editor of *Copeia*, Robert F. Inger, wrote to me on January 23, 1961 and commented: "As far as I can recollect, you must be the first herpetologist to have cracked *The New Yorker.* That is some sort of distinction."

The bite was featured in *Venomous Reptiles* (Chapter 5: When Snake Bites Man) by the well-known herpetologist and toxicologist S.A. Minton, Jr. (with M.A. Minton), published by Charles Scribner's Sons, 1969.

The December 1973 issue of *Today's Health* magazine carried a shortened version of the Berton Roueche *New Yorker* article.

While still at MRI they asked me to present a Staff Seminar on "Case Report of a Bite by a Red Diamond Rattlesnake." I was honored and did so on June 21, 1960 in the Spencer Auditorium.

My affiliation with MRI has had a lasting impact on my life and I will always treasure that association, even though each time I attend the annual retiree's luncheon I'm known as "the snakebite guy."

Incidentally, when I left MRI at the end of August 1960 they discontinued research with reptiles and gave them all to me . . . including Big Red.

SNAKEBITE!

The Day Big Red Lost His Temper

Author's note. More than a decade after Big Red bit me, we were still together. I was the Zoo Director in Topeka, Kansas and he was living a well-tended life in my house, an esteemed member of the family.

Jim Lapham, a staff writer for STAR Magazine, the Sunday magazine of The Kansas City Star, came to our modest house for dinner and to meet Big Red. His report appeared in STAR Magazine September 20, 1970. It is reprinted here with permission from The Kansas City Star.

It was the proverbial dark and stormy night when I first heard the story of Big Red.

We had just finished dinner and everyone was relaxing around the table at the home of Gary Clarke, director of the Topeka zoo. The wind spattered rain against the windows of the old, frame house.

The gaunt skeleton of an elm across the street, a dead patriarch, seemed to pose a threat now instead of holding an offer of shelter. The time seemed right for Gary to recite the horrible saga of Big Red.

Big Red was large and handsome and deadly. Just how deadly became clear as Gary narrated the chilling account of how almost 11 years ago a rattlesnake named Big Red had nearly killed him.

"And now," Gary said at the conclusion, rising from the table, "would you like to see Big Red?"

We knew that Gary had an extensive collection of skins, skulls, rattles and fangs and assumed it was some such relic we were about to see.

But it was to a bedroom that Gary led us. Everyone in the group suddenly became very polite, stepping to the rear, as Gary slid a big, plastic-fronted box into sight. Loosely coiled and staring at us was the same Big Red of his horror story.

With two keys Gary opened padlocks at either end of the box, lifted the lid and slid a snake hook under the dull red body. Big Red obligingly oozed out onto the floor. He was easily curbed by a touch of the hook and Gary lowered a smaller plastic box over him.

"He's used to this," Gary explained, "I use it when I clean his box. It will calm him down in a minute."

It did. Of all those in the suddenly small-seeming room only Gary and Big Red appeared calm when the box was lifted up. For you see, although Big Red brought him near death almost 11 years ago, he is still a well-cared-for, if lethal, member of the family.

The ordeal that Clarke endured because of Big Red left physical scars visible today. At the time, Clarke, a man too religious ever to consider suicide, nevertheless did not care whether he lived or died.

But the incident left no psychological scars to mar the relationship. Big Red, scientific name *Crotalus ruber ruber,* is a Red Diamond rattlesnake, and when it bit him, Clarke's first concern was, strangely, for the snake. He wanted to get Big Red back into his box without causing any trouble.

And this was the same snake and the same box that were now before us.

"I'd have him in the middle of the front room," Clarke said, "but Margaret (his wife) won't allow it. I'm not complaining, though. How many wives would live in the same house with a rattlesnake?"

On November 4, 1959, Clarke was working at the Midwest Research Institute in Kansas City as a lab technician. All he had planned to do with Big Red was weigh it. No assistant was immediately available, but it was a Wednesday, and Clarke's records all were based on Wednesday weigh-ins. He has the passion for scientific detail that made him loathe to disturb the rhythm of his records. Besides, he had weighed Big Red by himself on more than one occasion.

To weigh the snake, Clarke had to take it out of its box, put it in a snake sack, tie the sack and place it on the scales.

At 1:30 o'clock Clarke grasped the 52-inch-long snake behind the head with his right hand and at midbody with his left hand. The weighing sack was draped over the back of a chair.

Normally, catching and sacking the snake took about one minute. But this day Big Red kept curling his tail back over the edge of the sack every time Clarke would get him about halfway in, thwarting attempts to feed him the rest of the way into the free-hanging sack.

This fruitless activity continued for about five minutes, during which time Big Red tolerated the handling and remained relatively calm. Finally Clarke released his hold with his left hand in order to hold the sack open.

Hanging only by Clarke's grip behind its head, Big Red became angry and began to shake so violently that Clarke had to relinquish his hold on the sack to grasp its body again.

Again Big Red thrashed around and this time knocked the sack onto the floor.

His patience tried to the limit, Big Red for the first time opened his mouth and erected his lethal fangs. Clarke was reminded that these natural hypodermic needles could deliver in a split second three times the dosage of venom fatal to a human. He briefly considered returning Big Red to his box, but made the near-fatal decision to make one more try at weighing.

Clarke went to his knees in order to seize the sack in his mouth and Big Red tried to bite him twice. A muscular animal, Big Red seemed to be gaining strength, and, in his rage, continued his attempts to bite Clarke.

Even when the snake's mouth closed, Clarke noted, the fangs were still erect and completely exposed, free both of its jaws and protective sheaths.

"I clearly observed that on each side of the head both the old fang and the new reserve fang were being erected and apparently functional," Clarke reported.

A chilling sight, although snakes regularly shed and replace fangs as they do skin. At this particular moment Big Red looked doubly lethal, although delivery of a mere 140 milligrams of his venom could be fatal to a man.

Clarke finally succeeded in transferring the enraged rattler to the mouth-held sack, and rising to his feet, quickly twisted and tied the top. Big Red had never put up with this much manhandling before.

As Clarke straightened up, a part of the snake's body was supported on the floor and the upper part of its body was still in the air. This was something like the striking posture of a cobra but was not the coiled, ready position of a rattlesnake.

Big Red thrashed again, bumping against Clarke's leg. Because of the snake's upright position the fangs were protruding through the sack. They also stabbed through Clarke's trouser leg just below his left knee. The fangs caught and snake and sack hung there, the double thickness of cloth preventing it from closing its mouth.

In only the length of time it took the keyed-up Clarke to jerk the bag away he felt a burning sensation seeming to come, not from the wound itself, but welling up from inside his leg.

Big Red's fangs were still protruding through the sack and as Clarke swung it from his body it sprayed venom on his trousers and in a semi-circle on the floor. The quantity of venom visible led Clarke to believe he had received only a small dose.

"My first thought was that I could just put Big Red back in his cage and I wouldn't have to report him as a biter," Clarke said. At the same time he looked at his watch to determine the exact time of the bite. It was 1:45 o'clock.

Clarke was an old hand at handling poisonous snakes and had long ago determined that if he ever was bitten he would record the experience as completely as circumstances would permit.

It was literally the work of a minute to untie the sack and return the snake to its box. The double-padlocks were clicked shut and Clarke again noted the time . . . 1:46 o'clock.

The burning sensation in his leg was pronounced by now and Clarke picked up a snake-bite first-aid kit and walked 45 feet to the nearest phone, having decided he had better report the incident to his supervisor. He dialed the number, setting in motion an almost-comical panic reaction during which Clarke was calmest of all the participants. When he hung up it was 1:47.

He slowly walked 33 feet to a chair and sat down, becoming aware for the first time that the bite was bleeding freely. Three minutes after Big Red had fanged him Clarke had applied a tourniquet about two inches above the wound, just above the knee.

When help arrived at 1:50 Clarke had already prepared the affected area with antiseptic, and a single incision was made to start first-aid treatment. Because of the general excitement and Clarke's seated position this cut was made across his leg rather than lengthwise by one of those who had come to his assistance. This was more damaging to the tissue involved but otherwise did not hinder the effectiveness of the treatment. Clarke applied a suction cup to the wound.

The cup, Clarke observed, was effective, drawing out small bits of flesh as well as blood. At 2 o'clock an ambulance arrived and at 2:04 o'clock left with Clarke for the 4-block trip to Menorah Medical Center. At 2:07 he entered the emergency room.

Although Clarke had taken a test for sensitivity to horse serum when he began working with the poisonous snakes, and another intradermal test just before leaving for the hospital—both showing negative results—a third test was made in the emergency room. The antivenin administered to snakebite victims is obtained from horses that have been given nonlethal doses of snake venom.

In the emergency room Clarke noted the first sign of swelling near the wound and also felt a strange tingling sensation in his ears. The tourniquet he had put on was moved about three inches farther up his leg.

At 2:20 o'clock, 35 minutes after he had been stabbed by Big Red, Clarke was given his first injection of antivenin. Two more injections of antivenin were administered about 10 minutes later, a second incision was made and the tourniquet was removed.

Possibly influenced by the first cut, the physician ignored Clarke's pleas and made a second scarring transverse cut. In addition to other normal first-aid procedures, an injection of morphine was made to combat Clarke's growing pain. He then was taken to a hospital room.

That Clarke had by no means received all of Big Red's deadly venom had been apparent by the quantity spewed on the floor and on his trousers. Clarke still has the trousers, and a trail of dried venom running from knee to cuff is visible to this day.

Judging from the agony he suffered the next several days, however, there is reason to believe that the lightning stab of Big Red would have been fatal without the prompt treatment Clarke received.

There is no way, Clarke said, to describe the pain, its effect multiplied by a heightened sensitiveness of the injured leg.

For the next three hours Clarke lay in bed growing extremely weak, the pain in his leg increasing as it began to swell below the knee. He was given a second injection of morphine and a forth injection of antivenin.

By the time a physician examined his leg again at 6:45, exactly five hours after Big Red struck, the hypersensitizing effect of the venom was such that the mere breathing of the physician was like a painful gust from a hot blast furnace. The morphine was only mildly effective, and Clarke's leg pulsed with pain from just above the ankle to mid-thigh.

After two more hours Clarke began to experience short, spastic muscular contractions of the leg.

At 10:25 he was given a third shot of morphine but was unable to sleep because of the pain. By 12:25 in the morning Clarke was nauseated and the pain continued to increase.

Just after 1 o'clock in the morning, not quite 12 hours after the accident, Clarke vomited the entire contents of his stomach and reached, he said, the unquestioned low point of his life.

At this stage, scientist Clarke could manage only the briefest of dictated notes.

"I have never felt so sick nor experienced such extreme pain in all my life," is the bare testimony of his record.

Clarke has subsequently explained that there is really no way to describe the pain because it was of a totally different quality from any other. It was, he said, not the pain of a cut or the pain one suffers from getting hit or pinched, burned, wrenched, sprained or broken. It was, he said, like the sum total of all pain.

"The closest I can come to describing the way my leg felt is this," Clarke said. "It felt like someone had run it through a meat grinder and at the same time was boiling it in oil, pouring hydrochloric acid on it and was going back and forth over it with a blow torch."

Under such circumstances, Clarke said, time seems literally to stand still, utterly to refuse to move. The night was an infinity of unending seconds, none of which seemed to accomplish anything toward bringing it to an end but each brimming with its full content of pain.

Dawn revealed that his thigh was also beginning to swell, and blue, purple and yellow bruises were spreading and would eventually cover the entire leg. Despite the belated swelling of his upper leg, by the second night in the hospital his calf had swollen larger than his thigh.

This was to be another bad night and his thigh continued to swell, stretching the skin unbearably. In all, six slashes were made around his thigh early that night to keep the swelling from tearing and splitting the skin.

So powerful was the effect of Big Red's venom that it overrode the effects of local anesthesia injected at each incision. Insertion of the hypodermic needle itself was excruciating, and although the skin split apart at the touch of the scalpel Clarke could feel it running through his skin.

His scientific report summed this up in two words— "Extreme pain!"

"Actually, my thigh was just like a hot dog that had been roasted to the point where the skin is splitting open," Clarke said.

By 8:30 of that second night short spasms coursed over his entire body. At 8:50 he dictated the following:

"I do not feel as if I can endure this agonizing torture much longer. There is constant excruciating pain throughout my entire left leg."

This was 31 hours and 5 minutes after Big Red had stabbed Clarke.

At 10:15 that night Clarke received more morphine and more antivenin. This was another long night and even the weight of the sheet hurt his super sensitive leg. When photographs were taken of the leg, the heat emitted by the smallest flash bulb felt like a flaming torch was being pressed against it. When anything was done to dressings and bandages it hurt the leg. When nothing at all was done it hurt!

Clarke had been bitten early Wednesday afternoon and it was Friday night that his notes indicate that he felt the worst was over.

"If the rattlesnake venom does not kill me, I may starve to death."

His food intake up to this time had consisted of broth, Jello and tea, some of which he kept down. That night the swelling stopped and the pain eased a little.

After four days Clarke was able to bend his leg slightly. It was still sore, but the swelling was decreasing. After five days it was near normal size and he could move a few steps on crutches. The leg felt heavy and gave him great pain when he stood.

On the ninth day Clarke was able to limp for a short distance unsupported and was released from the hospital. He continued medication, and suffered from hives, but recovery was continuous. In addition to Big Red's initial bite, more than 60 other punctures with a hypodermic needle had been made, Clarke estimated.

This 60 to 1 ratio of venom to medication should be some gauge of the venom's strength.

A full six months after the bite, occasional local itching served as a reminder, and it was longer than that before his leg functioned under strain— such as protracted climbing—with the efficiency of the uninjured member.

A student of psychology as well as anthropology, Clarke was also presented with a perfect, if dearly bought, opportunity to observe certain of what he termed "ophidian phobic characteristics." The expression refers to the unreasoning and almost instinctive feeling of fear and revulsion so many humans feel for snakes.

This was apparent from the first phone call he made to report the bite. Had he suffered a simple chemical burn, or even blown up his whole section of the building, it would have been taken in stride by his fellow workers as simply the breaks of the game. But when he reported he had been bitten by a snake, his supervisor went into shock deeper than Clarke's.

While an excited but well-intentioned technician sliced his leg in the wrong direction, two other workers, deciding to take him to the hospital, searched feverishly for their car keys. Both impatiently emptied their pockets onto a desk top; the contents were mingled and neither man in snake-induced excitement could even recognize his own car keys.

Both decided to call for an ambulance at the same time, whirled, ran head-on into each other and made a jostling, Keystone Cops exit through a door to reach another phone.

Clarke later learned that as word of his accident spread through the building, work ground to a standstill. A small atomic explosion could not have caused more consternation.

In the emergency room he was identified to two nurses as a snake-bite victim. One nurse gaped at him and dropped a glass vial she had in her hand. The other recoiled and asked, "Is the snake with him?"

He shared a ward with three other patients and served as almost the sole topic of conversation for them and their visitors. "The guy that got bit by the snake" became a hospital curiosity.

One of Clarke's hospital roommates later told him that after his arrival he had a nightmare every night about being bitten by a snake. Clarke was attending college part-time and his instructor refused to accept snake-bite as a credible excuse for his absence.

Once a mother always a mother, and Clarke cherishes the reaction of his mother, Mrs. Charles F. Downs, of 7717 Summit street. For years she had been protesting her son's interest in snakes. At 3 o'clock the afternoon he was bitten and before the gravity of the accident was completely realized, she sent her son the following note:

Greetings Son,
Everyone here is simply ghastly with happiness since the rattlesnake finally bit you. I knew it was coming but could not foresee the exact date.
The doctors will undoubtedly stick you with long needles until you look or at least feel like a porcupine.

I hope the viper that tangled with you this afternoon was your favorite and that he feels worse than you do.

If you get worse, let me know.

Love,
Mother

Obviously no son ever outgrows the maternal I-told-you-so, and she had also been right in that the snake that bit him, Big Red, was indeed his favorite. Snakes are at best unresponsive creatures but, Clarke said, Big Red likes to have his back rubbed lightly and will even arch his back against his fingertips in much the manner of a kitten when receiving similar attention.

Big Red's presence at M.R.I., far from its West Coast habitat, was in order to duplicate—and refute—the findings of a previous test in which the heartbeat of snakes, including the Red Diamond, were recorded by means of implanted electrodes.

Clarke—rightly, it turned out—deduced that this implanting had irritated the snakes to the point that a true, resting heartbeat was never achieved. By wrapping the electrodes around the snake's body he got a much slower heartbeat.

The wavy lines of rattlesnake cardiograms, at rest and also during a strike, to the nonscientific would scarcely appear to have been worth the price Clarke paid.

When M.R.I. was finished with its tests Clarke was asked if he wanted his nemesis, Big Red, who would otherwise have to be disposed of. He did, has cared for it ever since and has lugged it over much of the Mid-West.

His personal animal collection was responsible for his eviction from a home he rented in Fort Worth, Tex., when he was animal department supervisor at the zoo there.

"I think it was more because of the alligator in the bathtub than it was Big Red," Clarke said.

Snakes are virtually blind but, as Big Red lay there on the bedroom floor, it was hard not to feel that it was staring at you.

"Big Red is a very well-adjusted snake," Gary said. "I'll never know his exact age, but he may set a longevity record. He must be 20 now and he's always been a good snake."

The fact of being a "good snake" is reason enough in Clarke's mind to continue to care for it.

"He didn't even see me when he struck that time," Clarke said. "It was just an accident."

Obviously Clarke suffers from no ophidian phobia. He does not fear Big Red, but he does have tremendous respect for the venom—modified saliva, really—that he carries in his poison sacks.

To the incredulous, Clarke explains:

"People are involved in car wrecks where fatalities occur, but they keep on riding in cars, don't they? Or they have hunting accidents, and people get killed with guns, but they still have a gun in the closet.

"I had an accident with Big Red, but why should that be any different just because he's a snake?"

Post Script: Big Red passed away in November 1974, regrettably while I was on my first Safari to Africa. To this day I carry his bite scars on my leg and his essence in my being. He was a very special snake.

Those 16 Little Yellow Pills

Jim Lapham's account of my encounter with Big Red was written some years after the incident itself, and I was by then zoo director in Topeka. But I'll return now to happenings in the summer of 1960.

Life after the now infamous snakebite took some twists and turns. Big Red was with me through many of them. In fact, he was the focus of a rather significant unexpected eventuality.

Earlier I mentioned that I presented a technical paper on the bite before a professional association in Chicago on June 17, 1960. Midwest Research Institute paid my expenses (bless them). It so happened that Margaret and I were married on June 11, 1960. So, I covered her costs to go with me to Chicago (by train) and that was our honeymoon!

Above and beyond the meetings (we attended every session) there were great zoos, natural history museums, libraries, universities, old bookstores and wildlife art galleries to explore. Although Margaret knew when she married me she had married the animal kingdom as well, this honeymoon served to confirm that fact, and she was a willing ally.

Now that I had the responsibility of a wife and strong prospects for a forthcoming family, it seemed important to get serious about continuing my college education. Despite my shoddy academic record, I enrolled at the University of Missouri in Columbia, Missouri (their main campus). Reluctantly I resigned from MRI. We moved to Columbia and found a one-room apartment with a hide-away bed in a quiet neighborhood at 705 Lee Street.

Since I had no car I was dependent on relatives and friends to move our meager possessions and my living reptiles, including Big Red and several other rattlesnakes. The landlord had a "no pets allowed" policy and it was tricky getting past him. Our apartment was on the ground floor at the front of this very old boarding house, and was quite compact. You could reach into the fridge while sitting on the toilet.

Margaret walked to her clerical job with the local health department and I walked to the campus for classes and my job of caring for the University laboratory animal colony (at 75 cents an hour). It was exciting being in the atmosphere of a major university, associating with faculty and graduate students, and becoming involved in various wildlife-oriented activities and organizations. My snakes proved to be popular and, with many requests for lectures and programs, I quickly became part of the community. It was great fun but I was not keeping up with my studies very well.

Then the roof fell in—literally. During a severe thunderstorm in the middle of the night rain leaked through the roof, forming a huge water pocket in our ceiling which quickly collapsed with a humongous crashing sound! Even the landlord heard it and was quickly pounding on our door, wanting to know what had happened! But we couldn't let him in until somehow we hid or covered all of the snake containers. This we did hurriedly but could not get the rattlesnakes to stop rattling. Fortunately the storm kept raging and the landlord was so upset with the damage that he never noticed. The next day I arranged to move my snakes (except Big Red, of course) to the University wildlife lab.

In March 1961 our first child, Janet, was born. This was a great joy for us but obviously Margaret could not continue to work. We now had additional expenses, our funds were nearly depleted, and I was failing in my classes. Besides, I was longing for the zoo.

On April 16, 1961 I wrote to Mr. Cully in Kansas City requesting a full-time position at the zoo. He replied on April 19 that all employees had to go through the city personnel department, but "as a satisfactory employee and an experienced one, I believe we will be able to put you on." Mrs. Cully knew my mother in Kansas City and on May 17 called her to say, "We are hiring very few but would like to have Gary and it might be a stepping-stone for him to get a better job somewhere later." And it came to pass. I returned to work at the K.C. Zoo on June 1, 1961.

We rented a small house at 4416 Bellevue in Kansas City, Missouri. Access to the basement was outside at the back through ground-level storm cellar doors. Inside it was dark and quiet; a perfect environment for my reptiles. (But the meter reader was afraid to go in by himself!)

The nearest bus stop was several l-o-n-g blocks down a steep hill. This was fine in early morning on the way to the zoo, but after a long hard day I dreaded walking up the hill with my backpack full of books. However, joy replaced exhaustion when I was greeted by my beaming bride and bouncing baby.

The zoo was more exciting than ever and my experience with primates broadened. Besides the mandrill baboon, I worked with a variety of monkeys: African green, Diana, red patas, spider, sooty mangabey, sapajou and rhesus, as well as three of the great apes: gibbon, chimpanzee, and gorilla.

As a species, gorillas were both a rarity and a challenge, so zoos were constantly developing better husbandry and management techniques. The first gorilla birth in any zoo occurred in Columbus, Ohio—a heralded event—on December 22, 1956. The four-pound female was hand-raised and named Colo. I mention this as it relates to a special event in my life.

During my time in the reptile labs at Midwest Research Institute I had still maintained contact with Mr. Cully at the zoo. He wrote to me at MRI on January 30, 1959 and commented: "I am enclosing a copy of the program for the Midwest Zoological Meeting in Columbus, Ohio, Feb. 8, 9 and 10. I do not know of a better place for you to meet with herpetologists (and zoo professionals) from all over the country, including Marlin Perkins of the Lincoln Park Zoo . . .

" . . . I will be glad to give you a hand in meeting the right people, but I am sure you will have no difficulty along that line."

How good of him to think of me in this regard, and what an opportunity! MRI granted me time off, I took the bus to Columbus and attended my first professional zoo conference. Yes, I did meet the giants of the zoo world at that time, men I had read and heard about, many of whom would become supportive colleagues in the not-too-distant future. Quite honestly, though, the big thrill was my personal one-on-one visit with Colo, who was just over two years old at the time. Here I was, a nobody, being snuggled by the biggest star in the zoological world! Incidentally, as of December 2006 Colo was still reigning at the Columbus Zoo, the mother of three and grandmother of 16.

Now back to the gorillas at K.C. Zoo. The developing male, Big Man, had grown to the point that keepers no longer wrestled on the lawn with him. Additionally, two young females, Katie (20 pounds) and Jeannie (18 pounds), had arrived on June 21, 1959, again as a gift from Deets Pickett. They were the darlings of the zoo with their distinctive personalities, and it was a delight to care for them and to watch their development.

During my time at the zoo, Big Man and "the girls" were kept separate because of age and size. But, after I left, the trio was introduced. Eventually this resulted in a number of offspring, including the female Tiffany, born to Jeannie on July 15, 1968. By October 1969 I was director of the Topeka Zoo and arranged for the acquisition of Tiffany as a companion for our young male, Max, but that is another story.

Besides gorillas, Deets Pickett provided other animals for the zoo, usually unsolicited and often unwanted . . . such as gaboon vipers.

GABOON VIPERS?

YES!

One day in July 1962 a heavy wooden shipping crate from West Africa showed up at the Kansas City Zoo labeled, "Gaboon vipers—Poisonous—Handle with Care."

Mr. Cully wanted *nothing* to do with this shipment, particularly since the snakes were POISONOUS. Besides, the zoo no longer exhibited snakes of any kind, so he offered them to me. I accepted.

WOW! Gaboon vipers! Absolutely one of the most magnificent species of snakes in nature.

Here! Now!

Formidable. That may be the best word to describe gaboon vipers. They can be four to six feet long with a body circumference of 14 inches and a weight of 18 pounds. The huge triangular head has two small horns on the tip of the snout, and their loud hiss is almost a low roar.

They can produce 450 to 600 milligrams of blood-destroying venom, of which 90 milligrams is sufficient to kill an adult human. Their impresssive size, prodigious quantity of potent venom, and the longest fangs of *any* snake (one and one-half to two inches) makes them one of the deadliest snakes in the world—yet one of the most beautiful.

With a geometric pattern of triangle and hourglass markings, their colors vary from dark and light shades of brown to buff, lavender and gold. In their natural habitat of dead leaves on the rain forest floor, this provides superb camouflage, making them difficult to see in the wild.

Seemingly sluggish, they will remain motionless in ambush for hours while waiting for rodents or ground-dwelling birds to approach, and then strike quickly with great force. Such a splendid snake!

Few people could imagine (and even less would really care) how exciting it was for me that evening to lug this travel-worn crate down to my basement, knowing full well that it contained two "crown jewels" of the herpetological world.

After their long journey I knew they would need water, to soak in and to drink. Accordingly, I prepared two deep metal drums with lockable lids to initially house them. The drums were set at an angle with shallow water on one side and a dry area on the other.

Whenever snakes are shipped they are first put in a cloth sack, which is then placed in the shipping container. The label on the crate indicated they were "baby gaboon vipers," but still, I had utmost respect for their potential danger and knew I had to be *v-e-r-y careful*. So, with great caution I pried open one corner of the crate and peeked into the darkness using a small flashlight. A stentorian hiss emanated from the shadows and, unexpectedly in the thin beam of light, was an **adult** gaboon viper staring at me, his massive head as big as my fist! *Both snakes were loose in the crate,* a burlap bag lying in shreds around them.

GASP!!! I was ASTONISHED!!! A jolt of electricity could not have stunned me more! Totally unexpected, and one of the few times I have been truly frightened!

After I caught my breath, and now that I knew the situation, I carefully balanced one snake at a time on the end of a long handled "snake hook" and safely transferred each viper to its own metal drum. Both quickly calmed and drank . . . and drank. They were fantastic specimens, and certainly *not* babies. I studied them for awhile, secured them for the night, and started preparing special living quarters (which housed them safely for many years). Big Red was *still* my favorite, but gaboon vipers . . . WOW!

*****

At the Kansas City Zoo I dealt with other species possessing long fangs—the big cats (and a few not so big). The Main Zoo Building exhibited African lions, Indian tigers, North American pumas and Asiatic leopards, as well as jaguars and ocelots from Central and South America.

A chute connected the indoor with the outdoor units of the Main Zoo Building, and a long, narrow, dingy tunnel gave keepers access to the transfer gates, which had to be manually operated. A one by six inch board bridged the open space between chutes and I had to "walk the plank" from one to the other. Standing on top of the chute, I would pull the heavy steel gate up and wait for the cats to transfer. In the open position the gate exposed a gap through which the cats could (and often would) thrust a paw, claws extended, and swipe at my leg. As dangerous as this was, we all knew how to "work the tunnel," and I never heard of a serious incident.

The Asian elephant exhibit dominated the far end of the building, with an outdoor yard adjacent to a refreshment stand in a shaded patio with picnic tables. The elephants were bathed with a high pressure water hose every day and then exercised through a series of basic voice commands to assist in management and veterinary care. Twice a year we gave them a coating of mineral oil to condition their skin, applied with a paint brush over their entire body (and a lot over ourselves, too). The elephants enjoyed it and afterwards they looked like they had just been cast in bronze!

A pair of hippos, occupying a large pool in the center, rounded out the residents of the Main Zoo Building. The male, Mark Anthony (Mark), arrived June 12, 1953 and the female, Cleopatra II (Cleo) on June 27, 1954. Both were estimated at four years of age on arrival.

They had a baby in October 1957, but more significant was their female offspring born at 1:00 pm on June 9, 1961 while I was caring for them. The baby was named Jiff at the time, but in May 1966 we acquired her for our new exhibit at Topeka Zoo, where she was renamed 'Peka-Sue. So, I've known her all her life and, yes, she was a beautiful baby.

After draining and cleaning the hippo pool I would place hay for them to eat around the land area. They also ate oats and fresh produce, and I had a daily ritual with Mark. When I brought the bushel basket full of vegetables, he would be waiting for me at the edge of the feeding platform with his huge mouth agape. I would then reach in and place a food item on his tongue, which he would chew a couple of times and gulp it down.

A bunch of carrots: chomp, chomp—gulp.

An entire loaf of bread: chomp, chomp—gulp.

A quantity of potatoes: chomp, chomp—gulp.

A whole head of cabbage: chomp, chomp—gulp.

A bundle of zucchini: chomp, chomp—gulp.

Mark seemed to cherish this, I enjoyed the interaction, and the visitors liked to watch.

Hippos are not the most energetic animals, but one week Mark seemed particularly listless for several days. I reported this and the consulting veterinarian came out, looked him over, but reached no diagnosis. Still, he thought some antibiotics might help, and calculated Mark's weight to determine a proper dosage. The little yellow pills were half the size of your smallest fingernail, and a total of 16 would be required. He asked me if I could get Mark to take them, and with complete confidence I replied, "Sure."

Most animals are creatures of habit and feel secure in the same daily routine. I figured our feeding ritual would be a perfect way to administer the medication. Hence, I cut a triangular plug in a head of cabbage and hid those 16 little yellow pills in the center, carefully replacing the plug. At feeding time I went through the normal procedures and placed the various food items in his mouth.

A bunch of carrots: chomp, chomp—gulp.

An entire loaf of bread: chomp, chomp—gulp.

A quantity of potatoes: chomp, chomp—gulp.

The whole head of cabbage: chomp, chomp—oops!

Mark gulped the cabbage down, but one-by-one he spit out each of those 16 little yellow pills! When I saw the first one I thought Mark coincidentally dropped it, but would still get the other 15. Then the second one dropped, and the third, and a fourth. It was now apparent that Mark Anthony was *intentionally* doing this! How did he know they were there? How could he maneuver his thick lips and tongue to discharge the pills and not the cabbage? The veterinarian and I looked at each other in exasperation. Outsmarted by a hippo!

My sure-fire trick had not worked and, despite our best efforts, we were unsuccessful in getting Mark to take the medication. A week or so later, though, he was acting his usual self . . . without those 16 little yellow pills.

Monkeyless Island & Polar Bear Parasites

Everyone poops.

What a delightful phrase. How better to describe a natural biological process of all living creatures.

Everyone poops. And it is a good thing they do, especially animals in zoos, as poop is a general reflection of the animals' overall well-being and an important way of monitoring the state of their digestive systems.

What can one tell from the dung, or feces, of an animal? (By the way, is the dung of a really rare specimen called "endangered feces?") But let's be serious about poop. First of all, is there any? Granted, different animals may go at different intervals, so the regular habits of each specimen should be noted, since an animal not defecating on schedule could indicate a problem. With newborn mammals it is critical they expel the meconium, the first fecal material. Next, when do they go, where do they go? Some species do it on the move and go all over the place; others always go in the same spot (a zookeeper's dream); and some go near or in water. One should be alert for any changes in the routine.

Once we have our poop it should be examined carefully: the shape, the size, the color, even the smell. Not all excrement "stinks" by the usual definition. Elephant dung, for example, smells like wet hay. Also one should look for signs of blood, parasites, or foreign objects. Most zoos ban balloons, plastic bags and straws so they won't be accidentally ingested by the animals. Periodically, stool samples are collected for lab work or veterinary analysis. All data then become part of the animal's permanent medical record.

So you can see that, even though zoo keepers are sometimes ridiculed and called just a pooper scooper, it is a very important responsibility.

Now that you know your poop, you should have a better appreciation of the following true story . . . and a lesson learned.

Peaceful Valley was the area of the Kansas City Zoo that contained the Waterfowl Lagoon, rock grottos for small mammals and birds of prey, the otter pool and the bear exhibits. It was an older area of the zoo, with some things built by the WPA in the 1930's. The bear units were set against a high limestone wall and enclosed with heavy steel bars curved inward at the top. Each had dens in the back and shift gates between, with pools and huge logs for the bears. Species exhibited were grizzly, American black, and polar bears.

To clean the units safely the bears would be shifted to an adjoining unit or temporarily held in the den. The keeper could then enter the exhibit and "hose it down" thoroughly, drain and fill the pool, hide food in various locations, rake leaves if necessary, etc. The polar bears were potentially the most dangerous and also the most troublesome. I had to be extremely cautious if they were in the adjacent unit since their reach was so long and they were always stalking me. And if not me then my hose. If they snagged the hose with just one powerful claw it was a goner! Believe me, you can not win a tug-of-war with a polar bear! The best you can do is disconnect the section they have (and nozzle if necessary) and save the rest of the hose. Then be prepared for the scorn of other keepers when they hear the polar bears outsmarted you . . . again.

One brisk fall day I was routinely hosing down the polar bear exhibit when something in the dung caught my eye. It was a weird orange color and protruding an inch or so. I stopped and looked closely. Geeze, what's this? I carefully pulled it out of the pile and oh-my-gosh! It was a worm, as big around as a pencil, and nearly four inches long. I had *never* seen anything like it from *any* animal or even in a parasitology book. I carefully set it aside and looked for more but found none. The stool itself looked normal and the bears seemed fine, playing their usual stalking game. Even so, this concerned me. Procuring a small paper cup from the service area, I placed the worm in it and proceeded directly to the zoo director's office.

Mr. Cully, who had long experience at the Bronx Zoo in New York prior to coming to Kansas City, stared at the worm for a long time, shook his head and said, "Gezsus, I've *never* seen anything like this." He placed an urgent call to the zoo's consulting veterinarian who immediately departed from the clinic at his private practice and sped to the zoo. Dr. Ashby, who had long experience with a wide variety of domestic and exotic animals, gazed at the worm for a long time, scratched his head and said, "Hmmm . . . I've *never* seen anything like this."

So this "never seen before" worm was carefully preserved in a specimen bottle and shipped to the School of Veterinary Medicine at the University of Missouri in Columbia for scientific analysis. How exciting for me to be involved in a small way in this zoological mystery that could make zoo history.

We all anxiously awaited the laboratory test results, but it took a while and, quite frankly, I was so involved with my daily responsibilities as a keeper that I forgot about it. Running a bit late one day I trudged down the steps of the Main Zoo Building with feed buckets and tools clanging. As I entered the keepers' service area, the entire zoo work force was lined up, single file, all the way past the lunch table to the assistant director's desk: maintenance workers, truck drivers, summer help, keepers—everyone! And I had to walk by each one. As I did, they made remarks like, "So you want to be a zoo director some day" or "And you're the one always reading animal books on your lunch hour" and "We thought you were smarter than that."

I had no idea what was going on. At the end of the line was the assistant director with the orange worm in the specimen jar on his desk. He said, "So you thought you could pull a fast one, huh? What are you trying to do, embarrass the zoo director and veterinarian?" For the life of me I did not know what he was talking about.

Then he explained. "This so-called polar bear parasite of yours is nothing more than a rubber fishing lure. Hell, any fool can see that."

Oohhh . . . I was astonished and ashamed. Boy, did I feel stupid . . . and deserving of the disdain and contempt from everyone. Uh-oh, what would Mr. Cully think? This could be the end of my zoo career!

Fortunately, it was not. Although the vet lab at M.U. thought it was an intentional practical joke and had a good laugh, both Mr. Cully and Dr. Ashby had been fooled just like me, and knew I was sincere. The zoo crew knew the whole story and were having a good laugh at my expense. I kept that worm in the jar and when I eventually became a zoo director, I put it on a shelf in my office to remind me that anyone can make a simple mistake.

Also in Peaceful Valley was Monkey Island. Built in 1945 for $32,500, it was a top exhibit of its type in the country: large, constructed from natural stone, irregular in shape with various levels and climbing equipment, well-landscaped and surrounded by a wide moat six feet deep with three feet of water. The large colony of sooty mangabey monkeys was always active and produced babies regularly, and they made the island one of the most popular attractions in the zoo.

Keeper access to the island was through a tunnel under the moat which led to night quarters for the monkeys hidden inside the rock work. The monkeys were fed each morning in the shelter, so they watched for the keeper to approach the tunnel access doors, chattering excitedly. Once the keeper disappeared in the tunnel the monkeys swarmed inside and were waiting, where they could easily be secured, enabling the keeper to safely go out onto the island to clean. Of course the visitors would point and remark, "Oh, that's a funny looking monkey." Ha Ha.

I'll never forget the morning of June 13, 1961. I came within sight of the island and there were no monkeys to greet me from afar. Strange, but maybe they were on the other side of the island. So I called to them. As I got closer and circled around the island, there were **no** M-O-N-K-E-Y-S, except one small female! There should have been 31. Whoa! Then I discovered there was *no water in the moat.* NOT A SINGLE DROP! Whoa again!

How could this be? Where in the world were the other 30 monkeys? What do I do now?

While standing there, dumbfounded, I heard a slight rustling of leaves in the cottonwood trees around Monkey Island—yet there was no wind. YIKES! The monkeys! Apparently they had walked across the dry moat, scaled the outside wall, and climbed to the top of the trees—tall trees. Now what?

Obviously I had to report this and rushed back to the Main Zoo Building, dreading to be the bearer of bad news even though it was not my fault, or at least I didn't think it was. (An inspection later revealed the old drain valve had simply failed.) All available personnel were assembled and armed with heavy gloves and a large "catching bag" on a metal hoop that was both cumbersome and impractical. Mr. Cully called the fire department. Using high-pressure hoses, firemen squirted water on the monkeys to chase them down; they jumped to other trees. At midday we spread fruits and vegetables around the island. Many of the monkeys came back to the island, and we caught eight. The others returned to the trees or hid in the bushes surrounding the moat. Then it rained—hard—and we humans were very wet and uncomfortable, but the monkeys seemed to enjoy the rain.

Decked out in pith helmets and rubber boots, we must have been a sight stumbling through thick shrubbery. It was rough going, especially with the unwieldy catching bag, but I did catch a monkey by covering it with my pith helmet! We chased several others back across the moat and onto the island. By nightfall we were exhausted and had caught only 15 monkeys. The others were asleep in the trees.

Somehow *The Kansas City Star* found out about all of this and sent a reporter to the scene earlier in the day. By chance he encountered me and asked about the catching bags. In my frustration I answered, "The bags are poppycock." This appeared in *The Star* (front page) the next day and all of the other keepers were going around uttering "poppycock" in a variety of accents and tones at different decibel levels. Mr. Cully called me to his office and inquired about the word—what it meant and why I had used it. Honestly, I didn't know; it simply popped into my head. At a loss as to how to answer, I shrugged my shoulders. He just smiled.

Eventually all the monkeys were caught, the drain valve was repaired, and Monkey Island was back in operation. But for the rest of my days at Kansas City Zoo I never lived down that happenstance use of the word poppycock. On reflection, I wish I had thought (on the unexpected spur of the moment) to use the word "balderdash" instead. Somehow it sounds a bit more sophisticated.

Keeper Characters of the K.C. Zoo

When you read about fictional characters you accept how preposterous they might be since they *are* fictional. However, when you actually know and work with preposterous characters it is not always obvious at the time. You may realize this years later after quiet reflection (which, I have found, is necessary in writing a book).

The keepers (and other staff) at the Kansas City Zoo in the late 1950's and early 1960's were something of a rogue's gallery, but not in a negative way. How would I define them? Certainly they were all authentic, yet difficult to typecast. They ran the gamut from eccentric to substantive to oddball to unparalleled.

But who am I to issue such epithets on these guys? If they were writing about me, I'd probably fit in all the above categories. Nevertheless, they were the *dramatis personae* of my early zoo career and a half century later they are still prominent in my stream of consciousness.

You've already met Willie, the north end keeper. And I mentioned Dan Watson earlier, but a few more comments are in order. Dan was a nerd before the term was in vogue. Studious and philosophical, he wore heavy-framed glasses with thick lenses and always hesitated in thought before he spoke or answered a question. We shared a lot of common interests (including reptiles) and I learned much from Dan. The most scientific of all the keepers, he did the best job of answering questions from the public, especially over the phone. He was career oriented and eventually became director of several different zoos.

A greater contrast could not be found between Dan and Ted, the hippo keeper. Dan felt the zoo existed for the public, Ted considered visitors a nuisance. Dan appeared well groomed, Ted looked sloppy. Dan was always seeking new solutions, Ted was set in his ways.

Ted came in an hour and a half early every morning and started his routine. By the time the rest of us showed up, Ted was in his rubber boots, baggy pants and old-fashioned strap undershirt, scrubbing away in the hippo pool. Not only would he scrub the hippo pool, he would scrub the hippos! YES! I don't know if they liked it, but they tolerated it. Instead of moving the hippos to the next pool, he went in with them (against the rules) and got away with it. In fact, when he took a "smoke break" he would sit on a hippo to have his cigarette!

Ted had lost his larynx to cancer, so to speak he held a vibrator to his throat which produced a low grumbling drone. Even face-to-face it was difficult to understand him; I can only imagine what he must have sounded like over the phone, especially to a caller who had dialed the zoo.

The number listed in the telephone directory rang the only phone in the Main Zoo Building. It was located in a small, unused office at the head of the stairs. This was in the days before answering machines, and if you were on schedule and involved with your morning routine, the last thing you wanted was to be interrupted to answer the phone—especially when it was probably a question like, "What time does the zoo open?"

When the phone rang everyone pretended they couldn't hear it. The elephant keeper would keep shoveling, the cat keeper would be engrossed in hosing the lion's den, and Ted would scrub the hippo pool harder than ever.

But the phone would keep ringing . . . and ringing!

Finally, when Ted could stand it no longer, and with a fierce glare, he'd throw down his scrub brush and stomp out of the pool, go behind the guardrail, around the corner and into the little office. You couldn't help hearing Ted's raspy-voiced side of the conversation. And you could imagine what the other party was saying. It went like this:

"Swope Park Zoo."

　　　Pause.

Then louder, "SWOPE PARK ZOO."

　　　Pause.

Even louder, **"SWOPE—PARK—ZOO."**

　　　Long pause.

Then emphatically, "WELL, I CAN'T UNDERSTAND YOU EITHER!"

　　　CLICK!

Ted would bang the phone down and storm out of the office in a rage.

A father-son team worked in the Main Zoo Building. Jim was head keeper, chewed tobacco, and looked after the Asian elephants and big cats. His son Clayton was quiet and reserved, did not chew, and took care of primates. Both were tall and thin and always looked neat and fresh despite the dirty work.

Then there was "Candy Kid," who reminded me of Howdy Doody from the early days of television. He carried a metal lunch bucket with a loaf of bread in the lower compartment and, in the space reserved for a thermos, a jar of peanut butter and a jar of jelly. Everyday at noon he made one P.B. & J. sandwich after another, and that was all he ever ate for lunch, day after day.

Harry the bear keeper, on the other hand, would put the hard, pre-pared pellets for primates called monkey chow in a bowl with milk and have them for *his* lunch. He had a long face, spoke with a drawl and at the end of every sentence emitted a little, nervous laugh. His ambition was to become a customs inspector, but he never could pass the required examination.

"Old Blue" wasn't really old and wasn't really blue, but always wore a blue shirt. He was assigned to maintenance and hence not required to wear khaki. He talked very slowly and it took him forever to get to the punch line of a joke.

Calvin was the truck driver and his daily routine was to collect manure from the storage boxes in various areas of the zoo and haul it to the dump. At the end of the day he washed the truck, taking great pride in its cleanliness. Calvin was quite muscular with a body builder's physique. He was deathly afraid of snakes and always eyed me with great suspicion.

Two of the older keepers, Bert and Doc, worked the Plains Animal Building and the feeding corral for the African Veldt. Bert seemed more like a Sunday School teacher in a Norman Rockwell painting than a zoo keeper. Bert's favorite expression when moving hoofed stock from one area to another was, "Hooey Hooey." We used to joke that he thought it was some special African chant. One day an adult male ostrich (which has a lethal kick) knocked Bert down and stood over him. It was a potentially dangerous situation, but Bert did not panic, stayed motionless and was safely rescued. Bert looked smart in his uniform and wore his khaki tie every day. Doc, on the other hand, may have been the most grisly looking keeper of the lot. Rumpled, unshaven, slouching with a long-ashed cigarette dangling from his lips, his mantra was, "Quittin' time and payday."

One of my best friends was Ronzell, a black man a few years older than me. He had a great sense of humor and we shared many common interests. I'm very protective of my books, but I trusted Ronzell with borrowing them. When I first started working at the zoo, we cut weeds together along the visitors' path around the African Veldt. Ronzell was a big guy with a prominent scar on his cheek resulting from some sort of fight. This was hard for me to imagine, as he was so laid back in demeanor, and even in speech. But Ronzell had ambition and capability. After I moved on to another zoo he worked his way up to Animal Curator in K. C. His career was cut short by his unexpected death at the age of 49 in 1985. I had met many of his family and I was honored they asked me to speak at his funeral. The service was so emotional I had great difficulty, but I think Ronzell would have been proud.

The Assistant Zoo Director was Virgil, who always seemed to squint as though the sun was in his eyes. In his capacity as foreman he had an aura of being stern, and most of the keepers cowed at his commands. Softhearted in reality, he worked me hard but helped me a lot, more like a gruff coach than a mentor. If Virgil had a nemesis it was Rex May.

Rex May, a high school biology teacher with a Dennis the Menace grin, only worked in the summer. I'm not sure he needed the money; he just liked being at the zoo—and liked to harass Virgil with his sharp wit and quick comebacks.

Rex would periodically publish a humorous, typewritten, homemade one-copy-only newsletter called *FAUNA & FECES* that was "Dedicated to all lost souls who call themselves zoo men." He had a Man of the Week column and in one issue featured Virgil. Some excerpts: "Yes, Virgil has been in on many firsts at the Swope Park Zoo. He answered the first phone call wanting to know what to feed a baby blue jay . . . he threw out the first fish to the sea lions . . . first to read the numbers on the Children's Zoo turnstiles . . . and first to smoke Marvels for a steady smoke.

"As Assistant Director his jobs are numerous. Among his most important ones are: watching the Chain Gang in action; turning on the basement fan; cleaning his lighter; cleaning his cigarette holder; cleaning his glasses; finding suitable shade in which to perform all of these acts; and, of course, seeing that all of the work at the zoo gets done RIGHT. (Or should I say THE ZOO WAY.)"

In that same issue Rex had the following want ads:

FOR RENT OR SALE: One grass whip and file—like new—never used. Write Bert, African Veldt, S.P. Zoo.

FREE FREE FREE! Used khaki zoo uniforms (slightly stained). Contact elephant keeper, S.P. Zoo.

GET a good cussing out. Call Mr. Lyons at Ja 0057(zoo's number).

Rex added inside humor to the zoo scene, but I'm not sure everyone appreciated it.

There was another keeper of note at the K.C. Zoo. We knew each other well but never worked together. He was six years younger than I, but was taller and weighed more. Still, I could honestly say, "He ain't heavy—he's my BROTHER." It was true. All the while I worked at K.C. Zoo, my brother Steve showed no interest. After I went to the Fort Worth Zoo in December 1962, and with no help from me, he started at the K.C. Zoo in April 1963, working with many of the same characters and caring for many of the same animals. Believe it or not, after I went to Topeka as director, Steve went to the Fort Worth Zoo. All our colleagues in the zoo world were hoping Steve would not come to Topeka as a keeper while I was there because then . . . I would be my keeper's brother and he would be his brother's keeper!

Steve also worked at the Tulsa Zoo for a year before going to Fort Worth Zoo in 1969 for the next 38 years. He was Curator of Mammals much of that time.

We get together now and then in Fort Worth and reminisce over a bottle of Lone Star about our experiences on the chain gang, or with various animals at the K.C. Zoo. He recalled that sometimes the hippo pool drain would clog and flood the keeper area in the basement of the Main Zoo Building, to the extent that we had to eat lunch wearing our rubber boots while sitting *on* (not at) the picnic table. Similar to my experience, one of

Steve's first duties was to clean the parking lot, but with more sophisticated equipment. Instead of my old wooden stick paper picker, Steve had used a short aluminum pole with a bicycle hand grip; and rather than my old gunnysack, he was assigned a fancy green canvas bag with white letters that said, "KEEP OUR PARKS CLEAN." One day foreman Virgil told Steve, "Don't come back 'till your bag is full." There wasn't much trash on the lot itself, so Steve took some out of the litter cans to fill the bag.

Whereas William T.A. Cully was the director, rather than a Swope Park Zoo keeper, he certainly deserves mention as a character—and I mean that in the most complimentary sense. He was born in New York City across the street from the Bronx Zoo where he got his first job in the pony ride ring at the age of 12 and then rose through the ranks to become Head Keeper of Mammals. He became zoo director at Kansas City in 1942, saw the zoo through the war years, and guided its development until his retirement in 1967. Always well dressed (often dapper with spats and Derby hat) he made the rounds daily and checked all areas of the zoo. Very conscientious of visitors' safety, he walked into the public area of the Main Zoo Building one morning at opening time and found the floor still wet and slick. Immediately he had Calvin bring a truckload of sand and dump it on the floor. After the keepers cleaned it up (an all day job) that floor was always bone dry *before* the building opened. Lesson learned.

Mr. Cully lived on the zoo grounds in a stone house on a hill overlooking Monkey Island with his wife (Mildred) and young daughter (Cathy). I thought this was neat, but he never had any time to himself. If a Park Board member was at the zoo on Sunday afternoon, he'd stop by the house and have Mr. Cully take his family on a tour.

The zoo office was a room in the house and Mrs. Cully served as his secretary/administrative assistant. She had a manual typewriter and used a green typewriter ribbon to match the green ink on the zoo letterhead. Mr. Cully closed his letters with "Zoologically yours" and signed his name in green ink.

Mr. Cully liked to experiment with new construction materials and used aluminum whenever possible because it did not rust or have to be painted (but it did have to be cleaned). He used two middle initials (T.A.), which his colleagues quipped stood for "tempered aluminum."

Modest and sincere, Mr. Cully was a true professional and universally respected in the zoo world. Both he and Mrs. Cully took great interest in my career and I'll always be grateful for their counsel and advice.

I was blessed to have another great teacher at the K.C. Zoo—Bennie Henry. He helped me to understand what I was learning from the animals and has been a lasting influence on my career and life. But I'll let Bennie's qualities speak for themselves as together we enter the world of the tallest and heaviest land mammals on earth.

Days on the African Veldt

I have a confession. Admittedly I am reluctant to reveal it even after lo, these many years, fearful that it might be misconstrued. Nevertheless, here goes.

Yes, I loved the crowds at the zoo. Yes, I enjoyed sharing insights with visitors about animals in my role as a keeper. Yet, my most treasured day of the entire year was the Tuesday after Labor Day in early September.

Why? Purely selfish reasons. The weather was usually perfect: blue sky, bright sun, gentle breeze. And almost no visitors! Vacations were over, school was in session, and I had the animals pretty much all to myself—especially on the African Veldt. At that time I had never been to Africa, and in my mind this had to be the closest thing to it.

I could always count on many memorable days in September. I don't mean to say those days were carefree, but when you are the only human on the African Veldt, and you are surrounded by a variety of African animals you admire and respect, and you are in direct physical contact with a magnificent pair of African elephants you know and love, and spiritually you are in another world, well—what else do you need?

The Veldt opened in July 1954, taking advantage of an abandoned quarry with its natural rock wall. The Veldt was a seven-acre area in the shape of Africa, with shade trees and a lake, developed for mixed species of wildlife. From an elevated walk along the perimeter visitors could look over the entire expanse. And what a scene! Living together were zebra, eland antelope, white bearded gnu, ostrich, about 40 cranes and storks of several species, and a pair of African elephants (always accompanied by a keeper). Maasai giraffe were on the Veldt as well, separated by a stockade fence, but visually part of the scene.

A Giraffe House was built in 1955 and an Elephant House was constructed in 1962. Both were shaped like African huts, as was the refreshment stand for the public. Not visible to visitors was the Plains Animal Building, which had twelve large stalls that served as night quarters for the hoofed stock and birds (and the elephants prior to 1962). The building was surrounded by a large feeding corral where the animals were brought in each day for a grain ration and a close visual inspection to check their condition. This management complex was actually outside the Veldt with access through a concrete tunnel hidden under the visitors' walk.

Managing such a group of mixed species required daily monitoring, and introduction of new specimens took time and patience. Many mammal births occurred, but as the males matured they were separated and maintained off-exhibit in breeding corrals.

The Kansas City Zoo received its first pair of giraffes on September 14, 1955. Spotty and Dotty were adults when I cared for them. In the latter stages of Dotty's first pregnancy I stayed up with her several nights, but then she delivered the baby late the following afternoon.

Curious yet cautious, giraffes can become apprehensive at the slightest change. In good weather they would go outside each morning and come back in each afternoon . . . if everything was just right. This meant fresh hay in the high racks, grain and sliced onions in the feed pans, and straw spread across the threshold of the doorway. One evening I was running late and forgot to spread the straw. Everything else was set and I opened the tall door, went into the outside yard, spread my arms and slowly walked behind them. They would approach the door and turn away . . . repeatedly. What was wrong? Oops! Realizing my oversight, I dashed in, spread some straw and went back outside. Spotty and Dotty sauntered in routinely.

Another time a sudden thunderstorm developed in early afternoon. Concerned that the giraffes might slip and fall in the mud, I rushed around preparing everything properly, donned my raincoat and stepped out in the pouring rain. Instead of going in the building the giraffes stood stock-still and stared at me. Oops again! They had never seen me in a raincoat, so off it came and in they went. I was drenched but they were safe.

The inside hayracks were 15 feet up on the wall at the back of the exhibit. To fill them I had to position a six-foot stepladder below a rack, carefully carry a pitchfork loaded with hay to the very top step, balance myself and toss the hay over the top and into the rack. It took several trips to fill each rack. In good weather the giraffes were outside and I worked without difficulty in the empty exhibit. In bad weather, however, there was no transfer stall, so I had to go directly in with the giraffes, which posed a problem.

With their liquid eyes and graceful movements, giraffes might appear to be gentle and meek, but adult males can be dangerous—even aggressive. Despite their skinny appearance, giraffes are big, powerful animals. An adult male may weigh over 3,000 pounds, with a head weighing 75 pounds. They can kick in all four directions—hard enough to kill a lion. When I stood on top of the stepladder, my head was up to Spotty's shoulder and apparently infringing in his space. He would move sideways, crowding and pushing me off balance until I would crash to the concrete floor. Or, he would swing his huge head at me, as males do toward a rival in a fight for dominance, again knocking me off the ladder. Believe me, a giraffe never seems so big as when you are flat on your back in a small space with an adult male towering over you! I couldn't blame Spotty, though, as the physical constraints of the exhibit design forced me to violate basic rules of giraffe behavior. And later in my career, when I had the responsibility of planning a new giraffe facility, this experience proved to be quite valuable.

Certainly the giraffes put me to the test, but no more so than the pair of African elephants, Casey and Lady. They arrived at the zoo on July 20, 1955. Both were 53 inches tall. Casey weighed 975 pounds and Lady 925 pounds.

It was so exciting to actually have a young pair of African elephants in Kansas City. I paid particular attention to them on my visits to the zoo noting their behavior and watching their growth and development.

By the time I worked with them on the Veldt they were over seven feet tall and Casey was on his way to becoming, in his senior years, the largest African elephant in North America—and eventually the oldest.

It may have been serendipitous, but I've always felt my association with Bennie Henry was destiny. He was, by far, the finest animal keeper I've known, with an innate understanding of animals. Small in stature and gentle in manner, Bennie was a patient and inspiring teacher. He enriched my life by his example and dedication.

Whenever a species new to the zoo arrived, Zoo Director Cully entrusted it to Bennie. In turn, Bennie would instruct other staff on the best method of care based on his insight, practical knowledge and common sense.

Unbeknown to Mr. Cully, Bennie began training Casey and Lady to respond to voice commands as part of their daily routine. It was not meant to be an act as such, but simply a way to facilitate Bennie's ability to work safely in direct contact each day with two immense and intelligent mammals. At a time when many "experts" said African elephants could not be trained (most circus elephants were Asian), here was Bennie utilizing techniques that are common practice 50 years later. No fanfare; no glory; just Bennie in his own quiet way doing what he thought was best for the animals.

Mr. Cully was surprised but impressed with what Bennie had accomplished. So impressed, in fact, that he asked Bennie to put the elephants through their paces each afternoon for the benefit of the public. Unbeknown to visitors, this was not a "show," but a demonstration of the mental and physical capabilities of these elephants. This was also quite valuable to all of us who cared for them.

Bennie trained me as well as the elephants. When I would give Casey and Lady their morning bath, I could say "steady" and they would hold still; or "down" and they would assume an upright position on elbows and knees; "over left" meant to lie prone on the left side; "over right" the opposite; and so on.

I could direct the hose stream to any leg—left or right, front or back—and say "foot," and the elephant would lift that foot high enough that I could examine it and then clean the pad thoroughly.

It was most important to "reward" Casey and Lady after each successful response—sometimes with food, but always with a verbal affirmation of "Good Boy" or "Good Girl." This was reinforced with a firm pat on the elephant's side to assure them they had done the right thing. Better yet, I would vigorously rub them—behind the ear, under the eye, or on the tongue—to renew trust and security. Years later, when I would make an occasional visit to see them, these same actions would elicit a loud but low grumble, a sign of contentment (especially from Casey).

Equipped with all of this tutoring from Bennie, I felt confident to be on the African Veldt by myself, responsible not only for this imposing pair of African elephants, but also for all the other species as well *and* any potential interactions between them. Bennie would eat his lunch in the keeper area of the Giraffe House. He advised me that if I had a serious problem or was in real trouble, to throw a rock on the roof and he would come and help.

I knew that Bennie had an invalid wife at home, and he had to give her complete care before and after work each day. He never complained, but I felt it was important that he have an hour to himself, so I was determined to never bother him.

But Casey and Lady had other plans.

Bennie had warned me that Casey and Lady knew what they could get away with, and would test me. Also, they loved to cheat, and I needed to be firm with my commands.

They started by chasing zebras. I would call them by name, and they would stop. Then they would team together and raid the bird feeders, which contained specialized grain and pellets. As though there was a pre-arranged signal (we now know elephants communicate with sounds below the range of human hearing), one kept me occupied while the other would sneak over to a bird feeder and quickly siphon the entire contents with its trunk—just like that! Again, I'd call their names and they would stop and come to me.

Their best trick, however, was to proceed to the middle of the lake in the Veldt immediately after "being naughty." They knew I would not come after them.

All of this was acceptable fun and games until Casey decided to put me to the ultimate test. In our direct physical association I would frequently lean against him as he munched hay, and he would often gently nudge me, no harm intended.

One day, however, Casey used a new behavior. He came up from behind and gave me a playful push. Different, but no problem. He did it again, more arduously. Strange. Then he did it with fervor, and continuously. Despite my protest, Casey was pushing me forward . . . and directly toward the lake! I needed Bennie's help—quick! I grabbed a rock and threw it on the roof of the Giraffe House.

Bennie strolled over in our direction and called, "Casey! Come here, Son. You, too, Lady."

They did. Bennie reached as high as he could, touched Casey's left tusk, and said, "Let's go."

The two experienced elephants and the one learner-keeper dutifully followed Bennie into the elephants' indoor quarters.

Bennie instructed me to put the elephants through their verbal routine and insure that they responded to each command precisely and completely. I said, "Follow," and together we walked a big circle around the perimeter of the stall. At first I was not aware that Casey was crowding me and the circle was becoming smaller! Bennie said, "You'd better do something." So I started over with firm commands and rewards and kept it up until I could stand alone in the middle of the stall and Casey and Lady would complete the full circle.

We went through the entire regimen, over and over again, until the elephants responded to each and every instruction precisely, and I was exhausted. When I opened the door to take them back out both elephants bolted off across the Veldt! Bennie said, "You'd better DO something." I didn't know what to do, so I yelled, "CASEY! LADY!" They stopped and came back to me like two giant puppy dogs. From that time on we had harmonious accord and mutual respect.

On one occasion this strong rapport probably saved my life. I was bringing the elephant pair out of the building onto the Veldt. Casey was on the outside, Lady to his left in the middle, and I was on her left side walking alongside the concrete wall. A sparrow flew over Casey and spooked him. His massive head flinched to the left and hit Lady, pushing her into me and smashing me against the wall.

It knocked every ounce of breath out of me and I just crumpled to the ground. No other keeper was around. I was helpless. This was the type of situation where they could have trampled me out of fear and excitement. But those two elephants just stood over me, nervous and confused, waiting for a response. Finally I got to the point where I could sit up and say to them, "It's O.K." And it was, thanks to our bond.

A primary rule of animal behavior (which I learned early on) is: when you think you've seen everything, or that you know it all—HA! Get ready! A case in point would be the interaction between Spotty, the big male giraffe, and Casey, the big male African elephant. One day on the African Veldt Casey was next to the heavy stockade barrier that separated the giraffes from the other animals. Spotty, on the other side, arched his neck over the barrier and hit Casey with his head, delivering a powerful blow that made a WHUMP sound.

In response, Casey reached up and wrapped his trunk around Spotty's neck, just below the head, and pulled it toward the ground. My heart stopped!

With 40,000 muscles in his trunk Casey could uproot a tree—or break a giraffe's neck! But a giraffe has tremendous strength and, before I could do anything, Spotty lifted his head, pulling Casey's trunk upward, and broke free of the grasp . . . much to my relief.

If I had not seen it, I would not have believed it.

Then the most amazing thing happened: Spotty again leaned over, but this time simply rested his head on top of Casey's head, and Casey just stood there, subdued. It was unusual dominant submissive interspecies behavior. I carried a small camera with me and fortunately got the photo. Twenty years later Dorothy Harvey, then editor of *Capper's Weekly,* a national newspaper published in Topeka, would run this photo in color on the front page in conjunction with National Zoo and Aquarium month.

Later a separate exhibit was developed on the west side of the Veldt for a pair of black rhinos, with indoor quarters in the Elephant House. More properly called the hook-lipped rhino, they have a strong, pointed-shaped upper lip adapted for grasping twigs and leaves. I found out just how strong their lip is one day when I backed against the bars of the transfer stall during cleaning and the male rhino hooked his lip in the rear pocket of my khaki trousers and ripped them halfway down my leg.

I would have been completely satisfied to spend the rest of my days on the African Veldt, but Mr. Cully was determined to develop my potential as a "general zoo man." His pride and joy was the Children's Zoo, and he put me in charge of it. Built by Park Department personnel in 1948, it was unique at the time (although children's zoos are commonplace today).

Mr. Cully liked to say that it could very well be named "The Children's, the Parents' and the Grandparents' Zoo," because it was a magical place for the "young at heart" who include all of us. There was no question it was popular. During 1960, from May through October, 778,462 visitors passed through the turnstiles.

In 1961 Hallmark Cards, Inc. donated funds for a "Birthday House" in the Children's Zoo and, yes, that also became my responsibility. We hosted five parties a day, seven days a week, and we were booked six months in advance! Once an entire kindergarten class of 71 celebrated birthdays in two separate parties, one immediately following the other. On some occasions I even dressed in a clown costume!

In July 1962 the Associated Press featured a story (with photo) entitled "Zookeeper Is Host To Tot Set" that ran nationwide. This generated great interest and I was asked to write an article for *American City Magazine.* It was published in their March 1963 issue under the title, "Birthday Parties at the Zoo." All this notoriety, and not because of my achievements with animals, but with people!

Kansas City was the site of the annual conference of the American Association of Zoological Parks and Aquariums in September 1962.

Mr. Cully was elected president of the organization by his colleagues. Among other duties during the conference, I conducted behind the scenes tours of the K.C. Zoo for delegates from across the country. I met many zoo directors, including Lawrence Curtis of the Fort Worth Zoo, who asked if I might be interested in a supervisory position at his zoo.

WHOA! I had not even *thought* of leaving the K.C. Zoo just yet. True, it would be career advancement with a higher salary. And our son, James, had been born in March, so we now had two children to support.

But everything was going so well, and I still had so much to learn, and I really loved this place, and . . . was I ready?

Pink Porpoises and a

Misunderstood Octopus

Ready or not, I had to consider this. Actually, I felt I had the ideal zoo situation in Kansas City. At age 23 I was on schedule with my plan to gain direct animal experience as a keeper until I was 30 or 35, then possibly a mid-level zoo position for another five years, so that perhaps by age 40 I would have the knowledge and skills to qualify for a director's position.

But now, an unexpected opportunity for professional advancement at another zoo had occurred. Geeze—what to do: was this the next best step for my career? Was I qualified for the position? There were so many things to consider . . .

Lawrence Curtis followed proper protocol. He had written a formal letter to me, but in care of Mr. Cully. That way his colleague, my boss, could decide whether or not to pass it along. Excitedly, Mr. Cully called me immediately. He had reviewed the proposal and felt it was something I should seriously consider, as the Fort Worth Zoo emphasized aspects of operation and exhibition dissimilar from the K.C. Zoo.

The contrast between the two zoos was dramatic. Kansas City Zoo was known for its extensive collection of large mammals (and its African Veldt); Fort Worth Zoo featured unique small mammals. Kansas City had waterfowl, ratites, penguins and flamingos; Fort Worth focused on tropical birds and raptors. Kansas City had discontinued reptile exhibits some years before; Fort Worth was just completing a state-of-the-art Herpetarium devoted to reptiles and amphibians. Kansas City had never exhibited fish; Fort Worth was one of the few zoos to have an aquarium complex on the grounds; Kansas City was a municipal operation through the Board of Park Commissioners; Fort Worth was administered jointly by a Zoological Association and the City of Fort Worth. These differences, together with Mr. Cully's encouragement and blessing, swayed my decision.

The position was offered to me on November 14, 1962. I accepted on November 15, at a salary of $285 a month.

What followed was a whirlwind! Lawrence Curtis wanted me to start on December 1. No problem with Mr. Cully, but I couldn't do everything necessary to move my family by then. Alas, I didn't even own a car!

Having decided to leave the family in Kansas City for the present, I scurried around to get myself to Texas. Taking only what I could carry in a suitcase, and leaving Margaret with not only two small children but with all the animals at home as well, I departed Kansas City by train at 10:00 pm on December 2 and arrived in Fort Worth at 8:40 am the next morning.

I was officially welcomed to the Fort Worth Zoological Park staff on December 3,1962.

The whirlwind continued. The new Herpetarium was in the final rush to open and for a week I helped with the finishing touches. On December 10, 1962 I was appointed Animal Department Supervisor, a curatorial level position, responsible for care of birds throughout the zoo. One humorous incident immediately comes to mind.

The City Market had offered the zoo free beets—bushels and bushels of free beets! The food budget was tight, and as an economy measure, the zoo accepted them. At the next staff meeting we were advised to feed beets to everything in the zoo. So we did.

The Tropical Bird House in the zoo contained "jewel box" exhibits, which were glass-fronted individual habitat settings for delicate tropical birds. After several days of eating beets the birds started passing red stools . . . all over the rocks, the branches, the sand, the glass . . .

My office happened to be in the Bird House and all day long there was a steady stream of zoo visitors poking their heads in the door saying, "Hey, mister, your birds are bleeding!"

That was the least of my worries. I still had to get my family to Texas. I rented a one-story house in Fort Worth at 2015 Granger. It had a dilapidated garage in back, which I didn't need, but would be handy for storage since the house had no basement. Although I could walk to work, someone from the zoo usually gave me a ride.

A commercial moving van brought down what furniture we had, plus my books, files and skull collection. My live specimens were the biggest problem. I found homes for everything except a number of really special reptiles. These included Ginger, the snapping turtle ("Ginger doesn't bite; Ginger snaps"); Schroeder, the alligator; Sam, the gopher tortoise; the two gaboon vipers, and Big Red. This was not the type of situation where you ask a favor from your father-in-law, especially since Margaret was pregnant with our third child.

Charlie Van Trease to the rescue! He was my snake-hunting buddy (and a captain with TWA airlines), who had offered to help. He drove all the previously mentioned reptiles, his wife and two children, my wife and two children, from Kansas City to Fort Worth in a small Ford station wagon in the dead of winter—and made it! What a hero! To this day he considers it one of the great adventures of his life.

In 1963 the Fort Worth Zoo had some of the "stars" of the Zoo World— people and animals. Many of the staff later advanced in the profession at other institutions. Zoo director Lawrence Curtis became director at Portland, Oregon, Oklahoma City, Oklahoma, and Riyadh, Saudi Arabia; general curator Frank Thompson was director at Evansville, Indiana, before starting an import business in Florida; herpetarium supervisor John

Mehrtens built and opened the zoo in Columbia, South Carolina; mammal keeper Tim Jones was appointed director of the Waco, Texas zoo; and reptile keeper Steve Dobbs moved to the Atlanta, Georgia zoo as curator of reptiles, and eventually advanced to director.

Animal stars included everything from aardvarks (first animal listed in the dictionary) to a giant pangolin (this particular one was later featured in LIFE Magazine). Some of my favorites were Blue Bonnet Belle the hippo, Queen Tut the elephant, Mike the gorilla, Tuffy the huge Kodiak bear, and the giraffes Goldie and Topper (he was a **giant** male). In addition there were a number of nameless animals: an electric eel, a beautiful cock-of-the-rock, an Australian lungfish, a spectacular giant Japanese salamander, and a South American Harpy eagle who probably hatched around 1957 and is still alive at this writing (2007).

While the Fort Worth Zoo did *not* have a yeti or a unicorn or a griffin, it *did* have a creature almost as mythical: a pink porpoise! This species (*Inia geoffrensis*) is also known as the Amazon fresh water dolphin, with a range throughout much of the Amazon River system and extending into the Orinoco drainage. It is a much more primitive form of dolphin than *Tursiops*—the well-known performing saltwater porpoises like Flipper. I say "mythical" in that the Indians around Leticia, the Amazon River border town between Columbia and Brazil, said that sometimes these creatures would come out of the river to sing songs so sweet that humans were enticed to the scene.

Despite their popular name, pink porpoises are not solid pink. Rather, they are pale whitish with a faint bluish-gray above and a pinkish cast on the underside. They have a bulging head, small eyes and a cylindrical tooth-studded beak with a fixed smile. Males are larger than females and adults range from 6½ to 8 feet or more and weigh 300 to 450 pounds.

A special addition was built onto the Aquarium, containing a large indoor tank allowing both above and underwater viewing. Overhead the ceiling was stippled with some curious form of stalactites, which always prompted visitors' questions. When the porpoises surfaced, they exhaled with a "Whoosh" through the blowhole on the top of their heads. They would blow a misty jet, often containing mucus, at least eight feet in the air. But when visitors were told that it was just porpoise snot it sort of detracted from the aura of these wonderful animals. Sometimes they would expel air underwater and a large bubble would rise to the water's surface.

Pinky, the female, was already at the zoo but Paddles, the male, was acquired shortly after my arrival. I was privileged to be on the 24-hour observation team when he was introduced into the tank. For a week I had night duty, yet was still expected to put in a full day at my regular responsibilities. However, it was *very special*, since I was the only human present with these two leviathans as they got acquainted night after night in a surrealistic series of aqua-ballets. Years later in the Amazon I had a sighting of this species in the wild, but it was not the same as these nights in the Fort Worth Aquarium with the pink porpoises.

This brings us to Ormsby, the octopus, described at the time in Fort Worth Zoo literature as "one of the weirdest and most fascinating of aquatic animals." That he was. But he was also much misunderstood. I know, as I was there. You may not believe what I am about to relate, but it is true— even *I* could not make this up!

First, realize that I had a temporary office in the aquarium, since the Bird House was being remodeled. It was simply a desk against the wall in the public area, hidden behind a temporary vertical partition. Hence, while no one realized I was there, I could not help overhearing comments by visitors. And keep in mind that an octopus is a cephalopod mollusk with a soft sac-like body surrounded by eight slender appendages, commonly called tentacles.

One day a school teacher with her class of elementary students was explaining, "Now, children, this is a leopard shark; now, children, this is a spitting fish; now, children, this is a sea horse." They came around the corner and there was Ormsby, suspended in the water with his eight tentacles hanging down.

The teacher let out a gasp and exclaimed: "Oh, children, come here quick!" I could hear the pitter-patter of little shoes as they all gathered around the teacher in great anticipation. Then, with solemn authority, she decreed: "Now, children, this animal is an octopus; and you can always tell when an animal *is* an octopus—just **look** at all those testicles!"

Skeletons in My Garage

Fort Worth was so much more than a cowtown. Besides the zoo, there were fine museums, a beautiful botanical garden and, yes—used book stores—good ones! And as a state, Texas offered a great variety of habitats (even a coast) and some unique wildlife. Everyone was most hospitable and I was invited weekly to reptile collecting jaunts, nocturnal armadillo quests, or meetings of the Zoo Fauna Association.

Texas also had zoos: large zoos, small zoos, old zoos, new zoos, public zoos, private zoos. I knew about them, had read about them, and wanted to see them all. Still, I had no car. Hence, on my day off I'd venture throughout the great state of Texas by motor coach (usually Continental Trailways). Visiting the Dallas Zoo was a simple day trip, but other zoos were far-flung and required careful planning, especially when I had just one day off.

Houston Zoo was a good example. After work I'd take a city bus to the downtown bus depot and board a coach for the overnight ride to Houston. On arrival the next morning I'd catch a local bus to Hermann Park and spend the day at the zoo taking photos, making notes, visiting staff, and watching the crowd. At the end of the day, tired but fulfilled, it was back to the bus depot for the overnight return trip to Fort Worth, then catching a city bus to the zoo in time for work (a bit bleary-eyed and unkempt).

Getting around town without a car became more cumbersome as our family grew. Our third child, Joyce, was born in Fort Worth and Margaret now had three small children to manage at home plus the assorted menagerie. Just going to the grocery store was a challenge. It was too far to walk so we had to take the bus. I can still visualize Margaret with the baby in a stroller and me responsible for the other two little ones. The five of us would clamber onto the bus with the stroller, huge paper sacks of baby food plus glass gallon jugs of milk, and all the while the driver would be shaking his head in disbelief.

Neighbors knew I worked at the zoo and would give a friendly wave in passing. My reputation spread when the *Fort Worth Star Telegram* ran a front page feature article (and my picture) on February 8, 1963. Headlined "Appetite Like a Bird?" it told of the zoo's birds and what they ate. It was well written and following are a few excerpts.

"Clarke has about 140 different species and around 500 birds in his care, ranging in size from the thimble-size red-legged honeycreeper to 8-foot tall African ostriches, which weigh around 300 pounds. The zoo has six.

"In a week's time, Clarke doles out to his 500 feathered friends about 20 heads of lettuce, a bushel of bananas, 250 apples, 200 oranges, 28 pounds of grapes, 50 pounds of carrots, seven dozen hard boiled eggs, 175 pounds of raw ground beef (eaten mainly by birds of prey and wading birds), 200 mice, 4,000 mealworms, 1,000 crickets, 300 pounds of hen scratch, 100 pounds of miscellaneous seed and between 150 and 200 pounds of fish."

Reading such an article made my position at the zoo seem idyllic. Not mentioned, unfortunately, was my staff of keepers who actually cared for and fed the birds (the really fun part). I was already into administration, which meant more supervisory and paperwork responsibilities, with less time for direct contact with animals. Still, as my neighbors read this article, my work probably seemed glamorous and was quite acceptable, since zoo birds were, to most people, innocuous. Please keep this in mind as the next innocent, but inevitable, unexpected eventuality unfolds.

Before I get to that, I would be remiss not to mention at least one more inside story pertaining to birds (or should I say "the" bird). We had several marabou storks from Africa. These are huge birds, nearly five feet tall with a massive bill and a bald head (what's wrong with that?). They feed on fish and carrion, often scavenging with vultures on large carcasses. Their daily diet at the zoo included fish, ground meat, and a vitamin/mineral mix, which the storks picked up with their long, strong, pointed bills.

Frequently they had social squabbles among themselves, usually harmless. Then one day a stork lost most of its lower bill in a fight, which meant it could not feed itself. Our ingenious veterinarian fashioned a prosthetic lower mandible using aluminum and attached it to what remained of the jaw structure. While this stork could not pick up food, he *could* catch it, so each day we hand-tossed fish and enriched meatballs to him. To visitors he looked like all of his companions. To the zoo staff, however, he was special, and known as the only animal in the zoo with . . . an aluminum pecker.

Now, as promised, the innocent, inevitable, unexpected eventuality! I shudder as I recall it!

The summer of 1963 in Fort Worth was hot—HOT—**HOT!** Our rental house had no air-conditioning and, despite floor fans droning day and night, we sweltered in the Texas heat and humidity.

At the zoo the huge male giraffe had died and I had assisted with the postmortem exam. I also asked for and received permission to acquire the head, neck and a front leg, as I wanted to prepare a partial skeleton for educational purposes. A friend on the staff had a pick-up truck and together we struggled to load the various parts, covering them with a tarp and driving to my house. For most of my osteological preparations I simply boiled the skulls and/or bones in a cauldron on the stove. This loosened the flesh, which I could then pick off, using various tools. But with a head weighing 75 lbs., a neck longer than I was tall, and a front leg long enough to reach the ceiling, this procedure was not practical.

However, I had in the backyard some oversized stock watering tanks I had used for turtles. We dragged those into the old ramshackle garage, filled them with water, and deposited the skull and bones to soak until the flesh fell off.

Not-a-good-idea . . . especially since it was sooo hot—HOT—**HOT!**

The garage had no windows. Not only was it dark inside, it was airless, oppressive and stifling. When I departed for work the following morning, the atmosphere was already ripe, and I thought that I might have to make another plan in the next day or two. My neighbors had other ideas and filed a complaint with the Health Department! That afternoon two inspectors (wearing face masks) knocked on our front door. Margaret answered in all innocence with three little kids clinging to her. The inspectors said something was dead in our garage and demanded access. Margaret bravely refused and, in spite of the putrid odor now permeating the air, shrugged her shoulders and calmly said, "I don't smell anything." Incensed, the inspectors stormed off the front porch vowing to be back the next day with a court order.

She immediately called me at the zoo. I quickly contacted my friend with the pick-up truck. Fortunately his parents had a farm outside town and said we could put the "artifacts-in-process" out in the pasture. It seemed like nightfall would never come, but finally under cover of darkness, we made the switch. Afterwards I did what I could to expunge or mask the stench in the garage. By the next day it was greatly reduced and there was no physical evidence of a skeleton, giraffe or otherwise. Even so, from then on some neighbors looked down their noses at us, while others kept their noses in the air.

But the real shock was yet to come—for my neighbors *and* me. The newspaper article on birds was benign and acceptable. But the column entitled "Dateline: Fort Worth" by Jack Moseley on Sunday, June 16, 1963 sealed my fate.

It was not Jack's fault. He did what is known as a "human interest" story about a guy who works at the zoo and has a zoo at home to boot. He opened with, "Visitors get a start when they enter the bathroom of the Gary Clarke home out at 2015 Grainger. They are usually greeted by Schroeder, the family's pet alligator."

He went on to recount some of the other animals and then dropped the bomb: "But Gary Clarke also keeps a few other personalities around the house. Big Red is a red diamond-backed rattler and he is kept in private quarters as are Gary's two other reptiles, a pair of African Gaboon vipers. These happen to be two of the world's most poisonous snakes."

That did it. Apparently someone called our landlord, whom we had never met. He lived in Seattle, WA and must have jumped in his car and driven non-stop to Fort Worth, where he burst into the house and evicted us!

After a quick negotiation he agreed that, if I moved the animals out immediately, the family could stay until I found another residence. With luck and help from friends outside the neighborhood, we quickly relocated to 2755 W. Canty to end a rather traumatic ordeal. Word spread throughout the zoo world and I even received a letter from the Cullys at Kansas City Zoo that started, "Well, finally 'Big Red' managed to run you out of your house."

Interestingly enough, they went on to say that Topeka, Kansas had contacted them about me with reference to their zoo. When I was still at Kansas City, Preston Hale, the Topeka Park Commissioner, used to visit me and say, "We could use a young fella like you over at our zoo." Now John Goodin, a Topeka florist and businessman, held that office. In the spring of 1963 Fort Worth hosted the Zoo Conference (as Kansas City had done in the fall of 1962). Mr. Goodin sent his Park Superintendent, Dennis Showalter, to the conference as his representative. Guess what? He extended an offer for me to come to Topeka!

Geeze! Just when I was getting established and learning so much at the Fort Worth Zoo, I now faced another major decision that would have far-reaching implications on my career and family. Thank goodness, no one in Topeka knew of the skeletons in my garage.

Part 2

Elephants, Giraffes, Hippos and

How to Stripe a Tiger

How a brand new Zoo Director and Operation Noah's Ark brought the charismatic megavertebrates to the Gage Park Zoo in Topeka.

The only meeting place that the civilized world has negotiated between the absence and presence of the wild is the Zoo!

—Charles Siebert

Courtesy of the Topeka and Shawnee County Public Library   **Art work by Alice C. Sabatini**

PART 2

Elephants, Giraffes, Hippos and

How to Stripe a Tiger

"Ameliorate the Rest Room"

There are a few classic lines that seem to live on: "Dr. Livingstone, I presume?" and "To be or not to be" and "Play it again, Sam" and, of course, "Toto, I don't think we're in Kansas anymore." I admit "Ameliorate the Rest Room" is far from classic, but by gosh, it has lived on, at least in my world.

Yes, I said it—worse yet, I wrote it—in a letter to the City of Topeka Park Department outlining what I felt needed to be done to improve the existing zoo facilities if I were to consider the position of Director. Actually, I listed six categories with a total of 32 points covering topics from animal care to operation and maintenance, new exhibits to long range plans, educational activities to public relations. But "Ameliorate the Rest Room?" What sort of verbiage is that?

Certainly what then served as a public "rest room" needed drastic improvement, but I guess I was trying to sound impressive or something. For years after that, whenever I was tempted to use a fancy word or phrase, I was reminded of . . . you guessed it—ameliorate.

Topeka officials invited me to visit the city, see the zoo, and talk about the position, all expenses paid (or should I say reimbursed?). I took the overnight Rock Island train from Fort Worth, spent the day in Topeka, and returned overnight to Fort Worth. Still in my files is a copy of the City of Topeka Voucher No. 1239 for job interview expenses: 1 round trip train fare-$28.30; 1 cab fare-$0.55. Total: $28.85.

It was good I had seen things with my own eyes. Even the local paper, reflecting on the zoo, once stated: "Topeka's zoo consisted of a scraggly collection of domestic types, a few monkeys and deer and a dusty bison." What I had seen on my trip was better, but not much, and elicited serious concerns on my part. This was coupled by dire warnings from friends and associates. Such comments as, "That zoo's a loser" and "I heard the humane society was going to close it down" and, worse yet, "Nobody goes to the zoo in Topeka; they all drive to Kansas City."

All this prompted the infamous aforementioned letter, weird phrase and all, which the Topeka Park Department reviewed in detail.

It fell to Dennis Showalter to be the point man in final negotiations. As Park Superintendent, he would be my boss (and an excellent one as it turned out).

All these years later I must confess that I established what I thought might be impossible demands—demands I felt Topeka would not meet and, hence, they would say no to me and then I would not have to say no to them. But my plan backfired; they were so sincere and tried so hard that in the end I couldn't say no.

Topeka offered $450 a month. I asked for $500. They offered a Zoo Curator position; I asked for the title of Zoo Director. The zoo had a reputation as a political football; I expressed anxiety about that. I did not ask for a list of specific concessions; that would have been unrealistic and impractical. Instead I asked for what I termed "professional freedom." By that I meant the leeway to make decisions and initiate actions in the best interests of both the zoo and the community. I asked that they grant me the authority and I would accept the responsibility. In other words: LET ME TRULY BE THE ZOO DIRECTOR. I did not want to be a puppet-on-a-string with City Hall pulling the strings. I did not want to hire the Park Commissioner's nephew as a keeper simply because he "just loves animals." I did not want to be forced to do business with a certain vendor because they supported someone in the last political campaign.

I just knew Topeka would not agree. But they did!

Dennis Showalter wrote: "Mr. John Goodin, our new Park Commissioner, is interested in keeping our Zoo on a high level, doing some expanding, and thinks you are the man for the job." In a subsequent letter he stated: ". . Gary . . . we will do what we can to meet your requirements. They seem very sound . . . we are currently experiencing problems in the zoo. We need a good man right away. Please answer promptly, as we feel we must find someone soon. I pledge my fullest cooperation to you in getting our zoo to the place where we all can be truly proud of it."

How could I turn down such an impassioned plea? Even with colleagues saying, "If you go to Topeka, Clarke, we'll never hear from you again." True, Dennis did not offer a million dollars; he offered much more. Note what he said, in writing: "I *pledge* . . . fullest *cooperation* . . . *our zoo* . . . we *all* can be *truly proud* of it." Key words in my opinion. I took him at his word, and accepted the position, to start in the fall.

It was with regret that I left the Fort Worth Zoo. My short tenure had been so productive. But I had little time to lament as once again I was thrust into moving family, furniture, animals, books, and parts of a giraffe skeleton to the Capital City of Kansas. We settled in at 300 Waite street near Auburndale Park, just off I-70 at MacVicar. Our small frame house had one miniscule bathroom, one floor furnace, no air conditioning, no basement or garage. But my wife Margaret, a homemaker in the truest sense, made it a home for our growing family.

By now it must be obvious that the real heroine in the early stages of my zoo career was Margaret. Having wild animals in the house was an accepted thing. The real test of our still young marriage, however, was moving from Kansas City to Fort Worth; then from one house in Fort Worth to another; then from Fort Worth to Topeka—all in less than a year—with no car of our own (we simply could not afford one), and by then with three little kids. Our fourth child, John, was born less than a year after we came to Topeka. To recap our children: Janet was born in Columbia, Missouri, in 1961; James in Kansas City, Missouri, in 1962; Joyce in Fort Worth, Texas, in 1963; and John in Topeka, Kansas, in 1964. At this point Margaret advised me, in no uncertain terms, that we were *not* moving again. So, we bought our first TV set, and I had the wings clipped on the stork at the zoo.

Margaret was a brunette, but I was a redhead (in my youth when I had hair) and the children all started out as redheads. One day as we walked out of church with the kids all in a row like stair steps, a lady looked at Margaret, then me, then the kids and said, "My, I've never seen the brand so strong!"

Yes, Topeka would be a good place to raise the family.

So, here I was, a brand new zoo director, first day on the job (October 1, 1963), at a beat up desk in the service area with the smell of thawing fish and cleaning fluids, eager for come what may, and the telephone rings. The conversation went something like this:

"Are you the new zoo guy?"

"Yes."

"Well, one of your prairie dogs is digging up my backyard. Come and get it."

My second phone call of the day was a different caller but same script, as was the third, and fourth, and . . .

It seems that the entire colony of prairie dogs had, one by one, dug under the fence of their exhibit and were loose—not just around the zoo, not just in Gage Park, but all over the surrounding neighborhoods in our end of town—an embarrassing problem no one had previously mentioned to me. At the time it was not funny, but as I think back now, well over four decades later, I can't help but crack a smile. Margaret kept a scrapbook from the beginning, and as I carefully turn the pages the yellowed news-print flakes and crumbles. Everything is vivid in my memory, but it's like reading about someone else.

*****

It was my good fortune to join a talented team at the Topeka Park Department in 1963. In addition to Mr. Goodin and Dennis, there was maintenance supervisor Griff, field office receptionist Katie Sherrow, horti-culturist Bob Foster, carpenter Mr. Walden, Woody the welder, forester Lester Terry and Ed Carmona the draftsman. These folks and many others put forth a great deal of effort at, and on behalf of, the zoo, with much behind the scenes, unrecognized work. I'm forever grateful to all of them for their contributions.

Six days after I started at the zoo a baby mountain lion was born and became more a part of the Clarke family than any other animal. This was the first birth for its mother, who was young and inexperienced. After several days of close observation, it was obvious the mother was not providing adequate care, which is not unusual with a first-born, either in or out of the zoo. Some zoologists feel it is like a "trial run," and may be nature's way of preparing the mother for future offspring.

We removed the baby from the mother in an attempt to hand rear it. Since the zoo had no special equipment or facilities to care for newborns, we took the cub home where we could prepare formula, sterilize bottles and provide 24-hour care.

The baby was a female and we named her Jenkins, in keeping with all of our children's names starting with the letter "J." The cub was blind, toothless and could be held in the palm of one hand. Since she was unable to regulate her own body temperature, we kept her in an Isolette and fed her every three hours. Once again, Margaret should get the (mountain) lion's share of the credit for raising Jenkins.

The Topeka Daily Capital featured a front page story and photo about Jenkins on October 15, 1963 after which the community followed her progress intently. By the time she made her debut at the zoo on Sunday, January 19, 1964 she was already a star personality. Jenkins continued to be front page news and, at five months, made a special appearance to an excited overflow crowd during the pre-school storytelling half-hour at the Topeka Public Library. By then she weighed 12 pounds and was on a solid diet, but still had her "baby spots" which faded as she matured.

Our plan from the first was to not make a pet out of Jenkins, and to transfer her back to the zoo as soon as she was ready. Active and playful, Jenkins soon reached the point where she was sharpening her claws on the furniture and climbing the curtains. That was when Margaret said, "O.K.—back to the zoo!"

Jenkins always remained extremely responsive and friendly as she grew to adulthood. Even when she was full-grown she would readily leap into my arms (sometimes nearly knocking me down). I guess she thought I always had caught her before, and I always would. She'd put one paw on top of my head and start licking—she had the roughest tongue! And she would purr. But she always kept her claws retracted. She was 100 per cent mountain lion, eventually had cubs of her own and raised them, but trusted me to examine her babies.

Jenkins belonged to the zoo and to the community. But from my family's point of view she was very special and always remained a part of our family, as we were all new to Topeka at the time.

It would be unfair to you, gentle reader, to close this chapter without some amplification about the "rest room" that needed to be ameliorated (that is a rather sophisticated word; look it up—I just did once again). Anyone who visited the Gage Park Zoo in the late 1950's/early 1960's probably can't help remembering that in the only building—the old green-house/monkey house—there was a toilet stool set against one wall in a public viewing area enclosed only by a plywood partition with no ceiling. The partition was low enough that one could peek over the top and observe the occupant in an embarrassing situation. I couldn't believe it! As I think back I realize that ameliorate was not quite the right word; maybe it should have been annihilate, or even eradicate, or better yet, liquidate!

In time we took all of those actions to the rest room, but that dogged word lives on to this day.

Acrimony to Achievement,

Garbage to Gourmet

I must confess that being only twenty-four years old was much too young to be the director of a real zoo, regardless of the fact that I had some practical experience and book knowledge. This was true even though the zoo in question was a small, little known zoo that people overlooked—or should I say *particularly* since it was a small, little known zoo that people overlooked.

True, I was already getting bald and could usually bluff my way throughout the community (and to some degree at City Hall), since I appeared a bit older and maybe wiser. But to the long entrenched Gage Park Zoo crew of four—a zoo foreman and three keepers—I'm sure I was just a "young whippersnapper." And it did not help that I was from out-of-town.

They were a bunch of crusty old guys who had run their little empire quite well without me, thank you very much. As holdover political appointees from a past administration, I understood their resentment of me . . . the new kid. I just wanted a good zoo; they just wanted status quo.

One keeper was the most paradoxical individual I'd ever met. He claimed to have worked in Colorado Springs at the Cheyenne Mountain Zoo, but I was unable to verify that. Anyway, he said that when he was there they had "the cleanest zoo in the world." Yet, he was the sloppiest keeper you could imagine. I never figured that out.

With a crew of four the zoo was actually short one person for one day each week. Here's how it worked. The zoo was divided into three areas (or "runs" as they were called): cats and bears, hoofed stock and water birds, and the monkey house/commissary. Each crew member worked five days a week but the zoo was open seven days a week. A relief keeper would cover an area for two days a week for a regular off keeper, then do it again for another regular keeper, but only one day a week for the last off keeper. The zoo needed 21 "work days" a week to cover all areas but only had enough keepers for 20, not to mention scheduled vacations and unscheduled sick days (lots of them, especially after payday). So, when I started as zoo director I was a keeper at least one day a week and usually more.

Not that I minded. I very much enjoyed working with this new set of animals and really wanted to know them on a close personal basis. There was so much to do to make this zoo "happen," and I was eager to get on with it. Since I had no office as such at the zoo, I established one at home and did most of my administrative and planning work there in the evenings.

In my keeper capacity I faced a considerable challenge. My fellow keepers knew all the inside secrets of the zoo and were reluctant to share them with me. Such things as: which drains clogged the easiest, what hydrants had the lowest water pressure, where the new rakes and shovels were hidden, which sections of hose always sprung leaks, the little tricks to get transfer gates to function, how to convince rusty padlocks to work just one more time, where the broken sewer lines were located, how to keep the gas furnace going, etc. But I caught on quickly.

And being a keeper enabled me to learn all the crew's sneaky antics as well: when they cut corners or covered up, where they cleaned unseen areas weekly instead of daily, how they improperly scrubbed water pans and pools, and of course the age old trick of leaving the dirtiest of jobs for the next guy—and I was the next guy more often than not!

Over time the little games ceased, a team spirit developed, and we **all** became better keepers. I felt I had gained some respect, even though I would never be accepted as a "good ole boy." But a zoo is more than animals and we needed to provide better visitor care as well, something the crew had not pursued in the past. I doubt they had ever looked at the zoo from a visitor's perspective, so one day we took a walk-through together on the other side of the guard-rail.

WOW! A lot of things immediately caught their eye: litter on the walks and lawns, weeds along fence lines, broken wires on guard-rails, spilled hay and bedding in public areas, mud on sidewalks, loose slats and protruding nails on park benches, many items that needed paint, old fallen branches and sticks, unsightly tools in view of visitors—you name it. Maybe the zoo physical plant was old and haphazard, but at least it could be **clean**. The crew started taking pride in the overall appearance of the zoo and, with new uniforms, developed more pride in themselves as well, especially when visitors took notice and said something.

While all of this was well and good, the zoo had a big problem—actually a lot of problems, but one in particular I considered quite serious. It was the way they were feeding the animals. Not just what was fed, but how it was procured. The only acceptable aspect of the whole system was hay, which was grown and harvested by the Park Department under Park Superintendent Dennis Showalter's supervision.

Otherwise, the keepers fed the animals what they *thought* the animals should have . . . or what they liked! And they obtained foodstuffs however and wherever they could, as did so many zoos in similar situations in that era. The first time I stepped into the walk-in cooler at the zoo I was appalled by parts of poorly butchered beef and horse carcasses stacked in the corner. What's this? It seemed the foreman monitored sheriff department radio calls and whenever a livestock truck was in a wreck the zoo rushed to the scene. Sawed off hunks of a carcass would be thrown to the big cats and the leftover bones hosed down the drains (which regularly clogged). Acquisition of produce was just as bad. The foreman would take the zoo's only pickup truck (which we needed on the grounds for daily operations) and spend hours in back of local grocery stores scouring through discarded boxes of rotten produce and stale bread.

Then there was the "mixed feed" ritual. Once again the foreman would be off in the coveted pickup to a co-op elevator considerably south of town to get the "special" grain mixture. This usually took half a day. I tagged along one time (complete with scowling and growling from the foreman) to see what took so long. Turned out the only thing special about the grain mixture was that the co-op owner was an old buddy of a previous park commissioner, and he and the foreman needed considerable time to chew the fat.

Shortly after that we set up accounts with established suppliers (who were happy to give the zoo a discount) and had quality foods delivered to the zoo. This not only saved time but enabled us to repossess the pick-up truck from the foreman.

We revised diets and initiated a system of diet cards with designated ingredients and amounts. Regardless of who was preparing food on a given day, it needed to be consistent. Even so it seems to be human tendency for keepers to give their favorite animals a "little extra treat" whether it is good for them or not. This makes it difficult to properly evaluate the general health or veterinary condition of an animal. Many zoos faced this situation, and little did I dream that the Topeka Zoo—of all the zoos in the world— would play a key role in the development and standardization of balanced prepared diets for zoo animals.

The longtime African lion pair, Willie and Wilma, were two of the most popular residents of the Gage Park Zoo in the 1960's. They regularly produced cubs, but their last two had what appeared to be a nutritional deficiency. Although the zoo had a local veterinarian on call, I decided to consult with a specialist, particularly since (by geographical good fortune) there was one in Topeka. I contacted Mark Morris, Jr., DVM, who headed a nationally recognized staff of animal nutrition experts in Topeka. As a research veterinarian, Dr. Morris developed the Science Diet line of pet foods.

Dr. Morris took the cubs to his research center for further studies. Sure enough, the cubs were suffering from a nutritional disease in which the long bones fail to grow properly. The cause of the disease was an imbalance between calcium and phosphorous produced by feeding just horsemeat or beef.

The disease had been known for 100 years and zoo cats frequently experienced it. The meat diet being fed to most zoo cats, even when supplemented with vitamins and minerals, was simply inadequate. House cats had been fed a balanced and adequate, single-source, prepared diet for 30 years. Why couldn't zoo cats be fed the same way?

Dr. Morris asked me if our zoo would be interested in a joint research effort to try to develop a prepared diet that would provide zoo felines with adequate nutrition. I answered, "Definitely."

It was a fascinating process. The wild felines at the zoo were divided into control and experimental groups. All animals were weighed and blood samples obtained. A rating system on flesh condition, stool formation and coat appearance was established. The research staff at Theracon Laboratories would develop various formulations and we would field test them at the zoo. Both the regular and experimental diets were carefully prepared and weighed, and daily records were maintained on amounts accepted by each specimen. Participating animals remained on exhibit during the entire project. The big challenge was not so much balanced nutrition, but palatability. House cats are notoriously finicky eaters, so imagine the problem with a B-I-G zoo cat! And we had to win over the keepers, who thought that feeding the cats anything but a big chunk of raw meat was just not right.

Eventually a prepared feline diet was developed and this led to other diets, for a variety of species, scientifically formulated to provide adequate nourishment from a single source. These were marketed nationally and internationally under the brand name ZuPreem, and utilized by dozens of zoos around the world. It was most gratifying that our small zoo could make a significant contribution to the zoo world and to the improved nutritional health of captive exotic animals. More importantly, we had solved the big problem of properly feeding the animals in our zoo.

On a personal note I might add that this collaboration resulted in a lasting friendship with Mark Morris, Jr. and his family. Over the years the Morris family demonstrated tremendous support to the continued progress of the Topeka Zoo. Long after my tenure they were instrumental in the development of a new Education Center and Veterinary Hospital, as well as exhibits for African birds.

Another bonus from my affiliation with Mark Morris Associates was the privilege of working with other research veterinarians, including Dr. Stanley Teeter (who consulted on hand-rearing "Teeter the Tiger"), Dr. Lon D. Lewis, and Dr. George Doering—all strong advocates for the Topeka Zoo.

How to Stripe a Tiger

Being the zoo director was not an eight to five, Monday through Friday situation. So much to do and so little time. The hours flashed by, seemingly at the speed of light. Days and nights melted and ran together in a continuous stream of events and frenzied activity. It was exhausting yet exhilarating and suddenly I realized I had been in Topeka six months already! Not a lot of time in some respects, yet great strides had been made with the zoo. With no car, I walked to work from my house to Gage Park, usually through the State Hospital grounds. When I had a meeting downtown at City Hall I would take the bus.

Important management practices and improved daily operating procedures were now in place and my thoughts turned to developing the zoo as a community resource. To do this, particularly in a modest municipality with limited resources, would require broad based support. In contemplating the best approach, I thought that a citizens' group, composed primarily of families, might be appropriate. Not a "zoological society" (which sounded scientific and reserved) but more a "friends of the zoo," open to all.

Good idea. However, I really did not know many people yet and I also realized it would take an inordinate amount of time to identify select individuals from all over town in various capacities to contribute their expertise to form such a group.

Enter Tom Root. He was President of the Topeka Active 20-30 Club, a group of young professionals in the community between the ages of 20 and 40, many with families. Their purpose was to provide service and improvements in Topeka, and they were good at it. Tom approached me and said the 20-30 Club would like to donate an elephant to the zoo. An elephant? Maybe someday, but that was not what the zoo needed now.

Wanting to take advantage of the 20-30 Club's offer to help the zoo, I shared with Tom my idea for a friends organization, and told him I thought the 20-30 Club could make it happen. He invited me to speak before the members and I welcomed the opportunity. What an enthusiastic and responsive bunch they were!

My program explained the purpose and value of a support group to help the zoo develop and realize its potential. I proposed that the 20-30 Club had all of the resources to form such an organization. This included an attorney to prepare the Articles of Incorporation and By-laws, and apply for tax-exempt status; an accountant to serve as treasurer; a printer to prepare membership applications and hopefully a newsletter; members who could make contacts with businesses and professions to solicit support for the zoo; and a ready-made charter membership!

The membership embraced these ideas and immediately voted for the club to pay the first year's dues for each of its members (45 total) in the new friends group. This created a treasury as well as instant membership. SUPER!

The Topeka Friends of the Zoo became official in April 1964. While the 20-30 Club continued its strong support, it also recognized the importance of involvement by non-club members. Tom Root served as President and Ted Reed as Treasurer, both 20-30 members, but J.B. Holland, an educator, served as Vice-President and Mary Hall, a librarian, as Secretary.

To get the new Topeka Friends of the Zoo (TFOTZ) known and established in the community we needed a project, one in which everyone could participate. And while the zoo was not ready for an elephant we certainly could manage a spectacular species that would be a first for us—TIGERS!

The Miami, Florida zoo had a young pair of Bengal tigers available and agreed to hold them until we raised the necessary $2,000.00. When we announced the campaign in May 1964 I had a large sign featuring the outline of two tigers displayed in the empty future exhibit. I had counted the stripes on a pair of tigers and calculated that each stripe cost $20.00. Each time TFOTZ received $20.00 in contributions we would paint a stripe on a tiger outline so visitors could keep track of our progress. When both tigers were completely striped we would reach our goal. Before that happened the Topeka Board of Realtors stepped forward and contributed the full amount. Talk about community support! Contributions received up until that time from other sources were deposited in the TFOTZ treasury for future projects.

But the community involvement went far beyond the fund raising campaign. TFOTZ then initiated a naming contest among elementary school children. The boys suggested names for the male tiger, and the winner was "Tabor"—an acronym formed from Topeka Board of Realtors. "Dacca" was the name chosen by the girls for the female—and therein lies an interesting tale. The young schoolgirl who submitted Dacca had read the name in a library book, *My Zoo Family* by Helen Martini, wife of the head keeper of the Lion House at the Bronx Zoo in New York. Mrs. Martini had hand raised three tiger cubs in 1944, which was then an unusual event. One of the three cubs was named Dacca. Subsequently, the Bronx Zoo's Dacca gave birth to a female cub who was acquired by the Miami Zoo. In true stranger-than-fiction fashion, Topeka's new cubs were purchased from the Miami Zoo, and our female Dacca was a granddaughter of the Bronx Zoo's Dacca. The twist to our tiger tale is that neither the girl who submitted the name nor the TFOTZ judges knew of the relationship between the two Daccas.

The cubs arrived June 11, 1964. They were six months old and so small they could fit through the feeding slot in the back door of their den. Tabor weighed 50 pounds and Dacca 39 pounds. As anticipated, they were an immediate hit with the citizens of Topeka. The tigers thrived and multiplied. In fact, none of us realized just how significant these tigers would be to our zoo and to the conservation of tigers, as you will see.

Just as important was the fact that the Topeka Active 20-30 Club, by establishing the Topeka Friends of the Zoo, had initiated far-reaching impacts on all facets of our zoo. Less than a year after TFOTZ's inception their accomplishments were numerous. In addition to the pair of Bengal tigers, they had helped the zoo acquire a female Himalayan black bear, two Aldabra giant tortoises, a pair of Australian dingos, a pair of rhinoceros iguanas, a coatimundi, a pair of Australian wedge-tailed eagles, two reticulated pythons, and numerous North American waterfowl. This was not just from direct funding, but through the involvement of private citizens and such organizations as the Topeka Noon Sertoma Club, Fraternal Order of Eagles, and Shawnee Sportsmen. TFOTZ sponsored baby animal premiers, a film series, special events and eventually the education program of the zoo. The first newsletter, in 1965, was called the *Friends of the Zoo's letter* and edited by Mary Hall. This evolved into *The Bear Facts* and Nancy Cherry became editor in 1969. In 1971, under the guidance of TFOTZ President P.K. Worley, *ZOO Magazine* emerged, with Nancy Cherry continuing as editor until 1989. Thanks to Nancy and the creative folks at Admark and Mainline printing, *ZOO Magazine* was highly regarded in the zoo profession and won numerous awards. And it was distributed to every school classroom in the City of Topeka as an educational service.

But, back to 1964. It was amazing how much had been accomplished at the zoo in just the first year. I did not realize this myself until I was invited to present a paper to the Annual Conference of the American Association of Zoological Parks and Aquariums in Houston, TX in October of that year. This would be a first for me—and what an honor! I was still an untested zoo director, and Topeka was such a small zoo, not really part of the national professional scene.

What could *I* say to this august group of senior associates, established leaders in the profession . . . the ones I emulated, the ones who had already built the nation's zoos and aquariums? Giving this considerable thought it struck me that one of the main reasons I had come to Topeka was because I felt the zoo—as bad as it was in some regards—had *potential*. It did. And with limited resources, but a helluva lot of enthusiasm, some of that potential had been realized my first twelve months. HA! Here was my theme!

Our zoo *was* off and running, and I wrote a twelve page paper entitled, "Utilizing the Potential of a Zoo." In researching the published proceedings of past AAZPA conferences, as well as the *International Zoo Yearbook*, I could not find that this topic had been addressed. Hence, I felt a philosophical introduction would be in order. Here's what I wrote:

"A basic animal collection plus a moderate physical plant equals not a zoo, but a municipal menagerie. In the truest sense of the word a zoo is more, much more, than just an animal in an enclosure. However, if the menagerie possesses the intangible quality known as potential, then it can come into being as a proper zoological park. Potential will enable a zoo to emerge from the dormant state and fulfill an active role as a recreational, educational, and cultural institution. The size of a zoo has little bearing on its potential. The important constituent is how well the zoo serves as a community resource. The Topeka Zoological Park is a good example of a municipal menagerie in a progressive community of 120,000 population utilizing its potential and developing into a small, but valid, zoological park."

Next was a brief background and history of the zoo, together with detailed reports on how the zoo was progressing, developing and functioning in key areas. Following are a few examples.

"A number of major improvements, both in physical plant and operational procedures, have been accomplished within the last year: all animal diets were revised; a chemical cleaning program was initiated; a strict veterinary program was developed; animal species were rearranged and grouped to facilitate more efficient care and cleaning; inadequate animal facilities were eliminated; improved winter shelters were constructed; work schedules were organized; big cat and bear displays were modified to afford additional safety for the keepers; adequate sewer lines were installed throughout the zoo; reptile exhibits were refurbished; a new hoofed area was developed for North American mammals; various outdoor enclosures were painted with colors other than aluminum, thus breaking the monotony and accentuating the animals on display; a service barn in the Children's Zoo was constructed from used brick; necessary files were established at the zoo."

Other sections of the paper covered recreation, education, conservation, community service and the future.

Accompanied with color slides, the entire presentation was well received and resulted in praise, encouragement, support and, I would say, acceptance by professional colleagues in my chosen field. What a grand feeling!

My final slide, however, did cause some confusion with one zoo director. I figured that most of the delegates (maybe all) had never been to Topeka, but probably had the stereotypical image of a little town in Kansas at the end of the yellow brick road. To add a bit of levity I concluded my program with a famous commercial slide of the well known, easily recognizable, often seen, night view of the strikingly illuminated skyline of Manhattan in New York—a tongue-in-cheek contrast to lil 'ole Topeka. Everyone caught on and had a good chuckle, except one. Dr. Ivo Poglayen of the Albuquerque Zoo approached me afterwards and, in all sincerity, said, "I never knew Topeka looked so impressive after dark."

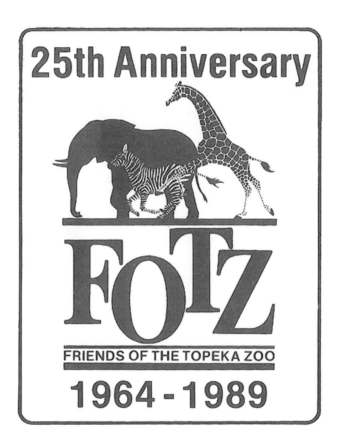

**By the time I retired from the zoo in 1989,
the Friends of the Zoo were celebrating their
25th Anniversary.**

The Hand-me-down Animal Kingdom

For many years it seemed that the zoo had been the stepchild of the Park Department. I don't mean this in a critical way; it was simply a practical reality. It did, however, result in a lot of hand-me-downs.

When the Park Department bought a new pick-up truck, the zoo received the old one; when the Park Department acquired a new typewriter, the zoo got the old one; when the Park Department hired a new man, the zoo . . . well, it wasn't quite that bad.

But when the Park Department did build a new greenhouse, yes, the zoo inherited the old one! Originally built in 1907 on what became the northeast corner of the zoo, the building had seen better days by the time it was converted in the 1950's into what was then called "the monkey house." Dark and dingy inside, it held several miscellaneous species but served primarily as winter quarters for alligators and the spider monkeys from monkey island. On my arrival in Topeka it was the only building in the zoo with public space . . . and home of the famous "ameliorated" rest room.

Spider monkeys from Central and South America not only have elongated arms and legs, but a lengthy tail as well that is prehensile, or grasping. The end of the tail lacks hair and is covered with tough skin. In essence, it is a strong "finger" with which they can pick up objects or cling to limbs and support their entire body weight to literally "hang by their tails." Such a common expression, it implies that all monkeys have this ability. Not true; only New World monkeys can do so. Monkeys from Africa and Asia use their tails only for balance in climbing and jumping.

From the care and management aspect, these quarters were certainly adequate. But from a visitor's perspective, as an exhibit they were piss-poor. Oops, I don't mean to use coarse slang (which it is, according to the Oxford English Dictionary). In reality, however, piss-poor may be the most accurate way to describe the situation at the time.

Upon entering the building it was not light and airy like a greenhouse; the glass roof had been replaced with solid shingles which blocked the light. Hence, a foreboding atmosphere engulfed the visitor as a first impression. A freestanding island of small haphazard snake units with no guardrail did not add a sense of security.

As a visitor proceeded into the darkened, clamorous depths of the building a hand would suddenly grab their arm—startling, but it was simply a spider monkey begging for food. Once the visitor recovered and continued, an unknown "somethingness" would violently seize them in a determined clutch, scaring the bejesus out of them! This time it would be a spider monkey tail, once again in search of a tidbit.

To move from the front part of the building to the back, the visitor had to go through a narrow aisle with spider monkeys on both sides . . . and the top! The spider monkeys could cross overhead and, yes, would frequently urinate on the visitors as they passed below! Whether this was intentional or not, I can't be sure . . . but I suspect that the outraged response of visitors may have encouraged this particular behavior among the monkeys!

The alligators, some of them rather large, spent their winter in a shallow pool at the rear of the monkey house. Visitors viewed them from a small footbridge. One night a torrential rain caused flash flooding throughout the city. The zoo was in the lowest corner of Gage Park, which had no storm drainage system, and was subject to all of the surface runoff.

Fearing the worst, I went to the zoo to check on things. The power was out in the old monkey house and, sure enough, the back section was flooded. Standing on the bridge with my flashlight I noted that the alligator pool was completely flooded with nary a 'gator in sight!

Where could they be?

In the darkness I could hear the sound of rushing water. Tracing it with my light beam I discovered a waterfall overflowing down the steps to the basement.

To confirm my suspicions I donned the chest-high waders used for the waterbird lagoon and cautiously descended into the basement, which was a catch-all storage area. It was *so* **dark**. The water was waist deep. Everything that could float was floating: paint cans, rags, pans, bowls, boards, plastic bags, empty feed sacks—you name it.

It was a sobering thought that lurking somewhere in the blackness among all of this debris were . . . the alligators. Then something bumped me and I nearly jumped out of my waders! WHEW! It was just a large bench plank, but the encounter resulted in a pronounced dampness inside my waders.

LISTEN! WHAT'S THAT? An emphatic hiss in the corner! In the light beam a pair of eyes glowing on the surface of the water . . . then another pair . . . and another. Here they were, all of the alligators content in their element. They would be safe until the water subsided and we could clean up and resume normal operations.

But, what to do with this old hand-me-down greenhouse? It was the only indoor space in the zoo, the only heated space for visitors in cold weather, as well as for those species that needed a controlled climate. As bad as it was, the zoo needed this building for now. As bad as it was, I could visualize an exciting and unique experience for visitors, employing proper exhibit design and techniques. This could be done with minimal expense and limited resources utilizing imagination, existing or donated materials and Park Department labor.

A good example was developing part of the greenhouse space for the small South American margay cat. This "exhibit" was formerly a menagerie cage consisting of bars and wire, painted a lifeless aluminum color. The visitor could look completely through the cage into the keepers' service aisle, and usually found it difficult to view the animal because of reflected light shining through from the back—certainly a most inadequate setting for such a beautiful and dainty creature.

Within a few weeks it was converted into a breathtaking exhibit. The walls were lined and painted a royal blue, and the front wire was painted a flat black to reduce glare. A large hollow stump was placed in the exhibit to provide a hiding place for the margay and thus afford her some security if needed. A log was situated diagonally from front to back, several feet above the floor since the margay is an arboreal species and spends most of its time off the ground. A piece of Utopia sandstone was used opposite the stump to add balance to the exhibit. A fluorescent light fixture was installed (hidden from the visitors' view) inside the exhibit and a silver-blue light tube was utilized for a nocturnal atmosphere. The margay is energetic mainly at night, and the soft "moonlight" encouraged her to be active during visiting hours.

The public response was enthusiastic which provided the stimulus to upgrade and 'professionalize' other exhibits. Two interesting small mammal species, a pair of Mongolian gerbils and a plains pocket gopher, were displayed in glass-fronted cutaway burrows. This enabled the visitor to observe the underground behavior of these animals. The gopher is native to Kansas but very few Topekans have seen it in the wild.

As work continued, the concept emerged to theme the former greenhouse the "Animal Kingdom" building by displaying representatives of every class of vertebrate animal—mammals, birds, reptiles, amphibians, and fish—plus selected species of invertebrates (animals without backbones). This would allow visitors (especially students) to study and compare living examples of the major groups in the Animal Kingdom all under one roof—hence the name.

Ringo, a giant Hercules beetle, was a main attraction of the invertebrate collection. The Hercules beetle is one of the largest in the world (over four inches in length) and native to South America. Other spineless creatures included giant African scorpions, millipedes, crickets, baboon spiders and their smaller cousins, the tarantulas.

At the entrance to the Animal Kingdom Building we developed a small, open Rain Forest exhibit consisting of vines, plants, moss, natural stone and a sparkling waterfall trickling into a crystal clear pool containing a variety of crocodilians and turtles. Directly across from the Rain Forest, an open flight display featured beautiful South American macaws, not retained by glass or wire.

Other exhibits in the Animal Kingdom Building consisted of various habitat settings: a bamboo forest for cobras, a hollow tree for screech owls, a desert scene for reptiles, and a jungle setting for tropical birds. Nocturnal animals, such as greater galagos and flying squirrels, were shown in a "red light" reversed activity cycle. These animals normally slept during the day, but red light appeared dark to their eyes and kept them active during visiting hours. At night a white light encouraged sleep, as they thought it was day. No animals were harmed by doing this.

One of my favorite exhibits was a natural stone grotto for giant pythons and boa constrictors. The glass was not evident, since it was recessed in the rockwork with balanced lighting on both sides that caused it to "disappear." Visitors could actually touch the rocks, vines, branches and plants extending from the exhibit into the public area. We even took a large log, sawed it in half and glued it together on each side of the glass, so that the visitor could, in fact, place their hand on the same log with a resting constrictor. A sign above the exhibit read: PLEASE DO NOT TOUCH THE SNAKES! Very effective!

Over time the Animal Kingdom Building exhibited some of the rarest and most unique species in the zoo, including golden lion marmosets, giant Indian hornbills, and mata-mata turtles.

I had always wanted to have a "signature" display and eventually one materialized: a "Living Tree of the Animal Kingdom." A plywood tree eight feet high and ten feet wide covered one wall. Cutout panels in the leaves revealed various exhibits depicting the five classes of vertebrates, with select representatives of invertebrates. Two labels accompanied each display: one on the general category of animal, another for the species shown. Very popular with youngsters, it was a classic example of painless education.

It was still an old building. But now it had a new look and a new purpose. The inadequate hand-me-down had become a classy fixer-upper.

Zoo Below Zero

The winter of 1965-1966 was *not* the winter of discontent. Things were going well and I was quite content. Our only building had been revitalized and new construction was in progress. In a four-season climate the public does not think of the zoo so often in the winter. To address this issue I drafted the following during my third winter in Topeka, and it was published in the Topeka Friends of the Zoo Newsletter:

There isn't any off-season at the Topeka Zoological Park. Regardless of the weather the zoo is open every day of the year.

Delicate small mammals, tropical birds and most reptiles are permanently displayed in heated quarters in the Animal Kingdom Building. While the alligators are moved outside in warm weather, they pass the winter in an indoor pool. They display little activity and refuse to eat even if food is offered to them since they have an ample supply of body fat stored at the base of their tail.

The rest of the animals in the zoo are maintained in outside exhibits year around, with dens, bedding, and shelters for protection. Most of them adapt very well to the Kansas winters. During heavy snows the Brazilian tapir and the Australian kangaroos come out of their heated shelters and romp and frolic, while the aoudads (Barbary sheep) from North Africa cavort on their snow-covered rock mountain.

The North American species seem right at home during cold weather and the mammals all grow a luxurious coat of hair. The bears find great sport in playing with the large chunks of ice that form in their pools. The big male Kodiak bear will take a piece of ice in his right paw, hold it against his jaw (as if he had a toothache), stand to his full height and vigorously shake his head and neck back and forth . . . still holding the ice to his jaw. Then he will flip it into the pool, dive in after it and repeat the activity.

A thick layer of ice forms over the large waterfowl lagoon but the ducks, geese and swans keep a small area free of ice by continuously swimming in this section. They seem to take turns, as there are usually some birds swimming and some birds resting on the snow-covered bank. Our herd of seven white-tailed deer is exhibited in this area, and it is a thrilling sight to see the entire group walking on the ice at the same time. Some of the deer regularly use the ice as a shortcut to the other side of the lagoon, and after a fresh snow it doesn't take long for the lagoon to be criss-crossed with deer tracks. The deer seem to instinctively know when the ice is too thin and only the smaller, lighter animals have been observed near the edge of the ice-free area maintained by the waterfowl.

On the night of January 28, 1966 the temperature in Topeka dropped to a record-breaking 9 degrees F. below zero. After listening to the weather forecast predicting the extremely cold temperature, I decided to put down my library book, leave my cozy home, and go out to the zoo to see how the animals were taking the weather. Also, I wanted to make sure they had sufficient bedding and that all heating units were operating properly. B-B-Brrrrr, it was cold! So cold the lock on the perimeter fence gate had frozen and I had to thaw it with a lighter before I could get into the service area. It was around 10:00 pm so I made my inspection with the aid of a flashlight. The fierce wind was biting through my parka; even with heavy gloves on, my hands were almost numb. As cold as it was I did not expect to see any animals outside.

Wild animals are amazing creatures and many will readily adapt to cold weather and seem oblivious to low temperatures. At the North American Exhibit the bison and elk were not in their shelter, but lying along the north fence contentedly chewing their cud. The eagles, hawks and owls appeared comfortable in their high sheltered perches. As my flashlight beamed into the pheasant runs the birds came out of their huts and stayed for some time investigating the light. The otters were snuggled deep in the straw under their rock shelter. The bears were all asleep in their dens except the male polar bear and the female Himalayan bear, who were outside.

At the South American area the llamas and rheas were all outside, and the three-month-old baby llama was nursing.

As I approached the carnivorous animals I shined the flashlight into the Bengal tiger exhibit. The female came out of the den and jumped up on her log. Our pair of Bengal tigers grew such a thick coat of hair in the winter that they looked more like Siberian tigers. The male African lion was waiting for me in the front of his exhibit as I passed by, but the female simply lifted her head and looked at me from the den. Both South American jaguars were asleep in the den, as were the bobcats and Canada lynx. Jenkins, the mountain lion, came out when I called her and wanted her neck rubbed. The coatimundis were rustling around in their den that contained bedding but no heat, and the mona and green monkeys were asleep in their heated dens.

All of the animals were warm and comfortable so, reassured, I went home to a cup of hot chocolate.

Winter weather is actually harder on the keepers than it is on the animals in the zoo. In extreme weather the keepers bundle up to the point that only their face is showing. Occasionally an animal will not recognize its keeper on sight in all the paraphernalia, and the keeper must speak to the animal so it will recognize his voice. During cold weather keepers maintain a constant supply of dry, fresh bedding in the outside exhibits, and make a continual check on the animal's drinking water to keep it free of ice. In addition to caring for the animals, zoo personnel have visitors to consider and must keep walks cleared of ice and snow.

The winter months are also a period of preparation for the coming spring and summer. Plans are developed for new exhibits. Existing facilities are refurbished and a great deal of "behind the scenes" work is accomplished. The Park Department builds new feeders for hoofed animals, improves service roads, and installs new lighting systems and heating units.

Educational activities continue during the winter. Zoo staff members present classroom programs throughout the city and science seminars throughout the state; they conduct guided tours of the zoo and give lectures to civic groups and parent-teacher associations. Zoo officials also utilize the winter months to negotiate with other zoos for new specimens that will be needed in the spring or summer.

All in all, the zoo below zero is a very busy zoo!

Pondering Pachyderms

After being in Topeka for only a very short while, I could tell if zoo visitors were local or from out-of-town simply by the way they phrased a frequently asked question—about elephants. Outsiders, expecting us to have them, asked, "Where are the elephants?" Topekans, knowing we did not have them, queried, "When are we going to get elephants?"

Pachyderms, or thick-skinned animals, have long intrigued people's imagination. They are among the most popular of all zoo animals because, in my opinion, of their large size, striking appearance and storied reputation. Pachyderms include elephant, rhino, hippo and giraffe. Giraffe? Yes, although not always thought of in this regard, the giraffe meets all of the criteria, including skin as much as an inch and a quarter thick!

With the day-to-day animal management and operation of the zoo now on a quality level, I devoted some of my attention to the future. It was important, I felt, to develop a master plan. Frank Thompson, Assistant Director of the Fort Worth Zoo, agreed to serve as a consultant. More than a "pretty picture," a proper plan would serve as a guide to the general development of the zoo and assure its growth in logical, orderly phases. And it would address such issues as visitor services, utilities, maintenance, storage, service areas, parking and traffic flow as well as animal facilities. Our first plan in 1964 called for two major new animal exhibits: a large mammal building for pachyderms and primates, and a rain forest building for birds and small mammals. In selecting pachyderms we planned on elephant and giraffe, but chose hippo rather than rhino because of their association with water.

Incidentally, when dealing with pachyderms, some fifth-graders once told me to guard against the three biggest veterinary ailments: a hippo with a toothache, a giraffe with a sore throat, and an elephant with a runny nose. Just kidding.

To be quite candid, if it had been my personal zoo, I would have built the rain forest first. Why? Because visitors, rather than just viewing animals in an exhibit, would be immersed in a naturalistic habitat amid vegetation and smaller free-ranging wildlife—something difficult to achieve (safely) with the giant animals of the world. And while visitors would be thrilled and impressed with a rain forest, they would invariably ask, "Where are the elephants? And hippos? And giraffes?"

But it was not my personal zoo, and I felt obligated to respond to public demand, so the initial facility would be for large mammals.

With the master plan in place, concept and design proceeded on constructing a home for those animals never before seen in Topeka—nor, in many cases, even in Kansas. The designated site was on the south side of a proposed central mall, with the future rain forest scheduled to be opposite on the north. Both sites were graced with stately trees.

Planning the architecture of this specialized structure was exciting. The facade would be characterized by simplicity, with clean lines and finished brick of light buff color. From the entry lobby, giraffes would be seen towering above visitors at the far end of the interior.

To create a spectacular impression, the first animal exhibit would be a bar-less enclosure for hippopotamuses. Visitors would have an unobstructed view over a large pool occupying the entire front section. The pool would feature an angled wall in a free-flowing curve to eliminate the "boxed" appearance, and rustic stone walls above the water level with pockets for plants. A sloped ramp would lead to a land platform behind the pool and both could be divided into two units if necessary. Two large drains would empty the pool in 15 minutes and six water inlets would fill it in 55 minutes, with an instantaneous heater warming the water in winter.

Next would be the elephant exhibit, with a high-pressure water line for bathing the elephants daily, and electric heating elements in the floor to keep it warm and dry. When I specified an oversized drain for the elephant exhibit, Topeka architects George Eicholtz and Bill Groth said, "My gosh, that's as big as a car wash!" My response was, "Well, elephants are as big as a car and we are going to wash them every day."

Between the hippo and elephant exhibits, but not obvious to visitors, would be a common transfer stall that could be used by either species, but primarily hippos. To avoid just a blank wall on the public side of the transfer stall, we proposed a glass-fronted display for the closest living relative to the elephant—the hyrax. This would enable Topeka to be the first zoo to show elephant and hyrax in association; we were flattered when many other zoos later copied us.

What the heck is a hyrax? And how is it related to the elephant? One visitor called it a "Hydrox," but that's a cookie! The hyrax is a small rabbit-sized mammal with brown fur, small ears and no trunk, which makes the relationship even more mysterious.

Zoologists agree that due to the skeletal structure, bones in the feet, chambers in the heart, the way the teeth grow, certain scent glands in the body—even the fact that males have internal testes and lack a scrotum—all of these characteristics indicate the relationship. What a super educational feature it would be!

Giraffes would occupy the entire southern end of the building. One large space could be divided into three equal units to manage a herd bull, female, and young, and have transfer space as needed. Specifications also called for a special floor to maintain adequate traction and keep the giraffes' hooves in proper condition. When the concrete floor was poured more than 200 lbs. of carborundum chips (an abrasive material) would be sprinkled over the floor and worked into the wet concrete with a wooden float. Then the surface would be "rough brushed" with a nylon bristled street broom and "dragged" with an iron-toothed rake to create grooves directed to wall scuppers leading to drains in the service aisle. A hayloft above the work area between elephants and giraffes would be convenient to drop hay down to elephants and place it in elevated racks for giraffes from a catwalk.

A subtle aspect of the design called for the floors of the elephant, hippo and giraffe areas to be elevated so the animals would be "on stage." Skylights would allow natural light to establish seasonal cycles complimented with supplementary lighting.

In the primate area the fronts of the exhibits would consist of a special glaze containing a plastic core with tempered glass laminated to each side—a modern, barless technique eliminating the jail-like atmosphere of traditional monkey houses. As a bonus it would provide better visibility for both visitors and animals, prevent litter or food from being thrown into the exhibit, and protect the primates from human diseases.

An animal diet kitchen with a glass window would allow visitors a "behind the scenes" glimpse of food preparation, with diet cards posted for various species. Also in this area would be a glass-fronted animal nursery unit. Visitors could see hand-raised babies being bottle-fed on special formulas, and could monitor their growth and development.

Because the zoo lacked so many basics, the new structure had to serve several purposes beyond the animal exhibits. Hence, the design also included a 60-seat Education Room, administrative offices, staff reference library, public telephone, refrigerated drinking fountain, and graphic panels. A special exhibit equipped with a mirror would allow visitors to view the most dangerous animal in the world . . . the one that has destroyed more wildlife and habitat than any other species!

Yes, planning the new building was exciting, as it would provide many essential dimensions missing in the current zoo. I felt that if we could make this dream a reality, it would not only fill a lot of the zoo's needs, but also serve as a catalyst for all good things to come. The projected costs were between $230,000 and $250,000—not a lot by today's standards but an enormous amount then for a modest municipality faced with the usual governmental issues and limited resources.

The City Commission was receptive to the project and its approval seemed assured. Then fate intervened. The final vote was scheduled for the weekly meeting on Tuesday, July 6, 1965. But on Friday, July 2, 1965 at 5:33 pm, a section of the Melan arch bridge over the Kansas River collapsed, sending several cars into the river and killing one man.

All capital improvement projects were halted and an immediate inspection ordered of *every* bridge in the city. This event, totally beyond our control and unrelated to the zoo, stopped us in our tracks. I was concerned about the long-term impact on zoo development *if* we could not push forward *now*. This called for a bold proposal: an admission fee. Let those who would visit the zoo (including out-of-towners) help develop new facilities through a minimal charge. This was not a new concept; most zoos (and other public attractions) across the country charged. But when a zoo has always been free it *seems* such a drastic step and it is bound to be controversial, even if the fee is modest. This I fully understood, and prepared a campaign to educate the public on the value and necessity of charging.

In reality, of course, there is no such thing as a "free zoo." It has to be paid for somehow, and a user fee is a logical part of the formula. When a zoo is free, people often take it for granted and frequently abuse the privilege. A fee induces a sense of responsibility and ownership, and places a value on the experience.

A fee would also address another issue facing the zoo—vandalism. Nationwide studies had shown that free zoos were more subject to various forms of vandalism. To help illustrate this point I prepared a poignant display entitled "The Museum of Human Stupidity." It contained objects actually found in animal enclosures at our—up until then—free zoo: plastic toys, balloons, coins, pens, small metal airplanes, rubber balls—any of which could be harmful. An admission fee would help protect delicate and valuable animals from teasing, injury or possibly death.

The zoo had no perimeter fence and people had access to the animals anytime. Prior to my arrival several incidents had occurred after hours. The zoo needed to be in a secure area with established hours when staff would be on duty.

The lack of a perimeter fence presented other major issues for the zoo. Without defined boundaries it was, in fact, a "drive-thru" zoo. For example, people could (and would) drive their cars directly past the bears! While this was a convenience for drivers, on Saturday and Sunday afternoons it was a serious safety concern for me. After observing excited youngsters trying to dart between moving vehicles to get closer to the exhibits, I spent most weekends patrolling the area to caution both children and drivers.

With endorsements from the Park Advisory Board and the Topeka Friends of the Zoo, the City Commission approved the project, together with the admission charge: a mere 25 cents, with children under 12 free.

Groundbreaking for the new building took place on July 31, 1965. This was an important milestone for the zoo. Now we had to go from pondering pachyderms to procuring pachyderms.

The State Journal – May 25, 1965

Gage Park Zoo for Education, Too

The City Commission is to be commended for approving plans last week for a new 10,500-square-foot animal building at Gage Park Zoo. If a contract is awarded in mid-June, the building probably can be finished by next winter. Architect George Eicholtz estimated construction will take about five months.

To the public, the most popular parts of the building probably will be facilities for an elephant, a hippopotamus and a giraffe as well as several primates. These are the kinds of exhibits which every zoo must have to measure up to the average zoo visitor's conception of a good zoo. But there also must be space for selected smaller species, and the new building will have it.

One of the most important rooms in the building will be a 50 seat education room. A primary justification for maintaining a zoo is it serves an education function in the community. Gary K. Clarke, Topeka's zoo director, has emphasized this fact and has talked himself hoarse, literally, conducting tours through the zoo and speaking to groups of children and adults.

Since Clarke took over as director, he also has stressed a need for orderly development of the zoo. The new building, replacing a drab structure at the east side of the zoo, will be the center around which Topeka's zoo of the future can be built.

Operation Noah's Ark

Absolutely, positively THE most successful, most phenomenal animal acquisition campaign by any zoo anywhere, anytime, ever—period!

Would you believe: one and one-half million assorted bottle caps, box tops, jar lids, bread wrappers, can labels and potato chip bags saved in a year's time to "buy" 17 new animals for the zoo in a city of only 120,000 people?

Topeka did it! And nobody but Topeka! Who else would—no, who else **could**—show such community-wide support? Who else could demonstrate such civic pride? Who else could muster such an overwhelming response? Who else, pound for pound, was the best damn zoo town in the country—heck, the world?

Only Topeka, with the help of northeast Kansas!

All of this may sound like boasting (it is) and even a bit far-fetched (it isn't). What it was, was "Operation Noah's Ark." To be candid, I thought of starting this chapter with something like, "With two new facilities coming on line—the Large Mammal Building, to be paid for by zoo admission fees, and the Australian Building, funded by contributions through Topeka Friends of the Zoo—the zoo was in a position to acquire exciting new species. But, how would we raise money for the animals?" Or, "Just as Noah collected animals for the Ark, the citizens of Topeka collected points that brought animals to the zoo." The latter was better (and true), but still did not do justice to what had transpired back in 1966.

What it was, was Operation Noah's Ark. And the only way to introduce the topic properly was as you have just read.

Based on a promotion that originated in Wichita, KS, the plan was brought to Topeka by Tom Root, first president of the Topeka Friends of the Zoo (TFOTZ). The key was coordination by *The Topeka Capital-Journal* newspaper, under the leadership of editor Lee Porter. A no-nonsense ex-Army officer, complete with a penetrating gaze, square jaw and crew cut, Lee epitomized the hard-boiled newspaperman with a soft heart. When we first met I was rather intimidated, but quickly developed respect and a true liking for him. There were numerous people from all departments of the *Capital-Journal* who contributed to Operation Noah's Ark, but Lee Porter deserves full credit as the catalyst and motivator.

Operation Noah's Ark was a unique cooperative project between Topeka residents and eleven leading product brands: Butter-Krust bread, Carey salt products, Guy's nuts and chips, Hill's Pet Foods (now Hill's Pet Nutrition), Ohse meat products, Planter's peanut butter, Ralston Chex breakfast foods, R-C Cola, Royal desserts, Tidy House products, and Super Oil Company. These fantastic sponsors agreed to pay for 17 new animals if the required number of points were accumulated within designated time frames.

It is important to note here that this marked the first association between Hill's and the zoo, a significant relationship that has lasted many decades and was critical in the zoo's later development. Hill's broad-based support went far beyond financial contributions, with employee volunteer participation, spirited leadership and confidence building, as you will see.

Operation Noah's Ark was on a city-wide basis (actually area-wide) and everyone was eligible to participate. The rules were rather simple: proof of purchase from each sponsoring product was worth one point toward acquiring an animal. A point was registered by turning in some feature of the product container—for instance a bottle cap, box top or wrapper. Points were accumulated at numerous point-collecting locations around the city.

These locations were any of the 13 Super Oil service stations in Topeka. Forrest Thurber and his team of "skippers" at each station had the challenging and unenviable task of collecting the points, evaluating them, and registering the city-wide total each month. They were the unsung heroes of Operation Noah's Ark.

The Topeka Capital-Journal kicked off Operation Noah's Ark on January 20, 1966 with a tall front-page photo of a giraffe and a special 24-page tabloid size supplement in both morning and evening newspapers. The supplement, entitled "The Wonderful Story Of Operation Noah's Ark for Topeka," was clever and engaging with super graphics, an abundance of photos, and creative full page display ads by the sponsors—a lot of work! (I still have my copy, stored in a cool, dark place.)

In addition to explaining the points program, the supplement contained: features on all of the species to be earned; stories on wildlife conservation; a map of collection stations; interviews with the park commissioner, TFOTZ President and zoo director; a brief history of the zoo; and a review of the master plan and photos of construction progress. WOW!

The program was scheduled to run for a year, during which 17 animals needed by the zoo could be earned, at 50,000 points each. One or more animals were to be earned each month. We had to carefully schedule the order for earning the animals to coincide with the completion of new facilities, availability of the animals and season of the year best suited for shipping each species. The day after each month's deadline all "points" were picked up from the various collecting stations and deposited in a huge 40-foot trailer for public display. On the side of the trailer was an illustration of a hippo with its mouth open and the words: HEY LOOK! IT'S THE NOAH'S ARK POINTS TRUCK.

Citizens were urged to increase the value of their points by accumulating a "full crew." This meant buying one each of the participating brands and turning in their point-counting features all at once. In this way, each point counted as five. Since there were ten firms sponsoring Noah's Ark, a "full crew" counted as 50 points instead of ten.

Groups were encouraged to turn in 30,000 points. This qualified them to name the animal of their choice. Individuals were urged to join the 1,000 Point Club, in which they could earn a free family membership in the Friends of the Zoo, with special privileges.

The progress of the contest, the earning of new animals and their arrivals at the zoo were big news throughout the entire year. Additional periodic newspaper supplements featured more zoo-oriented ads by the sponsors, progress reports, and pictures and facts of the animal species involved. This material contained great educational value and was utilized by schools to supplement classroom teaching. It is safe to say that a higher percentage of Topekans knew more facts about the hyrax (that comparatively little-known relative of the elephant) than the residents of any other community! Radio commercials, billboards, and grocery store promotions featured the Noah's Ark campaign. A "Noah's Barometer" (resembling a thermometer) was devised and divided into 17 graduations, each equal to 50,000 points, with the animals to be earned pictured alongside. Each month the barometer would rise to indicate the total number of points turned in to date and show what animals had been earned.

Every month more than enough points were turned in, even for some of the less spectacular animals. Species such as hippo and giraffe received the largest point totals. One Boy Scout alone turned in over 5,000 bottle caps. Topeka experienced a disastrous tornado during the campaign on June 8, 1966 but still made the goal by the deadline for that month. Concern that interest might decrease toward the end of the year-long promotion was unfounded. The last animals to be earned were a pair of chimps and the collection centers were deluged by more than 300,000 points!

During the course of the year more than one and one-half million points were turned in. People all over the surrounding area worked hard to earn the new animals for the zoo. Thousands of people—Cub Scout Packs, Brownies, Boy and Girl Scout troops, Sunday School classes, elementary and high school groups, civic clubs, families and individuals—all pitched in to earn the animals. Relatives and friends of Topeka residents sent points in from as far away as Kansas City, Chicago, even California.

Operation Noah's Ark met with greater success than anyone had anticipated, and provided a hippo, giraffe, cockatoos, hyraxes, mandrill baboons, emus, chimps, rheas, DeBrazza monkeys, and a python for the zoo at no cost to the citizens. Most of them were species entirely new to the Topeka Zoo collection, and many (including giraffe) were the first and only specimens in the state of Kansas! A second program followed with additional sponsors and renewed success. Animals earned included zebra, ostrich, camel, crowned crane, hyena, sarus crane, and beisa oryx. Once again, meritorious credit to *The Topeka Capital-Journal* for their continued initiative and leadership, and to the sponsors for their outstanding participation.

A win-win situation, Operation Noah's Ark was a valuable program that let everyone participate and thus feel a closer association with the zoo. Generating tremendous enthusiasm, it made the entire community "zoo conscious." It was an excellent reflection on Topekans and the support they gave to the zoo. And it let the sponsors contribute to a civic activity while promoting their respective products. Noah's Ark sailed through Topeka—twice—with joy and excitement for the zoo.

Our unprecedented community response caught the attention of the zoo world—internationally! I was invited (and honored) to present a paper in Mexico City at the International Conference of the Ibero-American Zoo Federation and the AAZPA (which I did) in March 1967. A number of other zoos, in communities larger than Topeka, copied our program, but none came close to emulating our success.

It had never crossed my mind what it might have felt like to be Noah. After this experience I gained somewhat of an insight. No, I did not build an Ark (I still don't know what a cubit is!); but I did build a zoo (Did Noah have to deal with building codes and competitive bids?). No, I did not round up all of the animals two-by-two; but I did acquire those specimens that were earned 50,000-points-by-50,000 points. And no, I did not endure a flood of water; but I did experience an unbelievable, overwhelming flood of enthusiasm to earn the animals. While I can appreciate Noah's ordeal, I am forever grateful that I had Topekans for my crew.

The Case of the Hesitant Hippo

IF: you have a large, exotic animal—let's say, a hippopotamus—AND: it won't do what you want it to—for example, walk into a shipping crate—BUT: you've tried every trick in the book, THEN: the thing to do (with no ifs, ands or buts about it) is simply wait for the news to spread and within a day or two you'll hear from thousands of instant experts across the country and around the world, each with an obvious solution.

WELL: this was not a hypothetical hippo in some supposed scenario—this was real.

The hippo in question was the five year old female at the Kansas City zoo, born June 9, 1961 while I was a keeper there caring for her parents. Now we were to be reunited, as she had been earned through Operation Noah's Ark and was destined to be the first animal in the new Large Mammal Building at the Topeka Zoo.

EXCEPT: she would not go into her custom-built crate! Everything had been planned in detail, and transporting hippos was usually a routine procedure. So routine that Mr. Cully, the Kansas City zoo director, had invited all the local news media to the big event. At 8:00 am on Wednesday, May 4, 1966 the hippo in question walked to the crate, hesitated for a moment, then laid down with her head just inside the crate and her torso anchored outside. And that was it! No amount of coaxing, encouragement or food could get her to move. We continued our efforts throughout the rest of the day, but to no avail.

The media loved it and the "hesitant hippo" (as they dubbed her) became first local, then national, and quickly international news. This, of course, prompted legions of armchair hippo psychologists to contact us from great distances with suggestions, opinions and advice on what could or should be done about the situation. Most were well intended, some were frivolous, and none worked. The hesitant hippo simply would not budge. At the end of the second day (Thursday) we were exhausted and frustrated. By now those following the story (which got bigger with each passing hour) fell into two groups: those who empathized with us, and those who found it humorous that we had a 3,000 pound hippo on a "sit-down strike" (they were in the majority).

Friday morning came and all of us directly involved were pretty much resigned to wait it out. There was, however, one last resort, suggested by Mr. Cully. It seemed far-fetched, even improbable. But nothing else had worked, so why not give it a try? We did. It worked! It worked! At noon on Friday the hesitant hippo stood up and calmly walked into the crate! It worked!

What finally did the trick? Would you believe . . . of all things—marshmallows? Yes! Marshmallows!

Our journey finally began from Kansas City to Topeka along the Kansas Turnpike. En route we made a brief stop at the West Lawrence service area. We drove up to the station and I asked the attendant if I could use his hose to wash down my hippo. The poor man appeared stunned—until he looked inside the crate. With a smile he got out the hose and we had quite a memorable 'splash party.' Then it was on to the zoo for a *proper* splash party in a brand new pool.

Now the hippo in question, no longer hesitant, needed a name. Keep in mind that she arrived in Topeka Zoo on May 6, 1966 but I did not know the full story of her fantastic name until more than forty years later, October 21, 2006. On that date I had three distinguished guests in town: Clayton Freiheit, President/CEO of the Denver Zoological Foundation; William Dennler, Director Emeritus of the Toledo Zoo; and Gary H. Lee, award-winning zoo design architect from Philadelphia. They had visited our zoo that morning, toured the Martin and Osa Johnson Safari Museum in Chanute that afternoon, and that evening the four of us were having dinner back in Topeka at the Capitol Plaza Hotel. The restaurant manager, Sharon McGuire, recognized me, and said she was the one that had named our hippo 'Peka-Sue, (and she was very proud of that fact over 40 years later). We all were intrigued as she related the story, and I asked her to write it down. Here it is in Sharon's own words.

"During Operation Noah's Ark, the 5th grade class of Most Pure Heart of Mary School filled two closets of carefully counted Butter Krust bread wrappers, Jell-O labels, etc. as part of a Social Studies project. Young determination earned enough points to purchase an animal for the zoo.

"The class picked a hippopotamus and held a contest to choose a name. I won with 'Peka-Sue. And yes, though it won because it sounded like Topeka Zoo, here is the secret I have held all these years. My mom had just taken me to see Disney's Fantasia, and my favorite character was the flirtatious, eyelash-batting hippo . . . and I thought of Peka Boo. My mom is the one who suggested Sue, and the rest is history."

'Peka-Sue was an instant star, attracting large crowds who were thrilled as she cavorted in her pool. Putting a porpoise to shame with her aquatic abilities, 'Peka-Sue would breach like a whale, then splash-dive and swim underwater making Olympic turns, and even roll over on her back with all four feet in the air! She would hold her breath underwater for as long as 5 minutes and 35 seconds. Visitors felt a close connection to her and bragged about how many Noah's Ark products they had consumed to help earn her.

To assist in her daily management, 'Peka-Sue was trained to respond to the ringing of an old fashioned, hand-held school bell, which she could hear even when fully submerged underwater. Early each morning her keeper would ring the bell to call her out of the pool. She would walk up the ramp and into the transfer stall to eat a grain supplement and take a nap while her pool was drained and scrubbed. By mid-morning her pool would be filled with clean water, with a crowd gathered awaiting her appearance. And she made it a "grand entrance." 'Peka-Sue scripted it like a theatrical production. *The Topeka Capital-Journal* wrote a fitting review as follows:

"She peeks out, studies the crowd for awhile and makes a slow motion entrance, walking with deliberate stride across the land area and down the ramp. At the water's edge, she pauses, then drinks. She moves into the water and walks—not swims—on the bottom and checks all four-corners of the pool. Then she settles down underwater for another nap.

"About every four or five minutes during her underwater nap, she pokes her nostrils to the surface—although she's still asleep—and takes a breath of air and sinks back to the bottom."

After her nap she would begin a period of intense activity and vigorous swimming. During the afternoon she would alternate between napping, swimming and watching her adoring fans. At 4:40 pm her keeper would place fresh produce on the land platform behind the pool and once again ring the bell. 'Peka-Sue would walk out of the pool and proceed to eat her apples, carrots, potatoes, cabbage and bread. She then had access to the transfer stall all night, where fresh hay was available. On those nights when I worked late at the zoo, I often slipped out of my upstairs office and stood in the dark by the hippo exhibit, listening to 'Peka-Sue swimming, snorting or munching hay.

In keeping with the zoo's philosophy of occupational activities for animals (today this is called behavioral enrichment), we tried a variety of things with 'Peka-Sue, including ducks as companions (she kept chasing them out of the water). What worked best was a small tree trunk. Or, as newsletter editor Nancy Cherry said at the time, " . . . happiness for 'Peka-Sue is a log!" Nancy observed the initial encounters and wrote the following narrative.

"The first day a log was placed in her pool, she spied it immediately as she came down her ramp. She swam to it, seemed to smell it, and proceeded to push it around with her nose. This was fun! It bobbed and floated and kept 'Peka-Sue busy all morning. She learned to push it to the bottom and nose it around the bottom. Sometimes she nuzzled it into a corner where it became wedged—so she opened her mouth and picked it up with her lips, just as a dog carries a stick. It wasn't long until all of the bark was off the log and floating in bits—much to the dismay of our zoo staff when it was time to clean her pool. Now the keepers removed the bark *before* they give her a new log!

"During the second week her log was placed on the land area instead of the water. She surprised the keepers by breaking her morning routine for the first time in anyone's memory. On this momentous occasion all her regular habits were forsaken for the log. She played with the log for ten mi-

nutes before getting her drink—and then she went back up the ramp and played for another forty minutes before she submerged. During the morning's play she rolled the log to the water's edge and eventually toppled it in. She stood poised on the edge watching the log, and appeared to be debating the merits of jumping in after it. By this time a large crowd had gathered—and we very nearly had some extremely wet zoo visitors! Fortunately, she decided not to leap—but in her impatience to get to her new toy she went over the side of her ramp!

"And so concludes another successful zoo venture—and we're pleased to report one happy hippo, a happy zoo staff, and several happy ducks!"

We had, of course, designed the facility for two hippos, but did not want a male as hippos breed so well in zoos it is difficult to find homes for surplus offspring. The Bronx Zoo in New York had an adult female (a few years older than 'Peka-Sue) available on loan. We accepted their offer and named the new arrival Submarie (I had always felt that was such a perfect name for a hippo). Hippos are social, contact animals and the two became great companions. Watching them together affirmed that hippos are not just big anonymous blobs. Each had her own personality and individual behavioral characteristics—as do all hippos.

Not one of the glamour species for field studies (like gorillas or elephants or giant pandas), hippos nonetheless are fascinating in their own way. They are well adapted to water (hippopotamus is Greek for 'river horse'), with only their eyes, ears and nostrils exposed while their massive body is hidden below the surface. The vibrissa, or stiff whiskers, around the hippo's muzzle can detect minute changes in water pressure to indicate underwater objects.

Despite their great size, the gestation period is only 8½ months. Babies are born on land or in the water, can swim at birth, and weigh 50 to 75 lbs. Recent studies have shown that hippos pick up sounds in the air as well as underwater, and have a range of hearing that far exceeds that of humans.

To know hippos—in the zoo or on safari—is a privilege. To know an *individual* hippo, as I have 'Peka-Sue, all her life (47 years plus at this writing), is special. During my tenure as zoo director, 'Peka-Sue remained responsive to my call. She would swim over to me as I knelt on the land platform, open her huge mouth to full gape, and allow me to pick the strands of hay stuck between her teeth and gums. And yes, she always expected her favorite treat—marshmallows . . . cherry-flavored, no less.

Tall Traveler on the Turnpike

On Wednesday, May 18, 1966 a strange caravan cautiously made its way north through Oklahoma toward the Kansas state line.

Leading the caravan was a heavy-duty truck pulling a hydraulic, tilt-down trailer. Following at a short distance was a blue patrol car with two-way radio, siren and red light poised for an emergency.

On the trailer was a tall—*very* tall—custom-made crate with an open top. Travelers on Interstate 35 craned their necks to see what was in the crate. At first glimpse, surprise or disbelief registered on their faces.

The man driving the truck gripped the steering wheel with strong determination as frequent gusts of wind threatened the security of his precious cargo.

The man in the patrol car showed concern as he watched for any sign of trouble, and the thunderheads boiling in the sky worried him. Although bridge heights had been checked and rechecked, anxiety rose each time the tall crate approached an underpass. But each time it slipped through untouched, just as planned.

At precisely 2:44 pm the caravan crossed the border into Kansas. In the crate, contentedly chewing his cud, was Twiga, the first giraffe in the state. His name meant giraffe in Swahili, and he was destined for the Topeka Zoo.

Park Superintendent Dennis Showalter was driving the truck, and I was driving the patrol car. As we neared the first toll gate plaza on the Kansas Turnpike, I pulled ahead to get the tickets for both vehicles. The attendant in the booth looked back (and up) and exclaimed, "Goll-lee! Where'd you get that giraffe?" I couldn't help but answer, "With S & H green stamps," a popular premium trading stamp at the time. The truth, of course, was more impressive than my attempt at humor.

Twiga was born in the Oklahoma City Zoo and valued at $5,000. He was not part of Operation Noah's Ark (although his mate would be), and we did not have the $5,000 to acquire him. And this put us in a most difficult quandary.

Twiga was only eleven months old, but already 8 feet, 10 inches tall. If we waited much longer, he would quickly grow too tall to fit under all of the bridges en route to Topeka. So, in addition to Noah's Ark, we announced an additional public fund raising campaign, "Operation Giraffe." It was not an organized effort—simply a plea for whomever to donate whatever they could. I advised the Oklahoma City Zoo of our intentions. They felt assured that Topeka would come through and authorized the transfer of the young giraffe on credit . . . and faith. I, too, felt confident that we could generate the necessary funds. But I must confess (now that the statute of limitations surely has expired), my thought was that even if we did *not* raise all of the money, Twiga would soon be so tall we couldn't send him back anyway.

Not to worry. Topekans *did* respond with lots of pennies, lots of $1.00 and $5.00 contributions, and several large gifts: $250 from the Fleming Co., $800 from the Topeka 20-30 Club, and $1,000 from Jim Clark Chrysler-Plymouth. By December 1966 we reached our goal. Good thing, as Twiga was now 10 feet, 2 inches tall.

There was another critical reason we needed to establish Twiga in his new home by mid-May 1966: we were slated to dedicate our brand new Large Mammal Building on Sunday, May 22, 1966. The only other specimen in residence was 'Peka-Sue, the hesitant hippo.

We *did* open the building on schedule, with only one hippo and one giraffe. This did not concern the community one whit: we had thousands of visitors!

Meanwhile, Operation Noah's Ark was going strong and had earned enough points for a female giraffe, Jan. Born in the Cheyenne Mountain Zoo in Colorado Springs, Twiga's mate arrived on August 26, 1966.

While the public's attention was focused on the arrival of new animals, many other aspects of zoo development demanded our attention: installing the perimeter fence, establishing a main entrance and designated exits, building and striping the parking lot (unglamorous, but so essential), as well as planning for new public restrooms and a snack bar. WHEW!

During those hectic days of spring and summer 1966, I was at the zoo 12 to 16 hours a day, seven days a week (unless I was on the road transporting animals). And while it was unfair to my understanding and supportive wife and young family, it was not a burden on me personally—it was a joy! Yes, sooo many things to coordinate; sooo many people to deal with; sooo many details to consider; sooo many spur-of-the-moment decisions that would have permanent consequences; sooo many new and unexpected situations.

On the other hand, sooo much was being accomplished—not just daily, but by the hour . . . even by the minute! As a youngster, yearning to be a zoo director, I thought all I'd have to do would be to make the rounds every day and check on the animals. HA! Now I was doing everything except that. But I could not have been more euphoric or exuberant. We were up to our eyeballs in making a zoo HAPPEN! Who could have envisioned that!

Certainly there were critical challenges. For me to do all that was necessary required an enormous amount of correspondence. This was long before computers, e-mail, faxes, cell phones, text messages, etc. Telephones did not have "direct dial" and long distance was expensive. I hate to sound so dated (and old), but in those days proper business correspondence was a neatly typed letter. I had no secretary at the zoo, had flunked typing in high school, and my hand scribbled notes were illegible (and remain so).

Nevertheless, all was not lost. A gracious secretary at the Park Department in City Hall, Esther Grout, took an interest in the emerging zoo (together with pity on me) and offered to help, with Park Commissioner Goodin's blessing. Believe it or not, I finally had a car (actually a station wagon to haul all of my kids *and* transport animals). I could drive downtown to dictate voluminous letters to Esther—letters for business in Topeka, or across the country, or around the world (there is a great deal of international communication in the zoo profession). But that took time *and* took me away from the zoo in Gage Park. This was not good. Esther was a sharp, experienced professional, and quickly learned the scientific names of animals and technical terms of zoobiz—even how to use the international date system (important for foreign colleagues), where the date comes first, then the month, followed by the year (such as 10 May 1966). This way the numerals are separated by a word (with no punctuation) to avoid confusion and misinterpretation. For example, in the USA we commonly list a date as 5/10/66. Is that May 10, 1966? Or is it October 5, 1966? The international date system is precise and leaves no question.

Esther not only grasped the nuances of the zoo world, but all of my idiosyncrasies as well, even to the degree that I could call her and dictate over the phone (not just a letter, but also a report or technical paper). Then all I had to do was go to the Park Department to sign things, which was much more efficient. All mail had to be dispatched through the City Hall mailroom anyway (with the exception of overseas postage, which I paid for myself).

But I digress. Back to giraffes, truly one of nature's more phenomenal creatures. If the concept of giraffe did not already exist, who in the world could come up with such an animal? Gangling legs, a disproportionate neck, so awkward in appearance yet so fluid in motion. With eyelashes so long they look false, the large, brown, soulful eyes of a giraffe are a distinctive attribute. Yet, their trademark peculiarity is the purple-black tongue. A giraffe's tongue is so long that they can stick it out and wrap it around your head!

Now, gentle reader, I want you to do something for me. This won't hurt, but it *will* help you understand and appreciate the tongue of a giraffe. Please mark your place in this book now, put it down, and procure a flexible tape measure. Take your time; I'll wait.

*****

Got it? Good. Thanks.

Now, stretch the tape to an extent of 20 inches. Hold your outstretched hands up to eye level and marvel at the length of a giraffe's tongue! Next, bring the tape measure to your forehead and encircle your head so your hands meet in back. Imagine this is a giraffe's tongue, which possesses greater mechanical power than the tongue of any other hoofed mammal. If it really were a giraffe's tongue you'd also experience large quantities of sticky saliva and whiffs of not-so-pleasant breath. But it would be worth it. After all, how many people have been kissed by a giraffe?

Giraffes use this remarkable tongue to eat. They will extend it around a branch, strip the leaves and pull them into their mouth. In Africa giraffes create a defined "browse line." Adults stretch as high as they can for leaves (sometimes 19 or 20 feet for males), and all of the trees in the vicinity appear as though they have been professionally pruned to this height (actually, I suppose they have!). The exact same thing happens in the zoo! Giraffes will maintain a precise browse line among the trees in the outside yard. Look for it on your next visit. It is particularly obvious in Topeka where one of my successors, Mike LaRue, expanded the giraffe habitat to include a great variety of trees, all now neatly pruned.

Giraffes are browsers, not grazers, and seldom bend to the ground to eat (hay and grain are placed at convenient heights in the zoo). Water sources, too, are elevated in the zoo. In the wild giraffes have to bend to the ground in an awkward posture for a drink of life-giving water. This prohibits them from seeing potential enemies, subjecting them to attack by predators. Hence, they may go for long periods without water, even when quite thirsty (I have observed this in Africa). This same fear of predatory behavior keeps most giraffes from lying down at night, and they frequently sleep standing up! In the zoo they feel so safe and secure that they lie down every night.

I so enjoy the wonder of small children as they gaze up at a towering giraffe. If you ask them to touch their own necks and guess how many bones are in it, most will say "one." Then ask how many bones are in a giraffe's long neck, and you hear a unanimous shout of "a hundred!" What fun to share with them that giraffes have the same number of neck bones as a person or a mouse—seven. And that giraffes have four compartments in their stomach and chew a cud just like a cow (watch for this on your next zoo visit). Giraffes can run up to 35 mph and kick hard enough to kill a lion, although their main defense is their great height and keen sight—they prefer to *avoid* danger and potential enemies.

Did you know that sometimes you display giraffe social behavior? How is that? Giraffes are basically a non-contact species. This means that generally they do not touch each other except for specific reasons: during courtship, during dominance battles between males, and in the mother/young relationship. Otherwise, they literally keep their distance. Watch a group in the zoo (or in the wild) and you'll note that giraffes generally maintain a minimum distance between each other.

Now observe people as they step into a crowded elevator and scrunch their shoulders together so they won't touch their neighbor. In our society we usually don't go around touching other people unless they are relatives or close friends. What happens when we unintentionally make physical contact, like bumping into someone? Immediately we are apologetic with, "Oh, excuse me," or "I'm sorry."

Knowing this about giraffes helps establish proper management in the zoo, starting with the design of facilities. Remember how we specified three stalls so we could transfer them and not have to go in with the giraffes when we clean? (And don't forget the difficulty I had as a keeper with the big male giraffe at the Kansas City Zoo.) During daily care we never touch them or brush them or make any direct physical contact. In essence, we try to adapt ourselves to their social behavior, so that we are accepted by the giraffes on their terms. Rather than try to make the giraffes think they are people, we try to make the giraffes think we are one of them. Granted, our necks are short and we don't have spots, but they seem to tolerate us as some funny kind of giraffe—and that is an honor!

The tallest giraffe on record was a male measuring 19 feet, 3 inches, although the average is 17 feet for males and 14 feet for females. Males spar by swinging their huge heads and battering each other. This appears graceful (almost playful), and while it is not life-or-death it is intense and can result in bruising, internal bleeding, broken ribs (or horns), even a knockdown. Most people do not think it is a "real fight." I have concluded the reason they don't is because (although they have underdeveloped vocal cords) giraffes remain silent, while most animals roar, growl, scream, bellow or produce some type of noise when fighting.

The first birth of a giraffe in a zoo appears to have been in London on June 19, 1839. Usually the mother stands during a successful delivery, although she may be in a partially squatting position. Normally a single young is born, although twins have been reported on occasion. Gestation averages 14 to 16 months, and at birth babies will be five to six feet tall and weigh 80 to 150 pounds. (Ladies, aren't you glad you are not a giraffe?)

The ancient Egyptians thought giraffes were a cross between a camel (which does have a long neck, but it is curved, not straight) and a leopard, which has spots. Some of the old Natural History books in my library list the giraffe as a "cameleopard," and even today the scientific genus and species is *Giraffa camelopardalis.*

A giraffe is a giraffe is a giraffe. Or is it? While there is just a single species, there are a number of subspecies—at least four and, according to some naturalists, as many as *twelve* (but I wouldn't stick my neck out on that). They range from the Sudan on the north to the Orange River in South Africa. Before we get into all of this, however, I should mention that albino giraffes have been reported in the wild, and my own Safari group observed (and Doug Hommert from St Louis photographed) a *white* giraffe in Tarangire National Park, Tanzania, in 1991. This animal was *not* an albino but did have blue eyes. Also, on July 25, 1967 a female giraffe was born in the Ueno Zoological Gardens in Tokyo, Japan, that was quite remarkable in that its coat was pale brown without any trace of the normal giraffe pattern, although both parents had normal coloration.

Each giraffe subspecies is distinguished by its geographical distribution and base color, as well as the size and shape of the pattern blotches. The most striking is the reticulated giraffe from northern Kenya and southern Ethiopia, with rich, chestnut patches separated by narrow white lines. Both Twiga and Jan were reticulated giraffes. Watch for different subspecies as you visit various zoos.

Regardless of subspecies, giraffes are head and shoulders above the other animals. To have giraffes in Kansas seems so natural. Standing and peering keenly at you with great curiosity, they transcend the form of mere animal and become gigantic, long-stemmed sunflowers bowing to nature's grassland sanctuary.

Trunk Line to the Elephants

Have you ever looked closely at the toenails of an elephant?

Not casually from a distance, but just at arm's length from your face for hours on end? And while carefully contemplating elephantine toe-jam, have you ever sat cross-legged in urine-soaked straw with bombs of elephant dung dropping all about you? I have.

And it was wonderful.

There's more. All the while, two (yes, two) elephant trunks were omnipresent around me, snaking along my arms and legs, dripping mucous on my head, encompassing my face, sucking/blowing in my ear, exploring down the front of my shirt. That, too, was wonderful.

And all well worth it, I might add, as I was in the back of a large transport truck traveling halfway across the country, bringing Topeka's first elephants to the zoo in July 1966.

Elephants, of course, were what had started an entire scenario of events that led to our zoo . . . well, truly emerging as a zoo. Elephants were the culmination of all the hectic, productive, rewarding, unbelievable activities at the zoo since my arrival several years before: cleaning the place up, organizing Friends of the Zoo, initiating basic education programs, developing community support, responding to visitors' requests, becoming active on a professional level. The crowning glory, the symbol of success, the mark of achievement, the validation of "zooness" were all represented by those prodigious, ponderous pachyderms—elephants. Not one, but two!

Although we had designed for two elephants, our initial plan was to acquire one specimen first and a second at a later date. However, at the AAZPA Conference I inadvertently bought two elephants instead of one. In all of the negotiations and permit documents and transport schedules and veterinary arrangements and miscellaneous details with different individuals over a period of several days, I struggled through what I thought were terms for one elephant, but it was for two. This was, indeed, a bit embarrassing to try to explain to my boss, Park Superintendent Dennis Showalter. He was most understanding, and pointed out that we could transport both elephants on one trip and save expenses. In addition, it would be best for the elephants as they are social animals and would have each other as companions for the trip. Both were female Asian elephants from the foothills of the Himalayas, a mountainous region where their existence had been threatened by shrinking natural habitat. To insure their survival they were designated for placement in zoos. Originally housed in a German zoo, the older one was now residing in upstate New York at the Catskill Game Farm. Catskill also offered to accommodate the younger one upon her arrival in the USA until we were ready for both animals.

Dennis arranged to modify a heavy-duty truck from the Topeka Forestry Department to transport the elephants, but I had no license to drive such a vehicle. Hence, he convinced the City Forester himself, Lester Terry, to drive the truck, while I'd be along to look after the elephants. Poor Lester. A really nice guy, he had no idea what he was getting himself into.

Since we had to drive all the way from Topeka to Catskill, I plotted a route that would enable us to visit *every* zoo possible between here and there! Lester was O.K. with zoos, but he was not what you would call an enthusiast. Worse yet, to do what I envisioned, we would have to visit zoos from dawn to dusk and then drive much of the night. He looked at me as if I were crazy, but agreed; said he could nap in the truck while I visited zoos. What neither of us counted on (but I should have known) was the incredible hospitality that would be showered upon both of us by zoo directors along the way.

This involved more than just a detailed behind-the-scenes tour of each zoo. It was also meeting the staff, reviewing the animal records, critiquing the breeding program and evaluating the master plan (all of which took more time than we had). Sometimes it entailed a hosted lunch with the board, or a visit to the local Natural History Museum, or cocktails and dinner in the director's home (all of which took even more time).

While I thrived on all of this, and Lester was politely tolerant, neither of us got much sleep en route to the East Coast. And when we reached the Catskill Game Farm (a hallowed zoological institution), the hospitality continued to an even greater degree—that is to say, in the "old world" tradition. I had only read about how European zoo directors bestowed lavish treatment on their colleagues. Now I was experiencing it from the legendary German zoologist Roland Lindemann himself, owner of Catskill Game Farm. And me, just a punk kid from Kansas! Even Lester was impressed, and mistakenly assumed I must have been a big shot in the zoo world.

But now, we had a challenging task and serious responsibility ahead of us. We had to safely transport these two young elephants from New York to Kansas. The larger animal (approximately four years old) was already named Sunda, after a region in Southeast Asia. The smaller specimen (estimated at one year of age) we called Toka: "To" for Topeka, and "Ka" for Kansas. Once we started, our plan was to drive non-stop to minimize the travel time for the elephants, despite the physical demands it would put on us.

Lester drove while I rode in back with the elephants, not only to insure their well being, but also to provide companionship and security—which meant a lot of touching and direct contact. I talked to them continuously and regularly provided food and water. While the side panels of the truck were so high that neither the elephants nor I could see out, the top was open and we could at least tell if it was day or night. Despite outside noises, we heard mostly our own sounds (which included a great deal of flatulence on the part of the elephants), together with wind and the hum from the tires of our vehicle. Once on the road the three of us had pretty well settled in to the rhythmic motion of the truck. While continuing to socialize with the elephants, I was watching the white vapor trails from jet planes as they dissipated in the blue sky above when, unexpectedly . . .

ItWasTheEndOfTheWorld!!!

INSTANT, COMPLETE BLACKNESS!

TOTAL, DEAFENING NOISE!

What was happening?

The elephants roared. I bolted to my feet and immediately reached out in the dark until I was touching *both* Sunda and Toka. As frightened as I was, my concern was to keep the elephants calm, if possible. I rubbed them and spoke in a firm, reassuring voice—hopefully loud enough they could hear me above the din.

Such sudden turmoil! Would it ever end?

And then, just like that, it was all over. What the—?

What we had just experienced, at 70 mph, was a tunnel on the Pennsylvania Turnpike!

Lester pulled over at the first opportunity to check on us. He had felt the elephants shifting their weight and wanted to make sure we were O.K. Anticipating the possibility of more tunnels, Lester said he would signal me by slowing down and tooting the horn as we approached. This would help as I could then start rubbing and patting the elephants in advance to pre-pare them.

As the time passed, hour-by-hour, and the distance was covered, mile-by-mile, the elephant urine flowed persistently and the dung-bombs plopped unabated. I had thought that spending so much continuous time on such an intimate basis with two elephants might actually make me feel somewhat like an elephant. True, I had the odor of an elephant, could make noises like an elephant, and was covered in authentic elephant mu-cous . . . but in reality I felt more like a proverbial dung beetle.

Lester stopped for fuel in Columbus, Ohio at three o'clock in the morning. I took my two buckets, went into the service bay where the atten-dant was changing a tire, and asked if I could get some water for my el-ephants. The guy looked me up and down—I must have been a sight, all bleary-eyed, grungy and disheveled—and finally said, "Uh—yeah, sure."

As I was filling the buckets, I overheard the attendant say to his buddy (with a scoff), "See that guy over there? He's watering his elephants!" They both chuckled. When I carried the water-filled buckets to the truck I could feel their eyes following me. About that time Sunda put her trunk over the side panel and stretched it toward my head. There is no way I could describe the surprised reaction of those two flabbergasted station attendants.

The remainder of the two-day journey was uneventful. We arrived in Topeka on July 16, 1966. Sunda and Toka, in good condition, quickly adjusted to their new home. Visitors flocked to the zoo. Some were those who, in the past, had asked about elephants. You may recall the questions from out-of-town visitors, "Where are the elephants?" and from Topekans, "When are we going to get elephants?" Now, at last, they could actually see bona fide elephants in the Capital City of Kansas.

Elephants, pinnacle of pachyderms, are such magnificent creatures! Their elongated snout, or trunk, contains 40,000 muscles (maybe more), and serves as a lifeline to the world. They feel with it, smell with it, eat with it and can pick up a tiny blade of grass or uproot a young tree. Elephants drink *with* their trunk, not through it (it is not a giant straw). They will suck water, three to five gallons at a time, into their trunk, lift it to their mouth and then squirt it down their throat. An adult will drink up to fifty gallons a day. Elephants are covered with stiff strands of hair over most of their body. It is thicker and obvious in young animals, sparse and less noticeable in adults.

Despite their huge size, elephants possess great balance. They appear to walk "flat-footed," but in reality are walking on their toes, due to the skeletal structure of the foot. Coupled with the fact that the hind foot always steps in the same place as the front foot, this enables them to walk on a beam no wider than their front feet.

Tusks are modified upper incisor teeth prominent in both sexes of African elephants, but found only in bull Asian elephants. The tusks of female Asian elephants are so small they are called tushes. All elephants have only four functional teeth at a time: a large molar in each jaw—upper and lower, left and right. These teeth are deep-set and seldom seen. If you know an elephant well enough, you can ask it to put its trunk up while you pull the cheeks open to reveal the teeth, each with a series of sharp ridges. When an elephant chews it is not an up-and-down motion like a human. Rather, it will grind food between its teeth from side-to-side. When a tooth wears smooth and becomes non-functional, it is shed as a new one grows in its place. During its lifetime an elephant will have six sets of teeth for a total of 24 individual teeth. If an elephant lives into its 40's, the final set grows into place and may last 15 years or so. Once this set wears out an elephant cannot masticate properly, and in the wild will starve to death (if it has not already succumbed to drought, disease, injury, predation, species conflict or poaching). Zoo elephants may live longer on specially prepared diets.

I often use a shed tooth from an adult elephant in my lectures. People are always impressed with its size (it weighs about seven pounds). As big as it is, however, a part of it is broken off. (I tell my audience that, "This is the tooth, the real tooth, but not the whole tooth, so help me God.")

Digestion is poor. One study showed elephants only digest 44% of what they consume (in contrast, a cow digests 67%). Hence, elephants have to eat greater quantities of a given food to gain the same nutritional value. They pass much undigested material, and elephant dung is not offensive in texture or odor—it is very fibrous and smells and feels like wet hay.

The tongue of an elephant cannot be extended like that of a giraffe. It resembles a slick rubber ball about the size of a cantaloupe. I have watched elephants take thick branches covered with long, sharp thorns into their mouth and proceed to chew and swallow them, thorns and all. How do they do it without injuring the tongue? I think I've figured it out. Having had direct personal contact with a number of elephant tongues, I noted they were extremely flexible, even yielding, while at the same time strong and covered with a thick coat of protective mucous. This enables an elephant to carefully manipulate the thorns, with the help of the trunk, inside its mouth so they can be swallowed whole. The thorns are undigested and passed in the balls of dung (properly called boluses). If you drive over an elephant bolus on safari, and the thorn is in an upright position, a puncture is almost inevitable.

In movies, the only sound elephants make is trumpeting (and if you listen closely, it often is the same sound track played over and over again). While they do trumpet, more often than not they grumble, squeak or roar (louder than a lion). And these are just the sounds that we can hear. Extensive studies have shown that elephants communicate with each other using sounds well below the range of human hearing.

In contrast to giraffes, elephants are social contact animals. They regularly make physical contact with each other—touching, rubbing, caressing and stroking with their trunks. This was a factor in establishing our daily management in Topeka. Our keepers worked in direct contact with the elephants. Every morning they were bathed with a high-pressure water hose and scrubbed with a coconut shell or stiff brush to keep their skin in good condition. When necessary, their toenails were filed with a large rasp. To develop a mutual trust between keepers and elephants, to assist in such things as veterinary procedures, and to provide occupational activity, Sunda and Toka were trained to respond to a variety of voice commands. During these sessions the keepers would pat and rub the elephants, sit on them—even ride them.

It may look easy to ride an elephant, but like most things that look easy, there is an art to it. How well I remember when Jim Lapham, of *The Kansas City Star Magazine*, accepted our invitation to ride Sunda.

Following are a few excerpts from his article, "The Art of Riding an Elephant," published on August 23, 1970.

"A trousers splitting kick and you are sitting atop the elephant's neck. With any luck at all your seat is far enough forward to be clear of the jolting, sharp, shoulder blades that lie just under the hide of the pudgiest of pachyderms.

"There is no point in trying by the feeble vehicle of the written word to describe the discomfort of such a ride.

"It is a nauseating combination of airsickness, terror, being caught in a washer-dryer and abandoned on a runaway roller coaster. That's at first. Then it gets rough.

"Regardless of how you feel immediately on alighting after your elephant ride, rule 13 of Zoo Director Gary Clarke's 16 basic guidelines for 'How to get along with Elephants' is invariably invoked. This is the rule where, when the elephant has done what it was told, it is given kind words, firm pats, and extravagant praise.

"With a heartiness you may or may not feel you slap the elephant on the shoulder, rub its cheek just under the eye, and assure it in convincing tones that you have just enjoyed one of the best rides you ever had on one of the best elephants you have ever ridden.

"And in my case, at least, that certainly was the truth."

Notwithstanding Jim's experience, if you have a chance to ride an elephant, do so.

Elephants hold great fascination due to their enormous size, unique appearance, and because they are *always doing something!* Watching elephants in the zoo, even for a short period of time, reaps many rewards. Moreover, one does not have to be a zoologist to appreciate their expressions of behavior. Simply observe elephants as they eat, drink, play, socially interact with one another . . . even as they sleep!

When visitors see an animal of any species asleep in the zoo, they often remark, "Oh, he's not doing anything."

WRONG!

Sleeping is but one of many behaviors that most living organisms (particularly vertebrates) demonstrate in a 24-hour cycle. It can be just as interesting as any other activity. Visitors seldom see diurnal species (those active during daylight hours) actually sleeping, but if you are so fortunate—ah. Elephants, for example, only lie down for three to five hours, usually at night. Sometimes, though, you'll catch them napping at midday, flat out on one side. Which side? Left or right? Is the trunk extended, or curled up? Is another elephant close-by, standing guard? Is the sleeping elephant snoring, showing signs of dreaming, or passing gas? When it awakens, how does it get its huge body back up on four feet? So many things to look for . . . and to learn.

Do elephants sleep standing up as well? They do. Hmmm . . . how can you tell? My personal observations reveal several indications. They stand very, very still, with their eyes closed. The tail will swish just occasionally, and the ears will flap only now and then. The trunk becomes so relaxed that the end not only touches the ground, but a segment folds back with the nasal openings pointing toward the front feet. They still seem to be aware of their surroundings and accept routine noises, but an unfamiliar sound will awaken them.

Elephants have an affinity for water that goes far beyond a life sustaining liquid. To watch them drink is engrossing, but after they quench their thirst, their child-like behavior (even in adults) is pure enchantment. With their trunk they will splash water gently or vigorously, blow bubbles underwater, or suck water into the trunk, pinch the tip and expel water in a jet. With their feet they will kick back and forth, resulting in huge splashes and waves. When elephants' skin is wet it appears quite dark, and after they stand in or walk through water it looks as if they are wearing boots. In warm weather they will blow a trunk-full of water on their belly or behind their ears.

In some regards you could say that elephants never grow up, as they love to play in the dirt. Digging a hole with their trunk or front foot, they take loose dirt in their trunk and throw it on their back or blow some behind their ears. Dust baths are another favorite activity. When their entire body is coated with a thick layer of fine dust, they sometimes execute one giant shake, causing the dust to float suspended around their huge form. If angled sunlight catches the dust just right, it creates a breathtaking halo—one you won't forget seeing.

Mud is a glorious substance for elephants, and a good reason to take your umbrella and visit the zoo on a rainy day. (Many zoos create mud in dry conditions as well.) Elephants will kick in the mud, throw it on their body with their trunk, even lie on their side and roll in it. While watching elephants in a full-fledged mud bath, they often become so absorbed and have so much fun that it makes you want to be an elephant!

Besides their involvement with water, dirt and mud, watch elephants as they interact with other aspects of their environment. They will rub against tree trunks or deadfalls, straddle a large boulder and scratch their belly (which may result in a squeaking sound), or walk around while balancing branches on their head. And always, they are investigating with their trunk, or sniffing the air to pick up various scents. Most interesting, of course, is interplay with other elephants: touching, rubbing, pushing, shoving, intertwining their trunks—even stealing food from each other!

You might be lucky enough to see their initial reaction to a totally new situation. I remember when Sunda and Toka encountered their first snow, which was a fresh layer several inches deep. Curious, yet cautious, they seemed reluctant to step on it, until they discovered the solid ground underneath. (By the way, if the association of elephants and snow seems unusual, remember how Hannibal crossed the Alps.)

Eating occupies most of the time in the daily activity cycle of elephants. When food is abundant, as it is in the zoo, they can be quite selective. Watch them as they take hay in their trunk, then shake loose the stems and proceed to eat only the succulent leaves. Or steal from their neighbor what apparently is the more desirable hay. Sometimes, with huge quantities of hay piled before them, I've seen elephants stuff their mouth full, then grab another batch in their trunk and hold it while nonchalantly chewing the first batch.

In the ordinary act of eating elephants display such joy. More than sustenance, eating seems to provide natural solace and security as well. When an elephant is truly relaxed and at peace with the world, it will place its weight on three legs while casually eating, and then cross one hind foot in front of the other. I have been privileged to see this carefree behavior both in the wild and in the zoo. It was so gratifying and, in every instance, it was a glimpse of elephant heaven.

Familiar to everyone, usually from childhood, elephants may very well be the most compelling symbol of the animal kingdom. Yet, so often they are depicted erroneously by movies, commercials, TV, and books. Furthermore, elephants in the wild are inaccessible and anonymous to most people, and might just as well be imaginary.

But *live* elephants at the zoo are *substantive* and actually present in real time as pure, living, breathing, eating, drinking, defecating, urinating, tangible individuals, and are part of our immediate existence. We relate to them on a personal basis, which inspires awe and affection. To be in the presence of elephants is simply magical. Treasure your time spent with the elephants when you visit the zoo.

The Little Zoo That Could

Topekans had seen an amazing transformation in their zoo by the fall of 1968. And this just a scant five years since some of my colleagues from zoobiz had said it would be professional suicide for me to associate with the meager municipal menagerie in Topeka's Gage Park.

Hold on! I'm not looking for a pat-on-the-back. The point is that this all took place because of one dominating force: com mu ni ty sup port. This was so important that I have tried to make six words out of two for emphasis! I simply happened to be in the right place at the right time (as they say) and my role was primarily that of cheerleader, a catalyst to spark motivation. And did the community ever respond! The people (especially the children) of Topeka and northeast Kansas made things happen because of their gumption, impetus, compassion and, most important . . . P-R-I-D-E.

I have long held that two phenomena can synergize a community in the development of self-esteem and spirit. One is a winning athletic team. When the Kansas City Royals won their only World Series title, people who had never attended a Royals game in their life were flying the colors. The other, of course, is a good zoo. Witness San Diego.

But a community does not have to be big, or rich, or be a terminal tourist destination, or a media center, or be in a sub-tropical climate, or a thousand other things in order to have a super zoo. However, the one element it *must* have is responsive and supportive people. Topeka excelled in this. And they took *pride* in their zoo.

The term community encompasses not only visitors and zoo members, volunteers and donors, staff and city officials, but also news media and civic clubs, students and tourists, merchants and vendors . . . anyone and everyone who values and wants to utilize the zoo as a community resource.

Indeed, there was much at the zoo to engender pride. Some of the most wonderful and spectacular animal species on this planet were right here in Topeka—alive and well for all to see—in facilities specifically designed for their husbandry and management.

The new ultra-modern structure for elephant, giraffe, hippo, chimpanzee, mandrill baboon and DeBrazza monkey, made the zoo a major focus in Topeka and a leading attraction in northeast Kansas. To use the phrase, the zoo was now on the map. Better yet, it was on the phone book! The cover of the 1966 Greater Topeka Telephone Directory featured the zoo in a full color montage with photos of a tiger, polar bear, giraffe and the new Large Mammal Building.

Another new exhibit was completed in 1967: the Australian Building. This was the result of fund raising efforts by the Topeka Friends of the Zoo ($12,000), the gratis time and talent of architect Robert Jones, donated materials, volunteer labor and assistance from the Park Department. Australian species included red kangaroos, wedge-tailed eagles, dingoes, emus, brush-tailed phalangers, greater sulfur-crested cockatoos, blue-tongued skinks, rainbow lorikeets . . . even an echidna, one of only two egg-laying mammals in the world (the other is the duck-billed platypus).

For a zoo of its size, Topeka had a remarkable medley of bears: polar bears, American black bears, Himalayan bears, Alaskan brown bears, grizzly bears and a Malaya sun bear. The polar bears were champion crowd pleasers . . . and crowd teasers. They shared with many zoo animals a common occupational activity: watching the people. They not only watched people, they learned more about people than people learned about them . . . and they learned faster!

On warm summer afternoons large crowds would gather in front of the polar bears and the pair would scheme as a team. One would stand on its hind legs to its full height and awe the crowd with its stunning size and beauty, while the other would discreetly mosey to the edge of the pool, pause momentarily, then suddenly plunge all of its 800 pounds into the water, drenching the unsuspecting visitors!

Everyone would jump back in unison, laughing and pointing at each other. Most people would wipe themselves off while looking embarrassed and, after a moment or two, move back up into the same position—and the polar bear would splash them again. It took some people three or four times to learn, yet the polar bear knew they would come back and was ready and waiting. It often made you wonder which was the more intelligent species.

Felines from around the world were represented: Bengal tigers from India, African lions, South American jaguars, Canada lynxes, Kansas bobcats, and from Central America, the ocelot and margay cat. Jenkins, the mountain lion (a North American species), was queen of the cats. Since she was born in the zoo, her litters were second generation zoo-born cubs.

In addition to Australia, the zoo had a couple of other geographical exhibit areas. North America contained bison, elk, deer, predatory birds, sandhill cranes, wild turkeys, gulls, pelicans, ducks, geese and swans. South America included llamas, rheas and Brazilian tapirs. Thanks to TFOTZ, new exhibits were on line for African species: zebra, antelope, ostrich and camel. The zoo now had six sections for final inspection on the handwritten daily report (remember, this was the pre-computer age).

TOPEKA ZOOLOGICAL PARK
Daily Activity Record

Date_____Day_____Weather_____Temp. Range_____

Animal Accessions:
(births, eggs laid-hatched, exchange,donation,purchase,collected; sex,age,size,cost, etc.)

_____
_____
_____
_____

Animal Removals:
(Exchange, sale, donation, euthanasia, death, escape; sex, age, size, autopsy results, etc.)

_____
_____
_____
_____

Breeding Activities:
(Mating, or mating behavior,estrus,pregnancy noted or suspected,nest-building activity, etc.)

_____
_____
_____
_____

Veterinary Data-Illness and Injury:
(Diagnosis,treatment,quarantine,inoculation,parasites,vomiting,diarrhea,appetite, etc.)

_____
_____
_____
_____
_____
_____
_____

Miscellaneous Animal Data:
(Diet changes,moulting,shedding,transfers,changes in procedures,unusual behavior, etc.)

_____
_____
_____
_____
_____
_____
_____
_____
_____
_____

See reverse side for Zoo Physical Plant,Miscellaneous Remarks, and Final Inspection:

Zoo Physical Plant: Buildings, Grounds, Equipment, Exhibits--Accomplished and/or needed.

Miscellaneous Remarks:
(Special projects, educational activities, attendance, guests, conservation activities,
research projects, community service, news media, etc.)

Total Attendance_____ Adults_____ Children_____
Admission Revenue $_____ Educational_____ TFOTZ_____

Final Inspection: Animals in satisfactory condition, facilities locked and secured, etc.
AREA   TIME   KEEPER   REMARKS

ANIMAL KINGDOM BUILDING_____

CATS AND BEARS_____

GEOGRAPHIC AREAS_____

HIPPO-PRIMATE_____

ELEPHANT-GIRAFFE_____

HOOFED STOCK_____

                              Approved By:_____
                                           Zoo Director

This wild and wonderful gathering of animals was rounded out by an amazing array of fabulous fauna in the Animal Kingdom Building, as described previously. Several fortunes and a lifetime of travel might not offer the variety of wildlife that could be seen in one day at the Topeka Zoo.

Civic pride in the zoo extended far beyond the animals. In addition to its general education programs, the zoo worked closely with the Veterans Administration Hospital and was the recipient of the annual Bell Award from the Shawnee County Mental Health Association for "outstanding contribution to community mental health" during 1966.

In 1966 Topeka was one of the first zoos to establish a group of trained volunteer educators, or Docents. Sponsored and initially staffed by the Junior League of Topeka, the program developed under the guidance of Nancy Cherry, a Junior League member, a TFOTZ Board Member and later editor of *ZOO Magazine*. Zoo Docents conducted guided tours and presented outreach programs in schools. The League also provided funding for educational graphics throughout the zoo.

Just as important as all of the new animals was insuring that the public understood and appreciated them. Keeping up with labels and graphics is a major challenge for every zoo of any size, but especially those on a limited (or non-existent) budget for such things. Don't forget: outdoor labels had to be able to withstand the rigors of the elements—heat, fading from the summer sun, rain, snow, freezing and thawing in winter . . . even daily bird droppings.

We came up with a system for labels, but it needed coordinated teamwork for it to be successful. Fortunately we had that! TFOTZ provided funds for us to buy blank heavy-duty plastic plaques. The zoo staff researched the text for each animal: basic information such as common name, scientific name, geographic range, natural history facts, and—something I felt was very important—a remark on the behavior of that particular species. Also, the background and personalities of selected individual animals were profiled. At this point our trusted associate, Ed Carmona at the Park Department, would physically engrave each individual plaque and it would be installed at the zoo. Visitors simply accepted them as part of what a good zoo should be, never once stopping to think what was involved to make all of this happen.

Ed Carmona deserves special mention. Not just for our labels; he was also the key staff person who had the best information on where all of the old water lines were in the zoo (and they often broke), as well as all of the rusty sewer systems (and they often clogged). Ed Carmona was truly one of the unsung heroes of the zoo in the early days.

But beyond the essential labels, the zoo needed fundamental graphics to tell the story of particular species and to help interpret the special dimensions of wildlife in the zoo. Keepers contributed a lot to the Topeka Zoo, and not just with suggestions in animal care. In this case, with graphics as well!

Keeper Harry C. Conwell, Jr., assumed the challenge of developing graphics in a zoo with no graphics department. Remember those giraffe neck bones that got me in trouble back in Fort Worth? I still had them and all along had intended to use them for educational purposes. Ah-ha! Here was the perfect opportunity. Harry made a life-size pattern-to-scale representation profile of an adult male giraffe, as well as one of a human and one of a shrew. Each was painted black and showed only neck bones. We located the graffic next to the indoor giraffe exhibit and titled it, "The Cervical Seven: a comparison of the world's tallest mammal, the world's smallest mammal and man—each having seven neck bones."

The Australian graphic featured a central plywood map of that continent with color codes to show the various vegetation areas, plus two side panels of aluminum photo plates. One described the postures, basic gaits and sexual behavior of the kangaroo. The other explained the three types of mammalian births: monotreme (echidna), marsupial (kangaroo) and placental (dog).

The year 1968 saw the initiation of another unique service for our visitors: The Zoo Question Box. This was a simple open-air booth staffed by a volunteer high school student trained to answer questions and dispense minor first aid, from 11:00 am to 5:00 pm, Wednesday through Sunday. Our first "Zoo Answer Man" was Ron Kaufman, who later became education coordinator at the zoo. Mark Pheasant assumed the post the following year and answered 5,105 questions between Memorial Day and Labor Day. Mark later became a keeper. Our Zoo Question Box evolved into the A to Z Shop (Answers to Zoovenirs) which, in addition to answers, carried film, posters, books and zoo souvenirs, with proceeds going to TFOTZ. Mike Coker operated the shop for several summers, later joined the staff and eventually became zoo director. Incidentally, the most frequently asked questions concerning animals were about elephants, snakes, and feeding times. The number one all-time question, however, was: "Where are the restrooms?"

Over time this led to a new dimension of zoo labels we dubbed FAQ's, or Frequently Asked Questions. We wanted to give the visitor a better insight into zoo animal behavior and zoo management practices. Some examples of FAQ's were: Why do giraffes lick? Do animals get bored? Will the cats have more room? Do you ever clean this pool? Why do gorillas vomit? The questions were more intriguing than the answers.

We also encouraged visitors to utilize the library as a source of animal information

From the time I arrived in Topeka, I was impressed with the Topeka Public Library. Long time Director Jim Marvin took it to great heights during my time at the zoo. The Head of the Adult Services Department at the Library, Mary A. Hall, was the first TFOTZ Secretary in 1964 and started a membership newsletter, *The Bear Facts.* Mary and I agreed that two of the most valuable educational resources in the community should combine efforts in a joint program.

Staff members of both institutions prepared annotated reading lists of books available at the Library that pertained to zoos in general and animal species in the Topeka Zoo. The general list was titled "The Seal of Good Reading" and the children's list was "Zoo's Who." Special education exhibits were prepared throughout the library, incorporating books, animal sculptures and zoological artifacts (skulls, eggs, horns, tusks, etc). Live animals from the zoo were taken to the library for story hours. I recall one giant tortoise who chose such an occasion to have an infrequent void of bladder contents, and the glee of pre-schoolers as they shouted, "He pottied a lot!"

The programs extended to surrounding communities that had a library but no zoo. Thus, the Topeka Zoo expanded its educational benefits outside its usual geographical limits to serve as a regional zoo through local libraries.

From the outset of my arrival in Topeka I felt it was essential to bring the zoo to the community, especially to students. Despite the press of other activities, I regularly spoke to groups and school classes. The importance of these programs (and our joint effort with the library) was reflected in a letter to me dated April 16, 1964 from Wilmer Moffet, Principal of Stout Elementary School in Topeka, who said:

"Dear Mr. Clarke:

"I want to use this opportunity to thank you for taking time from your very busy schedule to visit with our pupils about animals. The children were really thrilled with your pictures and the animals you showed them. When you read the letters that some of the second graders wrote to you, you will find that they learned many new concepts from your talks.

"Your personal cooperation with the public library and the schools is a completely new experience for the citizens of Topeka. You are to be commended for your educational program.

"We will all follow with a great deal of interest your zoo development program. I am sure we will see some real improvements under your leadership."

What an encouraging letter! And he sent a copy to Mr. John Goodin, the Park Commissioner.

In September 1965 I was honored to initiate a series of Science Seminars sponsored by the National Science Foundation and the Kansas Academy of Sciences. I spoke at the Linda Hall Library in Kansas City, Missouri, to an overflow crowd of more than 200 area students. Naturally, I had my old pal Schroeder, the alligator, forever a big hit, by my side.

Besides live animals, slides and artifacts, I had always felt it was important to give the students something tangible, something to take with them. Hence, I developed a series of outlines and handouts. One was entitled *Zoological Park Appreciation* and covered such topics as the history of zoos, zoos in a world scope, psychology of zoo animals, behavior of zoo visitors and functions of a modern zoo. A second addressed the research potential, scientific contributions and educational activities of zoos, plus career opportunities. Yet another contained a selected bibliography as well as a list of suggested projects to do while visiting a zoo. These were simple exercises to help understand the significance of an animal's appearance, sound, behavior, even odor. Much to my surprise, this all eventually developed into a program I called "Zoology and Peopleology" that was featured by the Associated Clubs/Knife and Fork Clubs on a nationwide after dinner lecture circuit. Over the years this enabled me to spread the fame of the Topeka Zoo in 45 of the 50 states.

One of the highlights of my developing speaking career was an invitation from the Provost of Raymond College at the University of the Pacific in Stockton, CA to speak before their High Table. I did so on November 21, 1967 at which the president of the California Fish and Game Commission presented me with a live pair of California quail for our zoo!

On July 11, 1968 the Provost wrote:

"Dear Gary:

"You will be pleased to know, I believe, that our High Table committee has asked me to extend another invitation to you to visit us. With such luminaries as John Kenneth Galbraith, Karl Schnabel, Lewis Mayhew, Arthur Clarke, Ralph Nader, Michael Harrington, Harry Edwards, and others, the students place you as, by far and away, the most interesting and exciting speaker of the year. (You are more than welcome to use this information in your public relations material!)

"Could you come in November for a presentation? If so, the 3rd, 10th, or 17th, would be most agreeable.

"It will be a pleasure to see you again, and I hope you can accept the invitation.

"It would be delightful if Mrs. Clarke could join you."

In addition to paying all expenses, they offered an honorarium. In lieu of an honorarium, I asked if they would pay expenses for my entire family (wife and four children) to travel with me to California. They agreed, and I requested long overdue vacation time, as this was a special opportunity. We took the train, both as an experience for the kids and because I was bringing (actually sneaking) along several animals (including Schroeder) to use in my presentation. All went well and afterwards I took the family (and animals) to San Francisco to see the zoo.

My professional involvement on a national level continued to grow. At the spring 1965 meeting of the American Association of Zoological Parks & Aquariums (AAZPA), I was appointed to develop a system of nation-wide regional zoo conferences conducive to smaller institutions and second level staff. I divided the country into five regions and the map was published in the AAZPA Directory. To get things started we hosted the very first regional conference in Topeka: the KANSAS ZOO WORKSHOP in September 1965. We had an attendance of 30 from three states representing seven zoos, one research institution, one university and two recreation commissions.

At the AAZPA annual conference in 1967 I was elected to a three-year term on the Board of Directors. Topeka was the smallest zoo with a member on the board.

The AAZPA represented primarily zoo administrators and managers. In 1967 another organization emerged: the American Association of Zoo Keepers (AAZK). Born/hatched at the San Diego Zoo, some zoo directors feared it was a union. Having been in contact with the organizer, I felt not— it was a national association of keepers dedicated to professional animal care, so I offered my support. Some years later they were looking for a location to establish their National Headquarters. With permission from the City and Park Department we provided rent-free office space, and many of our staff were involved. Suddenly Topeka was "the" address known to keepers across the country. In time, a TFOTZ Board Member, Susan Chan, become the Managing Editor of their Journal, the *Animal Keeper's Forum*. By the way, AAZK is still going strong 40 years later.

With all that was going on, I was again contacted by *The American City* magazine and asked to submit an article (with photos) about how our zoo had developed with the shared efforts of the public and the city. This was an excellent opportunity to commend the community and give much deserved credit to Park Superintendent Dennis Showalter and his staff before a nationwide audience. Under the title "Upgrading a Zoo," it appeared in the November 1969 issue and Topeka received a lot of recognition as a result.

More than just animals and buildings, the zoo had quickly evolved into a valuable civic asset and a living, dynamic community institution that played a vital role in the activities of Topeka and its citizens. It truly was the zoo that civic pride built, assisted by tremendous support from professional colleagues in the zoo world. An editorial in *The Topeka State Journal* of September 28, 1968 was titled, "Gage Park Zoo an Asset."

As I looked back then, it all was so much more than I could have ever anticipated. More than once I heard reference to "the little zoo that could." And while it was not apparent at the time, upon reflection now it is obvious that the local Gage Park Zoo was on the verge of becoming . . . the WORLD FAMOUS TOPEKA ZOO.

Part 3

Pampering Pregnant Giraffes and Changing Gorilla Diapers

A series of phenomenal firsts: first gorillas in Kansas, first giraffe birth in Kansas, first prize in ape art, first eagle hatchlings, record tiger litter, etc.

The zoo is a healing island of naturalness and reality in a megapolitan sea of artificiality and unreality. An island that can give the people glimpses of beauty and mystery, and even unexpected familiarity.

—William G. Conway
General Director
Wildlife Conservation Society

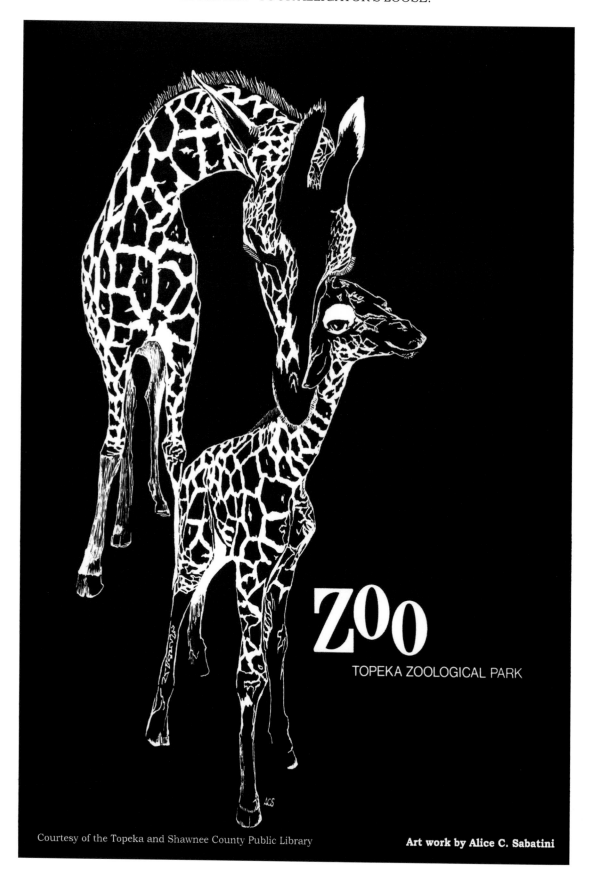

ZOO

TOPEKA ZOOLOGICAL PARK

Courtesy of the Topeka and Shawnee County Public Library

Art work by Alice C. Sabatini

Part 3

Pampering Pregnant Giraffes and

Changing Gorilla Diapers

Gorilla Diapers in the Sky
Max Loves Tiffany
Gorillas Star in *The NEW YORKER*
The Anxiety and the Jubilation . . .
　　　　Our First Giraffe Birth
D. James Orang, the Painting Primate
The World Responds
Ape Art: An Assessment
Eagles Hatch Golden Eggs
Zoo Directors Stand Alone
A Horse of a Different Color
Topeka's Terrific Tigers

As a teenage keeper in 1958 I had the privilege of caring for Big Man, the first gorilla at the Kansas City Zoo.
Photo from Gary K. Clarke archives.

Jiggs, the adult male Brazilian tapir at the Kansas City Zoo, weighed 500 lbs. His nose extended beyond his mouth to form a short proboscis.
Photo from Gary K. Clarke archives.

Drama on the African Veldt at the Kansas City Zoo: Casey, the African elephant, grabbed the horns of Spot, the Maasai giraffe—my heart stopped!

Photo by Gary K. Clarke

I feared Casey would break Spot's neck, but Spot was so strong that he subdued Casey! Such fantastic behavior!

Photo by Gary K. Clarke

Winter scene of the waterbird lagoon in Peaceful Valley at the Kansas City Zoo. Regardless of the weather, a zoo keeper's duties must carry on daily.

Photo by Gary K. Clarke

Matt, the male camel at the Kansas City Zoo, proved to be one of my great challenges as a young keeper. Yet, he taught me so much about the wiles and ways of exotic animals.

Photo from Gary K. Clarke archives

At Midwest Research Institute in Kansas City, Missouri, I devised a suction tube method for collecting mites into a glass jar from under a snake's scales (in this case a bull snake) for a project on the eradication of reptilian external parasites.

Photo by Midwest Research Institute

Big Red, the red diamond rattlesnake, inflicted a near-fatal bite on me at Midwest Research Institute in November 1959. It was my fault. Big Red remained a close member of my family thereafter.

Photo by
Midwest Research Institute

When I assumed my duties in Topeka as director in 1963, the zoo in Gage Park consisted of basic facilities.

Photo by Charles Van Trease

Exterior of the 1907 greenhouse that had been converted to the "Monkey House," the zoo's only heated building in 1963.

Photo by Charles Van Trease

Interior of the Monkey House, with free-standing small units for reptiles in the center.

Photo by Charles Van Trease

The abandoned Gage swimming pool was housing bison and elk in 1963. It was converted to the zoo parking lot in 1965.

Photo by Charles Van Trease

The first official Topeka Zoological Park staff photo was taken on August 31, 1966 with our two Asian elephants. Sunda is center stage with the smaller Toka partially visible to the right. The clean-shaven guy with the skinny necktie is . . . the author.

Photo by Henry Gund III

Schroeder, the alligator, was a popular and effective live teaching aid, as well as a marvelous ambassador for all wildlife, and the star of our new Education Room in 1966.

Photo by Swetnam & Grier

The hippo `Peka-Sue always responded to my visits . . .

. . . and expected her marshmallow treats!

Photos by Phil Lange

Jenkins, the mountain lion, was born six days after I started as zoo director in Topeka and hand-reared in our home.

Photo by The Topeka Daily Capital

The first gorillas in Kansas! Max (l.) was born in the Dallas Zoo on March 7, 1969 and arrived at the Topeka Zoo on September 29, 1969. Tiffany (r.) was born in the Kansas City Zoo on July 15, 1968 and arrived at the Topeka Zoo on October 15, 1969. Then Max had "Breakfast at Tiffany's."

Photo by Gary K. Clarke

This record litter of six Bengal tigers was born in the World Famous Topeka Zoo on June 15, 1973. All six were raised by their mother, Dacca, and accepted at an early age by their father, Tabor.

Photo by Gary K. Clarke

Max Falkenstein cuddled his namesake, Max the baby gorilla, in flight from Dallas, Texas to Topeka, Kansas, in September 1969.

Photo by Dr. Mark Morris, Jr., DVM

A baby llama from the zoo was a guest at the Topeka Public Library story hour in 1968.

Photo by The Topeka State Journal

Living art: head of Nyoka, the Gaboon viper.
Photo by Gary K. Clarke

Art in nature: face of Duke, the mandrill.
Photo by Ron Kaufman

One of my favorite activities as Topeka zoo director was sharing stories with Zoo School classes. Teacher Evie Green's students always had zoo jokes, animal riddles and original songs for me.
Photo by Nancy Cherry

The young male orangutan Djakarta Jim in my office with his original painting "Tornado" in January 1971.

Photo by The Topeka Daily Capital

Known in the art world as "D. James Orang," Jim would sit at a table, use a hand-held brush, deliberately select different colors and *then* compose his paintings.

Photo by Gary K. Clarke

Jim's fourth painting, "Train from Tokyo," painted on January 20, 1971 won first place in a state-wide art contest and generated world-wide attention. Although Jim painted unaided, the author had to title each painting.

Original non-toxic acrylic painting by D. James Orang

Sunflower, the first giraffe born in Kansas, standing 30 minutes after her birth on August 24, 1970. She was 5' 11" tall and weighed 130 lbs. First-time mother Jan was a perfect parent.
Photo by Gary K. Clarke

Sunflower at one day of age. The "horns" of newborn giraffes are *not* attached to the skull in order to ease the birth process. With time they become upright and fused with the skull.
Photo by Gary K. Clarke

Under the geodesic dome of the Tropical Rain Forest with a blue-and-gold macaw after being named Kansan of the Year in Recreation by The Topeka Capital-Journal in 1974.
Photo by The Topeka Capital-Journal

The stainless steel spider web at the margay cat exhibit in the Tropical Rain Forest was popular with visitors . . . and real spiders!
Photo by Gary K. Clarke

When the Tropical Rain Forest opened in 1974 it boasted the highest waterfall in Kansas!

Photo by Gary K. Clarke

The Topeka Zoo's 1982 holiday greeting card featured this lovely scene of the Tropical Rain Forest accentuated by a fresh winter snow.

Original oil painting by Marnie Wuenstel

What fun to roll out an authentic red carpet for Joan Embery, Goodwill Ambassador from the San Diego Zoo and Wild Animal Park (she said it was a first for her).

Photo by Nancy Cherry

Proudly touring the Tropical Rain Forest with Marlin Perkins. Marlin always looked so distinguished, particularly in contrast to my Zoo Power button, elephant necktie and shovel tie clasp.

Photo by The Topeka Daily Capital

Rolmar, a stallion Przewalski wild horse, under the Kansas sky at the Topeka Zoo's Conservation/Propagation Center at Forbes Field in Topeka in the 1970's.
Photo by Gary K. Clarke

A one week old Przewalski horse foal born at the Topeka Zoo's Conservation/Propagation Center. Note the erect mane from birth.
Photo by Gary K. Clarke

Zoo below zero!
Photo by Gary K. Clarke

Topeka Zoo's Arctic fox in its prime winter coat.
Photo by Gary K. Clarke

To me the zoo was like a secret garden where I could share in the enchanting lives of such wondrous and incredible animals as April, one of numerous Topeka Zoo-born giraffes.

Photo by The Topeka Capital-Journal

Gorilla Diapers in the Sky

So . . . by 1969 the zoo was on its way up! From a run-down municipal menagerie just a few years earlier to a dynamic community institution with unparalleled civic response, a major new exhibit facility with charismatic megavertebrates, a citizens support group with enthusiastic volunteers, an active professional staff with involvement on the national zoo scene, and a bright future.

Now did we dare think of . . . gorillas? Why not? They were periodically available, albeit expensive. But it was important that we be selective and acquire the appropriate animals, preferably a pair. Youngsters would be best, so they could grow up together in their home in the zoo. Additionally captive-born animals were desirable for a variety of reasons: their detailed records would be available (date of birth, parents, medical history, diet, growth rate, etc.); transport should be less difficult (no international flights and more direct accessibility); and reduced total cost (no foreign quarantine, customs fees, permits, etc.)

With these parameters in mind a silent search was initiated: reviewing other zoos' annual reports, checking animal inventories and birth records, discrete inquiries at zoo director's conferences. It was discouraging since gorillas that fit our criteria seemed to be non-existent.

I had just about given up trying to obtain one from an American zoo, so while on a study tour of European zoos I made several inquiries, but to no avail. Near the end of the trip I was woefully telling my tale to Larry Calvin, director of the Dallas Zoo, who was also on the tour. I said: "Larry, I've searched throughout America and Europe, and I just can't find a young zoo-born male gorilla." And Larry replied: "Well . . . we've got one." Good heavens! All this time the answer was literally right in my own backyard in the great state of Texas. HA! You never know how or when a gorilla may enter your life.

It was an infant male, born March 7, 1969 at the Dallas Zoo, hand-raised by their staff and still in diapers. He weighed 4lbs. 6 oz. at birth. On further confirmation I agreed this little guy would be perfect for our zoo, and the first gorilla to reside in Kansas.

The asking price was $5,000, which was quite reasonable for a gorilla, but a sizeable sum for our zoo. The next task was to find a donor. Rather than an individual, I thought we might have a better chance with an organization. I was a member of the downtown Rotary Club and knew of their service and support to the community. The president at the time was Max Falkenstien, a well-known area sports broadcaster. I reviewed the idea with him and he invited me to put my request before the Rotary Board of

Directors. The challenge now was to make a convincing case of how and why the Rotary Club of Topeka should spend big bucks on a gorilla for our zoo.

I gave it a lot of thought, came up with every conceivable tie-in from general to specific, and developed an outline for my presentation.

The Board was receptive but said candidly they simply did not have funds in their treasury to cover the entire amount. They suggested I make this same pitch to the entire membership at a luncheon meeting and ask for individual donations on the spot. This I did, complete with color slides and gorilla behavior impersonations.

The response was overwhelming! Members literally rushed to the podium and crowded around with wallets open, plunking down large bills with big grins, not wanting receipts or acknowledgements—simply eager to be a part of this momentous occasion. On the spot they contributed nearly the required amount and the club made up the difference. (For years after that, each time I spoke to this club, members sat with one hand on their wallets.)

When announcing the gorilla purchase at the club meeting on August 21, President Max Falkenstien said, "This is an excellent way to involve Rotary in the community. A gift of this nature will bring enjoyment to everyone—young and old—with the prospect of watching the little guy grow up. During the years he will attract thousands of people to Topeka. For these reasons the Rotary Board of Directors enthusiastically approved this donation."

One member, Mark Morris, Jr, DVM, already a strong supporter of the zoo, offered to fly his plane to Dallas to bring the gorilla back to Topeka (I said yes). It seemed appropriate that the Rotary Club of Topeka have the privilege of naming the gorilla, and they chose "Max" in honor of their president.

On the morning of September 29, 1969 four emissaries departed Topeka on a special mission: "Big" Max Falkenstien, Rotary Club President and Baby Gorilla Namesake; Lauren Nash, Topeka Park Commissioner and Godfather to Baby Max; Mark Morris, Jr., Gorilla Veterinarian, Photographer and Pilot; and Gary K. Clarke, Topeka Zoo Director and Professional Baby Holder. We flew in the twin-engine Gorilla Express (also known as Bonanza 5668 Kilo) to Dallas Redbird Airport, a general aviation field just ten minutes drive from the Dallas Zoo, whose staff provided ground transportation.

Outfitted in a clean diaper and diaper shirt, Baby Max was ready for the return plane ride. As we left the Dallas Zoo, Baby Max had his little arms wrapped tightly around me. Once we boarded the plane and were aloft, Baby Max relaxed and I transferred him to his namesake, Big Max, who embraced him fondly.

While Mark piloted the plane and Lauren navigated, Baby Max explored the contents of Big Max's pockets and then took a nap. On our arrival at Billard Airport in Topeka, Baby Max was greeted by excited reporters, dazzling flash bulbs, city commissioners and welcoming banners. Quite a reception.

A waiting vehicle whisked us to the zoo where Baby Max received a warm bottle from keeper John Wortman. As Mark Morris said, "For Baby Max, the day could not have ended better."

Baby Max immediately endeared himself to the community and his name became a household word with Topekans. Admiring crowds gathered daily at the animal nursery to watch him respond affectionately to his keepers and their T.L.C. When having his diaper changed Max was very patient. He didn't squirm or kick, but he did something no human baby could do. He grabbed and held onto his keeper with both hands-
and both feet!

One of his best tricks (which incidentlly showed his amazing strength) occurred when his keeper held Max by his wrists and swung him like a pendulum. Max would pull his feet up and over his head to perform a complete backward flip. He liked this so much he responded by pursing his lips and giving the keeper a grateful "whoo-whoo-whoo!"

The date September 29, 1969 will forever remain a historic date. Baby Max became the first gorilla to reside in Kansas, an important milestone for our zoo. And Big Max Falkenstien became the first human to change a gorrila's diaper while 8,000 feet over Kansas, no doubt a significant highlight in his illustrious career.

A GORILLA IN ROTARY

Rotary Club of Topeka
Board of Directors Meeting
5 August 1969

 I. Rotary Involvement With Zoos
     A. In the United States
     B. The World Over

 II. The Fascination of Gorillas
     A. Legend of King Kong
     B. First Known to Science in 1847
     C. Characteristics and Behavior
     D. Famous Gorilla Personalities

III. The Topeka Zoo and Gorillas
     A. In the Zoo Master Plan -- Time is Now
     B. Value to Zoo and Community
     C. First Gorilla in Kansas
     D. First Captive Born Pair in Any Zoo

 IV. What A Gorilla Can Do For The Rotary Club of Topeka
     A. Living Example of Rotary in Action!
     B. A Gorilla projects an image of masculinity, leadership, strength,
         and intelligence--all representative of our Club.
     C. 200,000 people a year will see the gorilla and the Rotary Club's
         name on the donation plaque.
     D. Couldn't buy interest and recognition it will generate.
         1. Star attraction of the Zoo, not just a Gorilla, but a Topeka personality.
         2. Continously focusing attention on the Club.
         3. Spectacular attraction for new members and out of town guests.
         4. Something people can identify with.

 V. Gorilla Participation in Committee Activities
     A. Community Service: The Zoo serves the community, so what benefits the
         Zoo benefits everyone.
     B. Rotarian Magazine: Examples of Zoo articles; Topeka Club and gorilla
         article.
     C. Program: A natural.
     D. Public Relations: See item IV; other aspects; Zoo publications.
     E. Rotopeka: Progress reports.
     F. Fireside Meetings: Focal point of discussion
     G. Classification: Establish a new one?
     H. Membership: Interest new members; make gorilla honorary member?
     I. Banner: Feature gorilla?
     J. Guest Introduction: Well, maybe not.

                                          Gary K. Clarke
                                          Zoo Director

Max Loves Tiffany

Our plan all along was to have a pair of gorillas. After all, we didn't want Max to grow up to be a bachelor, and it so happened that our sister zoo in Kansas City, Missouri (just 75 miles to the east) had a female named Tiffany who was born there on July 15, 1968. She would be ideal for Max and this time truly was in our own backyard, but also cost $5,000. We made the commitment to acquire her and I spent several months trying to figure out how to raise the money.

One day the Kansas City Zoo called and advised that we had one more week on our option; otherwise several other zoos were in a position to purchase Tiffany. That put me in a dilemma: how to raise $5,000 in a week's time to acquire Tiffany as a mate for Max.

I couldn't very well hit up—er, I mean ask Rotary again, and I didn't know of any other organization in town that could single-handedly respond to our need. So I simply made an announcement to the community through the news media. Overnight a spontaneous campaign arose throughout Topeka. Signs went up on billboards and marquees. They didn't say, "Help the zoo buy a gorilla." They simply said, *MAX LOVES TIFFANY.*" People started bringing jars of money out to my office from collections they had taken up at work, leaving them on my desk, and walking out. I didn't even have their names and addresses to write "thank you" letters. They just wanted to help buy Tiffany.

The mayor authorized all the fire stations in town as collection points, so that Bluebirds, Cub Scouts and others could make contributions for Tiffany within their neighborhoods. The Independent Insurance Agents of Topeka and the Topeka Restaurant Association both made major contributions. Many individuals contributed what they could, and one youngster decided to give all of his savings to the Tiffany fund. I even had a fellow call me at home one night—rather late, as a matter of fact. He said, "I am awfully sorry to bother you so late, but I would like to donate $1,000 to help buy Tiffany." I replied, "Believe me, it is no bother; call me anytime!"

In less than a week's time we had reached our goal—$5,000. And this fund drive occurred at the worst time of the year, right during the United Way Campaign. The Tiffany fund was not an organized campaign; it did not have pledge cards or team captains . . . it was simply the community responding to the zoo.

On October 15, 1969 the Kansas City Zoo brought Tiffany over to Topeka. We rolled out the red carpet (it was only three inches wide) inside the entrance of the zoo and she walked down the carpet in her diaper. We had a paper sign stretched across the doorway of the Large Mammal Buil-

Zoo Interest High—
Topeka Daily Capital
Friday, Sept. 5, 1969

Baby Gorilla's Arrival Awaited

The fancy of Gage Park Zoo visitors has turned from thoughts of elephants and giraffes to the coming arrival of a new baby gorilla.

The gorilla which will be

where it will be placed; and the answers to a dozen general questions about gorillas," Clarke said.

Most questions about the gorilla and other zoo animals

Most commonly asked question concerned the length of the gestation period of elephants.

Zoo Director Gary Clarke said the elephants are quite popular and the gestation period of an

Others wanted to know what you give an elephant with diarrhea. The answer to the latter was easy — lots of room, Clarke said.

Clarke said he is pleased with

Campaign for Ape Gets Large Boost

Gage Park Zoo's campaign to raise $5,000 for a female companion for Max, the new gorilla, received a big boost Monday with a promise of a $1,000 donation by a Topekan who asked to remain anonymous.

But the drive

the zoo in the attempt to chase Tiffany, a young gorilla at the Swope Park Kansas City.

$270 in Donation
Contributions

Baby Gorilla Fund Passes Mid Point

Topeka Capital-Journal
Wednesday, October 8, 1969

Called at Home

Gary Clarke, zoo director, said the donor telephoned him at home to pledge the $1,000 donation.

"He said, 'I'm sorry to have bothered you at home'," Clarke said. "I assured him it was no bother."

Clarke said the man told him he had just returned to the city and had read about the campaign in the newspaper.

The Topeka Fire Dept. is

Max, the gorilla who has become the greatest drawing card in the Topeka Zoo, was the object of many wide-eyed stares from Topeka school children this morning as he took a bottle from John Wortman, the

primate animal keeper at the zoo. Director Gary Clarke announced today that Max might be linked romantically with a female gorilla in Kansas City. The female's name is Tiffany.

—Staff Photo by George Olsen

Next Zoo Project May Be Getting Max Mate

$974 More Needed To Buy Tiffany

Topeka State Journal
Wednesday, Oct. 8, 1969

2 Topeka Daily Capital
Thursday, Oct. 9, 1969

Girl Gorilla to Join Max

A jubilant Gary Clarke, Gage Park Zoo director, announced late Wednesday the $5,000 drive to purchase Tiffany, the baby female gorilla at the Kansas City zoo, was more than successful.

Listing such donors as youngsters who emptied piggy banks, a boy who withdrew $100 in sav — with his parents' permission — Topeka Restaura Assn

Headliners at the Zoo

Topekans may grumble about high taxes, waste in government, the high cost of living and all the other pocketbook plagues they fall heir to; but they have proved that when they really want something, they shell out the money to pay for it.

Downtown Topeka Rotary Club set the stage a few weeks ago when it plunked down $5,000 to buy an eight-month-old gorilla from the Dallas, Tex., zoo for display in the Topeka Zoo.

Scarcely had the baby gorilla arrived and been christened Max when word was received that the Swope Park Zoo in Kansas City had a baby girl gorilla named Tiffany it wanted to place.

Max could use a girl friend, and if Topeka could get Tiffany, its zoo would be the only one in the nation to have a pair of born-in-captivity gorillas.

Trouble was, Tiffany also had a $5,000 price

Gorillas to Appear Topeka Debut

Topeka Daily Capital
Thursday, Oct. 16, 1969

ing of 'Tiffany' Djakart
ge Park Zoo

Tiffany Right At Home Here

By SUE WEBSTER

Wearing a blue sweater and clutching a yellow and white teddy bear, Tiffany arrived at the Topeka Zoo today.

A 15-month-old gorilla. Tiffany gave everyone an affectionate hug.

Comm. Kenneth Kern presented

Baby Gorillas Just Good Friend

(Continued From Page 1)

Pulse of the

Max's Ma Meets City Wedne

ding that said "Welcome to Topeka, Tiffany," and she tore that up right on schedule for the TV cameras!

All in all, it was a great day in the history of our zoo. The first day that Tiffany was in our zoo, we did not—I repeat, we did not—put Max and Tiffany together. We kept them separate all night long. And then, the next morning, we took Max into Tiffany's exhibit, so that Max could have . . . (are you ready for this?)—"Breakfast at Tiffany's." (I know . . . go ahead and groan.)

But there is more to the story than that. My love affair with Tiffany actually began with her mother when I was privileged to be a keeper at the Kansas City Zoo working with the gorilla trio of Big Man, Jeannie and Kate. Little did I dream at the time that someday I would be the director of a zoo that was lucky enough to have an offspring from Big Man and Jeannie, namely Tiffany. (Does that make me sort of a gorilla godparent?)

Tiffany had been raised by Jack and Jan Armstrong, then director and curator of the Kansas City Zoo. Tiffany was already an established personality in town since many Topekans had seen her at the Kansas City Zoo and kept up with her activities through Kansas City TV stations and newspapers.

John Wortman was the first keeper at our zoo for the baby gorillas. Prior to Tiffany's arrival John spent a week at the Kansas City Zoo getting acquainted with Tiffany and studying the care and handling of gorillas. Bill Gage arrived on the scene shortly after that to relieve John for other duties and became Topeka Zoo's Gorilla Keeper par excellence. Bill should get the lion's share of credit for raising the gorillas, although many of our keepers played an important role in the gorillas' development.

Max and Tiffany were the undisputed stars of our zoo, but their fame was destined to spread in a most unexpected way.

Tutoring Tiffany for Topeka

As mentioned in the previous chapter, John Wortman spent time with Tiffany at the Kansas City Zoo to help ease her transition to Topeka. Jim Lapham referred to this in *The Kansas City Star* on August 12, 1969. The column headline was "Tiffany's Welfare Aim In New Home," and following are a few excerpts.

"The number of persons who have heard the laugh of a young gorilla at play must be limited.

"There are all sorts of reasons why this is so. One is the fact that the sound is so low as to be scarcely audible at more than arm's length. It is a soft, huh-huh-huhhing. The most nearly similar familiar sound, probably, is that of a dog panting.

"Tiffany, the year-old gorilla at the Kansas City Zoo, is the source of young gorilla laughter in this area. And at the Kansas City Zoo throughout last week one of the keepers, probably unnoticed by patrons, was wearing the shoulder patch of the Topeka Zoo.

"He was John Wortman, and he was here, among other reasons, to make Tiffany laugh. He succeeded admirably."

*****

"This being a workaday world, Wortman did not spend a week in Kansas City on a keeper exchange program simply in order to play kitchy-coo with Tiffany. He also was studying the care and handling of several species that Topeka does not have but plans to acquire. Most immediate and prominent in that category, however, is Tiffany."

*****

"Tiffany squirmed with glee and grinned broadly as Wortman first jounced her on his knees and then swung her, face up, while she kicked happily at his chest. He placed Tiffany on her back and, while she held up hands and feet and laughed softly, spun her rapidly like a top.

"Wortman devoted much of his working time last week to being a companion for Tiffany. He was accepted immediately by the gorilla and Tiffany thus seems assured of having one good friend when she moves, probably next month, to Topeka."

Topeka Daily Capital, October 11, 1969

Headliners at the Zoo

Topekans may grumble about high taxes, waste in government, the high cost of living and all the other pocketbook plagues they fall heir to; but they have proved that when they really want something, they shell out the money to pay for it.

Downtown Topeka Rotary Club set the stage a few weeks ago when it plunked down $5,000 to buy an eight-month-old gorilla from the Dallas, Tex., zoo for display in the Topeka Zoo.

Scarcely had the baby gorilla arrived and been christened Max when word was received that the Swope Park Zoo in Kansas City had a baby girl gorilla named Tiffany it wanted to place.

Max could use a girl friend, and if Topeka could get Tiffany, its zoo would be the only one in the nation to have a pair of born-in-captivity gorillas.

Trouble was, Tiffany also had a $5,000 price tag.

Undaunted, Gary Clarke, director of the Topeka Zoo, set out to raise the $5,000 in five days. Despite comments from Doubting Thomases in the city, money flowed in like buttermilk. Before the deadline (Wednesday) had passed, more than $5,000 had been donated to buy Tiffany. The money left over will go to projects of Friends of the Zoo.

It all proves that when Topekans really want something, they go after it – and they're willing to pay for it.

Contributors to the Tiffany Hall of Fame as listed in the TFOTZ Newsletter, November, 1969.

Topeka Restaurant & Purveyors Association
Topeka Insurors
Dr. and Mrs. John Ashley
Master Robbie Fowks
Mr. and Mrs. C. S. Gavitt
Dr. and Mrs. Joseph E. Gootee
Mrs. Julia Hochstatter
Holwick, Inc.
The James Marvin Family
Quota Club of Topeka
The John W. Weber Family
Mr. and Mrs. Jack Bradley
Design Forum, Inc.
Jardine Jr. High Student Council
Liz and Lee Stratton
Potwin 6th Grade Class
Employees of State Motor Vehicle Dept.
Mr. Donald Chubb
Mr. H. C. Corbett
Mr. and Mrs. Preston Hale
Mr. and Mrs. John T. MacNair
McEntire Brothers Mattress Co.
Dr. and Mrs. Dean M. Miller
Dr. Gary J. Newman
Amy, Abby, and Betsy Thompson
Jamie and Russell Pollom
Trojan Construction Co.
Mrs. Lucile A. VanHorn
Mr. and Mrs. Les C. Walters
Zercher Photo, Inc.
Topeka West High Senior Class
Martha and Paul Klemme
Topeka West Junior High Class
Mr. and Mrs. Charles Craig
Pauline East Grad School
Topeka West High Sophomore Class
Mr. and Mrs. Max Bickford
Chapter FI of P.E.O.
Topeka High School, Room 123
Eisenhower Junior High School
Dr. Glenn Bair and Family
Mr. and Mrs. Russell W. Barnes
Mr. and Mrs. Marvin Cox
Heather, Ariel, Bonar and Eric Menninger
Beverly and Susan Menninger
Fredrick, John, Eliza, Marian, William
  and David Menninger
Freda J. Driscoll
Mrs. John Grimshaw
Major and Mrs. Herbert W. Hemmila

Mrs. Ted Hussey

Dr. and Mrs. Harry Kroll
Neon Tube Light Co.
Mr. and Mrs. John R. Peach
Mr. and Mrs. John P. Ransom
Miss Georgia Sue Reuter
Mrs. W. P. Snyder
Topeka Assoc. of the Visually Impaired
Lt. Col. and Mrs. Henry W. Williamson
Dr. and Mrs. Lonnie J. Bevens
Dr. Ben O. Evans
Mr. and Mrs. Edward Alberg
Mr. and Mrs. Philip E. Arnold
Rev. and Mrs. B. P. Bogia
Mr. and Mrs. Robert Bundy
Mr. and Mrs. Caleb J. Cochran
Mrs. Jessie C. Davis
Mr. Donald J. Gleason
Miss Lucy Good
Mr. and Mrs. William Higgs
Mrs. Dorothy E. Kendall
Mr. and Mrs. C. W. Larson
Mr. and Mrs. Ross Laybourn
Mr. W. E. Lindemuth
Mr. Roy McNish
Mr. Paul E. Palmer
Mr. and Mrs. R. D. Paquette
Mrs. Gladys M. Perry
Mr. and Mrs. R. H. Rogers
Mr. and Mrs. Don B. Rolley
Mr. and Mrs. Milo L. Schultes
Mrs. Charles J. Seel
Mr. Ray L. Stone
Mr. and Mrs. Howard Swanson
Mr. Robert C. Taggart
Mr. and Mrs. John Thiele
Mr. and Mrs. Clark Webster
Mr. Ben Lowther
Topeka West High School Faculty
Miss Helen Fish
Dorothy and Agnes Sieben
Esther Grout
Pat Towle
Mr. and Mrs. V. C. Allan
Mr. Verne Dow
Mr. and Mrs. Richard Frazier
Mrs. Jerri Massey and Girls
Miss Shellee Pendleton
Mrs. V. A. Wellborn
Ted Young
Master Troy Cummings

Miss Susan Halloran

Gorillas Star in *The NEW YORKER*

Dear Gary,

Could I get another one of those orang-painting papers that you so kindly sent me? So began a typewritten note dated Nov. 2, 1971.

It continued: *The editor has grabbed mine and I don't think I can get it back.* The note was on a 7x10 inch piece of beige-colored letterhead from *The NEW YORKER* Magazine, complete with the well known typeface and official logo. Just above the salutation, in small print was "EDITORIAL OFFICES" and, below that, the telephone number: "OXFORD 5-1414."

The writer of this note was a writer indeed, and a prolific one at that—author of 35 books (on subjects ranging from China to England to Africa to zoos), as well as a frequent contributor to *The NEW YORKER*. And she smoked cigars.

Her note to me concluded: *I am thinking of concentrating now on gorillas for a while. Have you any? I suppose I ought to get down to business and telephone everyone, but this is a good beginning.*

All the best – Yours,

And it was signed . . . Emily Hahn

Emily liked zoos ("I have liked them all my life . . .") and we had met at the conference of zoo directors in Los Angeles in 1968.

True to her word, she did concentrate on gorillas. Perhaps her note to me truly was "a good beginning" because her exhaustive account on gorillas, entitled "A Moody Giant," was published more than a decade later under "Annals of Zoology" in *The NEW YORKER*.

Part I appeared in the August 9, 1982 issue. Emily Hahn began with an engaging recollection of her first encounter with a live gorilla—a young female at the Bronx Zoo in New York City many years ago. With perception and scholarship she launched into the early literature on gorillas, followed by a detailed history of gorillas collected for museums and the first live gorillas imported to Europe and later America. Her engrossing profile from infancy of the young male who came to be known as "Gargantua the Great" of Ringling Bros. Circus fame is unforgettable.

It is so easy to read Emily Hahn that you sometimes fail to appreciate how difficult it is to write well. To me, that is the sign of a SUPERB writer.

Part II appeared in the August 16, 1982 issue. She started with the first gorilla birth in captivity on December 22, 1956 at the Columbus Zoo. Then she referred to the increasingly successful captive birth rates of gorillas up to that time and cited the first list of zoo born gorillas co-authored by zoo historian Marvin Jones and myself.

In her charming, casual way she proceeded to report on a series of visits to major zoos, with vignettes and anecdotes about their gorilla personalities, *and* the zoo personnel involved with them (also an exotic and amusing breed). In addition to the Columbus Zoo, others included San Diego (of course), Cincinnati, Colorado Springs, Denver, Oklahoma City, Lincoln Park and Brookfield in Chicago, Omaha, St. Louis, Central Park Zoo in New York and the Bronx Zoo, having come full circle. It was here that her infatuation with gorillas started, and once again she met that same female gorilla (named Oka), who by now was 33 and the second oldest of zoo gorillas.

Also on the list of prestigious zoos Emily Hahn visited was—you guessed it—the World Famous Topeka Zoo. At that point in time we did *not* have superstar gorilla personalities such as Colo in Columbus, the late Bushman of Lincoln Park in Chicago, King Tut at Cincinnati, Albert in San Diego, or even the infamous Gargantua of Ringling Bros. Circus fame. But we *did* have Max and Tiffany. Emily Hahn, true to her perceptive writer instinct, seemed to sense that this gorilla pair, even in a modest prairie state zoo, was significant. But maybe it is best to let Emily herself take it from here.

En route to my next stop, the Topeka Zoo, I was met at the Kansas City International Airport by Gary K. Clarke, the director at Topeka and another old friend. "What I find most fascinating about gorillas is the variation in their personalities," said Clarke, as we drove along the straight, flat road to Topeka. "Take Tiffany, our prize female. She could do a lot of things at four months that her half brother, The Colonel, couldn't do at five. At six months, he was walking gorilla fashion, on all fours. Then both of them, by the time they were nine months old, were walking upright." When Tiffany, at five months, was shown pictures of apes, he continued, she would pat her own mouth and then the mouth of the pictured ape, or do the same with her nose and the pictured nose. This was not really surprising, he said, because her mother, Jungle Jeannie, was very bright.

Emily had a love for the curious and the ability to bring to a story an aspect that others had not considered. I must admit she caught me off guard with a question as we proceeded to my house and continued our discussion.

We talked about gorilla behavior as the road sped by, and I asked about a phenomenon that had piqued my curiosity after I had observed it—or pictures of it—several times. I said, "Why do gorillas like to stand on people?"

Clarke looked surprised, and was silent for a while. "I don't know," he replied, at last. "I guess I'm so used to the fact that they stand on people that I've never wondered why." He went on looking thoughtful for a bit, then brightened up. "We'll ask around, shall we?" he said. "It'll be interesting, collecting theories."

At Clarke's house, he showed me some of his enormous collection of books and pamphlets pertaining to zoos. Many dealt with gorillas, and we looked at them for a long time trying to discover, among other things, why gorillas stand on people. We saw a number of photographs of the phenomenon, and even a few of gorillas standing on other gorillas—I believe there was one of the white gorilla, Snowflake, in Barcelona, standing on his black-gorilla companion's back—but nowhere in what is called the literature did we find any comment on, let alone explanation of, this strange habit.

The next morning, as Clarke and I drove to the zoo to visit Tiffany and Max, her mate, Clarke told me something about Tiffany's early upbringing at Topeka. In her enclosure, he said, she had had a playmate most of the day— John Wortman, who was then head keeper of primates. He wrestled with her, cuddled her, fed her, and generally kept her company. "A lot of infant gorillas used to die of marasmus," said Clarke. "The dictionary says marasmus is a 'general wasting away'—progressive emaciation, as in babies and children. In my opinion, it's due directly to a psychological condition. Keep a baby gorilla occupied and happy—with human company, if necessary—and it won't waste away."

At the Topeka Zoo, a very verdant place, I was introduced to John Wortman and other members of the staff. I asked my question: "Why do gorillas stand on people?" It evoked the same reaction it had always evoked— blank puzzlement, followed by a slowly shaken head. But Wortman came up with a theory, or, at least, a plausible term. "Playful dominance?" he suggested. Clarke and I agreed that this might be as good an answer as any.

We found Max and Tiffany chasing each other, with gorilla dignity, from one part of an outsize jungle gym to another. After admiring them through the glass—"See how different they are?" Clarke asked. "See how much more delicate her features are, even though she's bigger than Max?"—I attained an ultimate enjoyment that members of the public seldom experience: I was ushered into their enclosure, along with Clarke and Wortman. The little apes— each then weighed about fifty pounds—greeted us with great enthusiasm, pausing in their gambols to hug us, hang around our necks, or playfully wrestle. As suited her superior age, Tiffany was always the more forward of the two, but Clarke said that it was not only a question of age. Their temperaments were completely different. A small platform ringed one of the jungle gym's uprights, about a foot above my head, and as we talked I noticed Tiffany standing on it, eyeing me with a purpose clear to see. She was going to jump on me—fifty pounds of healthy gorilla. There was only time to realize it, not to move out of the way, but at the next-to-last second Clarke, too, saw what she had in mind. "Oh, no, you don't!" he said, and he reached up and pulled her down. He added to me, "And don't think for a minute she wouldn't have done it, either." A few moments later, he told me, "Look, I want to take your picture" and said, "John, give me a hand here, will you?" Following his orders, I bent over, hands on knees. Wortman put both apes on my back, and Gary Clarke took a photograph of two gorillas standing on me.

Ever the gracious guest, Emily wrote on May 16, 1972:

Dear Gary,

All unpacked and more or less caught up at last. This is to thank you and Margaret for your help and for making my trip so enjoyable. I have hung up one of the Max and Tiffany posters on the wall at home, and next week will bring the other one here to the office. I am also boring everybody to death, probably, with my conversation about gorillas. It was bad enough before, but now it is worse. Now to get to work on those notes . . .

If by any unforeseen chance any of the Clarkes come to England between June 15 and early in September, I'd be delighted to entertain them—separately or together. All the best to you from . . . and she signed it . . . Emily

So ended a most successful visit by the world famous writer Emily Hahn to the World Famous Topeka Zoo. It was a marvelous milestone for all—gorillas, writer, zoo staff, zoo visitors, and—last but not least—*The NEW YORKER* readers, many of whom were current or former Topekans. When the article was published ten years after her visit, the following is but one of the many fantastic letters we received.

Mount Prospect, Illinois
August 24, 1982

Gary Clarke, Director
World Famous Topeka Zoo
Gage Park
Topeka, Kansas 66604

Dear Gary:

We were very proud to read about you and the Zoo in <u>The New Yorker</u>. *We were proud that we are members of TFOTZ and have participated in many Zoo activities, including the first Zoo class for adults.*

During the seven years we lived in Topeka, we looked upon the Zoo as our own. We met there for lunch; we walked there in the summer when it was too hot to do anything else and in the winter when it was the only outdoor bit of Topeka with cleared walks. We knew most of the animals by name and we learned important lessons about observing animal behavior.

We were disappointed, though, that you didn't share Emily Hahn with Topekans. Her writing about animals and zoos in <u>The New Yorker</u> *has long fascinated us, and it would have been a delight to meet her.*

As we look back on our years in Topeka with fondness, the Zoo and our intimate relationship to it will occupy a special place in our thoughts. We send best wishes for Zoo/Tomorrow.

Yours sincerely,
Sherry Levy-Reiner, Ph.D
Fred N. Reiner, Rabbi

Thank you Sherry and Fred. Thank you Emily. Thank you Max and Tiffany. Zoos touch our lives in remarkable ways.

The Anxiety and the Jubilation . . .

Our First Giraffe Birth

Author's note: The following is the account I wrote at the time about our first giraffe birth; it was published in the September 1970 SPECIAL GIRAFFE ISSUE of our newsletter.

In May 1970 it was quite obvious that Jan, our female reticulated giraffe, was in the final stages of pregnancy. In June, members of the zoo staff started making friendly wagers on the date of birth. Some would not predict a specific time—only that it would be on a busy Sunday afternoon when the zoo was packed with visitors.

According to our calculations, she was scheduled to deliver in July or early August. The experience of other zoos had shown a gestation period ranging from 444 to 488 days, with a number of births occurring at 455 to 461 days. The shortest gestation we found was 416 days.

By mid-August our eager expectations had turned to weary anticipations. During July Jan was checked regularly throughout the night. A 24-hour "giraffe watch" was initiated in August.

Individual zoo staff members took turns staying all night in the Large Mammal Building complete with sleeping bag, transistor radio and flashlight. They did this willingly, not expecting to be paid.

When Jan passed the 460-day mark we felt it was a good sign, particularly since this would be her first offspring. A longer gestation period should insure a larger and stronger youngster at birth.

Twiga, our adult male giraffe, was the first giraffe in Kansas, arriving at our zoo May 18, 1966. He was born in the Oklahoma City Zoo on June 18, 1965. Jan was born in the Cheyenne Mountain Zoo on April 26, 1965 and arrived in Topeka on August 26, 1966.

On December 18, 1968 Twiga showed his first interest in breeding and Jan appeared to be in estrus for the first time. Both animals were a little more than 3½ years old. However, we felt proper management dictated that we wait for the right point in time to breed the animals, and that would be the spring of 1969. The first breeding could probably be achieved more easily in the outside yard as opposed to indoor quarters. By scheduling the breeding this way the young would be born in midsummer, hopefully during dry, warm weather. Also, we felt that if the animals were a little older they might produce a healthier first-born. We believed the added maturity on the part of the female would promote a more positive maternal behavior toward her first young.

Breeding activity was observed in April and May, with the last instance recorded on May 14, 1969. Jan did not come back into estrus after that, and we were quite certain she had conceived. Twiga was then 3 years, 11 months old and Jan was 4 years, 1 month old.

There are always a number of unknown factors in any wild animal birth. Since this was Jan's first young and the first baby giraffe to be born in our zoo, we had more than our share of unknowns. Many questions continued to run through our minds. Will the baby be full term? And born with no congenital defects? Will the female be able to deliver successfully, and unassisted? What will be her reaction to this first-born—will she become frightened and attempt to trample the baby, or ignore it, or reject it and not let it nurse? Will she accidentally step on it? All of these situations had occurred at other zoos.

In regard to the baby, would it be able to stand within a reasonable time after birth? It is most important for newborn ungulates to gain their feet soon after birth, and the mother often will tap the young with a front leg to encourage the baby to stand. It usually takes several attempts, and if it fails, this indicates some weakness or defect in the young.

With reference to first-born animals, Dr. Heini Hediger, in his highly regarded book, *Studies of the Psychology and Behavior of Animals in Zoos and Circuses,* (London: Butterworths Scientific Publications, 1955) states that: "...a considerable difference, as far as the mother-child relationship is concerned, may often be seen between the behavior of experienced mothers and those with their first-born young. This distinction is often indeed so sharp that the first birth might be considered as something like a dress-rehearsal, not counting for the propagation of the species, but a preparation for subsequent births. Efficient rearing of young often seems inadequately developed in primiparas (females pregnant for the first time); they are not mature enough and the young are not fully developed either. There is a lack of that intimate dovetailing of the behavior of mother and baby so that the weak baby soon dies, or is even stillborn." He goes on to state, "I have been able to confirm a similar state of affairs for many primiparas wild animals; immaturity on the part of the mother, and its typical fear of its offspring."

Since we were concerned with the baby dropping onto the concrete floor of the stall if it were born inside, we felt it would be best for Jan to deliver in the outside yard. We gradually let her become accustomed to going in and out while Twiga remained inside, then leaving her out all day, and finally staying out day and night. By early summer she was conditioned beautifully.

However, we were concerned about the frequent thunderstorms that Topeka experiences in hot weather. Throughout the summer many trips were made to the zoo at all hours of the night during unexpected severe weather situations to check on Jan's behavior and safety. High winds could cause branches to fall into the yard, or the excitement of a heavy thunderstorm at night could trigger the birth.

When Jan reached her 463rd day of gestation on August 19, 1970 her udder was well developed and appeared to be full of milk. For some time we had been able to see the baby moving internally. By now everyone directly or indirectly associated with the zoo was most anxious for the birth to occur. The zoo staff had lost a lot of sleep and even postponed vacations. When park department officials and Friends of the Zoo board members had to go out of town on business, they left phone numbers where they could be reached. All were afraid Jan would deliver while they were gone, and they didn't want to miss the big event after going through all of the anxieties of the long waiting period. With each passing day we just didn't see how Jan could go much longer, and the main question being asked of the zoo staff was, "*When* is that giraffe going to have her baby?"

On the evening of Monday, August 24, 1970 the entire zoo staff had assembled in the Large Mammal Building for a seminar on zoo exhibit philosophy. At 8:30 pm we all observed Jan, and although she looked extremely pregnant, she showed no signs of impending birth. Hence, we proceeded to the Education Room for the seminar. A little after 10:30 pm, the seminar was over, and one of the keepers took a flashlight back to the giraffe exhibit to make a routine check on Jan.

He immediately returned to announce, "She's having it!" The time was 10:43 pm. We had all been waiting so long for this moment that when it actually occurred, we found it hard to believe.

We rushed back to the giraffe exhibit and observed that Jan was indeed in labor. The calf's forelegs were protruding to the second joint and the nose was visible, with the surrounding amnion hanging several feet below. The calf's hooves were encased in eponychia (a shiny jelly-like skin) which protects the mother's birth canal.

General Curator Paul Linger scurried over to the service building for floodlights and extension cords, and keeper Bill Gage routinely stepped into the stall with Jan to gently coax her to the outside yard as planned. When she passed through the door, the amniotic sac broke at 10:50 pm.

Once outside, Jan became very excited and started running around the yard. Now that the moment of birth was near, all of the conditioning during the summer months meant nothing to Jan. I was afraid she might deliver in this state of excitement and either trample or reject the baby. So, even though our plans were to have the baby born in the outside yard, Jan's behavior indicated otherwise and I immediately (10:51 pm) instructed the keepers to let her back into the building.

We held her in the west stall while several keepers tossed hay down from the overhead loft and the rest of us spread it over the floor of the center stall for bedding.

At exactly 11:00 pm the remainder of the calf's head emerged to the neck. We finished spreading the hay and shifted Jan to the center stall adjacent to Twiga. Being next to the male seemed to have a calming effect on her, and several times she tried to eat some hay off the floor even though there was plenty in her elevated manger.

During the labor process the calf would periodically move its lips and tongue and blink its eyes.

The following notes of the birth were recorded by Ken Kawata, zoo management trainee.

11:35 pm — Jan attempts to lie down but does not. The calf's tongue moves.

11:36 pm — Jan bears down hard in an attempt to expel the infant. She also defecates.

11:39 pm — Jan is on the southwest side of the stall, facing north. The neck of the calf comes out. Jan takes a step forward.

11:40 pm — As Jan bears down hard the calf is delivered and drops on the hay. Jan turns around and faces southwest, then immediately begins to lick the calf. She starts to eat the fetal membrane. She lifts her right front leg and hits the floor with it, as if to touch the calf. Other than this behavior, Jan remains calm.

11:41 pm — Jan tries to tap the calf again.

11:42 pm — Jan eats membrane a little. The calf is breathing. It moves its head and neck.

11:43 pm — Calf lifts its head a little. Jan is still eating the membrane.

11:45 pm — Respiration of the calf is measured; it is 11 times in 15 seconds. Jan is still eating membrane. A leg of the calf is caught between the bars, and Paul Linger helps the calf remove it.

11:47 pm — Calf lifts its head three times with its eyes open.

11:48 pm — Calf sits, facing north. Jan, still in the same position, licks the calf's head.

11:51 pm — Calf tries again to stand. Jan remains calm.

12:00 Midnight — Calf tries for the seventh time to stand up and almost stands on its hind legs. Paul Linger helps calf, but it fell after one minute.

12:05-12:19 am — By the 12th trial calf stands up. Four minutes and 40 seconds later she tries to walk but is unable to do so. After eight minutes and 30 seconds, she starts walking, but soon stops. Jan continues to lick her.

12:45 am — Calf approached Twiga, the male, in the adjoining east stall. Twiga touched her muzzle with his lips through the fence. The heads of the three giraffes came together. Jan was continuously licking the calf.

12:52 am — Calf's unsteady gait was much improved.

1:41 am — Since the delivery, Jan has drunk about seven gallons of water.

Great joy reigned at the Topeka Zoo. Our first giraffe birth was a complete success—a full term, viable baby, very strong and already walking. Jan had borne her first young at five years and four months after a gestation period of 468 days (15½ months).

Since the baby was the first giraffe born in the Great State of Kansas (and a female at that), we appropriately named her "Sunflower." At birth she was 5 ft. 11 in. tall and weighed an estimated 130 lbs.

Keeper Ron Kaufman stayed the rest of the night and maintained a close observation on mother and baby giraffes. The following notes are from his detailed records:

2:14 am — Calf falls to floor and lies with head erect.

2:30 am — Jan is restless, nervous and hyper-alert. After three attempts the calf is back up on her feet.

2:46 am — Calf lies down.

3:15 am — Mother calm now.

6:32 am — Jan passes placenta (afterbirth).

7:00 am — Calf up. Jan is calm and eating.

Throughout the next day (Tuesday) Sunflower seemed to gain strength, although when she walked she resembled a mechanical wind-up toy. By Tuesday night we had not seen her nurse. This was our final major concern. We were prepared to bottle feed her the next day if necessary. It was shortly after 8:00 am on Wednesday when we first saw her nursing, much to our relief.

The response of the community to our first baby giraffe was overwhelming. All of the news media were most gracious with comprehensive coverage, and their reporting was interesting, accurate and educational. The event was carried by the wire services and featured nationally on the "Good News" program on ABC Radio Network.

The citizens of Topeka came to the zoo in droves and, coupled with people from the surrounding area, the zoo showed a record attendance. Crowds on weekdays resembled those on weekends. People who had not been to the zoo for years came just to see Sunflower. Many of the visitors would extend congratulations to the zoo staff, shake our hands, slap us on the back, and even ask if we were handing out cigars. (Actually, we were handing out carrots.) We received congratulatory cards and presents, some from out of town.

A successful giraffe birth is a significant accomplishment for any zoo. In our case, however, it was much more than that. Sunflower represented the success story of the Topeka Zoo over a period of six years. Such events don't just happen, but are the result of many people and organizations working together for a common goal.

Initial preparation for the birth of Sunflower dated back to 1964 with the development of the Zoo Master Plan. The first major phase was the Large Mammal Building, which was researched and planned in 1964-65, with special facilities designed for exhibiting and breeding giraffes. Construction took place in 1965-66, and the building was dedicated on May 22, 1966.

It was most important that we acquire the best specimens for this fine structure. We wanted a pair of pure reticulated giraffes, each born in an American zoo from unrelated parents, and approximately one year old. We carefully selected the animals from reputable zoos that maintained accurate records.

The next step was raising sufficient funds to buy the animals, which cost $5,000 each. Contributions and donations from the entire community resulted in enough money to buy Twiga. These ranged from a $1,000 gift from a leading business firm to a handful of pennies from a kindergarten student. Jan was earned by the citizens of Topeka through Operation Noah's Ark.

The park department built special crates and provided vehicles and personnel to allow us to bring the animals to our zoo. By the fall of 1966 we had established a fine young pair of giraffes.

During 1967 and 1968 the animals grew and developed well. They received daily care and attention from our dedicated keepers, regular examinations by the veterinarian, and the park department maintenance crew provided specialized equipment as needed.

When the animals reached sexual maturity in 1969 the zoo staff exercised careful management of the breeding and devoted attention to the many details necessary to ensure success. And finally in 1969-70, we all waited through the long pregnancy—468 days worth.

None of this could have been achieved without the full cooperation of the entire Topeka Park Department, who allowed us to operate the zoo on a high professional level. Additionally we had the devotion and sacrifice of our fine zoo staff, the untiring support of the Topeka Friends of the Zoo, and the wonderful response of the people of Topeka—the greatest zoo fans in the world. All of this reflected on Topeka as an outstanding community.

Those first few days after the birth of Sunflower I thought to myself: What a remarkable experience for these people, to be able to see this mother giraffe—a beautiful and unique species from a far-off land—very calm and secure, in perfect safety, caring for her newborn baby, just ten feet in front of them . . . and of all places . . . right here in Topeka, Kansas. It was just unbelievable!

As the weeks passed and I daily watched zoo visitors from all walks of life and every social and economic background admiring our beautiful giraffe family, I was instilled with a sense of pride and tremendous satisfaction. Sunflower was certainly one of the greatest attractions in the history of our zoo. In her first month she grew seven inches, to a height of 6 ft. 6 in., and at seven weeks measured 7 ft. 2 in. She was active, alert, and brimming with life and vitality—just a wonderful animal in every respect. And yes . . . we were going to keep her!

The Topeka Daily Capital

SATURDAY, AUGUST 29, 1970

Uncommon Sunflower

Gage Park Zoo has scored another first! Or perhaps it was Twiga and Jan, the first pair of giraffes in the state of Kansas.

Sunflower, their somewhat wobbly offspring, arrived late Monday night to become the first giraffe born in the state. Sunflower's arrival climaxed a three-week, 24-hour vigil and has stirred up a new interest in the goings on at the park's expanding zoological garden.

The baby giraffe, which is 5 feet 11 inches tall and weighs about 130 pounds, has stolen the limelight away from Tiffany, the baby girl gorilla who celebrated her second birthday anniversary last month. Tiffany created her own stir when funds weren't available for her purchase and Topekans contributed freely to obtain her.

Sunflower and Tiffany are only a few of the interesting exhibits at our zoo. Another exhibit obtained this month consists of four American great white pelicans. They were gifts of the Kiwanis Club of West Topeka, which paid $75 each for them after they were hatched in May on the Great Salt Lake breeding grounds in Utah. Named Joe E. Brown, Martha Ray, Paul Kiwanis and Spiro T. Agnew because of "their big mouths," they now are mixing with the geese and ducks on the waterfowl lagoon.

Zoo Director Gary Clarke has worked hard to make our zoo one of the best of its size anywhere. And he has had good support from Topekans, who started paying admissions in 1967 to help finance building of a large mammal building, where Sunflower's carefully planned birth occurred.

The zoo has been a popular recreation spot for a long time, and its attendance this year is expected to surpass the 188,722 visitors counted in 1969.

In May alone, a total of 34,834 persons were there and nearly 12,000 of them were youngsters in school groups. Of the May number, 8,500 were children under 12 years of age.

The exhibits afford most enjoyment for the children under 12 years of age, and they still are admitted free. Adults enjoy them perhaps almost as much, and they don't pay admission except during the summer months and on weekends during the off season.

All of us should make more frequent trips to the zoo. There is usually something new and interesting to see. And with its record of scoring firsts, Sunflower probably won't get to be the featured attraction very long!

D. James Orang, The Painting Primate

By January 1971 the Topeka Zoo had established a fine young group of great apes. With the arrival of Daisy, the female orangutan, we now had a pair each of gorilla, orangutan, chimpanzee and gibbon.

During the last half century in research projects and zoos around the world all ape species except the gibbon had demonstrated an ability to draw or paint. We felt it would be worthwhile to see if any of our animals could or would produce drawings or paintings.

A survey of the available literature revealed that of the three dozen or so great apes that had shown some artistic ability, only three orangutans were recorded in published reports, and I had received a verbal report of two others. Chimpanzees had been the most productive, gorillas next, and orangs last. And of the orangs, they reportedly had produced only a few paintings or drawings each. With this in mind, we were prompted to try our orangs first, rather than chimps or gorillas.

Daisy, our newest orang, was selected as the first subject. After consultation with several artists, it was suggested we use non-toxic acrylic paints. When we presented her with these paints, an art board and brush, she displayed no inclination whatsoever to paint. She would not even accept the brush when placed in her hand by Bill Gage, her keeper. Although discouraged, we were not surprised, since so few apes seem to be artistically inclined.

However, Djakarta Jim, our male orangutan and Daisy's mate, showed a keen interest in the entire proceedings. Jim took the brush and Bill showed him how to dip it in the water, then in the paint on the palette and guided his hand to the art board. Jim made a few strokes with the brush and became intrigued with the visual image being produced. He dabbed the brush in more paint and made long sweeping strokes (he even painted Bill a little).

History had been made! On January 18, 1971 Djakarta Jim produced his first painting entitled, "In the Beginning."

Many of the chimp artists had been finger painters, but Jim took readily to the brush, holding it in a "primitive grip," with his very long fingers completely encircling the handle and his thumb either up or down. The fact that an animal will use a brush, or a tool, was quite significant.

The next day Jim did two paintings, "Sunrise in Gage Park" and "Tornado." Now that he had learned what to do, he seemed to find great enjoyment in this activity. The following day (his third session) he produced two more paintings, "Train From Tokyo" and "Monday Morning."

The three sessions had lasted about 30 minutes each. After that Jim's attention span would wane and Bill Gage's patience would run out. Jim showed no particular color preference—he would eat any color!

Although the acrylic paint was non-toxic, Bill endeavored to wipe it off Jim's mouth before it could dry, and this became something of a game. Jim would dip his brush in the paint, show every indication he was going to continue his work, and just before the brush touched the art board he would slyly put it to his lips for a taste of paint. Bill and I both tasted the paint (it was terrible) and felt that Jim *had* to be attracted by the colors.

In his first three sessions Jim showed that he was ambidextrous. He painted with both his right and left hand as well as his right and left foot; sometimes with his right hand and right foot at the same time. Later we introduced Jim to a table and chair, and he sat at the table and painted with his hands only.

The monthly Board of Directors meeting of the Topeka Friends of the Zoo was held on January 20, 1971. I had prepared a brief presentation on the subject of ape art, and after explaining the project, I showed Jim's five paintings to the Board. Although our basic aim was to conduct the entire project in a scientific manner, we thought an additional bonus would be to offer some of his works for sale to help raise funds to pay for Daisy. The Friends of the Zoo still owed the Dallas Zoo about half of the $5,000 purchase price for Daisy. It was agreed that an art show at our zoo would be an appropriate way for TFOTZ to raise the money.

In the meantime, I took Jim's five paintings to Ed Carmona, the park department draftsman, to have them matted. While Ed was working on these, several officials from the Topeka Recreation Commission stopped by his office, and upon seeing the paintings exclaimed: "Hey, these are great! Can we enter them in the art contest at the Kansas Recreation and Park Association Conference in Hutchinson?"

We were reluctant to enter Jim's paintings in a state-wide art show because if we identified him as an orang we might be in trouble; if we did *not* identify him as an orang we might be in trouble. The TRC delegates persuaded me to loan them two paintings and entered them under the name D. James Orang, but did not specifically say he was an ape. Lo and behold, a week later we were notified that "Train From Tokyo" won first prize in the four to eight-year-old category!

It was never our intention to cause a furor in art circles, and in fact, one of the judges wrote a very understanding letter and said if she had known Jim was an orang before the show it would have made no difference in her judging as his was the best in his category.

Studies of apes around the world indicate that this form of artistic behavior is found only in young animals. Apes seem to lose the impulse to draw or paint as they reach maturity. For this reason, each of Jim's paintings was chronologically numbered, dated, titled and recorded in a Catalog. In addition, color photographs were taken to document each painting. A selected number of his paintings are in the permanent collection of the zoo. Daisy later began to show an interest in painting, two of which were in a style very different from Jim's.

In addition to Jim and Daisy's work, we planned to carry through our research with the other apes. We felt the gorillas and chimps should have a chance to try their hands (and feet) at painting—as a basis of comparison. We had inquiries from animal behaviorists, child psychologists and anthropologists, and made our material on ape art available to qualified individuals for research and study. In fact, Djakarta Jim even made the front cover of *Science Digest*.

Artists fear not: apes have been eating bananas for centuries but have yet to paint a still life of one.

The World Responds

As soon as the local media broke the story of Djakarta Jim's painting in February 1971, the wire services immediately picked it up and came to the zoo for pictures and information. Within 24 hours of the release of the story over the AP and UPI wires, pandemonium reigned at the zoo. A chain reaction was initiated that became more incredible each day. A file was established on the response from around the world including press clippings, letters and even radio tapes—the file soon filled one large briefcase. Following are several of the more interesting and unusual responses.

The immediate response was a call from CBS-TV in New York City to their local affiliate, WIBW-TV in Topeka, asking them to dispatch films to New York for network use. The second call was from an airline pilot friend of mine, Charles VanTrease, who was staying in a hotel in Pittsburgh, PA, and who had just seen Jim on television.

An NBC-TV morning panel show called "Jeopardy" referred to Jim by asking contestants, "For what art form did the state of Kansas recently award first prize to an orangutan?" One contestant immediately pressed the buzzer with the correct answer—painting.

A staffer from CBS-TV in Chicago called for a taped interview to accompany their film.

The educational television station in Wichita, KPTS-TV, sent a cameraman to film one of Jim's painting sessions. The film was shown March 21, 1971 on a program entitled "You're On." Primate keeper Bill Gage and I drove to Wichita and were interviewed live by Murray Coates during the show.

The night the news broke I received a call at 11:00 p.m. from radio station WGAN in Portland, Maine and was interviewed over the telephone on the Cole Wilkins Show. At 2:00 am I received a call from the Larry Glick Show on WBZ radio in Boston. Arthur Godfrey chatted about Jim on his morning radio show on February 28.

Jim's story made newspapers all over the world: *The Bangkok World*, *Pacific Stars and Stripes*, *International Herald Tribune*, *Honolulu Advertiser* and the *Miyazaki Nichinichi* (a Japanese daily published in Keeper Ken Kawata's hometown). The English edition of *The Japan Times* dated February 20, 1971 carried the following datelines on Page 5: Osaka, West Berlin, Bombay, Moscow, Jerusalem, Lisbon *and* Topeka, Kansas. The headline read: "He's Top Banana in Kan. Art World."

The *National Observer* of April 5 ran a photograph of Jim's prizewinning painting, "Train from Tokyo," to accompany a long story about Jim. Two newspapers that are read by school children, *The Weekly Reader* and *Junior Scholastic*, carried the story. As a result, letters from children all over the country were written to Jim with requests for his picture.

In addition to our TFOTZ "One Ape Art Show," Jim's paintings were requested for a month long exhibit at the Museum of Natural History in Pacific Grove, California. Another of his paintings was exhibited from April 28 to May 16 at the Animal Art Fair in Oklahoma City, sponsored by their zoo and the Oklahoma Zoological Society.

Requests to buy Jim's paintings came from such diverse places as Paris, France and Huron, South Dakota. (A lady in Huron offered $100 for one of his paintings.)

One of the most gratifying letters for our zoo staff was from Colonel Leslie Armen who was stationed in Oslo, Norway and read about Jim in an Oslo paper. Jim had been a pet of the Armen family when Colonel Armen was stationed in Indonesia. Colonel Armen wrote: "About a month ago I read an article in the Oslo newspaper *Verdens Gang* concerning Jimmy which was to the effect that he is painting, showing, winning and selling. Of course, I am quite proud of his achievements but not at all surprised. One has only to see him in action to recognize how talented he really is." The Armen family was delighted to find that Jim was world famous and Colonel Armen expressed the hope that they might be able to visit Jim again some day.

Another interesting letter was from Alleice Toldan, who was at Ohio State University, but formerly was with the Dallas Zoo where she had cared for Daisy for six months in the Dallas Children's Zoo. She was very happy to know that Daisy was at our zoo and had a mate.

A postcard from Milan, Italy appeared to be a request either to buy a painting or a photo of Jim.

A writer for National Features in Chicago, a free lance writer in Wichita, a writer for *Science Digest*, an author-artist team who wrote children's books—these were but a few examples of those requesting additional material about Jim and Daisy. How I envied the big zoos with a full-time public relations department to respond to such inquiries. And just when we thought it was safe to go back to routine zoobiz, interest somehow revived. Djakarta Jim's popularity gained strength and he continued as the zoo's leading newsmaker. *Science Digest* featured him in an article and he was pictured on the front cover in color.

A telephone call from the producers of "What's My Line?" developed into a trip to New York to tape a segment of the TV show. Not only that—the panel was stumped! Panel members Helen O'Connell, Arlene Francis, Gene Rayburn and Soupy Sales were told that I was Director of the Topeka Zoo and that an orangutan named Djakarta Jim had won a prize. The question posed to the panel was, "What was the prize, and why did he win it?" Before time ran out, the panel had guessed activities such as acrobatics, baton twirling and playing a musical instrument. After "What's My Line?" Moderator Wally Bruner informed a surprised panel of the correct answers, I showed five of Jim's paintings which I had hand carried (with some difficulty) on the airplane to New York.

While in New York City I delivered two paintings to the President of Steuben Glass, Arthur A. Houghton, Jr. Mr. Houghton was a collector of simian art and wrote to me asking to purchase two of Jim's paintings after reading about Jim in the *National Observer*.

The following week I was in Washington, D.C. to meet with some conservation officials. While there I presented one of Jim's paintings to the White House. President Nixon was out of town, so the painting was accepted by John Nidecker, deputy special assistant to the President, in a ceremony held at the White House and arranged by Senator James Pearson. The title of the painting—"Fourth of July"—of course!

Djakarta Jim certainly was doing his part to make the Topeka Zoo world famous!

APE ART: An Assessment

After the advent of Djakarta Jim, the zoo's male orangutan, as a painter of pictures, a variety of reactions from various segments of the public took place. In general it was a positive response, although the entire subject was somewhat misunderstood. Many people referred to Jim's works as "monkey paintings" (orangutans are apes, not monkeys) and felt that the project was only a clever idea to raise funds to pay for Jim's mate. Some members of the art community were offended, feeling that "ape art" made a mockery of human art. Yet some people realized that ape art had valid scientific and artistic functions.

Zoologists, animal behaviorists, child psychologists, and even some artists, are serious students of ape art. I realize that ape art as a subject, and Djakarta Jim as a painting primate, will always have critics. However, I would like to present a little background on the subject so everyone may have a better understanding of ape art.

Paintings produced *by* apes, rather than portraits of them, represent a unique and biological approach to art. Humans have long recognized art in nature—the design in a peacock's feather or a butterfly's wing, the stripes on a zebra or tiger, the intricate skin pattern of a giraffe or gaboon viper. But it is only since the beginning of the twentieth century that people become intrigued with art in nature in the form of paintings and drawings by monkeys and apes.

Of all the members of the animal kingdom, the primates are the only group that have demonstrated the intelligence and ability to make patterns or designs with available materials. (Elephants have done so with *provided* materials and verbal instructions.) Simply observe the animals in our zoo—how many of them have made marks in the sand or soil, produced intentional patterns in the snow, or utilized their food or feces to draw on the walls or floor of their exhibit? None—except the great apes! Anyone who has seen our gorillas and orangutans in their glass-fronted exhibits can attest to their excellent finger painting ability—especially just after the keepers clean the glass!

As interesting as this spontaneous behavior is, it is even more interesting that apes will produce a true finger painting when supplied with paper and paints. But of greater significance is the fact that these animals will use a human "tool" or instrument, such as a brush or a pencil.

Some investigators surmise that the ape artist eliminates the recognizable subject matter from his/her work and instead concentrates upon the relationship of form, color, lines, movement and texture for aesthetic impact and emotional suggestion. Does this imply that it is an intentional act? If so, it is a rather sophisticated psychological construct and raises some very interesting questions.

The earliest known example of infrahuman picture making occurred in Moscow in 1913, in an important study by Madjejeta Kohts and Joni, her young chimpanzee. Joni's early scribbles compared with her later drawings showed a greater visual control involving a deliberate intersection tendency. Since that time over three dozen chimpanzees, gorillas or orangutans, and at least four capuchin monkeys, produced well over a thousand paintings and drawings without assistance or guidance. More importantly, these animals did not receive any rewards of food or favor that are frequently used in animal training. They found the impulse to paint or draw self-rewarding and often more powerful than other impulses until they reached sexual maturity. Such painting is not an accidental occurrence, such as dipping a donkey's tail in paint and holding a canvas behind him while he swishes his tail. (Human artists have been known to dump paint onto a canvas and drive a vehicle back and forth over it to produce a finished work.) Rather, it is a deliberate action on the part of the animal.

Ape art may seem improper to some members of the art community, but it does have artistic and scientific validity. After all, if a machine can produce paintings (some computer paintings are quite interesting) then it really is not so strange that a living creature, with a high degree of animal intelligence and closely resembling humans in physical structure, can produce a unique art form in its own right.

Drawings and paintings by primates are not the only art form found in the animal kingdom. The variety of natural sounds ranges from the musical notes of songbirds to the underwater singing of whales. A professor of biology and an acoustics engineer recorded the cries and rumblings of these huge creatures communicating underwater. Although originally recorded for scientific study, the sounds were composed into a symphonic album entitled "Songs of the Humpback Whale." These whale sounds may be technically considered "songs" as they do obey meter and maintain pitch. They also repeat themselves in patterns similar to the patterns in the playing of human musical instruments.

Paintings and drawings by apes are considered by some as a vital art form. Anthropoid artists provide a source of really simple aesthetic material which is invaluable to art theory. At minimal levels the primate painters show aesthetic variation, composition control and calligraphic development. They vividly demonstrate the basic fundamentals of aesthetic creativity. Their pictures seem to have an intriguing relationship with the scribbles of very young children and provide an important source of material for the analysis of human art.

An excellent study of the picture-making behavior of the great apes and its relationship to human art may be found in *The Biology of Art* by Desmond Morris (New York: Alfred A. Knopf, 1962). Morris formerly was Curator of Mammals at the London Zoo, then became Director of the Insti-

tute of Contemporary Arts in London. In his book he recognized six biological principles of picture-making which universally apply to all artists
from Leonardo to—well, to D. James Orang. These are:

1. The Principle of Self-rewarding Activation.
2. The Principle of Compositional Control.
3. The Principle of Calligraphic Differentiation.
4. The Principle of Thematic Variation.
5. The Principle of Optimum Heterogeneity.
6. The Principle of Universal Imagery.

Ape art may represent a new rugged dimension in fantasized art. For
some artists, abstract form discloses inner emotions as the picture con-
jures the phantasm of the hidden psychological world of imagination.

Even without all of these intellectual interpretations, ape art is just
fun.

Eagles Hatch Golden Eggs

The flight aviaries for our American golden eagles reflected the fact that we were a "park department zoo." They consisted of two large pipe frame and chain link baseball backstops welded together to form an enclosure measuring 50 feet in length and 25 feed in width, with a height of 25 feet at mid-point. While not very attractive, they were extremely functional and the eagles thrived (and we had ZuPreem Bird of Prey diet).

So much so, in fact, that Topeka became the first zoo in the world to successfully hatch and raise the American golden eagle!

Frank Kish was our associate curator at the time, and I'd like to quote from an article he wrote for the May-June 1971 issue of *ZOO Magazine.*

"In 1969, two of the three eagles at the Topeka Zoo formed a pair and began nesting in their enclosure. At that time we built a structure to support a nest which we hoped they would build. Loads of branches were placed in this structure (and on the ground) and the two paired eagles then began adding material to the nest. The other eagle was removed from the enclosure.

"On March 23, 1969 we observed one egg in the nest. Two more eggs were laid at later dates. After having allowed sufficient time for the eggs to hatch, we opened the eggs and found them to be infertile.

"In 1970 the same events took place, except that we removed the three eggs from the nest for artificial incubation. The female parent laid two more eggs in a few days, and these were left for her to incubate. None of these five eggs hatched.

"We had about given up hope in 1971 but our eagles had not. Although the eagles' area had been isolated from all visitors in previous years, in 1971 we did not consider the isolation necessary.

"Then on May 2, 1971 (a sunny Sunday morning), Keeper Mark Pheasant, responding to what sounded like the cheeping of a young bird, climbed the side of the exhibit and noted a newly hatched eaglet with two eggs remaining in the nest.

"After learning of the news excitement ran high at the zoo. Photos were taken of the nest's contents, and the female fiercely defended her nest. At this time the area surrounding the eagles' enclosure was fenced off from all visitors in order to prevent any defensive reactions on the part of the female parent which could have resulted in accidental injury to the young and the two eggs. The second young hatched three days later. The third egg remained in the nest without hatching.

"The male parent shared incubation with the female while she took time out for eating and maintaining her plumage. After the young had hatched it was the male exclusively who brought food to the nest for some time. Nest building, nest repairs, probing the nest bowl in which the young lived, sanitizing the nest, bringing food to the nest, feeding the young, brooding, shading the young from the sun, sheltering them from rain and defending the nest against intruders were the more prominent activities that occupied the parents while rearing their young. By May 30, 1971 the two young had grown to the size of a large domestic hen. They resembled a ball of cotton candy when viewed from a distance.

"We consider the successful breeding of golden eagles one of the most significant events ever to have happened at our zoo. It served as an example, provided guidelines, and aroused interest for the breeding of these and other birds of prey in captivity. At a time when wildlife populations are seriously endangered, having a captive breeding population may help save a species from complete extinction."

*****

The Bean Award. One of the most coveted awards in the zoo and aquarium field is the Edward H. Bean Award, named in honor of the first Director of the Brookfield Zoo in Chicago and one of the deans of the American zoo profession. The awards are given for the most notable birth or hatching in each of four categories: mammal, bird, reptile/amphibian and fish.

The awards are presented each fall at the Annual Conference of the American Association of Zoological Parks and Aquariums (AAZPA). We are very proud of the fact that our zoo received the Bean Award in the bird category for the hatching of an American golden eagle in 1971.

In conjunction with this award a companion award is given to the keeper or keepers most responsible for working with the animals.

Keepers Ken Kawata and Mark Pheasant of our zoo each received this award from the American Association of Zoo Keepers.

World Book. Our golden eagles made the *World Book!* In their 1972 Year Book, which is the annual supplement to the *World Book Encyclopedia*, the hatching of the golden eagle at the Topeka Zoo in May 1971 was reported under the listing "Zoos and Aquariums: Notable Births."

*****

An update: American golden eagle propagation at the Topeka Zoo has continued through the years (even into the second generation), with a total of 59 chicks hatched by 2008. Many hatchlings were sent to other zoos for further breeding, and three eagles were provided for a release program in the wilds of North Carolina. But here is the best part.

In 1985, with the endorsement of the U.S. Department of Interior, Fish and Wildlife Service, the zoo and the Prairie Raptor Project began a program to reestablish golden eagles in our home state. The project is a joint venture with the Kansas Wildlife and Parks Department, Westar Energy, and Turner Enterprises (which manages the Z-Bar Ranch, location of the release site). All captive hatched eaglets are banded and radio tagged for continual monitoring by interns.

As of this writing (2008) a total of 31 birds have been released. More than a landmark conservation effort, it is a source of pride to know that the golden wings over Kansas were hatched at our zoo in Topeka!

The Topeka Daily Capital

THURSDAY, MAY 13, 1971

Another 'First' for Zoo

Topekans have another reason to be proud of the Gage Park Zoo, now that two American golden eagles have been hatched there. They are the first captive hatching of this kind of bird and the first in the Western Hemisphere of any form of golden eagle.

It is a breakthrough for the future conservation of this rapidly disappearing species and, as such, has gained world-wide attention of ornithologists.

Those going to the zoo will be unable to see the young birds close up for some time, for it is important not to disturb them until the eaglets obtain some growth.

But there will come a day when they will be on public display and crowds can enjoy them.

It's the second time in recent months that Gage Park Zoo has gained international fame.

Early this year Djakarta Jim, the 5-year-old orangutan, became famous as a artist, after having won a statewide art contest for youngsters.

So good are his paintings, as a matter of fact, that more than $1,000 of them have been sold.

Topeka's Gage Park Zoo is one of the finest small zoos in the nation. Animals, birds and other wildlife are attractively displayed for the enjoyment of the public. Number of species is greater than that in the sprawling Swope Park Zoo in Kansas City.

People crowd around to see Peka Sue, the hippo; to watch the elephants perform, and to admire Sunflower, the baby giraffe which also was born at the zoo here.

From antelope to zebra, Gage Park Zoo has a wide variety of interesting specimens.

The growing popularity of the zoo is attested by the fact that it attracts visitors from over the state and nation. And many more will want to see the eaglets once they are on display.

Zoo Directors Stand Alone

It was just like one of those scenes from the old movies—you know, a bunch of folks in the back room talking in low voices and obviously up to something clandestine. The only difference was, these folks were fighting for their professional lives, and it was no secret.

The Scene: the annual conference of the American Association of Zoological Parks and Aquariums (AAZPA)

The place: Salt Lake City, Utah

The date: September 20, 1971

On this historic occasion the membership of the AAZPA voted overwhelmingly to follow an independent course of action. Since 1966 AAZPA had been a branch of the National Recreation and Park Association. AAZPA was originally established in 1924 in association with the American Institute of Park Executives, the forerunner of NRPA. So, for our first 47 years, we were "chicks hatched in the wrong nest," as many of my colleagues used to say.

During the week of that conference in 1971 the talk centered around nothing but whether we should split from NRPA. Although I was still a young whippersnapper in zoobiz, I was fortunate enough to have served on the AAZPA Board and at that moment was president-elect. I was all in favor of our going independent, but hated to think about how we would operate without all the support services we seemed so dependent upon through NRPA. Not only that, but our aquarium colleagues had been making noises about whether or not the last "A" of AAZPA was getting its just due. They were thinking of splitting from the AAZPA in favor of the American Society of Ichthyologists and Herpetologists. I personally felt that the aquarists were a vital element of AAZPA and we needed them. The rest of the Board felt the same way and appointed me to convince the aquarists to stay with us. They did, and our vote to separate from the NRPA truly unified the zoo and aquarium professions.

After we split from the NRPA we legally did not exist—and I was now President! We had no constitution or by-laws, no headquarters, no paid staff, no committee structure, no publication, no treasury, and no membership! We were told by the NRPA that they were unable to extract our membership list from their computer. But there was no need for fear. The camaraderie and spirit of my colleagues was strong, and they responded with enthusiasm before I could catch my breath. Each of us on the Board contributed $25 out of our own pockets to establish our initial treasury of $250. Those original investors in the AAZPA were: Les Fisher, Director, Lincoln Park Zoo, Chicago; Bill Braker, Director, Shedd Aquarium, Chicago; Gunter Voss, Director, Toronto Zoo; Louis DiSabato, Director, San Antonio Zoo; Dan Moreno; Director, Cleveland Metroparks Aquarium;

John Werler, Director, Houston Zoo; Lamar Farnsworth, Director, Hogle Zoo, Salt Lake City; Ron Blakely, Director, Sedgwick County Zoo, Wichita; and Robert O. Wagner, Director, Jackson Zoo. At the final banquet a steady parade of members came to me to volunteer.

Bob Wagner said he would create a new membership list from scratch and serve as treasurer. Karen Sausman (Director, Living Desert Museum) said she would edit and distribute a newsletter. Don Davis (Director, Cheyenne Mountain Zoo) said he could have his zoo issue a billing for membership dues. The Accreditation Commission was established and Bill Conway (Director, New York Zoological Society) served as the first chairman.

So here I was, President of our national professional organization, returning home to Kansas to try to bring some semblance of order to this sudden mishmash of events we had brought on ourselves. And I didn't even have a secretary.

Back in Topeka I had already worked out a system with one of the secretaries at the Park Office in City Hall whereby I could dictate correspondence over the telephone, she would type it up, then I would go to City Hall and sign it and put it through the postage meter. Hill's Pet Products (bless them again) responded to my request for a special donation to print AAZPA letterhead.

Even with the help and support of the entire North American zoo and aquarium profession, I knew I couldn't survive a year trying to run the AAZPA—out of Topeka! Three months later we were successful in our quest to hire Margaret A. (Peg) Dankworth as our first Executive Director. She was familiar with, and had worked with AAZPA, as a staff member of NRPA (she was always on our side). The Wheeling, West Virginia Park Commission was good enough to contribute office space for her at Oglebay Park. Peg not only got us off and running but was instrumental in establishing the AAZPA Management School. Fittingly, there is now an annual scholarship awarded in her honor each year.

Peg told me at the outset that she would help us get started but only work for three years. She kept her word, and fortunately we were able to convince Robert O. Wagner, then director of the Jackson, Mississippi Zoo to become our Executive Director. Bob had a promising career as a zoo director and I've always appreciated the fact that he gave this up to serve our profession on a national level. A Management School scholarship has been established in his honor as well.

Eventually the AAZPA became AZA, the Association of Zoos and Aquariums. From its humble beginning AZA has developed into the largest and strongest zoo and aquarium organization in the world. I would say the $25 investment made by each of the ten people in 1971 has paid many dividends.

American Association of Zoological Parks and Aquariums

EXECUTIVE OFFICES AT OGLEBAY PARK,   WHEELING, W. VA. 26003   AREA CODE 304 - 242-2160

RESOLUTION OF APPRECIATION TO GARY K. CLARKE

WHEREAS: The American Association of Zoological Parks and Aquariums, by vote of its membership in Salt Lake City, Utah, in September 1971, separated from the National Recreation and Park Association and became an independent Association for the first time in its 48-year history; and

WHEREAS: The Association began its reorganization without assistance nor funding and relied totally on the cooperation of the members and the leadership of the Board of Directors and especially the President; and

WHEREAS: Gary K. Clarke, the newly elected President, gave unstintingly of his time and abilities to give dynamic leadership during this critical transition period.

NOW THEREFORE BE IT RESOLVED: That the Board of Directors of the American Association of Zoological Parks and Aquariums, meeting in Tucson, Arizona, April 15, 1972, and acting in behalf of all members, hereby extends deep appreciation for the tremendous service of its President, GARY K. CLARKE, and commends him for his tireless and unselfish leadership; and

BE IT FURTHER RESOLVED: That the success of the Association and its reorganization is attributed to his leadership and will long be remembered and recorded in the history of AAZPA.

attested by:

Margaret A. Dankworth
Executive Secretary

A non-profit, tax-exempt organization dedicated to the advancement of zoological parks and aquariums for conservation, education, research, and recreation.

The State Journal

page of opinion

Thursday Evening, January 13, 1972

My great concern is not whether God is on our side; my great concern is to be on God's side.—Abraham Lincoln.

The zoo's a paying investment

Few municipal operations can make such a claim—but the zoo is doing quite well for itself financially, Topekans are pleased to know.

Increased attendance for 1971 brought in revenues more than 50 per cent above the year before.

That means not only continued improvements in an already top-notch zoo, but additional nestegg for an eagerly awaited tropical rain forest which will give a whole new dimension to the natural exhibits in the years ahead.

RIGHT NOW, as 200,000 visitors in the last 12 months would indicate, there's plenty to see. Director Gary Clarke, a real professional in his line, and a competent staff of assistants have worked tirelessly to add variety to the zoo population and on innovations to show the exhibits to best advantage.

Only recently, a horse became the rarest animal in the Topeka Zoo—a somewhat startling statement until it is explained. Clarke was able to obtain on loan from the Chicago zoo a purebred Przewalski, whose breed is recognized as the only surviving authentic wild horses in the world. Only 182 remain.

Between its birds and the burrowing animals, the Topeka Zoo has an abundance of rare species and noted individuals. Among those are Max and Tiffany, the first gorillas in Kansas. Sunflower, first giraffe born in the state, is another.

And don't forget Djakarta Jim, world-renowned as a painting orangutan after he won an art contest for youngsters and one of his works was presented to the White House.

While commercial enterprises are relegated to the yellow pages, the current Southwestern Bell telephone directory features zoo animals in full color on its front cover, and calls attention to the rare birth in captivity of Bengal tiger quintuplets here last year.

Rare eagles have been hatched successfully; other births have supplemented the acquisition of new attractions with such regularity that not to visit the zoo at least a couple of times a year any more is to miss part of the show.

IN ADDITION TO TOURS for groups, conducted by volunteer guides, the zoo continues to upgrade its educational and informative programs, lately adding "graphics" to better explain special features.

Paid admissions for 1971 were more than $47,000, giving the zoo ample funds to meet its payment on the Large Mammal Building and to earmark some for contemplated improvements.

Besides support from the Topeka area, the zoo is patronized by hundreds from outlying areas, and tourists—who are not only enjoying their visits here but helping build a noteworthy local attraction.

A Horse of a Different Color

Note: In late 1971 our zoo had the opportunity to acquire a significant endangered species—the Przewalski wild horse. Our first stallion, Rolf, eventually became the oldest living Przewalski horse in the world, and his arrival ushered in a significant propagation program both at our zoo and its satellite conservation centers. The following were my thoughts at the time. G.K.C.

There are some 650 original Rembrandt paintings in existence, but only 182 Przewalski horses—one of the rarest animals in the world! Also know as the Mongolian wild horse, this splendid creature formerly was believed to have followed many other species into the absolute, irreversible emptiness of extinction.

Every day is an exciting day at the zoo, but it is doubly exciting when another zoo calls long distance and asks the question, "Would your zoo be interested in accepting a Przewalski horse?" As tempting as it is to say "yes" immediately, a number of factors have to be considered before a decision can be reached.

The ultimate contribution a zoo can make to a rare and endangered species is to propagate that species to ensure its survival. This is particularly true of animals that are threatened or extinct in their natural environment. We were being offered a single animal and there was no guarantee we would be able to obtain a mate in the near future. However, conservation education is another important responsibility of zoos. Although people can read about animals and see them on film, nothing replaces the living animal to make a lasting impression. The immediacy and reality of an endangered species on exhibit in the zoo contributes to an awareness and knowledge of that animal.

Since very few people in this area have the opportunity to see the Przewalski horse (the nearest ones are in Chicago), it was decided to accept the offer. The Chicago Zoological Park at Brookfield, Illinois, had two males but could only use one as their herd stallion. As a result, our zoo was privileged to receive on loan the Przewalski stallion Rolf. The Przewalski horse is the only authentic wild horse surviving in the world today. The so-called "wild" mustangs of the western United States are not true wild horses, but feral animals—a domesticated species living back in the wild.

The Przewalski horse is a stocky animal, light bay or yellow dun in color, with a narrow dark stripe down the back, and occasionally faint stripes on the legs. Lower legs, mane, and tail are black, and the muzzle and abdomen are usually pale or even whitish. The head is heavy and massive, with Roman nose and powerful jaws, while the ears are small and neat. In winter the coat becomes long, thick and heavy, with cheek tufts prominent, while in summer the hair is short and sleek. Average height is four to five feet with a weight up to 600 pounds. Other noteworthy characteristics of the Przewalski include the short, stiff mane that is totally erect; the absence of a forelock; the short hairs on the upper third dorsal surface of the tail; and uniformity in color and markings.

The Przewalski horse dates back nearly one million years. This original horse was the last stage of the wild horse species before man began to establish domestic varieties by planned breeding. From *Equus przewalskii* a straight line leads back along the road to *Eohippus,* primeval horse of the Eocene Period. Some authorities feel that the Przewalski is one of the ancestors of many present day breeds of the domestic horse.

Previously evidenced by the European fossil record, this horse was re-discovered in 1879 by the great Polish-Russian explorer Nikolai Mikhailovich Prjevalsky. It was named in his honor by the Zoologist S.J. Poljakov of the Imperial Academy of Science in St. Petersburgh, who first described the animal for science in 1881. The horses depicted by Stone Age man in the Glacial Period were probably the Przewalski. One horse drawing from the cave of Lascaux, France, discovered in 1940, is approximately six feet high with a stiff, black mane.

The first living Przewalski horses were collected in 1899. The present world captive population originated primarily from two breeding herds at the Zoological Gardens in Prague, Czechoslovakia and Munich, Germany. The Catskill Game Farm in New York state obtained one half of the Munich herd (7 animals) in 1956 and has become the primary breeding center in the Americas, with a second major breeding group fast developing at the San Diego Zoo.

All known Przewalski horses are recorded in the International Studbook of The Przewalski Horse, which is the world pedigree registry for the species. This is maintained at the Prague Zoological Garden and is the result of dedicated conservation efforts of zoos throughout the world. It is edited by Dr. Jiri Volf and contains a complete registry of all living specimens in captivity as of January of each year.

That the Przewalski horse is alive today, and a living specimen may be seen in Topeka, clearly demonstrates an important function of modern zoos: saving animal species threatened with extinction through captive propogation and conservation education.

In 1956 there were only 36 Przewalski horses in zoos. By 1971 there were 182 specimens known to exist, with 35 in the United States at six zoos, including Topeka. (By 2008 the horses totaled 1600.)

Rolf is truly a magnificent animal, and it is a joy to watch him display his various forms of equine behavior. He is responsive to his keepers and has adjusted well to his daily routine in our zoo. It is a stirring sight to see this prehistoric animal cavorting in the fresh snow, as Przewalski horses have done for eons in the desolate regions of Mongolia.

The Topeka Daily Capital

WEDNESDAY, JUNE 30, 1971

Zoo Babies Draw Crowds

It's little wonder the turnstiles are clicking merrily at Gage Park Zoo.

There are a lot of attractions to be seen there, the latest being five tiger kittens, making 14 altogether which have been born at the zoo here in recent years.

Then there's the survivor of two baby golden eagles hatched at the zoo and for which a special day of recognition was held recently. It is rare indeed when golden eagles are born in captivity, giving it special interest.

Among other baby animals is Ralph, a five-months-old Alaskan brown bear born at the zoo, and Sunflower, the giraffe, almost a year old.

Also being seen for the first time this season are a pair of 250-pound termite-eating sloth bears.

Still drawing crowds is Djarkarta Jim, the five-year-old orangutan who has gained international fame as an artist after having won a statewide art contest for youngsters.

The standbys of the zoo retain their interest: Peka Sue, the hippo; the elephants, lions, monkeys, antelopes, zebra, reptiles and so on and on. As a matter of fact there are more different species of animal and birds at Gage Park Zoo than there are in Swope Park in Kansas City.

If you haven't visited the Gage Park Zoo lately, do so. It is interesting and instructive.

There are many Topekans who have the zoo habit, going there frequently. For them it is a show which never is boring because of the attractive way in which the exhibits are maintained.

Topeka's Terrific Tigers

Our first tigers, Dacca and Tabor, thrived after their arrival as youngsters in 1964. It was wonderful watching them grow and develop, and take their place as star attractions along with the lions, jaguars and pumas.

We fed all of our big cats the ZuPreem diets, and had them on managed breeding programs. Adult breeding animals were placed together after the first of each year so that litters would be delivered in the spring, the babies would be on exhibit during summer, and old enough to be transported to a new home in another zoo in the fall. Although a female big cat could produce up to three litters a year, we thought one litter a year was adequate. This allowed the mother animal to gestate for three months, lactate for three months, and rest for six months. It was a very workable management plan. Breeding dates would be observed and recorded, gestation periods calculated, and delivery dates anticipated with regularity. Generally, the regular keepers would simply observe through the back den door to see how the mother was doing and how many youngsters she had. Very seldom would any of the big cats need assistance in delivering their young. Dacca had her first pregnancy in 1967, and usually had two or three cubs per litter.

In 1970 a unique situation developed. The day of delivery arrived (May 13) and the keeper came up to my office a little after 8:00 am to report that Dacca had started her delivery. Later he reported that she had had her second cub, and by noon a third cub. At this point everything was routine.

A little while later the keeper reported that Dacca now had four cubs! While that was a first for us, it had happened in other zoos. But, by the end of the day he came back to report, "You know, she has had five cubs in this litter!" I rushed out to the exhibit and peeked into the den myself to make sure that he had not counted some of the cubs twice. It was difficult to distinguish individuals in this little pile of squirming stripes, but sure enough, there were five cubs! I then rushed back to my office and checked the *International Zoo Yearbook* (annually published by the Zoological Society of London), as well as inventories and annual reports from other zoos. I could find only one other zoo in the world in which a female tiger had delivered a litter of five cubs, and that was a zoo in Sweden. Even with this many cubs, Dacca raised them all—on her own!

The next year rolled around and we wondered whether Dacca would repeat her performance. The day of delivery arrived, the keeper came up and reported: she's had her first cub . . . her second cub . . . her third . . . fourth . . . fifth! Five cubs again, two years in a row! Not only did she have them but once again she raised them without our help!

If a female tiger in the wild were to deliver a litter of five cubs, the runts of the litter would probably perish. The mother would be out finding food, protecting territory, and watching for enemies. The stronger cubs would compete for adequate nourishment, and the weaker cubs would perish. In anticipation of this in the zoo situation, we had infant isolettes warmed up and our substitute formulas ready. Each day we checked for runts, but there were none. All five cubs were fat and sassy.

The next year we wondered, would she—could she—do this again? If so, that would be fifteen cubs in three years' time on a once-a-year breeding program—a most unusual circumstance. There was great anticipation around the zoo, and all the staff were taking bets with each other: "Oh, I bet she does; no, I don't think she can," and so on.

The much anticipated day of delivery arrived. The keeper came up and reported: "She's had her first cub . . . her second . . . her third . . . her fourth . . . she did *not* have five cubs that year. She had *SIX!*

Not only did she have them, she raised them. And not only did she raise them, we were able to let Tabor, the father tiger, back in with the mother and cubs. Here was this 450 pound male Bengal tiger, sitting in the middle of the exhibit, while the six cubs climbed upon his head, chewed on his ears, slid down his back, chased his tail. It was truly a glorious sight.

Over time this pair of Bengal tigers produced nearly three dozen cubs and many were sent to zoos across the nation and around the world. Some were even named "Topeka." It is interesting to note that in 1939 there were 40,000 Bengal tigers in India. By the 1970's, there were less than 1500. In my lifetime alone, Bengal tiger numbers in the wild have shrunk literally to the point of no return. There are more tigers alive and well in the zoos of the world than remain in their native habitats. This is a sad reflection on the status of our natural world. It also places an awesome responsibility on zoos holding the last viable genetic stock for the future survival of the species. Topeka's terrific tigers certainly have made a significant contribution.

NOTE: The Greater Topeka Southwestern Bell Telephone Directory issued in November 1971 featured a color photograph of two of our young tigers on the cover.

Part 4

Growing a Tropical Rain Forest . . .

in Kansas?

Who?

What?

Where?

When?

Why?

. . . and How!

. . . the zoo really is . . . not just a haven for animals . . . not just a place to have fun. It is a place where people can be surrounded by nature instead of concrete, and see and hear and smell other living creatures instead of automobiles.

—Peter Crowcroft
Former Director
Toronto Zoo

Art work by Alice C. Sabatini

Courtesy of the Topeka and Shawnee County Public Library

Part 4

Growing a Tropical Rain Forest . . .
in Kansas?

The State Journal

page of opinion

Saturday Evening, May 27, 1972

To fulfill the dream of one's youth; that is the best that can happen to a man. No worldly success can take the place of that.—Willa Cather, novelist.

Busy times at the Gage Park Zoo

School children from a wide area around Topeka are on almost constant safari to the Gage Park Zoo this month, enjoying its many fascinations these warm spring days.

Young visitors are running from 1,300 to 1,600 daily and at times there are more school buses than cars in the parking lot, observes Gary K. Clarke, zoo director.

Besides Kansans, many are from Missouri, Oklahoma and Nebraska. During the present school year, more than 200 group tours have been personally conducted, reaching a peak now.

These youngsters, and all others 12 and under, are admitted without charge, while regular patronage continues to mount steadily, assuring the zoo of fees sufficient to add regularly to its exhibits.

IN THE FIRST FOUR months of 1972, attendance has been 14,000 above the same period last year, Clarke reports. Total for 1971 was more than 200,000, an amazing figure in view of the fact that the drawing power of most zoos is regarded as good if they equal the population of the city in which they are located.

Gage Park Zoo is sure to be setting ever-increasing records in the years to come, with its unique and realistic tropical rain forest now assured as a new central feature by 1974.

This week, the City Commission accepted a bid of $103,875 from a California firm for the 100-foot diameter clear plastic dome which will be one of the main components of the rain forest enclosure.

With that on order, architects now can finish their specifications for the base and walls of the building, with a view to awarding the construction contract later this year. Additional months will be necessary to move the jungle foliage, birds, mammals and reptiles into the natural setting and allow them time to become acclimated before it is opened to visitors.

THE RAIN FOREST is being built without tax money. Gate receipts to the zoo already have gone into a sinking fund, to be augmented by bonds to be retired from admission revenues. In other words, the fine new attraction will be paid for by those who visit and enjoy its exhibits.

Distinctive features will include weathermaking machinery to produce the right levels of humidity and heat, artificial thunderstorms with sound effects and lightning, and a 17-foot waterfall. Footpaths will allow exploration of the beauties of the natural environment at close range.

When the tropical rain forest becomes a reality it will prove once again there's always something new to bring visitors back to the Topeka zoo—a formula Director Clarke and his staff have pursued to excellent advantage.

Groundbreaking Giraffe Baby

Friday, November 3, 1972 promised to be a more exciting day at the zoo than usual. Groundbreaking ceremonies for the Tropical Rain Forest were scheduled for 3:00 pm.

For several weeks preparations had been underway for this event. The construction site had been cleared under the supervision of Park Superintendent Dennis Showalter. The office of Park Commissioner Lauren Nash had extended invitations to officials and dignitaries. The architects, engineers and contractors had prepared their remarks. Members of the Zoo Explorer Post were ready to serve as hosts and hostesses. Representatives of various youth organizations (Scouts, Camp Fire Girls, etc.) were coached on how to turn the first spade of earth. Zoo Docent Chairman Ann Hedquist and her staff had prepared the Education Room for a post-ceremony reception, and P. K. Worley, president of the Topeka Friends of the Zoo, was all set to serve as master of ceremonies. Everyone was looking forward with anticipation to this long awaited event, and there was a genuine air of festivity at the zoo.

Activities at the Clarke household that morning were quite hectic: six of us taking turns in one bathroom, Margaret preparing breakfast, the four kids getting ready for school, and me gearing up for the excitement of the day. After several weeks of dreary overcast weather, I was relieved to hear the forecast predict clearing and sunshine by mid-afternoon—just in time for the groundbreaking.

I had kissed my family goodbye, and was preparing to head out the door for the zoo when the phone rang. My wife answered, and, in an excited voice on the other end of the line, Keeper Ken Kawata shouted: "Emergency! The front legs are halfway out!" Oh, no—that could mean only one thing: Jan, our adult female giraffe, had started delivery of her second baby. And, today, of all days! I told Ken I was on my way.

It was about a five-minute drive from my home to the zoo and during that time a thousand thoughts raced through my mind. We had known Jan could deliver any day, and the zoo staff had maintained a volunteer around-the-clock "giraffe watch" for several weeks. A number of people had lost quite a bit of sleep as a result.

Since this was Jan's second offspring, we did not have to contend with all the unknown factors associated with the birth of Sunflower, her first-born. Everything was in readiness, and we were prepared to cope with the many variables that could occur. However, we felt reasonably sure that if it was a normal delivery and the baby was viable, Jan would show proper maternal behavior. Jan was in her 458th day of pregnancy. The gestation for Sunflower had been 468 days, so she was ten days earlier this time. (And, oh yes—we have that Tropical Rain Forest Groundbreaking today, too.)

I arrived at the zoo in record time. Keeper Bill Gage had already started the video tape camera, as we hoped to record the birth on tape. In addition Zoologist Mike LaRue and I were taking both black and white photos and color slides. General Curator John Wortman, who missed the birth of Sunflower, had left the previous day for a zoological meeting in Houston, and would miss this birth, too.

Jan was in the center stall with ample bedding on the floor. Twiga, the male, was in the east stall and Sunflower on the west side. At 7:49 am the baby's head protruded. Both Twiga and Sunflower were very curious and tried to sniff the fetus as Jan would walk by.

At 8:10 am Jan went into pronounced contractions, and was heard to utter a low moan. Many of the old natural history books state that giraffes are mute, and the belief existed even among many zoologists that giraffes were incapable of producing a sound. (Ahhh . . . what we can learn from zoo animals.)

The neck of the fetus was extended halfway. The moment of birth occurred at 8:12 am. Immediately Jan turned around and started licking the calf. The calf's eyes were open, and breathing was confirmed at 8:13 am Jan started to consume the amniotic membrane, a positive sign.

By 8:25 am the baby made its first attempt to stand. Numerous attempts followed and the calf finally gained its feet at 9:01 am. At 9:21 am, after being up and down several more times, the calf took its first step. By 9:31 am the calf was walking around its mother. At this point the baby seemed in good health and Jan was acting quite normal. The labor period was a bit shorter than for Sunflower, and the calf was progressing much faster. It nursed just one hour and thirty-one minutes after birth, whereas Sunflower did not nurse until she was over 32 hours old. Jan finished passing the afterbirth at 3:44 pm.

The zoo settled down into its regular routine by late morning. Last minute details for the groundbreaking were attended to, and a large crowd had gathered by mid-afternoon. Just before the ceremony started the sun broke through the clouds to shine brightly on the festivities. Everything went according to schedule and the Tropical Rain Forest was officially underway. During the reception afterward the videotape of the complete birth sequence was shown continuously in the Education Room. Good weather held over Saturday and Sunday and the zoo recorded its best attendance to date for a November weekend.

It was determined that the calf was a male, and he was named "Lauren" in honor of the park commissioner. Sunflower, who had been the "baby" since her birth on August 24, 1970 suddenly was just an older sister. All attention was now centered on the *new* baby in the giraffe family.

Afterword . . . In working with a living collection of wild animals one experiences a gamut of emotions—from the pinnacle of joy to the depths of frustration. Such was the case with our giraffe family.

Our joy and pride in the new baby giraffe increased with each passing day, and we were all so pleased with his progress. Things seemed to be going even better than with Sunflower, until December 16, 1972. On that day the calf was listless. The consulting veterinarian for large animals was called to the zoo to examine Lauren. Preliminary diagnosis indicated a minor gastric disturbance and medication was prescribed. The next day a blood sample was obtained and subsequent laboratory analysis showed a normal reading.

The baby's condition remained about the same during the week. The keepers and staff worked very closely with Lauren and, although he really did not appear to be in a life-and-death struggle, it certainly was a concern that the condition persisted. The veterinarian administered daily treatment, and by December 22 Lauren actually seemed to be responding.

We were somewhat encouraged by the calf's general behavior, but his unexpected death on December 24 was a disastrous conclusion to a series of routine events. One always feels so helpless and defeated in a situation such as this.

Even though it was Christmas Eve, arrangements were made for Curator John Wortman and Zoologist Mike LaRue to take the baby giraffe to Kansas State University Veterinary School for a thorough post mortem, complete with tissue sections and laboratory cultures. Unfortunately, the eventual results were inconclusive.

The loss of a young animal like Lauren distresses everyone, especially those who work on a close daily basis with the animals in the zoo. I recall the death of a baby camel I was bottle raising when I first started in the zoo profession as an 18-year-old keeper. I was left with a feeling of bitter frustration. The wise and experienced zoo director I worked under at the time admonished me never to become too emotionally involved with the animals in my care. But as I write this now, on Christmas Day 1972, I can't help having that same feeling.

To the AMAZON!

The Amazon—an improbable world, an incredible river! And to understand it, one really has to experience it. I had the privilege of doing so in the summer of 1973. The timing was perfect, as we were in the final stages of developing our Tropical Rain Forest at the World Famous Topeka Zoo. The purpose of my trip was not to "bring-em-back alive," but to gain firsthand knowledge of the tropical rain forest so that we could better interpret our exhibit to the public.

The University of California Extension Division conducted a series of International Programs on Natural Environment Studies. I participated in their first such course on the rain forest entitled, "Land and Life: The Ecology of the Amazon." Instead of bringing back any live specimens, I brought back 1,200 color slides, 18 hours of tape recordings, and thousands of impressions.

As a novice in the Amazon, I had a lot to learn. Although I had read and studied and made every preparation, I was in for some quick lessons. On our first day in the town of Leticia, right on the banks of the Amazon River, at the mutual borders of Columbia, Brazil and Peru, we were supposed to rest so we would not experience 'tropical lag'. However, I was so anxious to actually experience the rain forest that I just couldn't wait. So I donned my jungle gear, grabbed my camera equipment, rushed into the little patch of rain forest next to our compound—and promptly tripped over a vine in my eagerness! First lesson learned: despite the excitement of the moment, you must be patient and observant.

It didn't take long to learn my second lesson either. I was extremely concerned about protecting all my delicate equipment (camera, tape recorder, binoculars) and at the same time keeping myself clean and dry. In very short order I forgot about myself and worried only about my equipment. After a day in the humid rain forest I was so hot, so exhausted, and *so* wet—it was raining on the outside and I was sweating on the inside—that I gave up keeping myself neat and clean. I was covered with sunscreen oil, mud, mosquito repellent, foot powder and sweat. And rain, rain, rain! My Arid Extra Dry became Tropical Extra Wet. But, I was in a *real* tropical rain forest and it was great!

I found that there were four basic essentials I needed for survival in the Amazon. The first was drinking water; second was enough food from day to day; third was an adequate supply of batteries, because when the sun goes down the light goes out in the rain forest; and fourth was that good old stand-by survival item—toilet tissue! (We were advised not to use the sandpaper-like leaves that are common in the forest.)

In addition to those basic essentials, there were a number of other items that were equally important. Chief among these were plastic bags—

big plastic bags, little plastic bags, plastic bags, and more plastic bags. I used them for everything. A hammock is also necessary, as the rain forest floor is so wet a conventional sleeping bag is of no use. Not only that, but one would be swarming with insects. An Amazon hammock is not the neat, flat type you can get at Sears, but more like a cocoon that just swallows you up and completely shuts out the rest of the world. It also gave me a backache when I tried to sleep on my stomach.

Life in the Amazon is truly life in a different world. There was no press of hectic daily activities, no rigid schedules or demanding deadlines to meet, no telephones, or newspapers, or TV. Many of the things that were so dominating in my life in Topeka seemed so unimportant in the rain forest.

Frequently I am asked what was the one thing that I missed most while in the Amazon. It's probably not what you think it would be. After I was in the jungle for about a week, there was one thing that I developed a craving for, one thing that I thought about, that I dreamed about, so much so it became an obsession. It was on my mind constantly. I take it for granted here in the States, but I would have given almost anything for just one. The one thing . . . that I craved the most . . . was a pure, real, unadulterated, honest-to-goodness American Coca-Cola!

They have their own type of soda pop in Amazon towns such as Leticia. It's called Gaseosas—and it gives you gaseosas! It tastes like the lowest quality U.S. soft drink product that has been sitting uncapped in the sun for two weeks. No, it's worse than that. I guess my craving was obvious, because when we returned to Leticia after a spell up river, I was approached by a local resident who, with a big smile, offered to sell me a bottle of Coke. Wow! There it was! The real thing, as they say. Oh, it was beautiful: the bottle, the color, and even though it was hot, I didn't care. So I paid a premium price for it, popped the cap off, guzzled it down—and it was Gaseosas! In a Coke bottle! YUK!

Another lesson learned was that the image most people have about a tropical forest, usually from the movies, is totally erroneous. Yes, the jungle is teeming with life, and all of the star animals one hears about—jaguars, anacondas, piranhas, electric eels—are there, but not as your major concern. It's the LITTLE animals that give you the BIG problems . . . the insects! Ants in particular. If you pause for a moment and lean against a tree, they swarm up your arm. Or if you are just so tired that you have to sit down and rest, your clothes are immediately infested. And remind me sometime to tell you about the candiru and the lantern fly!

One of my most memorable moments was the first time we penetrated deep into an area of primary rain forest. I simply had to stop for a while and soak it all in. Although birds and insects were present, it was really very still and quiet. A gentle rain was falling and the green leaves glistened as the water dripped from them. With the low light level the surrounding lush vegetation overwhelmed me. As I looked up at the giant trees towering above me, I felt as though I was an intruder in Nature's cathedral. It was difficult for me to imagine how anyone could lose respect for this reservoir of life and intentionally destroy it.

Finding and observing animals in the rain forest was often quite frustrating. Mammals were few and far between. Birds were a quick flash of color in the corner of my eye. Reptiles and amphibians utilized protective camouflage to the extent that I would pass right by without seeing them. However, fish were seined out of the muddy Amazon and insects were attracted to light traps. And the jungle was alive with activity at night: leaf cutting ants in a diligent parade, bats fluttering about in whimsical patterns, tree frogs filling the air with a resounding chorus.

The Amazon area is a land of paradoxes and contrasts. Whereas the undergrowth of the rain forest is a world so narrow that you seem to suffocate, the Amazon River is so open and wide that your heart and mind go soaring. The canopy of the forest shuts out light to the forest floor, but on the river there is no shade and you broil in the equatorial sun. One does not travel far by foot, and a dugout canoe is the main means of transportation. The Amazon River is the highway and its thousands of tributaries are the roads and streets.

Being on the Amazon River at night is a bit scary until one gets used to it. There are no reflected lights from cities and you are engulfed in utter blackness. Your dugout canoe is so low in the water and the current so swift that you feel like a minute fallen leaf in this vast river sea. A backwater tributary offers yet another experience. The water is still and the rain forest is close on either side. The air is filled with the ever present chorus of tree frogs. On a cloudless night the trees are silhouetted and bathed in moonlight, while the huge expanse of sky is filled with hundreds—thousands—millions of dazzling stars. You don't even want to talk; a human voice sounds so out of place.

Part of our time was spent on Santa Sofia Island No. II. A privileged highlight was spending most of one day in the nesting area of the hoatzin, a rare and almost prehistoric bird. On our return to base camp that night we were in a canoe in the middle of a lake in the middle of an island in the middle of the Amazon where we witnessed another glorious sunset. With the ever-changing clouds, Nature paints a new masterpiece each evening. It was a magical moment, one I wished would last forever.

I went to the Amazon expecting to experience the true rain forest primeval, the richness of jungle plant life, the variety of unique and secretive creatures, and the world's greatest river. All these expectations were met. But I also returned with an unexpected and profound admiration for the people of the Amazon. The culture of the Indians may seem strange and incomprehensible to us, but I'm sure ours is even more so to them.

The children of the villages were a great delight to me, and I to them. They were so amused at the tall stranger with reddish skin and carrot-colored hair talking into a black box (my tape recorder) that they followed me everywhere. And while we could not speak the same language, a smile served as a most effective means of communication.

I grew more than a beard in the Amazon—I gained a personal insight into this fascinating part of our world and a new introspection of myself.

The State Journal

page of opinion

Saturday Evening, April 6, 1974

How about a visit to the zoo?

These are busy days at the Topeka Zoo. Lots of things are happening that make it interesting and which will make it more exciting in days to come.

Last Sunday brought a rush of visitors, and parking lots were full. Gary Clarke, zoo director, expects visits to increase as spring progresses.

Work is going on rapidly on the new tropical rain forest area and it should be completed by June. Special lightweight stone has been put in place for the waterfall, and plumbing is being connected. Tropical plants, some of which have grown in Gage Park's greenhouse since 1969, are being moved in. Plans are being completed for the animal, bird and other occupants.

One part of this area makes a good place for bird egg incubators because humidity and temperature are controlled. The zoo carries on a considerable hatchery operation — incubating more than 250 bird eggs each year.

Old standbys like Max and Tiffany, the gorillas, are still in the zoo and new animals and birds will be appearing. Most recent arrivals are emus, hatched recently. They are an Australian species, related to ostriches. And there is a new giraffe.

The zoo especially welcomes student visitors. Thirty-five women volunteers or docents are available to take groups through on guided tours.

So it is a good time to see Topeka's zoo if you haven't already been there — or to make a return trip. If tomorrow is a fine day, a zoo visit would be an interesting way to spend the afternoon. Like many other features of Topeka's parks, the zoo is an asset to the city.

The Topeka Daily Capital

Viewpoints

Friday, May 24, 1974

A Dream Come True

Topeka's pride is showing today — and with good reason.

This is the long-awaited day the new Tropical Rain Forest building at the Gage Park Zoo will be opened to the public.

For years, it has been a dream in the mind of Gary Clarke, nationally known director of the Gage Park Zoo. It has been in various stages of planning since 1969. Ground was broken in 1971 and final plans were drawn in 1972.

Built entirely with funds derived from zoo entrance fees, the Tropical Rain Forest is part of a planned zoological complex which includes a Large Mammal building and later will accommodate an aviary and other special sections, possibly a new reptile building.

The unique structure is round, 100 feet in diameter with a 10-foot wall and a geodesic dome which is 30 feet high. Within the building, which is equipped to maintain tropical temperatures and humidity, will be found tropical vegetation and tropical birds, animals, fish and reptiles.

The Rain Forest building is constructed so the wild life appears to be roaming and living in natural surroundings without cages or other controls. But the spectators are separated from the animals by almost invisible nettings.

In later months and years, when the vegetation has grown more lush it will provide areas where there is constant shade as there are in the Amazonian Rain Forest in South America. Some of the trees, now about 10 to 12 feet tall, will grow enough to reach the roof. Then the building will appear to blend with its surroundings.

For the benefit and direction of visitors, there will be a "stand-up" theater where slides will be presented automatically to show them how and where to find the various animals and what to look for.

A visit to the Tropical Rain Forest building is a must for all residents of the Topeka area, and it will be obvious that the construction and planning of the Rain Forest exhibit is a tribute to the ability, imagination and determination of Gary Clarke.

Trials and Tribulations of the Tropics in Topeka

If you think building your dream house would be a challenge, how about creating a tropical rain forest . . . in Kansas? Then install a few hundred unpredictable wild-animal residents *and* keep the whole climatic system thriving even in mid-winter! Surely along the way you'd experience more than a few headaches and surprises. Believe me, we did.

It all started with the master plan in 1964. After the first major exhibit for large mammals, the Tropical Rain Forest (the TRF) was designated to be the next major feature of the revamped World Famous Topeka Zoo. For the next five years we tossed around ideas and reviewed the literature available on every facet of the project. Our research confirmed that it would be one hellacious challenge to develop a rain forest in a prairie climate.

A feasibility study in 1969 detailed the general concept: a circular structure under a domed roof, with visitors walking among tropical plants and free-ranging animals. There were rain forest exhibits in a number of zoos, even some walk-through free-flight aviaries. But up to that time no one had achieved an entire complex dedicated to the total environment that we envisioned—it would truly be our "dream house."

Intensive planning began in 1971. *Everything* had to be researched. The planning team represented all facets: architects, engineers, zoologists, horticulturists, and city officials. Groundbreaking took place November 3, 1972. I spent several weeks in the Amazon in 1973 gathering field data to assist in the interpretation of a rain forest for zoo visitors. Of all things, record breaking rains in Topeka slowed construction progress, but gradually the dome took shape. When construction was completed horticulturist Bob Foster created an instant jungle and animals were introduced. Dedication of the TRF took place May 24, 1974.

The Tropical Rain Forest is 100 feet in diameter with poured-concrete walls 10 feet above grade. An aluminum framework of geodesic design, 31 feet high at midpoint, covers the circular area. A total of 240 triangular panels of clear acrylic are inlaid in the frame to form a Crystogon dome. These panels permit 85 percent solar energy and 92 percent natural light transmission, which promotes not only green vegetation growth but blooming plants as well. There is no floor, as such, in the building except for the undulating visitors' path through the graceful vegetation.

Although major emphasis is on Amazonia, the total exhibit theme is a generalized global rain forest with a diversity of forms from several continents. Each display represents a specific niche: Forest Floor, Jungle Stream, Jungle Clearing, River Isle, Backwater Tributary, Upper Canopy, Jungle Pool, Forest Undergrowth, Treetops, Amazon River Bank, Bates Falls (named for Henry W. Bates, an early explorer of the Amazon region), and Lake Yagua (named for an Amazonian Indian tribe).

Since the TRF is modest in size, most of its residents are medium to small. Many animals range freely throughout the entire domed area while others are maintained in moated or low-walled exhibits. The latter group includes those that could be dangerous to visitors, damage plants, or create social disputes with other species.

Entering the Tropical Rain Forest is an adventure. Immediately you are aware of the tropical climate and the awesome roar of the waterfall. Automatically you pause, as it truly is a breathtaking experience. Brilliantly colored macaws are squawking, while an iguana lizard leisurely strolls across the footpath. The vegetation is overwhelming and towers overhead. You are in another world—an atmosphere totally different from the outside environment you just left. Totally enveloped in a living jungle, it seems impossible that you are still in Topeka!

Despite our careful planning, I guess I should have expected the unexpected. Why should the Topeka Zoo be immune to that inevitable reality of dream-house building? We had erected a structure that was supposed to maintain tropical temperatures through severe winter weather as well as a comfortable environment in the midst of typical Kansas summers, when temperatures actually soar higher than in many real rain forests, and humidity is just as bad if not worse. Space travel aside, earthly mechanical systems are still subject to malfunctions.

We also had the challenge of maintaining a delicately balanced collection of varied plants and animals. Although we may know the biology and behavior of a given species, animals are still individuals. Our years of zoo experience have demonstrated that animals often do all the things the natural history books say they can't . . . or won't.

One of the least expected events occurred shortly after the TRF had been opened to the public. Late one night, after the zoo was closed, Curator John Wortman and Keeper Bill Gage were recording the water temperature in the Amazon River Bank exhibit. There are no overhead lights in the clear plastic dome; all was quiet and dark. Suddenly the entire building exploded with light—blinding light! Bill Gage dropped to the ground and shielded his eyes with his arms. John Wortman looked around with a dumbfounded gaze. Sleeping birds were awakened abruptly, and the nocturnal mammals immediately scurried for shelter. The TRF was in total havoc!

What in blazes happened?

It was only the police helicopter getting a bird's-eye view.

The next day I talked to the Police Department helicopter pilots and explained the serious consequences that could result from powerful lights unexpectedly flooding the building. Of course they had not meant any harm and were extremely apologetic. They explained: "We've been watching the progress of your building. We saw the walls go up, the dome take shape, the interior exhibits develop, and the plants put in place. It is such a beautiful sight, especially from the air. And at night it lights up like a sparkling jewel. We just love to look at it, but from now on we'll only fly around the perimeter so as not to frighten the animals."

Unusual occurrences have become usual in the TRF since that first surprise . . . especially with the animals.

We tried South American Urucca jays the first couple of years. They did well and even nested. Then trouble began. They started dive-bombing keepers in the area of the nest. The keepers solved this problem by wearing hard hats. Next the jays took to dive-bombing zoo visitors, zeroing in on people as they entered the building. The jays were such troublemakers that we finally had to remove them and send them to the Jungle Building at the Sedgwick County Zoo in Wichita.

We once had a South American troupial (which looks something like a Baltimore oriole—the bird, not the baseball player). He managed to get above the protective screen at the top of the dome and couldn't get back down. After rescuing this bird several times, and to save ourselves future trouble, we sent him to the Jungle Building at the Sedgwick County Zoo.

We received a trio of small-clawed otters from the Riverbanks Zoological Park in Columbia, South Carolina. They were beautiful specimens— but afraid of water! We encouraged two of them to swim by placing their food on a stump in the center of their pool. When the third one didn't catch on we sent him also to the Jungle Building at the Sedgwick County Zoo.

Our original plan was to have green iguanas ranging free in the TRF and rhinoceros iguanas confined to one of the enclosed exhibits. The green iguanas not only adjusted but reproduced, incubating their eggs in the forest floor soil. Contrary to our plans, however, the rhinoceros iguanas learned to overcome a four-foot-high wall. After chasing them through the "jungle" a few times, we decided to let them loose in the building. We did have a few concerns: that they might bite a visitor, they might harm other animals, and they were so heavy-bodied they would damage some of the younger or smaller plants. But the plants grew large and strong, the iguanas did not bite any visitors, and they proved to be compatible with other species.

One year some Rothschild's mynah eggs were hatched in the rhinoceros iguanas' favorite perching log and the chicks would stick their heads out of the nest hole within inches of an iguana's mouth. We watched with great concern to assure that the iguanas did not attempt to harm the chicks, and were surprised and relieved that the big lizards ignored the birds.

Initially, we had intended to exhibit cotton-headed tamarins (a squirrel-sized primate that looks like a living troll doll) in the Backwater Tributary—an open area surrounded by a water moat. The tamarins were on exhibit during the day, and every night exited through a hole in the back wall that led to sleeping quarters and nesting boxes. This gave us management control over the animals, enabling us to do such things as hold one off exhibit or separate a pregnant female. But it didn't take long for a newly planted rubber tree to grow to the point where the tamarins could use it to leap across the water moat. In fact, the first time that happened I was "showing off" the building to a visiting professional colleague, who assumed it was a regular occurrence.

For a while we kept the rubber tree trimmed back and caught the tamarins whenever they leaped across the moat. Then we decided to let them free-range throughout the dome, an idea that has worked well ever since even though the tamarins do eat a few plants here and there and have been implicated in robbing some birds' nests. Eight little tamarins were born in the TRF (four sets of twins) over the next few years. We usually tried to show a family group of six animals: the adult parents, an older pair of weaned twins, and a younger set of twins riding on their parents' backs. The tamarins had access to all areas of the building, and it is a spectacular sight to see the entire group high in the dome leaping from branch to branch. Probably our greatest loss occurred when a pregnant female tamarin ventured to the ground in the Amazon River Bank exhibit and apparently stepped on a log that turned out to be a caiman. We really didn't know the circumstances surrounding this loss and decided the chances of a repeated incident were extremely remote, so the tamarins remained free to range through the trees in the TRF.

Acceptable social interaction between various species of animals occurs on a regular basis. The tamarins seemed to delight in teasing the macaws by pulling their tail feathers. The Rothschild's mynahs would chase away a green iguana if it got too close to their nest. One sometimes could see several species of birds, a giant Indian fruit bat, and a Malabar squirrel at the same feeding station. By the time the two-toed sloths would arrive there was little left, so they were fed elsewhere.

Interestingly enough, our black crakes—starling-sized, long-legged birds—nested successfully in the ground cover of the Amazon River Bank exhibit, inhabited by five caimans.

The red-crested cardinals once built a nest in a tree overhanging the water of the River Bank exhibit (and within reach of zoo visitors, had they known the nest was there). One day a green iguana climbed out onto that branch and stepped on the nest, knocking the eggs into the water. Keepers retrieved the eggs with a net and placed them back into the nest, which they tied onto a branch. The cardinals continued their incubation and hatched two out of the three eggs.

Although we felt that capybaras (aquatic rodents weighing up to 150 lbs.) were probably too large to place in a walled exhibit, we tried them anyway. They *were* too large for the space. We substituted pacas, slightly smaller South American rodents, and single specimens worked well. Our experiences with pairs were unsuccessful because the females would chase the males out of the exhibit, and the males would then roam through the building nibbling on delicate plants. It is not an easy task to recapture a two-foot-long rodent in dense vegetation. Once one jumped into the Lake Yagua exhibit, with a keeper in hot pursuit. The paca dropped beneath the surface and the keeper stood in the water with his net poised. The paca swam under the waterfall and disappeared, while the keeper stood there ready . . . and waiting . . . and dripping.

The acouchis, tropical rodents much more delicate than agoutis (which are related to pacas), thrived in the TRF. They, too, began to reproduce after a period of adjustment. Eventually, as a simple means of population control, we decided to leave the mother and youngsters in the exhibit and let the male range free throughout the TRF. The exhibit's four-foot wall would maintain their separation. When the female became pregnant we first considered an immaculate conception, but then discovered that the male had been jumping over the wall at night to visit the female and jumping out the next morning before we arrived. Where there's a will . . .

From the beginning two fears haunted us at the TRF: What would happen if we lost heat during the winter, and what would happen if we lost cooling power during the summer? Well, both of these fears were realized.

On February 1, 1979 we had a boiler-room fire that resulted in the loss of all heat in the building. Normally our temperature cycle ranged from 80 °F or higher during the day to 68°F at night. The fire occurred not merely on the coldest day of the year, but on the coldest day of the *century* in Topeka (minus 23°F). The fire destroyed the primary boiler and disabled the secondary boiler, but at least it was confined to the boiler room and did not damage the exhibit area.

As soon as the Fire Department left, about 9:00 am, we were faced with the task of providing life support systems while emergency repairs were made on the secondary boiler. Rather than move the animals out of the building (even if we could have caught them), our plan had always been to maintain minimum heat in the total environment to save both plants and animals. The temperature in the building had dropped rapidly and a layer of frost had formed on the dome. The latter served as insulation and reduced further heat loss. But it was frightening to stand there and see our breath.

We immediately set up two portable propane heaters and kept a close watch on the plants and animals. Thermometer dials dropped below the scale, which bottomed at 50°F. The temperature approached the freezing point, but fortunately it was a clear day with bright sun and the solar gain helped raise the temperature back to an acceptable level.

The secondary boiler was back on line by 5:00 pm and the temperature was stabilized. Damage to the boiler room was placed at $25,000. Our only losses were several lizards and a few plant species that suffered thermal shock.

On June 4, 1979 a power surge occurred throughout our section of the city, shorting out the transformer serving the TRF. It was already noon on a very hot, humid Kansas summer day, and the loss of power shut down the cooling fans and ventilating system. The transformer was beyond repair, and our emergency generator failed to operate. The building temperature rose rapidly and the thermometer dials registered above 95° F. The heat was unbearable to zoo visitors and staff alike. Even the sloths, who normally dote on jungle mugginess, descended to ground level seeking a more comfortable environment.

We disconnected all of the electrical controls on the ventilating louvers around the building and opened the louvers manually. For more ventilation, Head Keeper Ron Kaufman climbed up on the outside of the dome and propped open a section of roof panels above the interior bird screen. Fortunately the TRF is surrounded by tall shade trees, and a gentle Kansas zephyr produced some air movement inside. The following day the transformer was replaced and the system was again operational. We now knew what would happen "if."

But along with unexpected problems came unexpected rewards. The following is taken directly from an entry by Ron Kaufman in the zoo's Daily Report of November 2, 1976: "*TRF Keeper had unparalleled pleasure of chewing out a photographer (female) and her female model (clad only in a bikini and a glowing blush) in front of Lake Yagua. They had thrown a towel over the end of a branch overhanging the water, and the model had waded in for some pictures. Two Chilean flamingos and three cattle egrets were scared out of their gourds. Keeper R.K. (scowling on the outside, cheering on the inside) gave the girls a stern lecture. Apparently, it was a project for a photography class. This is certainly a rewarding job. . .*"

We had our trials and tribulations in the TRF, but our real achievement probably was the integration of free-ranging mammals, birds, reptiles, and amphibians. As of this writing (1979) six of our ten mammal species have access to the entire building. Although the Giant Indian fruit bats usually roost during midday, they are a most spectacular sight when they fly around the TRF dome in late afternoon.

As I reviewed the first half-decade of the TRF, it had developed into more than even the most visionary members of our staff imagined. Yet I felt that we were still learning how to operate the exhibit properly and that we had not yet begun to realize its tremendous potential. The Tropical Rain Forest was alive and vibrant and offered unlimited opportunities.

Special Note*:* In 1974 the American Association of Zoological Parks and Aquariums (today the AZA) established an annual Exhibit Achievement Award to recognize and honor the most significant new exhibit in a zoo or aquarium. The award is not for architectural recognition. Rather, it is for outstanding achievement in the area of exotic animal display, exhibit technique and design innovation. At their annual conference in Philadelphia that year the first Exhibit Achievement Award was presented to the Topeka Zoological Park for the Tropical Rain Forest. Although it had been most satisfying to see the response of the visiting public to the TRF, it was extremely gratifying for the zoo staff to be honored and recognized by professional colleagues.

I would like to extend credit and appreciation to key members of our planning team; architects Charles Burton and Don Depew of Ekdahl, Davis, Depew, Persson, P.A., and mechanical engineer William Latimer of Burgess, Latimer and Miller.

Topeka

ZOo

RULES FOR JUNGLE WATCHING

MOVEMENT FRIGHTENS WILDLIFE;
ALWAYS MOVE SLOWLY

ANIMALS ARE MASTERS OF CAMOUFLAGE;
TAKE TIME TO OBSERVE EACH AREA
CLOSELY FOR HIDDEN CREATURES.

MANY RAIN FOREST ANIMALS ARE
QUITE SECRETIVE;
BE PATIENT UNTIL THEY COME
OUT OF HIDING.

MUCH LIFE IN THE RAIN FOREST IS ABOVE
GROUND LEVEL; LOOK CAREFULLY FOR
ANIMALS IN THE TREES

NOCTURNAL ANIMALS SLEEP DURING THE
DAY; UNDERSTAND AND RESPECT
THIS NATURAL BEHAVIOR.

YOU ARE A GUEST IN NATURE'S REALM;
PLEASE EARN THE PRIVILEGE TO
RETURN AGAIN.

TROPICAL RAIN FOREST

The Tropic of Kansas

Author's note: Since the Tropical Rain Forest was a new concept at that time, I felt it was important to document the philosophy of the original exhibit themes. Each area was carefully researched and there was a definite rhyme and reason why we designated a particular habitat and featured certain wildlife species. I wrote the following in 1974. G.K.C.

A Rain Forest in Kansas? Yes!

The Tropical Rain Forest in the Topeka Zoological Park represents a one-half million dollar project that spanned a decade from initial idea to grand opening.

It is unique in that an entire structure is devoted to one single ecological concept—the tropical rain forest. The visitor experiences a complex world of luxurious green vegetation and exotic animals living together in a skillfully developed, delicately balanced community.

The Tropical Rain Forest is the ultimate in zoo exhibit technique as it incorporates and interrelates live animals, live plants, habitat settings, climatic conditions, cultural artifacts, visitor participation, interpretative graphics, and audio-visual learning experiences. It is a sparkling jewel in the City of Topeka and a major attraction in the Midwest region.

Habitat Themes and Animal Life

Although the total exhibit theme is a representative rain forest with a diversity of forms, major emphasis is upon the Amazonian rain forest. All species of mammals, reptiles, amphibians, fish and invertebrates are South American. While many of the birds are Neotropical, some of them are from other equatorial regions of the world, as are many of the plants.

Each of the exhibits in the Tropical Rain Forest is representative of a specific habitat and titled as such. Instead of simply having a standard macaw exhibit, or a snake exhibit, each exhibit is developed along a habitat theme with the animals as one part of the total environment. Periodically some animals will be changed and different species may be seen from time to time. The following is a brief listing of the exhibits and animals as the visitor normally would see them on a tour of the TRF.

Bates Falls

Entering the Rain Forest on ground level is an emotional experience as one is immediately caught up in the atmosphere of the tropics—the humidity, the towering vegetation, the birds in free flight, but most of all the thunderous impact of Bates Falls, the dominant feature of the interior. The waterfall is named after Henry W. Bates (1825-1882), who explored the Amazon River basin a century ago, and Marston Bates (1907-1974), a noted naturalist who contributed much to our present day knowledge of the tropics.

River Isle

Islands of various sizes in the Amazon River are constantly being formed and eroded away by changing currents and flooding. This River Isle represents such an island. On the island perches are scarlet macaws and blue-and-gold macaws, which are among the largest members of the *psittacine* or parrot family. In the pool surrounding the island are young caimans, mata-mata turtles, and a variety of other aquatic turtles from the tropics.

Forest Floor

Although tranquil at a casual glance, the shadowy forest floor is teeming with activity from thousands of minute organisms. Many of the larger rain forest species also are ground dwellers and spend most of their existence on the forest floor. The beautiful crowned pigeons, large powder blue birds with distinctive red eyes, can be seen among the plants.

Jungle Clearing

This exhibit represents a natural open scar left by a giant fallen tree. On the ground, sometimes partially hidden in a tree cavity, is the acouchi, a secretive rodent of the rain forest. The impressive rhinoceros iguanas, largest of all iguana lizards, frequently perch on the fallen logs. And blending in with surrounding vegetation are the Amazon parrots.

Hidden Creatures

Just as in the Amazonian rain forest, many of the prevalent creatures are hidden in the natural camouflage provided by the trees and plants and blend in so well with their surroundings that it is difficult to see them. However, close and patient observation will reveal such hidden creatures as iguana lizards, marine toads, and various species of tree frogs, among others.

Jungle Stream

A cut-away underwater view features the yellow anaconda, a large constricting snake native to the jungle streams of the Amazon Basin.

Backwater Tributary

Penetrating deep into the jungle are countless tributaries that support a major river system like the Amazon. Cotton-headed tamarins, also known as cotton-topped marmosets, are the small active primates living in the trees. On the ground, usually partially hidden, is the paca, a brown rodent with white spots running down the sides of the body.

Upper Canopy

Up the steps is an overlook presenting a panoramic view of the entire Rain Forest and an excellent vista for photographers. The Upper Canopy represents the highest level of growth found in the stratification of a rainforest.

Birds in Free Flight

Brightly colored exotic birds live in a free flight environment. Bird behavior may be observed continuously to gain a better understanding of social interaction, territories, feeding stations and nesting sites. Among the free flight birds are: Rothschild's myna, red-crested touraco, San Blas jay, troupial, red crested cardinal, Urraca jay, Schalow's touraco and a variety of finches.

Tree Tops

Many animals live their entire lives in the tree tops. This exhibit features a huge tree that reaches from the floor of the Rain Forest to the top of the geodesic dome. The tamandua, or lesser anteater, sometimes can be seen on eye level from the Upper Canopy, demonstrating its climbing skill and prehensile tail. The two-toed sloth frequently is seen hanging upside down asleep in the tree. The South American prehensile-tailed porcupine may also be featured.

Jungle Pool

Small pools of standing water contain fairly simple plant and animal communities. These pools are frequently inhabited by small clawed otters. Yellow crowned night herons inhabit the pool area, and the cavity nest of the Bali myna is in back of the pool.

Forest Undergrowth

The inner depths of the jungle are almost cave-like in atmosphere because only flecks of sunlight penetrate through the upper canopy. The small and secretive margay cat is viewed through a stainless steel spider web in a nocturnal setting.

Lake Yagua

A small lake in the center of the Rain Forest beneath the waterfall has been named after one of the Indian tribes of the Amazon—the Yagua. Of all jungle life, the species most endangered by man is man himself—the forest Indian. Only a few thousand survive. Of 230 known tribes, 87 are already extinct.

Amazon River Bank

One of the most spectacular exhibits depicts a section of Amazon River bank with lush vegetation and trees overhanging the water. An adult pair of spectacled caiman, South American relatives of the alligator, live in the exhibit and have shown breeding activity. The water is four feet deep and frequently the caiman will float on the surface or sink to the very bottom and remain underwater (motionless) for up to three-quarters of an hour. Other endangered species of caiman may be established for conservation and breeding purposes.

*****

It should be noted that selection of animals for our Tropical Rain Forest intentionally avoided the large, showy species commonly seen in zoos. We felt it was important to acquaint the visitor with the more modest sized and possibly lesser known inhabitants of the rain forest ecosystem.

Thus, instead of the massive jaguar we chose the delicate margay cat; instead of the common anaconda, giant of all constricting snakes, we chose the shorter yellow anaconda; instead of the large spider monkey we chose the small marmoset; instead of the impressive black caiman we chose the medium sized spectacled caiman; and instead of the bulky tapir we chose the small agouti and acouchi.

These examples reflect the philosophy of species selection prevalent in the development of this living natural environment exhibit.

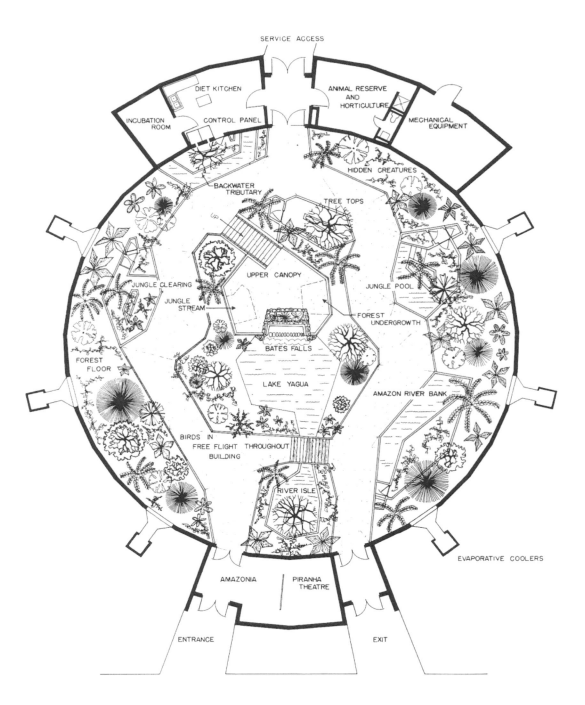

Tropical Rain Forest

A Whimsical Web

During the plethora of meetings in planning the Tropical Rain Forest, one of the challenges the zoo staff faced was how to retain the margay cats in the Forest Undergrowth exhibit. Glass was excluded because of reflection and air circulation problems. We really didn't want to use the standard cross-hatch wire mesh that was practical but somewhat unattractive. I was groping for a more naturalistic barrier when Keeper Vince von Frese popped up and said, "Well, how about a stainless steel spider web?"

WOW! What a great idea!

But how to get it done? And who to make it? I had never heard of such a thing, particularly as a barrier for a live animal.

In checking with the architects, we learned that even if the building contractor could do it, it would be beyond the budget of the project. In the course of events Zoologist Mike LaRue arranged with Topeka Metal Specialties to fabricate a man-made spider web—as a gift to the Rain Forest. Mike designed a life-sized pattern, six feet square. The welders spent approximately 33 hours in welding time and used about 225 feet of stainless steel wire. The entire project was valued at $675.

Spider webs are an integral part of the rain forest, and one of nature's most unique structures. They possess great strength, infinite variety, tremendous beauty—and ours was a work of art. Never to our knowledge had a zoo tried this technique of enclosing felines, and it proved to be a successful innovation in zoo display. It created more interest and comment among zoo visitors than any other Rain Forest exhibit, thanks to Hank Gerdes, president, and Melvin Davis, general manager, of Topeka Metal Specialties.

To top it off, we found real spider webs in our stainless steel web. Not only did the margays accept it, but the spiders just loved it!

Instant Blizzard over the Rain Forest

It was a clear, crisp, cold day in January 1978 with a mere six inches of snow on the ground when our distinguished guests from North Carolina landed at Forbes Field. They had flown to Topeka to study the Tropical Rain Forest in depth as representatives of the North Carolina Zoological Park and Advisory Council in Asheville. Included in this study group were Robert Fry, Zoo Director; Les Schobert, General Curator; and Dwight Holland, Curator of Design, of the North Carolina Zoological Park. Accompanying the three zoo personnel were Dr. C. J. Snow of the Advisory Council for the Zoo; and architects Hyatt Hammond and Alvis O. George, Jr.

The North Carolina Zoological Park in Asheboro is a state zoo (one of two in the U.S.) managed by their Department of Natural Resources and Community Development. It was one of the newest zoos in the country, and still under construction. Their master plan called for a large aviary, and they had been visiting zoos in the U.S. and Canada to observe facilities of this nature. They had heard of our Tropical Rain Forest and wanted to observe this exhibit with free ranging birds, mammals and reptiles. Thus, the visit to Topeka was arranged.

Though primarily interested in our Rain Forest, they seemed to enjoy seeing all of the zoo, and had to be torn away from the gorillas!

Upon entering the Rain Forest and making the instant transition from our midwest winter to tropical jungle, one of them commented, "Toto, I don't think we're in Kansas any more!"

They spent the remainder of the day inspecting the Tropical Rain Forest—not only from top to bottom, but from corner to corner. They toured the kitchen, the quarantine room, under the waterfall, off exhibit areas-- even the boiler room. Questions flew, cameras clicked, notes were taken, and a real brainstorming session took place all afternoon between our North Carolina visitors, members of our zoo staff, and Don Depew, our Rain Forest Architect.

In a telephone conversation prior to their trip to Topeka, the North Carolina delegation had been advised to bring warm clothing and wear boots because of the snow on the ground here. During the course of their afternoon in the Rain Forest they periodically shed layers of clothes, and discovered just how uncomfortable woolens can be in a tropical environment. Around 4:00 pm one of the keepers came in the Rain Forest and whispered to me that another winter storm had moved in— four inches of fresh snow already had fallen with four more inches forecast by midnight. Due to high winds it was drifting badly.

Because of the condensation on the dome of the Rain Forest we were unable to detect the changing weather conditions outside the building.

Our guests finished the tour of the facility at 5:30 and donned their winter jackets, sweaters and coats while still perspiring. We opened the exit doors and SWOOSH!—we almost lost the North Carolinians in a large snow bank. "WHAT HAPPENED?" they yelled in unison. "Nothing unusual," I replied. "You *are* in Kansas, now!"

As I drove them to their hotel they remarked on the beauty of Gage Park in winter, and said they were quite happy to be chauffeured. They wondered if I was driving on a road or just wandering across the snow through the park. I assured them we were on a road, though at times *I* was not sure as the visibility was zilch. Once they were snugly ensconced in the hotel, they relaxed and renewed their discussions about plans for their new Aviary.

The following day dawned bright and sunny with over eight inches of new snow on the ground. Back to the zoo they came, and discovered their boots were not adequate for that much snow. In spite of the adversities they seemed to enjoy their Topeka experience and took it all in stride. Wonder what they told their families when they returned home?

Crocodile Watching at its Best

"Are they real?" This was one of the more frequent questions that people asked about the West African dwarf crocodiles in the Riverbank Exhibit in our Tropical Rain Forest in 1985.

I guess it is logical, in that visitors frequently spend no more than 30 seconds—possibly a full minute at most—watching the crocodiles and expecting them to be demonstrating some spectacular behavior. Usually the crocodiles are motionless.

Here are a few hints for proper crocodile watching at the World Famous Topeka Zoo (or any zoo). As soon as you enter the front gate, make a beeline for the Tropical Rain Forest. Immediately proceed to the Riverbank Exhibit and note the position and/or activity of the crocodiles. If they are on the land, observe whether or not their mouths are open or closed. See if they are in the shadows or the sun. Look to see which way their bodies are positioned in relation to the sun and the pool. If the crocodiles are in the water, note if they are floating on top, hanging vertically in the water, or resting completely under water on the bottom of the pool. If they are swimming, see if they are using their tails, their legs, or a combination. Then make a note of the time of day, the position of the sun (or even if it is shining), the angle of the light that filters into the crocodile exhibit, and the general temperature and atmosphere of the Tropical Rain Forest.

Proceed then to different areas of the zoo to observe other animals. An hour or so later, stop by the Tropical Rain Forest again to see if there have been any changes with the crocodiles. Take note of all of the items mentioned above, and once again, check the time of day, the angle of the sun, and whether or not it is filtering into the crocodile exhibit. Then proceed once again to other areas of the zoo and forget about the crocodiles awhile.

Just before you leave the zoo, stop by the crocs one more time. Hopefully, several hours have passed, the day has progressed, and conditions have changed in the crocodile exhibit. Once again follow the hints mentioned previously and chances are you will see that there has been a great deal of change and movement among the crocodiles.

Obviously, it would be good if you could perch yourself at the crocodile pool and watch them continuously. Since they don't show a great deal of movement in a short time span, this might be a little boring. Hence, the method of stopping by now and then will enable you to keep track of activity and behavior in the crocodile exhibit and still enjoy other areas of the zoo. It's something like a time-lapse photography sequence. Actually, you could make a series of photographs to document their varied activities.

Certain days of the week are more exciting than others for crocodile watchers. If you check with the Tropical Rain Forest Keeper, you can find out when the pool is scheduled to be cleaned. As water drains from the pool, the crocodiles generally seek refuge on the land area. Or, you might want to be present at feeding time—this usually stimulates a variety of behaviors.

So, to answer the initial question: yes, they **are** real. And, as we have observed, they move more than you might think **if** you know how to watch them. The Tropical Rain Forest at the World Famous Topeka Zoo truly provides crocodile watching at its best.

Some Thoughts on the Zoo

of Tomorrow . . . Today

Author's note: I presented this paper at the International Union of Directors of Zoological Gardens at their 30th Conference held at the Cheyenne Mountain Zoological Park and the Denver Zoological Gardens in October 1975. It is interesting to note the philosophies and plans for the future of our zoo at that time.

Topekans love their zoo. There can be no doubt about that. Interviews and surveys may confirm it, but all that's really needed to convince anybody is to simply observe Topekans proudly showing their children or guests around the zoo. Ask the public why they like the zoo so well and you could get any number of answers. Many comment on its compact size and how easy it is to see the whole facility without tiring. Others cite the diversity of animal species displayed or mention the fine educational programs. Some like being able to get close to the animals, while others remark about the zoo's neat and clean appearance. Many especially like the pleasant, relaxed, landscaped setting.

In 1966 I was thrilled and excited as we dedicated our Large Mammal Building. I was a comparatively new zoo director and it was my first major exhibit. Although we had a modest budget, the Large Mammal Building was a modern facility that was biologically adequate for animals, workable for keepers, and well accepted by both the visiting public and professional colleagues. In 1976, on its 10th anniversary, this building will be rededicated and renamed "Animals and Man" as part of our new Master Plan. A major graphic will explain how humans are linked with the world of animals.

We are proud of our zoo and its role in the community. And during the last decade we have made some tremendous strides in programs and exhibits, with the Tropical Rain Forest serving as a crowning glory. But despite all of our accomplishments, there remains much that needs to be done—some of it spectacular and appealing, some of it unglamorous but necessary. Our zoo is suffering from growing pains.

We need more adequate utilities and service areas, centralized administration, and expanded educational facilities. We have storm drainage problems, a confusing visitors' traffic pattern, and visual pollution from areas surrounding the zoo. The big cat and bear units are old and outdated, the gorillas and orangutans have outgrown their quarters, and the present Animal Kingdom Building is on borrowed time.

Few zoos can build everything at once, and most zoos continually live with the past as they rebuild and redevelop new facilities by phases. With today's better-educated and more sophisticated visiting public, most zoos are no longer satisfied to show animals in taxonomic groups. Zoos now are developing unique approaches to animal exhibition. One example is the zoogeographic theme in which Australian species are shown in the same area, North American animals are shown in a given area, etc. The Milwaukee County Zoo has expounded upon the predator-prey relationship, where they show African lions in relation to zebras, etc. The Bronx Zoo in New York has demonstrated real pioneering efforts with such innovative exhibits as the World of Darkness and the World of Birds.

The philosophy in zoos today is to reduce the number of animal species and develop a specialized collection. This is easy to say but hard to do. One has full realization of this difficult task when one gets into master planning a zoo. It means that you intentionally are *not* planning on showing some animal species that may have been in your zoo for years—species that frequently are big favorites with the visiting public. As a zoo professional, it seems difficult to give up some of these animals, particularly when your thinking over the years really has not been along these lines. But reality demonstrates it is impossible for a zoo to show all species of animals.

If you consider there are approximately 50,000 species of vertebrates, of which 5,000 are mammals (the most popular and dominant group in the majority of zoos), even the largest of zoos cannot begin to exhibit 500 species, just one-tenth of the mammals. The San Diego Zoo, with two facilities totaling 1,928 acres, a huge staff, wonderful climate, large attendance and a multi-million dollar budget, shows a total of only 280 species of mammals as listed in the current Directory of the American Association of Zoological Parks and Aquariums. And THAT is a BIG collection—undoubtedly one of the largest in the world. With this in mind, it stands to reason that a zoo such as Topeka's cannot begin to expect to show everything. And this has great bearing on the future of our zoo. The zoo of the future should exhibit fewer animals, and select them for the purpose of a unique theme and presentation.

In Topeka we have chosen specialized habitats as the basic theme of our Master Plan for future development. Eight major areas are planned:

Tropical Rain Forest - an existing walk-through facility devoted to a single ecological concept with emphasis upon the Amazon.

Northern Realm - a huge ice cave bridging the Bering Strait to include the frozen northlands of America and Eurasia.

Ngorongoro Crater - exhibited species will be only those found in this collapsed volcano, a microcosm of African wildlife.

Kansas Prairie - representing the vast, undisturbed grasslands of North America as they existed a century ago.

Animal Kingdom - a variety of animal life will compare the similarities and differences of the animal classes in select specialized habitats.

Animals and Man - an existing facility of large mammals redeveloped to reflect the multi-faceted relationship between animals and humans.

Discovering Apes - special emphasis on gorillas and orangutans with visitors walking through simulated habitats and extensive interpretive graphics.

Water Bird Lagoon - this popular group of birds will be shown in a natural setting with numerous islands and various water levels.

These major exhibits will be complemented by an orientation plaza, multimedia-education center, restaurant and gift shop, as well as administration and operational complexes.

Master planning involves some *very tough* decisions. It also forces one to be a visionary. A good master plan probably should cover about a ten-year period. This means that in 1975 you have to visualize and plan for a zoo (some of which might not be built until 1985) that still won't be dated in a decade and will be a progressive zoo. This is a challenging task, especially with limited finances. But it is a necessary task if a zoo is going to live up to its professional obligations.

Our dedicated and loyal visitors have been tolerant of our inadequacies. The Zoo Master Plan charts greater service to the community. The plan is far-reaching and progressive, yet realistic and attainable. And it stresses excellence rather than size. The Zoo Master Plan provides the vehicle by which we can truly live up to our boastful slogan of being "The World Famous Topeka Zoo."

*****

Press release, May 15, 1976

WORLD FAMOUS TOPEKA ZOO
Rededication of the
Large Mammal Building Into
Animals and Man
As part of
ZOO/Tomorrow

The Large Mammal Building dedicated May 22, 1966 was the first major exhibit in the Topeka Zoo. During the last decade nearly two million people have enjoyed and learned from this facility, and the animals therein. An important feature of the building was the Zoo's first classroom.

At long last the Zoo was able to show hippopotamus, elephant, and the first gorillas, giraffes and orangutans in the State of Kansas. Special highlights include 'Peka-Sue, the hesitant hippo; Djakarta Jim, the orangutan artist; Max and Tiffany, gorilla personalities; Sunflower, the first giraffe born in Kansas; and Tembo, the newly-arrived African elephant.

Over the past ten years the building has served the Zoo well as a focal point and nerve center of activity. During that same time Zoo exhibit philosophy in general has advanced at a rapid pace, and the Topeka Zoo in particular has made many forward strides.

In ZOO/Tomorrow, the Master Plan for the Topeka Zoological Park, the Large Mammal Building plays a vital role in the future of the Zoo. Through changes and additions it will develop from a "building" into an "exhibit complex." The function of simply showing large mammals is outmoded, and the entire theme will be redefined, primarily through an interpretative graphics program. To reflect the exhibit's emphasis on the multifaceted relationship between animals and humans, its name will be changed to "Animals and Man."

On the Tenth Anniversary of the Large Mammal Building, May 22, 1976 at 2:00 pm, a rededication into Animals and Man will take place. It will link the past with the future and initiate the implementation of a major aspect of ZOO/Tomorrow. The ceremony will be highlighted by the unveiling of a "super impact" theme graphic. This will redefine the exhibit and set the tone for future development. The new graphic is a gift from the Topeka Friends of the Zoo.

The Mayor, City Commission and Topeka Friends of the Zoo officials from 1966, together with the architect, contractor and others, will be invited to participate with today's City officials and TFOTZ Board in the ceremony. Many of the Topekans who were present at the 1966 dedication may want to relive this historic event. Those who were secondary students then might bring their own children now. It will be a significant and festive occasion.

TOPEKA ZOOLOGICAL PARK
Animals and Man Graphic

Text:

Every living organism plays its role in a dynamic community. Man, one species among a million, is linked with the entire world of animals.

From the beginning of man's existence on the earth, he has had a dependency and interrelationship with other species of the animal world.

These relationships, such as the predator prey cycle, reflect the delicate balance which exists in nature. When this balance is upset or altered in any way, the ripple effect involves many species.

The most severe problem facing the animal world today is the extreme pressure being exerted by the loss of habitat, which threatens an increasing number of species. Increased public awareness and determination to solve this problem are the only hope we have of preserving these complex relationships.

Presidential Appointment

The State Journal

a page of opinion.

Tuesday Evening, November 15, 1977

Truth never yet fell dead in the streets; it has such affinity with the soul of man, the seed however broadcast will catch somewhere and produce its hundredfold. — Theodore Parker, American theologian.

High marks for Topeka Zoo

Gary Clarke's nomination to a new, 15-member National Museum Services Board illustrates not only Clarke's impressive accomplishments in zoology, but also speaks well of the citizen support Clarke has received from Topekans over the years.

Clarke, director of the Topeka Zoo, was nominated last week by President Carter to represent all zoological directors in the nation on the board, which was created by a 1976 law. The board will establish policy for the Institute of Museum Services, founded by the same law.

Specifically, the board will review and pass on institute funding for museums and zoos in a broad spectrum. Funding by the institute includes grants, matching funds and loans. The board will therefore be responsible for the handling of millions of dollars.

Fortunately for Topeka, the board position will allow Clarke to keep his job as zoo director here. Topeka, incidentally, is the smallest city represented on the list of nominees.

Clarke must be given the greatest portion of credit for building Topeka's zoological gardens into what they are today. Topeka's zoo takes a back seat to none in quality of its exhibits and in its educational and recreational value.

That's because Clarke and his staff don't see a zoo as a sideshow or a jail for animals. Exhibits are designed and maintained as much for the animal's comfort and safety as for the zoo visitor's edification.

The Topeka Friends of the Zoo also deserve credit for the help they have given the zoo through the years, particularly in insuring that the zoo has remained a self-supporting enterprise.

Topekans can be proud of Clarke and his singular honor, as much as they can be proud of supporting one of the best zoological parks in the world.

A Matter of Degree

Previously I have alluded to my shoddy academic pursuits. After high school at De La Salle Military Academy in Kansas City, Missouri, I started and sputtered at several institutions, then finally fizzled.

The fall semester of 1956 found me at Rockhurst College in K.C., MO. After two years my grades were mediocre at best. (My English instructor at the time, Mr. Knickerbocker, would be flabbergasted to see this attempt to draft a manuscript.) During my time employed by Midwest Research Institute I attended night classes at the University of Missouri of Kansas City, but did not do well.

Despite all I had learned at the zoo and MRI, a formal education still seemed important to me. I took a bold step in the fall of 1960 and moved to the University of Missouri in Columbia, complete with my new bride and collection of living reptiles. I was active on campus (and in the community) and associated mostly with graduate zoology students—but I did not study. It took only two semesters to flunk out—the low ebb of my academic career. Maybe a university degree was not for me.

So, in the spring of 1961, with a new baby and no money, I limped back to Kansas City and returned to the zoo full time. My zoo career flourished at Kansas City, Fort Worth, and Topeka, with college the furthest thing from my mind.

I did, however, frequent the University of Kansas in Lawrence, particularly the Museum of National History. One evening, in the mid-1970's, I attended a lecture about the Galapagos Islands. While waiting for it to start, I thumbed through a schedule of classes. Much to my surprise, I found a Department of African Studies listed. One of the courses offered was "Independent Field Study." That sounded intriguing!

Within a week I had met with the Chairman (a scholarly Nigerian) and learned there were no formal classes; rather, the student submitted a proposal for a study project in Africa and, if approved, wrote a paper due by the end of the semester. It would be the basis for the final grade, and I could earn from one to six credit hours, depending on the complexity of the project and the length of the paper. I qualified as a "special student" and signed on!

My topic addressed the impact of western civilization on the traditional cultures of East Africa, and I conducted the field work on my next safari. I decided to go for six hours credit, and that required an enormous amount of research and literature references. It was work . . . but it was rewarding. I finished just a few hours before the deadline and, regardless of what grade I might receive, I had a sense of accomplishment.

And I got an A!

That prompted me to audit some night classes at Washburn University in Topeka, particularly in subjects that interested me: geography, anthropology, psychology, and Kansas history. Several faculty members (Terry Booth, Jim Byrnes) said, "Why just audit? Why not go for credit that could apply toward a degree?"

Hmmm . . . I had not thought of that, but why not?

Suddenly I was a student again, and this time a serious one. The faculty said not to waste my time with zoology courses or public speaking—tackle some new areas. That was good advice.

My duties as zoo director usually extended beyond the standard workday, so I had to make some adjustments with regard to evening meetings, volunteer activities, etc. Then another unexpected situation pressured me into an accelerated schedule: my oldest daughter was a senior in high school and planned to attend Washburn University the next year. In no uncertain terms she wanted me *out* of Washburn before she started as she would be embarrassed to end up in a class with her dad!

So, despite working full time and with four teenagers in the family, I took 15 credit hours a semester, with classes on weeknights from 5:10 pm to 9:40 pm and on Saturdays from 8:00 am to noon.

At 40 years of age I graduated in the class of 1979 (much to the relief of my daughter), earning a Bachelor of Arts degree in sociology with a concentration in anthropology and a minor in psychology.

All of my children attended Washburn, and one year all four were there at the same time. When I received a request from the university president to contribute to a fund raising campaign, I replied that I currently was paying tuition for four full-time students—a senior, a junior, a sophomore, and a freshman—and that was about all I could do. He understood.

I am proud to be a graduate of Washburn University—it's a matter of degree.

Part 5

Beware of Low-leaping Kangaroos

A bit of Zoology, with stories of wild animals in and out of the zoo. And a bit of Peopleology, with stories of famous personalities in and out of the zoo.

The Zoo is a weird, wonderful, exciting, frustrating, glorious, rewarding, disheartening, beautiful place to work.

—Theodore H. "Ted" Reed
Director Emeritus
National Zoological Park
Washington, D.C.

ZOO
TOPEKA · KANSAS

Art work by Alice C. Sabatini

Part 5

Beware of Low-leaping Kangaroos

The Care and Feeding of a Necktie Zoo

We all know what happens when two women appear at a social gathering unexpectedly wearing identical dresses. But what about two zoo or aquarium directors who show up wearing the same animal-design neckties?

In December 1982 I moderated the first World Symposium on the Future of Zoos, sponsored by the Indianapolis Zoological Society. Two members of the distinguished panel—John Knowles, director of the Marwell Zoological Park in Great Britain, and Murray Newman, director of the Vancouver Public Aquarium in British Columbia—entered the room together wearing identical musk ox neckties designed by Calgary zoo director, Peter Karsten. When this faux pas was pointed out, they complimented each other on their impeccable taste.

Zoo people are notorious for festooning themselves with clothes and jewelry related to wildlife, though the items are not actually made of skins, horns, or the like. At professional conferences you might spot rings, bracelets, tie tacks, cuff links, earrings, and lapel pins fraught with furry, feathery, or scaly motifs. Apparel with animal prints includes ladies' skirts, blouses, raincoats, and purses, and, of course, gentlemen's neckties. I dare say that most zoo directors have an assortment of animal neckties, but all have a few *cravates ordinaires* in their wardrobes. I am no exception. When I want to travel incognito I choose a subdued paisley rather than a tie with dancing pink elephants.

My tie menagerie has mushroomed with time, enlarged not by personal purchases but by gifts from friends and relatives aware of my grand animal passion, and it expands by leaps and bounds during the holiday season.

Many zoos choose a particular animal to symbolize their institution—a logo that surfaces on "designer" ties. I've collected many of these specialties from colleagues, and I always wear them with pride—from the St. Louis Zoo's stylized kudu to the Buffalo Zoo's buffalo.

Some of my favorites have migrated into my closet from Africa and depict the prominent large mammals of that continent in clever designs. One, from Hwange Safari Lodge in Zimbabwe, excels in its sheer elegance: a solitary silvery blue elephant stands in the center of a solid blue "plain." It manages to coexist peacefully with other members of Africa's Big Five which grace my collection: lion, Cape buffalo, rhino, and leopard—collectively considered the most dangerous by hunters. On a trip to Africa I wore my rhino tie to a meeting with an official of the Zimbabwe Game and Conservation Department, who wore a department waterbuck tie. We cast covetous glances at each other's neck pieces and, before you could say "duck soup" we had negotiated an agreement, untied our knots, and traded on the spot! So much for standing on ceremony. (Consider the possibilities for international relations if only ties were designed to be swapped by heads of state.)

"Novelty" is an apt description for many ties on my rack. The Miami Zoo's veterinarian—who has a fondness for sharks—contributed a gaping toothy specimen, which has been dubbed Jaws. A ferocious Bengal tiger leaps out at you from another, making me look like a walking billboard for the Ringling Brothers Barnum & Bailey Circus. (Many of my colleagues insist that I am able to achieve this effect without wearing a tie of any sort.) My rack is also bursting with gaudy ties bedecked with strange and wonderful animals and plants—my rainforest collection. I own ties with little green frogs and purple polka-dotted monkeys, and one with what look like paper-doll mice hooked together.

I would be remiss not to mention the rest of my elephant herd. I have three elephant ties with the same pattern in different color combinations. I have to make a disclaimer whenever I wear one to assure people that it simply reflects my fondness for pachyderms and is not a political statement. Maybe someday a donkey will trot its way into my wardrobe—provided it doesn't balk at elephants for companions.

An endangered species is the only way to categorize my most prized tie possession, as there are only 50 known to exist in the world. It features the caterpillar of the gypsy moth and has quite a story . . .

Wildlife author Roger Caras broadcasted regularly on nationwide television and radio. One September he was taking a nighttime trip into the Connecticut woods with Noble Procter, an ornithologist who specialized in owls. Roger was hosting the radio show and, with a special call, Noble would summon owls and talk to them as they perched on branches overhead. He could even imitate a dying animal, which helped attract these birds of prey.

In the course of the evening, Roger detected a noise in the forest that resembled gently falling rain, a sound Noble identified as frassing. Frassing occurs only during a gypsy moth infestation, when thousands of gypsy moth caterpillars excrete en masse onto the tree leaves.

Roger later wrote a radio script about his experience with frassing, pointing out that we generally do not pick up such natural noises because we are not listening to the sounds of life. In fact, some people may go through life without ever hearing frassing.

There happened to be a Peter Frasse Company on Long Island, New York that dealt with heavy industrial materials. The company president heard Roger's broadcast and wrote to him requesting a copy of the script. The man was so intrigued he special ordered a limited edition of 50 custom-made gypsy moth caterpillar neckties to give to his best customers. Roger ended up with two of the ties.

The first time I saw him wearing one was at the 1982 World Symposium on the Future of Zoos. I was most impressed, not only because of its rich blue color and distinctive red-and-yellow caterpillar, but because it was one of the few insect ties I had ever seen and the only one I'd come across featuring a caterpillar! I told him how much I would like to add it to my collection. He confided that originally he had had two, but William Conway, general director of the New York Zoological Society, had already appropriated one.

Several months later I dined with Roger in New York City. He was again wearing his frassing tie. As we sat down he whispered, "Don't worry, Gary, before this evening ends I will be tie-less." And yes, as we left he whipped off his cravat and presented it to me. Quite a sacrifice!

I've had a few close calls with my animal neckties—beyond the traditional drop of gravy that seems to wind up on most. I was wearing "koalas" one summer day when I stopped at a self-service gas station. As I pulled the nozzle from the tank some gasoline spilled and the wind blew my tie right into its path. OMIGOSH! The gas reacted with the material, instantly turning the lower half of my gold-and-brown tie purplish black. I quickly jumped into my car and raced to the cleaners.

They applied first aid, assuring me they'd do what they could. Several days later my koalas came home in nearly perfect condition. If light hits the tie just right you can see that the creatures on the lower half have lost a tinge of color around the edges; otherwise, the koalas' attempt to get "tanked up" left them unscathed. WHEW!

Every animal collection is an exercise in care and management, and my necktie zoo is no exception. To care for my charges, I have a tie clip in the form of a miniature shovel. I'm the envy of my colleagues because I must have been the only zoo director in the country with such a shovel for cleaning up. As for feeding, I periodically offer the animals small portions of hot fudge or that special sauce that drips out of a Big Mac.

This evening I am scheduled to go to a rather important social function, so I better wrap this up, go home . . . and tie one on.

One of Those Days!

There's an old saying that goes, "When it rains, it pours." This is true not only for salt, but also in zoobiz. Here is an example.

The day starts when the elephant and giraffe keeper calls to say his wife has had a baby and he can't make it in today. The assistant director has a scheduled day off, the general curator's position is vacant, and the secretary has taken a long-planned vacation day for a school activity. So, my immediate task is to juggle the schedule to see that all areas of the zoo are covered.

The Animal Kingdom Building keeper can fill in for the elephant and giraffe keeper, and the keeper trainee can work the Animal Kingdom Building. However, the groundskeeper then has to assume some of the keeper trainee's duties, and no one is left to clean the public restrooms. I'll have to do that.

On my way out the door the phone rings (I'm answering phones today, too), and it is an animal transporter who says he'll be at our zoo soon to load up a male wildebeest and a male eland antelope scheduled to move to another zoo. Geeze, now we'll have to make preparations for that and we're already shorthanded.

The weather is beautiful and the zoo is filled with thousands of elementary school students from all over the state who have come to the zoo for their annual spring field trip. Several times during their visit they descend upon the refreshment stand to refuel themselves with hot dogs, cotton candy, popcorn, and you name it. Unfortunately, because of local university and high school final exams, we have no student help in the stand except for one temporary part-time person. The food service manager comes in to help out, and I'll try to stop by if I get a chance.

Unfortunately, I don't think I'll be able to help out as the Dallas Zoo just called and at this very moment they are waiting at the south tollgate of the Kansas Turnpike with a male giraffe in a crate destined for our Forbes Field Conservation/Propagation Center. Well, there goes the assistant director's day off and he immediately heads for the Turnpike to meet them. The maintenance man and head keeper prepare all the necessary equipment that will be needed to unload the giraffe, and they leave the zoo for Forbes.

In the meantime, I am working the base station of our two-way radio system and taking the morning call-in reports from the keepers throughout the zoo. One of them calls and says that our female eland has just delivered a baby. About that time, a lady in rural North Topeka calls and says there is a rattlesnake in her basement, and would I please come out and catch it?

I look at my watch and it is only 9:15 am. I can tell it's going to be one of those days.

Such is the curse—no, the blessing—of being the director of a modest sized zoo.

Warning above the office door of Zoo Director, Gary K. Clarke

Zoo Artist: Alice Sabatini

A longtime feature of *Reader's Digest* was "The Most Unforgettable Character I've Ever Met." If they had retitled that to "The Most Gracious Lady I've Ever Known," then the late Alice Sabatini would have won hands down. And a "wish list" idea of mine led not only to a continuing friendship with Alice and her family, but an enhanced association with our Topeka Zoo that spanned more than two decades.

All of the "big" zoos issued posters, and I felt it was important for us to do so as well, even if we were just "a little guy." Zoos had posters to commemorate special events, for awareness and promotion, and to add an artistic dimension.

I researched the philosophy and basic principles of posters, which was fascinating in and of itself. A poster should be understood at a glance and combine immediate visual effectiveness with concise communication; it has to compete for attention in confusing surroundings yet give a direct message to the viewer.

Successful poster design is quite a challenge and not every artist could combine the qualities of interest, understanding and ability all in one. A special artist was needed with unique talents, one who was willing to contribute his or her talents (and necessary time) to the zoo, as this poster project was not a budgeted item.

Enter Mary Hall, who was the first secretary of the Topeka Friends of the Zoo (TFOTZ) in 1964 and editor of the *Bear Facts* newsletter from 1965 to 1969. Mary and Alice Sabatini were friends of long standing, and Mary knew that Alice loved the zoo and felt she would be the ideal artist. Mary was right. She introduced us and Alice and I immediately were on a common wavelength. (Mary called it "imaginative understanding and intelligent interest.") We agreed the poster should have emphasis on animals, reflect the dignity of the zoo, be directed at all age levels, be eye-catching, and be instantly recognizable.

Alice made preliminary sketches of several species (llama, gorilla, eagle, elk) but I was immediately struck by the impact of her baboon sketch. I felt it vividly expressed the intangibles of a fascinating animal. She then refined it and decided a line drawing would be more effective and come across stronger than a gouache or dry brush. Alice had such insight into the project and commented, "A poster *has* to be functional—a painting does not; but a poster should be more than just functional. If it does what it's supposed to do, and still continues to seem 'fresh' each time I look at it, then I'm pleased."

But after Alice finished her pen and ink artwork, we still needed to complete the project, and once again the Topeka community was most generous. Mainline Printing made the negative; Midwestern Paper Co. furnished the paper; Victory Life Insurance Co. made the plate and did the printing; Capitol City, Inc. donated the mailing tubes; TFOTZ paid the postage for worldwide distribution to other zoos; and Mary Hall documented all of this for posterity (thanks, Mary). A great example of a "wish list" item fulfilled at no cost to the zoo!

The first poster for our zoo was issued in 1969 and I never tire of viewing that classic baboon image. Over the years it has grown on me and I find it just as intriguing now as I did the first time I saw it.

More importantly, the reaction of the zoo world at the time was most gratifying. Here are a few excerpts from letters I received.

Cincinnati Zoo: " . . . your poster is excellent. It will be included in the International Zoo Poster Exhibition being shipped to zoos across the nation. You do have the greatest knack in the world for getting things done at absolutely no cost!"

Cheyenne Mountain Zoo: "We congratulate you on your first poster. It demonstrates what can be done with limited funds substituted by professional stimulus and considerable enthusiasm. It is a well done poster and we pay homage to its originators."

Milwaukee Zoo: "Thanks for your new zoo poster. You are certainly to be congratulated on your interest in the various phases of your zoological park as it affects the community."

Oklahoma City Zoo: "I was delighted to receive your poster. As usual, Topeka is making excellent progress."

Phoenix Zoo: "I think your poster is most attractive and good public relations for your zoo."

Lincoln Zoo, Nebraska: "Thank you for allowing us to be among the first recipients of your new zoo poster. It is just great! It follows the modern concepts of art and shows your thinking and approach to zoo management."

Barcelona Zoo, Spain: "We received the poster of your zoo. We congratulate you very sincerely for the selection of the theme and for the originality of your interpretation."

This unique poster led to a series of artistic endeavors by Alice for the zoo. Many are featured in this book and I am grateful to the Sabatini family for permission to use them. Her work enhances the quality of my efforts, just as it added a special dimension to our zoo.

While certainly she was Alice Sabatini: Zoo Artist, of greater significance is that she was the most gracious lady I've ever known. A lasting tribute may be found in the collection of her work at the Alice C. Sabatini Art Gallery at the Topeka and Shawnee County Public Library, Topeka, Kansas.

The Snake That "Plays Possum"

Date: *22 April 1961*
Time: *1035 hours*
Location: *Roman Nose State Park, Blaine County, Oklahoma.*
Conditions: *Mild weather; sun shining, sky partly cloudy; periodic gusts of wind; temperature in the 60's F*
Activity: *Slowly cruising in jeep while observing, recording, and photographing wildlife*

Stopped for an adult Eastern hognose snake (Heterdon platyrhinos) AOR (alive on road), approximately 30 inches long. Stepped out of jeep with camera in hand to photograph specimen, which had crawled off to the side of the road and was lying coiled flat on the ground. As soon as I took the first picture, the snake started hissing, and spread the skin on the neck until it was quite flat. It then struck at me several times but with its mouth closed. As all of these tactics failed to frighten me off, it then went into its "death act."

The snake started writhing and twisting as if it were in terrible agony. It reminded me of a snake I had once seen run over by a car in front of me. And then it went into, apparently, the final throes of death, and slowly turned completely on its back, with mouth open and tongue extended.

I watched it for several minutes, and there were no visible signs of life. I touched it, and got no response. Finally, I picked the snake up by the tail and carried it around; it dangled completely limp by my side. But, when I placed it back down on the ground on its belly, it immediately flipped over onto its back into the "dead" position.

These notes were taken from my field journal, and record my first observation of the letisimulation (or "death-feigning") phase of the defensive behavior in hog nose snakes. Death-feigning is the most spectacular aspect of the stereotypical defensive behavior of this species, but there are actually three phases that a hognose snake may go through in response to the presence of a person, or predator.

The first of these is the attempted escape, or retreat phase. As my jeep approached, the snake was already in this phase and it was crawling by utilizing wide convulsive loops of the body. Sometimes a specimen will attempt to "freeze" and depend upon its protective coloration to blend in with the background. I did not observe this particular behavior and, of course, the snake was quite obvious in the middle of a blacktop road.

Next is the threatening phase that can be subdivided into several behavior components. "Spreading-neck" is a bluffing posture and occurred after I took my first picture and the snake spread the skin on each side of its neck. Well developed ribs on the anterior body are extended to accomplish this posture. The snake was hissing loudly as it was filling its lungs and expelling air to alternately swell and narrow the entire body. The second component was not demonstrated by this specimen, but it is known as "concealing head" with the head concealed under a part of its body or its coiled tail. The third component of the threatening phase, that of "pseudo-strikes," was quite obvious. If all of the above fail to scare or discourage a person, then the snake pulls out all stops and goes into the most dramatic of all behaviors—death-feigning or letisimulation. In addition to the behavior exhibited by the specimen I observed, hognose snakes may regurgitate and/or defecate and possibly produce a secretion from the anal musk gland. The ultimate behavioral response would seem to be the ability of the snake to have the mucous membrane that lines the mouth hemorrhage and cause the mouth to become bloody.

How do herpetologists explain this behavior? Dr. Dwight R. Platt conducted an extensive study of the natural history of hognose snakes which was printed in the University of Kansas Publications, Museum of Natural History, Vol. 18, No. 4, July 7, 1969. There seems to be both a physiological basis and an adaptive value. The movement of a relatively large object apparently is the stimulus that initiates defensive behavior in hognose snakes. The escape and threatening phases evidently are instinctive, based on responses predominantly in the central nervous system. Death-feigning is primarily a nervous response initiated by a higher level of fear or flight tendency than the other phases of defensive behavior. The snake faints, and temporarily loses consciousness.

In addition to humans, both domestic and wild ungulates (hoofed animals) kill hognose snakes. Very little is recorded in the literature of the response of predators to the defensive behavior of hognose snakes, so the interpretation of the adaptive value of this behavior is speculative at this point. However, if just a few more snakes survive because of this defensive behavior, adaptively it will be maintained. The snake appears larger and more aggressive in the spreading-neck posture. The pseudo-strike probably discourages and may postpone an actual attack by a predator. Death-feigning is the most mysterious of all, and an adequate explanation has not been agreed upon by herpetologists. However. I subscribe to the theory that an animal may be left for dead by a predator, either man or animal, and afterwards escape. In spite of all we DO know, there is more that we DON'T know about the snake that "plays possum."

And Now the Gnus, Weather & Sports

Dateline: Topeka, KS (ZPW) i.e., Zoo Press Worldwide.
The scene: any of the local newsrooms in Topeka (newspaper, radio, television).
The caller: the local zoo director.
The callees: any of the reporters at the desk in the local newsrooms.
The dialogue:
Rrrriiiiinnnnnggggg!

"Newsroom."

"This is Gary Clarke at the Topeka Zoo."

"Yes."

"We have a gnus—'Bulletin'."

"A news bulletin?"

"Yes."

"What is it?"

"It's a new gnu."

"What the heck is a noo-noo?"

"Well, you know the gnus—Weather and Sports?"

"Yes, we report them all the time—that's our job."

"No, no—I mean the African antelopes called wildebeests that are also known as gnus—and sometimes called the crossword puzzle animals."

"Oh, yeah."

"Well, our adult gnus, Weather and Sports, had a bulletin. . . ah, er, I mean a baby. . . that we have named Bulletin. Get it?" (Note: various reactions by local reporters at this point; the printable ones follow.)

a) "Oh, geeze Clarke, I should've known."

b) "Hey, wow! That's really cool!"

c) "Well, maybe we can do something with it."

d) "I feel like Abbott and Costello doing 'Who's on First'."

e) "I still don't get it."

"This is the first baby gnu to be born in our Zoo, and I thought it was a 'gnus-worthy' event." Groan.

"We thought of naming it 'Six O'Clock' gnus or something like that. If it had been premature, we could have called it 'Early Gnus'."

"Sigh . . ."

"Anyway, its parents were born at the Fort Worth Zoo and arrived two years ago. The male baby, Bulletin, is their first offspring."

I went on to explain that someone once dubbed gnus the "clown princes of the plains". This phrase is very descriptive of the way these animals run in their native East African habitat. During migration periods when they move from the Ngorongoro Conservation Area and Serengeti National Park in Tanzania to the Maasai Mara Game Reserve, literally thousands of gnus can be seen across the horizon. When they are galloping (or galluping, as I call it) in great herds, displaying their peculiar gait with long beards flowing in the wind, they truly do remind one of clowns. But their abrupt stops and synchronous wheeling (sudden turns) as they are running add to their comical appearance. While fun to watch, their speed and synchronous wheeling when a predator is nearby are vital to their survival. This same behavior occurs at the zoo each morning when the gnus are released from their nighttime quarters in the barn into their outside yard—even though no predators are around.

By now the reporters complained that I had given them more gnus than they wanted, and they called a halt.

Reporter overheard to switchboard: "From now on, when the zoo calls, no gnus is good news!"

The Gnus of the Day

By Charles Osgood

Charles Osgood is a radio and television commentator. He has broadcast daily on CBS Radio Network since 1971.

Script from Newsbreak, CBS Radio Network
Broadcast Nationwide on
Labor Day, September 4, 1978
Courtesy of WIBW AM, Topeka, KS

The Topeka, Kansas zoo has a brand-new baby Gnu,
The Zoo Director happily reports.
Bulletin's the baby's name, which is something of a game,
Since the parents' names are Weather, yes, and Sports.

We will be back with what is new with this latest breaking Gnus
And the news behind the news that may be in it.
First, a moment we must take for this commercial break.
We'll have Weather, Sports and Gnus in just a minute.

Though we realize full well
That the "G," with which you spell Gnu,
Is not supposed to be pronounced,
We'll pronounce the silent "G," do it purposely, you see,
As the birth of a new Gnu we here announce.

For when one announces Gnus, while delivering the News,
It can be a bit confusing now and then.
For a Gnu is but a Gnu, even when the Gnu is new,
While news is who and what, where, why, and when.

In Topeka, at the Zoo, they had not one Gnu but two.
And Sports was one, and Weather was the other.
And the Gnus is good, not bad, that Sports is now a dad,
And Weather's happy now that she's a mother.

The Director of the park is a man named Gary Clarke.
He's the one you'll find there passing out cigars.
For a little baby Gnu is quite welcome at the Zoo
And is likely to become one of the stars.

It was Friday of last week that the birth, of which we speak,
Occurred there at Topeka's city zoo.
And the Gnu, who is known as Sports, had a new Gnu to report.
There were three Gnus now, instead of just the two.

Little Bulletin is short, so you'd expect a short report,
And his little tail is white as driven snow.
Gnus are antelopes, of course, rather smaller than a horse,
All of which, I'm sure, you folks already know.

Sports and Weather, from Fort Worth, that's the city of their birth,
Aren't rare Gnus, unusual to speak of,
Common Gnus, to speak the truth, so while still within their youth,
They were shipped from Fort Worth over to Topeka.

There were no Gnus over there, so they bought the Fort Worth pair,
And they studied until they really understood Gnus.
They were glad to make the space, for it's surely not the case,
No, it's not the case, that no Gnus is good news.

Now, Topeka's baby Gnu does what all new Gnus must do,
It stays very close to Weather, every second.
And the papa Gnu named Sports,
Is quite proud, by all reports,
Though I do not know how Gnu pride can be reckoned.

So Bulletin, the Gnu, welcome there! How do you do?
And may I pass along some good advice?
You will find this to be true, be you any kind of Gnu.
It pays to be polite and to be Gnice.

Very often, we may say, on a Monday holiday,
There's very little news out on the street.
But to pay the proper dues at delivering the Gnus,
A female Gnu can simply not be beat.

And Gnow this message.

The Ooooo-Aahhh Bird

I have a nickname for the ostrich: the "oooo-aahhh" bird. Because when the female ostrich lays the world's largest egg, she reportedly goes "oooo-aahhh." And there's the story about the boy ostriches chasing the girl ostriches across the desert. When the girls hid their heads in the sand, the boys said, "Where'd they go?"

Both of these stories indicate the superficial vein with which the ostrich is often regarded. This image is perpetrated by various cartoon characters and such motion pictures as "HATARI" with its famous scene of adult ostriches chasing people all over the animal compound to the tune of "Your Father's Feathers." But let's take a look at the ostrich as it really is.

There are six geographical races of ostrich, all members of a single species. They differ from one another slightly in size and in skin color of the bare thighs, head and neck. The size and texture of the eggs differs with each geographical race, and an expert could probably identify the race just by the eggs. The eggs vary from white to yellowish, and their hard shiny surface is pitted with superficial pores of different sizes and shapes.

Even though it is the largest egg in the world (measuring six to eight inches long and weighing up to three pounds), the ostrich egg is nearly the smallest in relation to the body size of the bird laying it, being about one percent of the adult female's body weight.

Frequently I use a drained ostrich egg shell in lectures and demonstrations. Many people will not accept the fact that it is real because it looks so much like fine porcelain. They often ask, "Where did you get it?" We reply that we acquire them directly from the manufacturer—there is no middleman involved. One of the drained shells in my collection is neatly lettered: "EGGSTRA BIG."

A female ostrich lays from 10 to 12 eggs in a large depression scraped out in the sand to form a nest. Several females may lay their eggs in a common nest, numbering up to 25 or 30 thirty eggs. Incubation is primarily performed by the male, who sits on the eggs every night. The female incubates during the day, as her dull colors afford better protection. The sun also helps keep the eggs warm.

After 40 to 42 days the young chicks hatch, already a foot tall. They are soon able to travel with their parents and will grow a foot a month until they reach five or six feet when the growth rate slows down. In three or four years they will mature, at which time they may reach eight feet in height and weigh up to 345 pounds.

Young chicks, when threatened with danger, will stretch out flat on the ground, necks extended, and feign death. This behavior probably gave rise to the myth that ostriches bury their heads in the sand to hide from danger.

Five fossil species of ostriches are known, the oldest dating back about 50 to 60 million years (the early Tertiary Period). These ancient birds lived as far north as the Mongolian deserts and occupied southern Europe and Asia as well as Africa. Until recently ostriches ranged from the Arabian and Sahara deserts southward throughout Africa. Today most wild birds survive only in the protected national parks of Africa.

Ostriches may travel in bands of ten to fifty birds and live in open, arid country. Their exceptional height allows them to share a mutual alliance with such large grazing mammals as zebras, gnus and antelopes. These browsing animals stir up food items for the ostriches (insects, rodents and small reptiles) while the giant birds keep an eye out for approaching danger. They also eat fruits, plants and seeds. Ostriches, as with the other ratites (rhea, emu, cassowary and kiwi), lost their power of flight many millions of years ago. Although they all probably descended from birds that once flew (including the fossil elephant birds of Madagascar and the New Zealand moas), they are now too heavy-bodied in proportion to their rudimentary wings to fly. However, they still retain the necessary characteristic that enables birds to fly—hollow bones.

Alert and shy, ostriches have some fighting ability, but depend mainly on their speed to escape their many predators. They can run over 30 miles per hour and change direction with amazing agility. When pressured, they can be quite dangerous, kicking out and down with powerful legs. Their heavy toenails can slash a lion or a man wide open.

Ostriches do well in captivity and have been known to live about 50 years. They are untrustworthy and, because of their large size, can be dangerous to work with. A loud hiss and a booming roar comprise the voice of the ostrich.

The ostrich claims a unique distinction, particularly for a bird. It has the largest eye of any animal in proportion to the size of its head. The eyes of diurnal birds can produce a sharper picture over a broader area than human eyes. In fact, if birds could read, it is believed they could read this entire page without once shifting their eyes. An ostrich can see clearly for 100 yards in open country.

Such an amazing creature. Next time you see one you can "ooooo" and "aahhh" over this amazing bird.

Straight From the Horse's Mouth

World Conference III on Breeding Endangered Species in Captivity was held in San Diego in November 1979. Immediately after this conference a special meeting was held for North American Breeders of the Przewalski horse. A great spirit of cooperation clearly prevailed among Przewalski horse breeders in North America.

Our zoo was unique in that we were a repository for this species from two other zoos. The Chicago Zoological Park in Brookfield, IL, had loaned us the stallion Rolf, who was born in Munich, Germany and was the oldest known Przewalski horse in the world. Also on loan from Brookfield was the mare Colleen, born May 16, 1973. The Memphis Zoological Garden had placed the stallion Rolmar on breeding loan to us. He was born at the Catskill Game Farm in New York state on August 20, 1973. Rolmar and Colleen produced their first youngster Rococo (a male), in our zoo on May 8, 1978.

Several days after the Przewalski horse meeting, Jan and Inge Bouman from the Foundation for the Preservation and Protection of the Przewalski Horse, which was based in the Netherlands, visited Topeka specifically to see our horses and facilities. Founded on March 21, 1977, one of the main functions of the Foundation was to administer and keep up to date a system of information on all Przewalski horses, living and deceased. This provided for basic management of the Przewalski horse in captivity, and was based on data and elaborations from the International Studbook maintained by the Prague Zoological Gardens.

We had made preparations for the Bouman's visit and were looking forward to their arrival on Thanksgiving Day. Not only could they see the horses and our zoo for the first time, but they could join with us in celebrating a uniquely American holiday. Prior to visiting Topeka they had a scheduled stop in Colorado. The first real blizzard of the season swept through the Rockies the Tuesday before Thanksgiving. In checking the national weather maps I was concerned that airports might be closed and commercial flights cancelled.

My home phone rang on Wednesday evening and the voice on the line said, "This is a fixed wing aircraft pilot and I am now over Salina, Kansas and I have the Boumans on board. We are scheduled to arrive at Forbes Field in 30 minutes. Can you meet them?" Imagine my surprise upon receiving a call at home from an airplane! I rushed to the airport and the Boumans were waiting when I arrived.

The Boumans filmed Rolf at the zoo since he was a noteworthy animal. However, they were even more impressed with the zoo's Conservation/Propagation Center located off-site at Forbes Field south of Topeka, and the large two-acre paddock where we had moved our breeding pair, Rolmar and Colleen.

Our weather through November had been glorious—clear skies, bright sun and warm temperatures. On Thanksgiving the winter storm from the west moved in and the weather was horrendous. The Boumans took it in stride although I wish they could have seen our zoo under better conditions. While we were at the zoo's Conservation/Propagation Center the wind swept across the prairie and made us feel like we were in Mongolia—which was perfect for the horses. Despite the adverse weather conditions, the Boumans carried on with their work of filming all of our horses (both movies and still photos) and documenting the facilities. Later that afternoon we treated them to our traditional Thanksgiving dinner. We talked turkey and Przewalski horses.

Of Olifonts and Loxodonts

If you think this is about elephants, you're wrong.

Ever since Tembo, our African elephant, arrived in 1976 and zoo visitors could visually compare her with Sunda, our Asian elephant, the most frequent comment made to me has been, "Gee . . . I never realized there was such a *difference* in elephants."

This usually prompts the following conversation:

"Did you know that an African elephant actually isn't an elephant?"

"It isn't?"

"For that matter, an Asian elephant might not be considered an elephant either."

"Really?"

Well, then—what is this creature we've always called an "elephant"?

It's not what it appears to be, and reminds me of the old oriental fable of the six blind men who, invited to feel an elephant, described it as a wall, a fan, a tree, a snake, a spear, and a rope, depending on which part of the elephant each one touched.

The word 'elephant' includes two quite different living animal species, inhabiting different continents, and varying considerably in size and appearance. They also show vast differences in behavior and psychology.

That most impressive and awesome of animals, the African bush elephant, is also the largest of the living land mammals. Males will average 10 to 11 feet in height (with the record being 13'2") and weigh up to 12,000 pounds. Females average 8 feet and weigh over 6,000 pounds. Both sexes have tusks. The famed Jumbo of London Zoo and Barnum Circus fame was a male African elephant.

Male Asian elephants average 9 to 10 feet at the shoulder and may weigh 10,000 pounds. Females, which do not have tusks (but do have small tushes), average 7½ feet in height with a weight of over 7,000 pounds.

Characteristic of the African elephant are huge, flapping ears, sloped forehead, swayback and two finger-like projections at the tip of the trunk. The Asian elephant is distinguished by its proportionately smaller ears, bulbous head, high-ridged back, and only a single finger-like projection on the end of the trunk.

So much for the physical differences; now to the heart of the matter. And I must agree with zoo visitors' observations on African and Asian elephants—there *is* quite a difference, but it's more than just physical.

During the past 60 million years a bizarre group of more than 300 trunk-bearing mammals flourished and spread over the land surface of the globe. Today the only two survivors are the Asian elephant *(Elephas maximus)* and the African bush elephant *(Loxodonta africana*)*. Please note that these animals are not only a separate species, but also are in a different genus. The genus name *Loxodonta* means "slanting-toothed ones."

Proboscidea is the name of the natural group, or scientific order, to which all the elephants of the world belong, both the extinct and living species. The name *Proboscidea* is derived from the lengthened nasal appendage, or proboscis, which is commonly called a trunk and is the elephant's main distinguishing feature.

The late Ernest P. Walker, in his monumental work *Mammals of the World,* refers to elephants as "proboscideans." This sounds logical until one takes into consideration that a number of other mammals with long snouts may also qualify for the term, though certainly to a much lesser degree. Examples that readily come to mind include elephant seals (wonder how they got that name?), proboscis monkeys, tapirs, and certain small insectivores (elephant shrews). Thus, in my opinion, the term cannot be restricted simply to elephants, and we have to come up with something else.

At this point I would like to emphasize that not all zoologists agree with what I am about to relate (and some may not care).

In 1955 the late Ivan T. Sanderson, well known naturalist, lecturer, and natural history writer, published a beautiful book entitled *Living Mammals of the World.* In the section on elephants he refers to the African animal as the African Loxodon, or sometimes just Loxodons, a derivation of the scientific genus. (Note the absence of the letters *t* or *a* on the end of the word.) He never explains why he uses the term—he simply uses it. In the successive years with hundreds of published elephant references since, it has not become common (or possibly not accepted) terminology in the literature, or anywhere else for that matter. But it makes sense to me, and I'd like you to know why.

Sanderson expounded on his elephant terminology in a volume entitled *The Dynasty of Abu* published in 1962. Abu is his name for the entire kingdom of the elephantines, living or extinct. He goes into great detail on his search for an appropriate term, how he found it in Dr. Wallace Budge's *Dictionary of Ancient Egyptian Hieroglyphics,* and why it is significant for this purpose. So Abu is his general word for *all* elephants, but he does not use it in a specific sense, such as the Asian Abu or the African Abu.

In an attempt to explain why Asian elephants and African elephants should not be called elephants, Sanderson resorts to a sort of analogy. He says that although both Cadillacs and Volkswagens are generally considered motorcars, few would insist they are of the same specific class. Yet if we were asked to define the differences, we might find it difficult to explain unless we were mechanics or engineers.

Sanderson then relates that since Asian and African elephants once had a common origin long ago, we cannot begin to define them until we learn more about that common ancestor. He laments that, in the meantime, we are stuck with the word "elephant," just as we are with "motor-car," and he doesn't think we can do anything about it. And then, in a bit of wishful thinking, he declares: 'Would that the old spelling for one could be revived —namely, "olifonts" for those pachydermatous creatures that to-day inhabit the Oriental Region of Asia; and that the scientists' term, "loxodonts," could be adopted for the somewhat similar-appearing creatures of Africa'.

So there you have it. On your next zoo visit you can see for yourself—Sunda, our Asian Olifont, and Tembo, our African Loxodont. And won't you have fun explaining this to friends and relatives! Asian elephants, African elephants, olifonts, proboscideans, pachyderms, or just plain whatever they be and whatever you call them—still glorious, dignified and royal.

*Recently the African forest elephant has been classified as a separate species (*Loxodonta cyclotis*).

Welcome Joan Embery

Joan Embery, Goodwill Ambassador from the San Diego Zoo and Wild Animal Park, visited the Capital City of Kansas and the World Famous Topeka Zoo on February 27, 1980. She came under the sponsorship of the Topeka Friends of the Zoo for a special membership program arranged by president R.E. "Tuck" Duncan. Her day in Topeka was a full one, and she did much more than just a membership program. Joan received the red carpet treatment everywhere she went, literally and figuratively.

Joan had a major problem getting here. She didn't just hop on a flight from San Diego—it wasn't that simple. Because of heavy rains in southern California her home was surrounded by water, and she started her trip by boat—the only way she could leave. But she was determined to get to Topeka—come hell or high water! And she did—close to midnight.

Early the next morning, as she entered our zoo, the first thing she saw was our marquee that read, "Welcome Joan Embery to the World Famous Topeka Zoo." Then, much to her surprise and delight, I rolled out a section of red carpet!

The news media were on hand and Joan was photographed and interviewed by *The Topeka Capital-Journal*, recorded two radio programs and was interviewed on video tape by WIBW-TV for their Early News Show. After meeting the press she made a brief tour of the zoo with a quick look at the construction site of Discovering Apes. She has a special fondness for equines and was most interested in our zebras, onagers and Przewalski horses. Then she reviewed the Zoo/Tomorrow Master Plan.

After a hot chocolate break she observed the elephant training session and was quite impressed, particularly with the fact that our zoo had trained both an Asian and an African elephant. Next on her tour was a stroll through the Tropical Rain Forest. She appeared totally enthralled with the exhibit—especially with the number of free-ranging animals. In fact, she enjoyed the Rain Forest so much it was difficult to tear her away in time to make her live appearance on KSNT-TV's Noonday Show. As part of her interview, film clips from her appearances on the Johnny Carson Show were shown. Also, she responded to questions from the studio audience during the telecast.

From there she was whisked to beautiful downtown Topeka for a luncheon with members of the TFOTZ Board of Directors high atop a bank building overlooking the State Capitol. During this meeting she discussed the role of zoos in conservation and education, and described some of the programs at the San Diego Zoo. Then it was back to the zoo for more touring, and off to Forbes Field to see the zoo's Conservation/Propagation Center. There Joan was met at the security gate by Metropolitan Topeka Airport Authority Director Gary Richert and his staff. She was then conducted on a tour of the zoo's facility. She saw the giraffes and ostriches in their winter quarters, but again was most impressed with the equine area. Because of her particular fondness for Przewalski horses, Joan was pleased to see our young pair, Rolmar and Colleen, in their large paddock.

After touring Forbes, she was driven back to the zoo to review the plans and models of Discovering Apes, which was currently under construction.

After dinner at my home she browsed through my collection of zoo literature and memorabilia of the San Diego Zoo dating back many years, some of which she had never seen before.

Then she was rushed back to the hotel to prepare for her program. TFOTZ members started arriving more than an hour early, and it was standing room only by the time the program started. I couldn't wait to introduce Joan as being from that "other" world famous zoo.

After her program she was very gracious and stayed for nearly an hour signing autographs and chatting with TFOTZ members—despite the fact she had to rise at 5:30 am to catch her flight back to San Diego, and then a boat to her home. In her thank you note she remarked that she would always have fond memories of her visit to the World Famous Topeka Zoo.

Addenda:

To learn more about Joan and her career I suggest reading her book, entitled *My Wild World* ,written with Denise Demong, and published by Delacorte Press in 1980. I'm grateful to Joan for being kind enough to send me a quote to use on the dust jacket of my first book, *I'd Rather Be On Safari,* in 2001. She wrote: "I'm so envious of Gary; he's living his dream and sharing Africa with others."

Marlin's Visit

Name: Marlin Perkins
Address: Wild Kingdom

That's the entry in the Zoo's Guest Book dated May 17, 1980. And it marked a very special day for Topekans and the Topeka Friends of the Zoo.

Long before he took office for his 1980 term, TFOTZ President R.E. "Tuck" Duncan approached me (with a gleam in his eye) and said, "I want to do something really spectacular in 1980. Do you think we could get Marlin Perkins for a day at our zoo?"

I replied that knowing Marlin as I did, I was certain (even without checking with him) that he would make an appearance in Topeka if he could work it into his schedule—and that is a tall order.

At an age when many people have been retired for a decade, Marlin was extremely active in his second career as a television personality and star of Mutual of Omaha's Wild Kingdom. Traveling with a production crew to film on location, Marlin journeyed to the far corners of the globe to capture the "wild kingdom" for his program. In fact, he had spent several weeks in the Galapagos Islands just prior to his Topeka visit.

At the Annual Conference of the American Association of Zoological Parks and Aquariums in St. Louis in the fall of 1979, I asked Marlin if he thought he might squeeze Topeka into his schedule for a day or two. He indicated the spring of 1980 was a good possibility. During the ensuing months he maintained contact with me by phone or letter when he was in the country. Finally a firm date was set, and it happened to be on the tenth anniversary of his last visit to our zoo in May 1970.

Although born in Carthage, Missouri, Marlin spent several years of his boyhood growing up in Pittsburg, Kansas. He attended the University of Missouri at Columbia for two years and then started his zoo career in St. Louis in 1926 sweeping sidewalks for $3.75 a day, six days a week.

Eventually he was promoted to Curator of Reptiles at the St. Louis Zoo, and in 1938 he became Curator at the Buffalo Zoo, New York. He was appointed Director of the Lincoln Park Zoo in Chicago in 1944, and then became Director of the St. Louis Zoo in 1962. He retired from that position in 1970 and was named Director Emeritus of the St. Louis Zoo.

While Marlin's time in Topeka was rather limited, he was on the go constantly—thanks to the hectic schedule prepared in advance by TFOTZ. O.C. Backhaus, General Agent in Topeka for Mutual of Omaha, was good enough to serve as a chauffeur for Marlin, and drove him to the WIBW-TV studio for an appearance on the Early News Show. Then it was off to the zoo for a tour of the Tropical Rain Forest. In the TRF, Nancy Perry of KSNT-TV taped an entire program for her Noon Day Show, Vickie Hawver conducted an extensive interview for *The Topeka Capital-Journal*, and both KTPK and WREN radio taped Marlin's reminiscences of his early days on radio in St. Louis. After a short rest break, Marlin spent the evening at the zoo greeting TFOTZ members.

Vickie Hawver's interview ran in the Capital-Journal with the title "Perkins explores Topeka Zoo jungle." In it she wrote that as Perkins observed the jungle-sounds and sights of the Tropical Rain Forest he marveled, "This is pretty fancy. Not all zoos have something like this." Marlin also commented to Vickie, "Zoo people feel this is a coming zoo. All of our colleagues in the zoo field have great respect for Gary Clarke."

The entire day Saturday was spent at the zoo and Marlin had an opportunity to review the construction progress on Discovering Apes. However, most of his time was taken with meeting zoo visitors.

At one point in the afternoon the line in the Animals and Man building extended from the inside giraffe exhibit, around the corner by the elephants, past the hippos, out the front doors and across the mall to the Tropical Rain Forest. Despite the continuous flow of people, Marlin was extremely gracious, taking time to sign autographs and pose for photographs.

It was a great day for our zoo, thanks to the Zoo Docents, TFOTZ Board and Zoo Staff, who made it a success. And "Tuck" Duncan probably is *still* smiling.

Reflections on Marlin

Marlin Perkins was the only zoo director ever to make the cover of TIME magazine. It was the July 7, 1947 issue and he was Director of the Lincoln Park Zoo in Chicago at the time. The cover story profiled many of America's prominent zoos and contained four full pages of color photos of significant zoo animals.

The article featured the male gorilla "Bushman," called Lincoln Park Zoo's "star of stars." The American Association of Zoological Parks and Aquariums had proclaimed Bushman "the most outstanding and most valuable single animal of its kind in any zoo in the world." He was valued at $100,000—twenty times more than any other gorilla.

Marlin was a pioneer in early television. The weekly program "Zoo Parade" was broadcast live when Chicago had only a few hundred TV sets. This evolved into Mutual of Omaha's "Wild Kingdom," filmed on location around the world and still in syndication.

I had the privilege of working with Marlin as a zoo consultant on various projects around the country. To travel with him was a kick. *Everybody* recognized him with that shock of silver-gray hair and distinguished moustache. And everyone felt they knew him on a first name basis. People would flock around him as he walked through airports, yell and wave as he toured zoos, interrupt his dinner at a restaurant for an autograph, even talk non-stop to him in the men's room. Yet he was always gracious and sincere.

In the late 1970's when I was still a rather young zoo director from a comparatively small zoo, I drove to St. Louis with my family for a "busman's holiday." Professional courtesy is such that you advise a colleague when you plan to visit his or her zoo, or announce yourself upon arrival. This always results in overwhelming hospitality with your host showing off every service area and quarantine barn in the zoo, ending up in the office to review attendance figures and the next phase of the master plan. Since our four children were all under ten years old, I felt they might find this more than a little boring, so at the St. Louis Zoo I opted to skip protocol and go incognito.

Oops! I got caught.

As big as the St. Louis Zoo is, wouldn't you know that Marlin would spot us from a distance, rush over in his electric cart and say, "Why, Gary, what a pleasant surprise! Hop aboard and I'll give your family a tour."

Bless his heart, it was *not* a zoo man's tour of the zoo. Marlin showered his attention on the children, with the grand finale being a train ride on the extensive St. Louis Zoo Railroad. The kids had a blast.

Not long after that (May 1970) Marlin was in Topeka as the keynote speaker at the first national conference of the American Association of Zoo Keepers, hosted by the World Famous Topeka Zoo. I invited him to join us for a home cooked dinner at my house. The children (Janet, James, Joyce and John) lined up by age in the living room to greet him. They were scrubbed and primed for his visit. They remembered him from their zoo tour and knew he was famous as they watched him every week on Wild Kingdom. To start the conversation I said, "Children, you remember Mr. Perkins." With that our youngest (John) said, "Oh yes; he's the train man from St. Louis." Marlin loved that story and asked me to tell it whenever we were together.

You're a Zoo . . . WHAT?

by Evie Green, Zoo Docent, 1975

Author's note: Evie Green served for many years as both a Zoo Docent and a Zoo School teacher.

When I tell people I'm a Zoo Docent,
They usually respond with a surprised, "You're a Zoo—*What?*"
And I always wish I could answer them like this . . .

Yes, I *am* a Docent at the World Famous Topeka Zoo!

Where else could I meet a bus load of excited school children
And have the privilege of guiding them through the Zoo?

Where else could I cram *so* many animal facts in my head
And hope to say them correctly to my wide-eyed eager listeners?

Where else could I feel so special as when a handsome young
Kindergartner asks, "Can I hold your hand?"

Where else could I forget the cares of the day so quickly
As in the delighted squeals of children watching lion cubs at play?

Where else must I keep as much on my toes,
As holding the interest of a large group of hot, thirsty fifth-graders?

Where else could I converse with the Zoo Staff between tours
And learn something new and exciting each time I do?

Where else could I see the miracle of life more clearly than watching our
female Bengal tiger (an endangered species) with her six beautiful cubs?

Where else could I feel as secure in the future of our world as in this
constant parade of intelligent and compassionate young students?

Where else could I feel as happy as waving goodbye to a group I hear one
of them yell, "Tell Max and Tiffany I'll be back!"

Where else could I feel the pleasure I do as I open a fat envelope of thank
yous and colorful drawings from an appreciative group of boys and girls?

Yes, I *am* a Docent at the World Famous Topeka Zoo . . . *And I Love It!*

The State Journal

a page of opinion

Thursday Evening, July 20, 1978

If half a century of living has taught me anything at all, it has taught me that "nothing can bring you peace, but yourself." — Dale Carnegie, American biographical writer.

Topeka Zoo: class, laboratory

Those who see zoos only as modified prisons where helpless animals are locked behind bars for people to gawk at should take another look and perhaps a leisurely visit to the Topeka Zoological Gardens.

More than just being a source of recreation, a zoo under proper management is primarily an educational institution. Topekans can take pride in making that claim for their zoo.

Topeka's zoo is not only a classroom in the figurative sense — it actually has a classroom, replete with desks and blackboards. Topeka school children having completed the sixth grade are offered the opportunity to learn zoology in a project sponsored by Topeka Friends of the Zoo docents.

The classroom experience offered by the zoo is perhaps the most tangible, down-to-earth manifestation of a zoo as an educational tool. But parents who have ever given it any thought, long have realized that a good zoo used properly is one of the best educational tools to be found in any city.

The Topeka zoo classes teach, for instance, that polar bears have hollow hair, or how to tell the difference between a male and a female box turtle. The secret to the success of the classes is that docents are able to make zoology fun and interesting. Instead of sitting in a schoolroom reading about snakes, the students have a chance to handle a snake in the zoo class.

And they have learning games, jokes and get to change the subject when they want.

Of course Topeka's zoo offers even more than that. To the community, the zoo is a source of pride, a place Topekans make a point to take visiting friends and relatives. To the scientific community, Topeka's zoo has a shining international reputation for excellence, contributing significantly to the efforts to preserve endangered species of animals.

Topeka's zoo — recreation center, living garden, scientific institution and classroom — serves its community well. Topekans would find their time well spent to make regular visits to the zoo, because there's something new there all the time.

Sombras en el Mundo de los Gatos

(Shadows in the World of the Cats!)

Jaguars are the third largest species of the big cats—outranked in size only by tigers and lions. They are the largest of the New World cats and have a very extensive range: from 40 degrees south of the equator up to southwestern United States, though they generally are thought of as a jungle cat. As a matter of fact, "Jungle Cat" was the title of one of the Walt Disney True-Life Adventure Features filmed some years ago. Photographed in the Amazon, the story theme revolved around a pair of jaguars—one of which was black.

The black color phase is referred to as melanistic. Melanism occurs when there is an abundance of black pigment. Leopards (particularly those from India) frequently have melanistic phases. Melanism is less common in jaguars, and few had been seen in zoos until the 1970's. The pattern of rosettes (or spots) common to all jaguars also exists on black jaguars, although obviously it is not so apparent. When the sun is shining it is easy for the visitor to see the rosettes gleaming through their black fur. Both black and spotted cubs can be born in the same litter from two spotted parents.

In 1979 our zoo received two black jaguars on loan. The male, named Darth, came from the St. Louis Zoological Park, and was two years old. Leia, the female, was from the Jacksonville Zoological Park, and was five years old. Both animals were shipped by air. General Curator Craig Dinsmore and Animal Supervisor Mike Coker drove to the Kansas City airport to pick up Darth. Several weeks later Craig and another keeper made the same trip to transport Leia. Although the Topeka Zoo had exhibited spotted jaguars in the past, (they produced several litters of cubs), this was the first opportunity for the zoo to display black jaguars. We were indebted to both the St. Louis Zoo and the Jacksonville Zoo for this opportunity.

The two black jaguars were exhibited in a double unit on the east walk opposite the outside elephant yard. They were most interesting to observe, as their temperaments were so different. During the day, Darth was quite active and was outside the den much of the time. An inquisitive and intelligent animal, he appeared to greet both zoo staff and visitors as they approached the exhibit. A large stump of wood that probably weighed 75 pounds stood in the exhibit. One day I was making rounds with Craig and noticed the stump was inside his den. When I questioned Craig about why the stump was inside the den, he replied, "Darth pulls it around everywhere with his claws and drags it in the den to a certain spot all the time—and then he crouches down behind it and peers out with those glowing yellow eyes to watch activity outside. If someone comes by, usually he comes bounding out of the den—which startles keepers as well as visitors. The keepers move the stump out, but he will drag it right back in the den! Gives you some idea of the strength of this robust animal." On the other hand, Leia was more shy and retiring. During the day she spent more time in her den, and when she was out, she frequently made threat gestures—with her ears back and snarling. While making rounds at night, Craig observed that she was more active and often was out of her den.

Darth and Leia proved to be a popular temporary exhibit and eventually were returned to their respective zoos. However, their uniqueness stimulated my thinking on a possible "WOW!" exhibit. Imagine taking a path through lush tropical vegetation culminating in two habitat settings opposite each other, with one featuring black jaguars and the other—white tigers! Although we never pulled that one off, we did feature a white tiger as a temporary exhibit during our 50th Anniversary Celebration in 1983.

The Fascinating Miracle of Kangaroo Birth

I'll never forget the out of town schoolteacher who brought her group of third graders to the zoo. She did not want one of our docent tours, but wanted to explain the animals to the class herself. When she arrived at the Australian area (across from the bears at that time), she started to elaborate about kangaroos. About this time a pair of our red kangaroos started breeding. Naturally the children were very curious and wanted to know what the animals were doing. Instead of referring to our *Zoo Guidebook* or the illustrated graphic describing kangaroo behavior, the teacher became flustered and avoided the question by saying, "Oh, goodness children, I don't know. I think they're just fighting. Let's go look at the bears." One of our keepers happened to be close by and said to her, "That won't do any good, lady, because the bears are fighting, too."

There may be some humor in that incident but there is also considerable pathos. What her students were deprived of was the fascinating miracle of kangaroo birth.

A newborn kangaroo is no larger than a navy bean and weighs 1/30th of an ounce. A half dozen could fit in a teaspoon.

The estrus cycle of the female red kangaroo is 35 days (she comes into heat every 35 days). Let's assume we have a female in heat, she is bred by a male, and conceives. The gestation period is 33 days. The baby is not born in the pouch; it is a vaginal birth like any other mammal. Immediately after birth the tiny baby crawls up over the fur on the mother's belly into the pouch, using tiny sharp claws on the underdeveloped front limbs. The journey takes about three minutes.

The pouch is not a pocket as is commonly shown in cartoons, but more or less an internal, expandable bag. Inside this bag it is dark, moist and warm—a secondary womb where the baby can continue its development. Kangaroos are marsupials; marsupium is Latin for pouch or bag.

Now we are going to do something that few people have ever had the privilege of doing: we are going to look carefully inside a mother kangaroo's pouch and observe her newborn baby. We see a little pink blob of protoplasm: it is hairless, blind, the hind legs and tail are mere buds and the front legs are simply stumps. It does not look like a baby kangaroo; it does not look like a baby anything. In fact, at this stage the baby does not have enough strength in its jaws to suck, so it attaches its mouth to one of the four mammary glands located inside the pouch, and the nipple swells inside the baby's mouth so the baby cannot drop off. The milk automatically drops into the baby's mouth.

As fascinating as that is, the story doesn't end there. Two days later it's the 35th day again, and the female may come into heat, be bred, and conceive. A second baby starts its development but does so for only two days and then goes into suspended animation. Meanwhile the first-born continues to grow and develop in the pouch. When it is about five months old it looks like a miniature of the adult with a long tail, back legs and ears. It pokes its head out of the pouch and is ready for solid food.

At first the baby peeks out in a tentative manner and is easily frightened, but as it grows and gains security it becomes fearless as long as it is near the pouch. The first excursions out of the pouch are brief and it will jump back in the pouch headfirst when frightened. Soon it grows to the point where it will not fit in the pouch and simply sticks its head inside to nurse.

At this time the chemical composition of the milk that the mother is secreting changes, and this is a signal for baby number two, who is still in the womb, to continue its development. It does so for another 31 days to complete the gestation period of 33 days.

It is born and, just like the first baby, crawls into the pouch—but attaches its mouth to a different nipple. Then the mother secretes milk of the original chemical composition through this mammary gland for the second baby. So, at any one time a mother kangaroo may have two babies—one in the pouch and one out of the pouch (but still nursing)—and she is producing *two different types* of milk for her babies.

Now you can understand what the students were deprived of at the most opportune time when the teacher did not explain kangaroo reproduction. She had the best teaching aid in the world—the living breathing creature. Some people may feel that children in the first, second or third grades are "too young," but I disagree. We think it is important for the zoo to present animals truthfully. We have explained kangaroo reproduction to young children and even shown them color slides of baby kangaroos in the pouch. We feel that this has meaning and significance to the youngsters. I recall one instance when I was in a local grocery store and a seven-year-old recognized me, rushed over, grabbed my hand, looked up and said, "I remember how a baby kangaroo is born!"

These children are eager to learn, hungry for knowledge, thirsty for the truth—yet what do they learn about animals? If you watch some of the cartoon characters on TV you see Magilla Gorilla, Peter Potomus, Yogi Bear: animals wearing neckties, driving cars, talking like people. That's not a true representation of animals, and children gain a gross misconception. Why make animals something they are not when in reality they are far more fascinating just being themselves. What could be more fascinating than the miracle of kangaroo birth?

A Maasai on Safari in Topeka

Note: In 1974 I led the first African Photo Safari sponsored by the Topeka Friends of the Zoo. Successive safaris resulted in many positive benefits for our zoo. The following is but one example. G.K.C.

"Obo osupuko, olitobikie inchu." These words greeted Tepilit Ole Saitoti of the Maasai tribe as he arrived at the airport on his first visit to Kansas— halfway around the world from his native lands of Tanzania and Kenya.

The above quote in the Maa language is from the *Wisdom of the Maasai*, and translates into, "A man's home is wherever he is." Since the Maasai were nomadic, the meaning of this proverb is that you should be as content with your present location as with your birthplace. Thus, our hope was that Saitoti, during his visit, would feel as much at home in Kansas as he did in his native Maasailand in East Africa.

Saitoti was in Topeka to give an illustrated lecture on his people presented by the Topeka Friends of the Zoo in cooperation with the L.S.B. Leakey Foundation. The lecture, held on February 15, 1981 was co-sponsored by Bryan World Tours and Alpha/Omega Books in Topeka.

Knowing how important cattle are to the Maasai, I had a surprise in store for Saitoti. Instead of going directly from the airport to the zoo or to my house, I drove out of Topeka to a rural area and parked just off the road by a pasture full of cattle.

Saitoti rolled his car window down and we both sat in silence. With great intensity he looked at the cows, he listened to the cows, and he smelled the cows. Never speaking, he seemed to be communicating with each cow on an individual basis. After awhile his eyes welled up and a tear rolled down his cheek. Finally he broke his silence. "Thank you," he said with a reverent voice. "You are the only one who has done this for me."

Saitoti had been one of 36 children from his village picked to attend a government boarding school. His father chose him instead of his other brothers and stepbrothers because he believed Saitoti would return to the family village after finishing school. He was eight years old and, as he described it, "It was very painful to leave home." In one conversation he explained it was more than the mental pain of leaving his family and the tribal traditions he had grown up with—it was also the physical pain of such things as wearing shoes.

After eight years of school he returned to his family manyatta and became a Maasai warrior, which he considered a great honor. Then fate and opportunity intervened.

At the age of 20 he accepted a request to work as a ranger and guide for the Tanzanian National Park Service. After four years of duty, he was selected by a visiting film crew to play the leading role in a National Geographic documentary entitled, "Man of the Serengeti." As Saitoti reflected in a media interview during his stay in Topeka, "Again, I was in the right place, at the right time." Although the filming took place in the Serengeti, Saitoti was flown to Hollywood to help in editing.

His first trip to the United States convinced him that he wanted "more school." It was not easy for a man of one culture to become a man of two cultures. But since he was a Maasai warrior he felt an inner confidence and self reliance. He found a benefactor who paid his expenses to attend one semester of college in the U.S. as a special student. He did so well that he became a full time student. During the course of his education (in Germany and the U.S.) he obtained assistance from various benefactors, including the Rockefeller and L.S.B. Leakey Foundations, and the World Wildlife Fund. Saitoti's eventual goal was to write about his people.

In February 1978 he returned to his home in Africa to write. His book, *MAASAI: THE LAND AND THE PEOPLE*, probably is the most in-depth portrayal of the Maasai ever published. It is far more than just a coffee table book. Beautifully written, it goes into great detail about the Maasai way of life from childhood, manhood (and womanhood) to elderhood. It is a book to be savored, and read more than once. The outstanding color photographs and artwork were by Carol Beckwith. It was published by Abrams in 1980.

Actually, it was the book that led me to Saitoti in the first place. On each of our safaris to East Africa I always scoured the bookstores in Nairobi, Dar es Salaam, or wherever I was for literature about the wildlife and peoples of Africa. Finding accurate information on the various tribes and their traditional cultures sometimes is difficult.

One of my good friends in Kenya was Jonas L. Ole Sademaki, Manager of Little Governors Camp in the Maasai Mara Game Reserve. Jonas himself was a Maasai, and I asked him about accurate literature concerning his tribe. Immediately his face lit up and he said: "There's a brand new book out that is absolutely the best ever written, and it is **by** a Maasai—he is one of us. His name is Tepilit Ole Saitoti, and he is a close friend, just like a brother to me. In fact, he is in the States right now on a lecture tour."

We discussed the book and Saitoti, and I decided to try and make contact on my return home. I did so through the L.S.B. Leakey Foundation and was able to visit with Saitoti by telephone between his lectures. He was receptive to the idea of coming to Topeka since he would be with a friend of Jonas'. I then made arrangements with the Leakey Foundation for Saitoti to lecture to the TFOTZ membership—and we were fortunate, as it was his last open date for this series.

TFOTZ President Marshall Clark and a large army of volunteers worked very hard to make Saitoti's visit a pleasant experience. The response to his lecture was more than anyone could have predicted, with a warm reception from the overflow audience. Saitoti's recitation of his personal experiences, along with Carol Beckwith's original color slides from the book, were a perfect combination for a very moving program.

Having been to Maasailand on numerous occasions, it was nice to have Saitoti as a guest in my home. We spent hours pouring through the literature on Africana in my personal library, and listening to actual recordings of tribal songs and dances. Far into the night we spoke of peoples. . . and cultures; of life . . . and family; we were serious sometimes . . . and we laughed a lot; and we shared personal thoughts and feelings as two men from different cultures on opposite sides of the earth, yet with mutual respect.

Just before he left Saitoti told me that prior to his visit he had never heard of Topeka, and the main reason he accepted the invitation was because Jonas had friends here. He really did not expect much, and was overwhelmed with Kansas hospitality. I think he summed it up when he said: "Now, I will always remember Topeka. The people are wonderful. Topeka is an echo of humanity."

A Friend Remembered

He was a good friend . . . a true friend. The kind who simply accepted me as I was, tested me at times, but was never judgmental.

We met in the mid-1950's, when we were both young and in our formative years. He was from Africa, and always carried with him the wisdom of that ancient continent. In his own way he imparted much of it to me.

For the first decade or so of our acquaintance we associated regularly. After that my career path caused a geographical separation of many miles, yet our lives were entwined and his impact on me was strong and lasting despite the distance.

As we both moved through the aging process into the later stages of life, our bond grew stronger—at least from my perspective. As naturalist John Muir once wrote: "Friends get closer and dearer the farther they travel on life's journey."

Periodically I would drive several hours to visit him, often taking along some of my other friends to meet this special individual. They were always impressed with his dignity, despite his over-sized ears and rather long nose.

My friend had only a single name: Casey. He was an African elephant and lived for nearly half a century at the Kansas City Zoo.

In the mid-1950's the professional baseball team in town was the Kansas City Athletics. The team owner played a role in acquiring a pair of African elephants for the zoo, so fittingly they were named Casey A and Lady A. The female always retained the "A" in her name, but the male became simply Casey. Some said he was named for the famous baseball slugger in the poem, "Casey at the Bat," while others felt his name reflected the pronunciation of the initials K.C., a frequent nickname for Kansas City.

Phil Small, owner of Parkview Drug Stores, was also instrumental in Casey and Lady A coming to Kansas City. I met him once and still have his business card, measuring only one half inch by one quarter inch to reflect his name. The K.C. Zoo arranged for the African elephant pair through Fred J. Zeehandelaar, the famous wild animal importer.

How well I remember the day, July 20, 1955 when Casey and Lady A arrived in Kansas City. After being shipped by sea from Africa, they were driven by truck from New York City to Kansas City. Before going to the zoo in Swope Park they were scheduled to make their debut at an Athletics baseball game. I was 16 years old and took the bus to the old Municipal Stadium. There they were, still in shipping crates, between home plate and the pitcher's mound. I really couldn't see much, just two little trunks snaking out, sniffing the air and feeling around the crates.

Even so, I was thrilled to actually be looking at live African elephants right here in Kansas City! All too soon the truck took them to the zoo. Casey's weight was listed at 975 pounds, with Lady A at 925 pounds, and they both were 53 inches tall. Their age was "guesstimated" at four years or so, although I suspect they were younger. Still, Casey's birth year was usually listed as 1951.

For the next two years, on my regular visits to the K.C. Zoo, I made a special point of spending as much time as possible with this young pair of African elephants, getting to know their personalities, watching them grow and develop. During the winter they were kept inside the Main Zoo Building, but each summer they were exhibited on the African Veldt. My first summer at the zoo, 1957, I saw them daily, usually on my lunch hour, as my duties were elsewhere in the zoo. The summer of 1958 was my first direct experience with Casey and Lady A, under the tutelage of that wonderful teacher, Head Keeper Bennie Henry.

While working full time for two years at Midwest Research Institute I made periodic visits, but none at all during my two semesters at the University of Missouri in Columbia.

In June 1961 I returned full time as a keeper at the Kansas City Zoo, and had a wonderful reunion with Casey and Lady A. The new rhino and elephant building was completed in 1962 and then the elephants resided permanently on the African Veldt. My training under Bennie Henry continued and I was promoted to what I considered to be the most desirable and prestigious position in the zoo: senior keeper of the African Veldt. Living and working day after day with Casey and Lady A resulted in a rapport I shall always treasure. From the anticipated morning bath, through roaming the Veldt together much of the day, to the bedding down ritual each evening—these shared experiences strengthened our friendship and mutual deference.

For almost a year—late 1962 to the fall of 1963—I was hundreds of miles from my Kansas City elephant friends while at the Fort Worth Zoo, but then moved to Topeka, and once again was able to make regular visits.

Over the next 30 years there were significant changes at the K.C. Zoo. William T. A. Cully, the zoo director I had worked under, retired and eventually passed away, as did my mentor, Bennie Henry. Lady A died around 1971 and was replaced with another female African elephant, Penny. But my friendship with Casey continued.

In his prime Casey was considered the largest African bull elephant in North America with an estimated weight of 12,000 to 14,000 pounds. In due course he became the oldest African bull elephant on the continent. As time passed he mellowed and I could relate to some of his age-related problems: sinus infections, intestinal disorders, arthritis, dental trouble, even cataracts. The zoo responded with excellent veterinary care.

I had retired from the zoo profession in 1989 to lead safaris full-time. However, the staff of the Kansas City Zoo extended every courtesy when I came to visit Casey, and I was very appreciative. By the year 2000 it was public knowledge that Casey was "wearing out." Curator of Mammals Conrad Schmidt was most gracious and would call me whenever there was a change in Casey's condition. On each visit I thought it might be my last. Casey remained majestic in attitude and behavior, but aging was noticeable.

At last the end came for Casey in September 2003 at the estimated age of 52. Yes, I was sad. But I will forever cherish my special relationship with a remarkable animal. Casey will always be a friend remembered.

Part 6

Orangutans! Oranguclans!! Orangunannies!!!

Unexpected orang destruction, after hours with baby red apes, a visiting white tiger, and World Famous at fifty.

. . . my heart is warmed whenever I think of your wonderful work with the Zoo—that great Zoo where so many children and grownups, too, have so much pleasure.

—Karl Menninger, M.D.
In a letter to Topeka
Zoo Director Gary K. Clarke
October 24th, 1977

Courtesy of the Topeka and Shawnee County Public Library   **Art work by Alice C. Sabatini**

Part 6

Orangutans! Oranguclans!! Orangunannies!!!

Has Topeka Gone Ape?

Talk about eyecatching!

The front cover of the March 1979 issue of *Topeka Magazine* had a brilliant red background and featured a sketch of a giant ape with an actual photo of *my* face for its head! Below this illustration, in yellow letters, was the title of the headline story: "Has Topeka Gone Ape?"

Uh-oh. I knew what this reflected; my most difficult battle to date as zoo director—new facilities for our two great ape species (orangutans and gorillas)—was a controversial issue.

Inside an extensive article by reporter Rosie Rebek outlined the exciting next phase of our master plan, as well as the opposition to it. "If you liked the sights and sounds you experienced in the Tropical Rain Forest, you're going to love what will happen in the Discovering Apes building," she wrote. She detailed how zoo visitors would step into an elevated tree house in a simulated Bornean jungle to view orangutans in their treetop habitat, and then *walk through* the outdoor gorilla habitat in a glass tunnel, the first exhibit of its type in the world.

In what I referred to as the labor pains and difficult birth process we go through with any new zoo project, the construction cost estimate had doubled in four years—from $556,000 in 1974 to $1.14 million in late 1978. That was when Mayor Bill McCormick said he'd heard from people who objected to spending $1 million "to discover what apes do in their spare time." He recommended the project be put to a vote of the public.

I strongly objected. While I had no doubt that Discovering Apes would win voter approval, any further delay would result in yet *additional* construction costs. Besides, the general obligation bonds for the building would be supported with revenues generated by the zoo, not tax money. Topeka Friends of the Zoo had raised over $50,000 for plans and specifications, which were being finalized by Topeka architects Phil Coolidge and Greg Allen. We were ready to proceed (and behind schedule, as far as I was concerned).

Park Commissioner Butch Felker, always a staunch supporter of the zoo (along with Finance Commissioner Jim Claussen), called Mayor McCormick's suggestion for a public vote "a political move" at the commission meeting of December 5, 1978. On December 12 the commission rejected the public vote proposal, and authorized the project by a 4-1 vote, with the mayor voting against it.

Despite the novelty of the cover, the *Topeka Magazine* article was actually quite beneficial. It explained how Discovering Apes would not only provide an enriched environment for the orangutans and gorillas, but also necessary behind-the-scenes animal management and husbandry facilities. The visitor experience would be unique, and the building would increase the zoo's educational dimension. In addition the article told how our zoo served the community as a year-round resource.

Author's Note: Orangutan is from the Malay *orang* (person) and *hjutan* (forest).

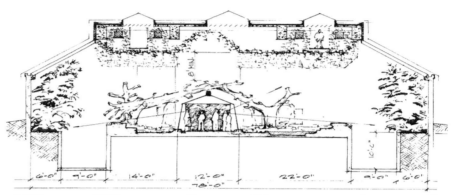

Has Topeka Gone Ape?

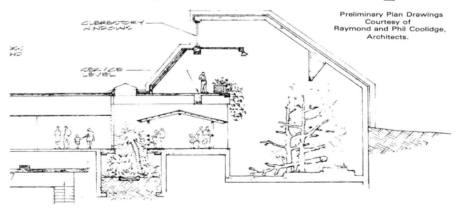

Preliminary Plan Drawings
Courtesy of
Raymond and Phil Coolidge,
Architects.

Twisted Trophy Tire Tactfully

Triggers Terrific Tropical Trees

As a parent, I was surprised at how fast my four human children grew up, and impressed at how big and strong my boys were as teenagers.

As a zoo director, I was even more surprised at how quickly our young orangutan pair developed, and particularly impressed with the size and strength of the male as a teenager.

Djakarta Jim, under the name D. James Orang, was busy in his early years producing prize-winning paintings, playing with Daisy, the female orang, and interacting with members of the zoo staff. We had to discontinue direct contact with the staff as Jim grew older because of his strength. It was not a question of Jim intentionally trying to hurt us. He was an orang and assumed we were as strong as he was, so he played and wrestled accordingly.

In providing the orangs with various items for occupational activity and behavioral enrichment, we had to be selective and insure they were not harmful to the orangs, would not damage the primate exhibits in the Animals and Man building, and hopefully were tough enough to withstand Jim's strength. One item that fit the criteria was a steel belted radial automobile tire. Jim loved it!

Now, if you have ever changed a tire, you know how heavy and awkward they are to handle. And if you have taken the tire to a service station to be repaired, you've seen the heavy duty compressed air machines used to manipulate such a tire, together with the accompanying loud noises.

Well, you can imagine our amazement when we came in one morning to find that Djakarta Jim had taken his tire and literally twisted it like a pretzel! I'm really not sure how to describe it. It may be the closest thing I've seen to a tire being tied into a knot.

Our first reaction was to "untwist" it. HA! Even the strongest among us was not able to undo the deed Jim had done. Then I had an idea for better use of *this* particular tire (we could easily get another one for Jim). Discovering Apes, our new and larger facility for gorillas and orangutans, was in the final planning stages. The main feature in the orang exhibit would be an extensive vertical space filled with specially designed and constructed tropical trees for the orangs, with public viewing from a bamboo treehouse at treetop level. We used the tire as a prop to help raise funds for the trees. It generated dozens of contributions from individuals, organizations and companies throughout the community.

The city commission had already approved this project, but I wanted to emphasize how our apes had outgrown their existing facilities. So I took the twisted trophy tire to a city commission meeting to tactfully demonstrate the importance of the new facility for our growing great apes.

The commissioners viewed it incredulously. After a long silence, one of them asked, "You mean that big male orang at the zoo did that?" To which I replied, "There's no one else at the zoo who could!" While they were shaking their heads in disbelief, I added, "If you think this tire is something, you should see the car!"

When Discovering Apes opened in 1981, we placed the tire on permanent display in the orang area.

DONORS TO THE ORANGUTAN TREE FUND – 1980/1981

Independent Insurance Agents of Topeka
Rotary Foundation of Topeka
Mr. & Mrs. Louis Pozez
Mr. & Mrs. S. Lee Pozez
Rita Ochs
Catharine Menninger
Breakfast Optimist
Mr. & Mrs. Richard Hanger
The American Companies, Inc.
Mr. & Mrs. Anderson Chandler
D.G. & L.B. Lothson
The Security Benefit Group of Companies
Brewster Place Service Fund
Cecile Hyland
Mr. & Mrs. Erich W. Noethe
Brent & Brock Hilpert
Gerald M. Gardner
Clara A. Zeller
Georgia Sue Reuter
Mrs. Bob Brock
Delta Theta Chi
Dr. & Mrs. Lorne Phillips
Margaret F. Schwartz
Alice Krumm
The Andes Company
Mid-States Solar Research Company
Myron & Rachel Seeley
R.E. Grene, M.D.
Georgia J. Burns
Coral Witter
Richard & Suzanne Hill
Andy Hill
Tom & Ann Gregg
Melvin & Nancy Cole
Lee & Bueltel Construction Co., Inc.
Howard & Lora Reineman
William & Martha Kauffman
Jerry McDonald
Carl & Patricia Monk
Giles & Komoro Thielman
Dairy Queen No. 3, 6, 8
Lee & Bueltel Construction Co.
Hill's Pet Products
Marjorye Heeney

DONORS TO THE ORANGUTAN TREE FUND (CONT.)

Kansas Lions State Convention
Mr. & Mrs. Don Engesser
Art Cherry, M. D.
Henry Blake, M.D.
William Bogue
Bill Rudnick
John Ashley, M.D.
Max Bickford
Joe Casper, D.D.S.
Gary Clarke
Hurst Coffman
Warren Corman
Howard Dexter, D.D.S.
Henry Hiebert
Balfour Jeffry
Bruce Johnson
Malcom King
Jim Maag
Harry O'Riley
William Palmer
Richard Petro
Charles Sheetz
Jim Taggart
Harry Turner
Bill Zagar, D.D.S.
Mr. & Mrs. William H. Griffiths
Ford & Cathy Ross
Emil & Sallie Kleinholtz, Jr.
Topeka Kennel Club
Brownie Troop No. 325
Friendly Pioneers
Jim Bush
Mrs. Robert H. Clark
Winter Hostesses of VA Volunteers
Seaman Congregational United Church of Christ
Neighborhood Children & Hudkins Family
Cool Clydes Miniature Golf Course
Bob & Karen Coe & Family

Out on a Limb With Djakarta Jim

PICTURE THIS: You are a zoo director in a medium-sized mid-western community and your zoo has just completed a $1.2 million exhibit called Discovering Apes that has been 10 years in development. It will feature orangutans and gorillas. Your staff and a host of medical, dental, and veterinary volunteers have successfully moved a pair of gorillas and a pair of orangutans into the new facility's off-exhibit areas. Your Friends of the Zoo organization has gone the extra mile, with volunteers raising $63,000 for special steel-reinforced concrete trees for the orangs. It is July 1981 and, in your nearly 25 years in the zoo profession, you can't remember a time that has been more jam-packed with excitement.

At this moment you have a select gathering of invited board members, volunteers, staff, primate behaviorists, public officials, donors, and representatives from the news media lined up for the introduction of the orangs into their new treetop home. This is a special VIP preview just one week before the official dedication and public opening of the building.

All eyes are riveted on the door as Djakarta Jim, the oh, so impressive adult male orang, slowly enters the exhibit . . . and, after swinging around a bit, he promptly crumples one of the specially designed steel-reinforced concrete tree branches . . . in front of **everybody!** Not a good day to be the zoo director.

Yes, we knew that Jim was strong (all orangs are strong—at any age and of either sex). He had demonstrated his strength in a variety of ways: yanking welded metal rings off the wall in his previous exhibit, picking at the concrete block walls with such force that the aggregate in the block literally exploded, and, of course, the infamous twisted tire. But this was a demonstration beyond comprehension.

In designing the new orangutan exhibit as part of the Discovering Apes complex we took great pains to specify extra-strength, heavy-duty materials in all of the off-exhibit holding areas as well as in the main animal exhibit space. Architect Phil Coolidge participated in a brainstorming session with our staff, Zooplan Associates, and primate specialist consultants. In addition, Phil visited a variety of great ape facilities in various zoos, learned to know our orangs on a first name basis, and gained a true appreciation of the strength of these animals. Thus, when the project went out for bid we all knew that the design concept was sound from the point of view of materials and strength.

The reaction of general contractors submitting bids was interesting —and probably should have been expected. They said we could save "a helluva lot of money" if we could reduce the strength of the materials specified. Surely, they claimed, those orangs aren't that strong. We invited them over to the Animals and Man Building to view the existing facilities that had housed the orangs for over a decade. We took them behind the scenes and Djakarta Jim came up to the transfer gate and started doing his "song and dance" by vigorously rattling the metalwork, which produced a deafening noise—as if the entire building was collapsing!. The contractors faces turned ashen and they fought to get to the nearest exit. Jim quickly made believers out of them. After that experience their universal question was: "Are you *sure* you have designed that new facility strong enough?"

Well, the building was built to the original specifications and we were quite pleased with the quality of construction. Jim tested the off-exhibit facilities in every conceivable way, and we were confident they would stand the test of time. The final aspect of the exhibit was a series of artificially constructed trees to create a free-standing forest for the orangs.

The poet Joyce Kilmer once said, "only God can make a tree," and he probably was right. But the trees that God makes are easily torn up by orangs like Djakarta Jim. There were a few specialist contractors around the country who had developed techniques to construct artificial trees that were quite realistic. This had been done in other zoos and we went through the process of carefully evaluating the types of trees we felt would be appropriate for our orangs. We considered fiberglass, or a fiberglass and concrete combination, and finally decided on steel reinforced concrete trees.

After the trees were built we held a series of open houses for TFOTZ members and the general public. Children and adults alike climbed all over the trees (some to the very top) and played "Orangutan for a Day." In fact, it was so successful that some people said we should have built a second set of trees just for people. Also, it turned out that the visitors in the public viewing space found those other visitors swinging in the orang exhibit to be one of the more interesting species they had seen on display at our zoo for quite some time. In the course of these activities, we had lots of folks—big, strong folks—who "tested" the orang trees for us by swinging and climbing on them, and gave us their seal of approval that these high strength, steel-reinforced concrete trees were more than adequate for the orangs. (Years later I watched fathers point to a specific tree and tell their children, "I climbed that very tree one time.")

The big day arrived and the multitudes assembled in the visitor's bamboo tree house to watch the orangs enter their new exhibit for the first time. It took awhile to get them out of the off-exhibit holding areas (they liked it back there) but finally Djakarta Jim emerged in all his magnificence. He was truly a superb animal—with prominent cheek pads and throat sac characteristic of an adult male Bornean orangutan—in his prime at 273 pounds, with an arm span of eight feet and a hand that measured 12 inches from wrist to fingertip!

Jim immediately climbed through the trees, and it was a glorious sight. Early on he started pushing and pulling on certain limbs, and a couple of them seemed to "give" a few inches. Some of us looked at each other quizzically, but assumed that maybe there should be some resilience in the branches. Jim went everywhere—upper levels, lower levels, big branches, small branches, climbing and brachiating branch to branch from one end of the exhibit to the other. It was a tremendous demonstration of the phenomenal physical capabilities of orangutans as a species.

Motion picture, videotape and still cameras were clicking away. The zoo staff was very excited that the orangs finally were in their new home, and that Jim immediately adapted so well. The Friends of the Zoo board and various volunteers that were present were beaming with pride for the contribution they had made to this fantastic new exhibit.

I was again expressing thanks and gratitude to the various donors who had contributed sixty-three thousand dollars (yes, $63,000!) for this jungle of concrete and steel trees. And then **it** happened.

Jim went over to the branch that he had tested earlier and, with what seemed to be very little effort, gave it a quick jerk. It made a popping sound, and the concrete cracked at the base of the tree trunk. Oohs and Aahs emerged from the crowd, and I felt a sudden attack of diarrhea coming on. We all watched in anticipation to see if that's all Jim was going to do, but it wasn't. He again pulled on the same branch and concrete cracked in the middle, with good sized chunks crumpling to the floor below. Jim then started bending the branch, and the steel reinforcing rods had about as much resistance as a long piece of licorice on a hot summer day. In utter disbelief we all watched, and Jim continued to work on some additional branches—all of this in front of God and everybody. Mind you, the cameras are rolling, the board members and donors are present, and this thing that just wasn't supposed to happen, **was** happening!

Immediately we moved Jim off-exhibit and I got on the phone long distance to the specialist contractors, who couldn't believe it either. I was bombarded from every side with the question, "What are you going to do now?" (You could tell people were glad it wasn't *their* problem.) There really was no choice; the trees had to function. They were guaranteed, and the out-of-town contractor immediately dispatched a crew who came and repaired the damaged trees and strengthened all the others just to be sure.

Now, let me explain about these trees. In creating this environment for the orangs, we did not want just a series of thick, vertical tree trunks with short, stubby limbs. We wanted trees with extensive horizontal branches of proper proportion at different levels to provide a real network so the orangs could utilize the vertical space we had created. The texture, bark, and color of the trees resembled those found in Indonesia. We also specified that the branches not be attached to the walls of the exhibit—we truly wanted a free-standing forest, with the orangs having access to every nook and cranny.

Specifications of that type made it difficult in the design and construction of the trees. And, while we acknowledge that Jim may have been stronger than we anticipated, it seems that some of the branches may have been a little longer and a little thinner than they should have been, particularly since their basic strength was in the attachment of the branch to the trunk. We were concerned that in "redoing the trees" the specialist contractor would simply turn them into trunks and stumps.

Fortunately that did not happen. The contractor did an excellent job of retaining the aesthetic value of the trees and the flowing network of a free-standing forest. Those who had not seen the trees previously did not know the difference. It is even difficult for those of us who had seen the trees "before" to see much change "after."

As soon as the contractor finished, we reintroduced the orangs and the trees held just fine. In the meantime, I had contacted most of the contributors to the Orangutan Tree Fund and assured them that it was not *their* branch that broke. The entire episode delayed our grand opening for two weeks, but it also stimulated tremendous interest in the zoo, the Discovering Apes project, and especially in Djakarta Jim—who was now known as "Super Macho Orang No. 1." In fact, TFOTZ issued limited edition T-shirts with this title and Jim's picture.

For the official dedication we constructed a large papier-mache tree and, instead of a standard ribbon cutting, we had a "branch breaking."

*****

One of the VIPs assisting us with the development of Discovering Apes was Terry Maple, Ph.D., Professor of Psychology at the Georgia Institute of Technology. He was also a Collaborating Scientist at the Yerkes Regional Primate Research Center of Emory University and author of the book *Orangutan Behavior.* Terry was in Topeka to train a group of volunteers, coordinated by Susan Chan, who would document the behavior changes of our apes in the new exhibit compared to the old facility. And he witnessed Jim crumpling the steel reinforced concrete branches. He later said he felt sorry for his human friends at the zoo, but "Jim's manipulative prowess was downright exciting! I can honestly say that witnessing Djakarta Jim's unleashed power was one of the genuine highlights of my research career."

Thanks, Terry.

'Go Ape' Days at the Zoo

Actually, we had two such days at our zoo.

The first one took place on Sunday, October 17, 1977 several years before the opening of Discovering Apes first phase, the orangutan exhibit. Sponsored by Topeka Friends of the Zoo, its purpose was to stimulate interest in the proposed Discovering Apes facility, generate new TFOTZ memberships, and provide unusual experiences for our zoo visitors.

It was fun for staff and volunteers to dream up new and different activities. In a reversal of routine procedures, we admitted everyone to the zoo free—but, they had to join Topeka Friends of the Zoo to leave, or pay the full admission price. It sounded a bit risky but turned out to be a successful gimmick.

Starting at noon we had local news media personalities on display in one of the current ape exhibits, and they could only get out after visitors donated a set amount of money to TFOTZ.

Kids were encouraged to make a zoo poster and bring it for display, there were drawings for door prizes every hour, and everyone had a chance to contribute ideas for the proposed great ape exhibit.

But the big event of the day, the real attraction, an occurrence of historic proportion never before and never again seen at our zoo, was . . . (drum roll, please) . . . Dr. Bob Menninger, President of TFOTZ, and Harry "Butch" Felker, Topeka Park Commissioner, being dunked in the hippo pool! YES! It happened! (We *did* clean the pool first, however, and the hippos were *not* in it.) These two gentlemen were such good sports for a great cause and will live in the annals of zoo history.

The other occasion was called "Let's Go Ape Day at the Zoo." Held on Sunday, September 26, 1982 it was sponsored by Hill's Pet Products to recognize their 75 years of business in Topeka. They wanted to do something for the Topeka community and chose the zoo for their celebration.

Hills provided free admission to the zoo, as well as free T-shirts, free balloons, free coin banks, free pet food coupons, and a "Name the Apes" contest.

Phase one of Discovering Apes was complete and Hill's had purchased two new orangutans for the zoo. Hill's explained: "We are donating two orangutans to the Topeka Zoo in recognition of our 75th year in Topeka and to honor our outstanding pet food employees in Topeka and Los Angeles and our pet chemicals employees in Miami."

The winning names for the new female orangutans were Maku and . . . Hill-da!

What a great way for Hill's to celebrate their 75th Anniversary. Congratulations! And a special "Thank You" from the World Famous Topeka Zoo.

A Ghost-Like Tiger

With the zoo's 50th Anniversary approaching in the year 1983, I felt it was important to mark the occasion in a special way. Certainly we would have a public celebration—hopefully the biggest party ever held in Topeka. But we needed something else—maybe a guest celebrity animal as a limited featured attraction. Previously we had black jaguars on loan . . . so this time how about a white tiger?

Yes!

Our neighbors in Omaha at the Henry Doorly Zoo had three of the 21 white tigers in North American zoos at that time. Would they be willing to loan one to us for our Golden Zoobilee?

Yes!

The wonderful people at Hill's Pet Products in Topeka (such fantastic angels of support for our zoo) agreed to sponsor all expenses.

What is a white tiger? It is not a true albino, but a mutant whose parents carry the recessive gene for white offspring. Its fur is chalky white and the stripes range from chocolate brown to gray, although some have been born almost totally white with very few stripes. All white tigers have icy blue eyes. They are one of the most beautiful of the large cats.

The first white tiger in any U.S. zoo was the famous Mohini ("Enchantress") who arrived at the National Zoo, Washington, DC, in 1960. Her father was Mohan ("Enchanter"), who was captured in the wild in May 1951 and raised by a Maharaja in a palace at Govindgarh, India in the State of Madhya Pradesh (formerly Rewa). Mohini was born in the palace in 1958 and was purchased for $10,000 by a businessman for the children of the United States. Because of the rarity of this animal she became an instant star in the National Zoo's collection.

Before she went on display at the zoo she was taken to the White House lawn for President Eisenhower to see. Mohini was dirty from her long travel from India and reportedly the President asked who was going to give her a bath? Like any good cat she did the job herself—by licking her coat.

So, who was the rare white tiger to be on loan to the World Famous Topeka Zoo? He was a robust three-year-old male born in the Omaha Zoo. Both of his parents were normal orange colored tigers, but carried the recessive white gene. His name was George.

GEORGE!!!

I mean . . . George? With all due respect to a fitting name for a person, how do you expect to captivate the imagination of the public with a white tiger named . . . George?

I called my friend and colleague Lee Simmons, the Omaha Zoo Director, and respectfully asked permission to bestow a more appropriate agnomen on this splendid specimen while he resided with us.

Permission granted.

Instantly a name popped into my mind: Ramar, the white tiger. Ahh . . . that's better.

Ramar, the first and only white tiger in the 50 year history of our zoo, was on exhibit for one month only: May 15 to June 12, 1983. During that time Ramar was a star in the community and over 50,000 visitors came to see this "ghost" of a tiger.

On his return to Omaha, however, he was just George again.

Golden Zoobilee: The Zoo's 50th Anniversary

The World Famous Topeka Zoo celebrated its 50th Anniversary, or "Golden Zoobilee," on Sunday, May 15, 1983. Hill's Pet Products of Topeka sponsored the entire event. The star attraction for the day was Ramar, the white tiger on loan for a month from the Henry Doorly Zoo in Omaha, Nebraska.

To commemorate the occasion, we had a number of special activities: the first 5,000 visitors received a piece of birthday cake; free balloons were distributed to the children; a limited edition commemorative poster was given away; children were invited to bring birthday cards to the zoo for display; and everyone was eligible to submit their entry in a "count the stripes on the tiger" contest.

The weather was beautiful and it was anticipated that the zoo might surpass its one-day attendance of 5,094 visitors set on May 25, 1974—the day the Tropical Rain Forest opened. The main gates of the zoo opened at 9:00 am and by 10:30 the first 1,000 people had passed through. Shortly after noon we had reached the 4,000 mark and knew for sure that we would set a record, as the crowd was picking up. By mid-afternoon we had surpassed the 11,000 mark, and when the gates closed at 5:00 pm we had recorded a grand total of 14,254 visitors!

This not only doubled, but nearly tripled our former record. Our attendance was equivalent to 12% of the population of the city of Topeka and 10% of the county population. We surpassed in one day the entire attendance for the previous month (April 1983), and achieved 8% of the total attendance for the previous year (1982). R.L. Blakely, Director of the Sedgwick County Zoo in Wichita, was present for the occasion and acknowledged that we surpassed his record and had recorded the largest single day attendance of any zoo in the state of Kansas.

There were other telltale signs of our record attendance. The traffic jam at 6th and Gage at one point was reportedly three blocks long. A line of people—four abreast—extended from the white tiger exhibit in Animals and Man all the way down the mall nearly to the entrance. Our entire stroller fleet turned over four times. We had to place an emergency order with our soft drink supplier for 25 additional tanks of premix. And by mid-afternoon the toilet paper supply had been completely exhausted in the ladies room.

At the end of the day the zoo staff sat down, looked at each other, and said: "Wow! Would you believe? If someone had told us in the morning that we would have that many people today, we would have been scared to death . . . and better prepared. But we did it!"

We anticipated that the zoo grounds would be a mess. Sure, you could tell there had been an enormous crowd at the zoo, but it was an orderly crowd that respected the zoo, and the grounds were virtually spotless. We were so proud of our Topeka visitors, as we always are.

Sincere appreciation was extended to volunteers from throughout the community, particularly those from Hill's Pet Products, as well as the Topeka Friends of the Zoo, the Topeka Parks & Recreation Department, the Topeka Zoo Staff and the Zoo Explorer Post.

Our Golden Zoobilee was a golden success.

Author's note: for an excellent history of the Topeka Zoo up to 1983, see "50 Years of the Topeka Zoo" by Nancy Cherry in *A Park in the Country—Gage Park's Century* published by the Shawnee County Historical Society (P.O. Box 2201, Topeka, Kansas 66601) as Bulletin No. 76, December 1999, Douglass W. Wallace, Editor.

Society of Animal Artists in Topeka

In recognition of the World Famous Topeka Zoo's 50th Anniversary Golden Zoobilee in 1983, the prestigious Society of Animal Artists held their Annual Juried Exhibition and Sale at the Mulvane Art Center on the Washburn University campus during October 1983. The Show was sponsored by Hallmark Cards/Topeka, the Mulvane Art Center and Topeka Friends of the Zoo.

The weekend beginning on September 29 was an exciting (and sometimes exhausting!) one for the artists, judges, and scores of volunteers from the Mulvane and TFOTZ. The judging was done on Friday, and that evening during the Awards Banquet the eight winning artists were presented with engraved medallions. Rather than Best of Show, or 1st or 2nd place prizes, the Society gave Awards of Merit to the artists.

On Saturday a preview of the exhibition was hosted by the Mulvane Women's Board. In keeping with the nature of the show, the theme of the preview was animals. The centerpiece on the refreshment table was animal oriented, and animal crackers were served with punch. During the preview a pianist in the galleries played songs featuring animals.

Immediately following the preview the artists and judges came to the zoo for a tour. Many of the artists went behind the scenes with keepers to take study photos for future work. In the evening a reception was held in the Discovering Apes lobby, hosted by Topeka Friends of the Zoo. To the delight of our guests, the orangutans were on display and were having a watermelon feast. According to the thank you letters the zoo received from the artists, this was one of the highlights of their visit in Topeka, as it was something they had not seen before.

Sunday was the grand opening of the show at the Mulvane with over 60 paintings and sculptures on display by artists from around the United States, Canada and South Africa. Many of the artists were still in Topeka and mingled with the visitors to explain their techniques in sculpting and painting.

The exhibition was a successful venture with countless people visiting the galleries during the month, including school groups.

Topeka Friends of the Zoo welcomed the opportunity to work in close association with the Mulvane Art Center. A quality exhibition of animal art enabled the zoo to expand its cultural horizons.

Judges for the Society of Animal Artists Exhibition were: Ernest Hagler, Director, Kansas City Zoological Gardens; Jim Hunt, Director, Mulvane Art Center, Washburn University, Topeka, Kansas; Don Lambert, Executive Director, Arts Council of Topeka; Professor Timothy Mitchell, Department of Art History, University of Kansas, Lawrence, Kansas; Professor Edward Navone, Chairman, Department of Art, Washburn University; Nancy Perry, KSN-TV talk show hostess, Topeka, Kansas; Marla Prather, Curator of Painting/Sculpture, Spencer Museum of Art, University of Kansas, Lawrence, Kansas; Jim Ramberg, Outdoor Writer, *The Topeka Capital-Journal*, Topeka, Kansas; Gary K. Clarke, Director, Topeka Zoological Park.

Awards of Merit were presented to the following artists: Shane Dimmick of Evergreen, Colorado, for "Teddies," an ink drawing of a mother bear nudging a tattered teddy bear; Guy Coheleach of Jensen Beach, Florida, for "Manchurian Chase," a painting of two tigers running in the snow; Jim Morgan of Mendon, Utah, for "Flooded Field," a painting of three Canadian geese at sunrise; Diane Pierce of Bonita Springs, Florida, for "Zebra Duikers," an oil painting; Dennis Anderson of Stockton, Missouri, for "Fishing Tackle," a bronze sculpture of a bear catching a fish; Joseph Sheppard of Camden, Delaware, for "Rabbits," an oil painting of five rabbits munching on pea pods; Nico Vosloo of Cape Town, South Africa, for "Etosha Dawn," a print of two elephants in a surrealistic scene; and B.J. Martin of Sarasota, Florida, for "Zarafah," a multipatinated bronze depicting two giraffes on the run.

The Oranguclan and the Orang Gang

Djakarta Jim, Daisy, Sabtu, Rango . . . and then—Hill-Da, and Maku.

These were the members of the World Famous Topeka Zoo's 1982 Oranguclan. With the addition of two new female orangutans, we now had a total of six Bornean orangs on exhibit together in the new Discovering Apes building. For many years the zoo exhibited Djakarta Jim and Daisy, our original pair and perennial favorites with zoo visitors. During this period, we only had space for a pair. But once Discovering Apes opened in 1981, we had a facility that would comfortably house a half dozen of these second largest of the great apes.

And what a spectacular sight to see all the animals on exhibit and in the trees at one time. Even I was impressed. Charlie Zin of *The Topeka Capital-Journal* (and a well-known punster) said that we have so many orangs in Discovering Apes now that we should consider renaming the building the "Hairy Simian Corral."

The best time to see the Oranguclan in action was when the building first opened at 10:00 am each day. The keepers put forth a great deal of extra effort to stimulate activity among the orangs. On some days they would place little clumps of hay in the crotches of the trees. The orangs would pick through the hay, eat little tidbits, even place the hay on their heads. At other times the keepers would hide seeds and raisins in the trees or smear honey on the upper branches. The orangs curiously explored the trees at all levels, seeking out the hidden treats, and smelling and licking the branches for the honey.

Now and then the Rain Forest keepers brought fresh cuttings from various tropical plants, including giant banana leaves. The orangutan keepers draped these throughout upper levels of the concrete trees.

Five of the six orangs would come out of their night quarters and spend a great deal of time in the trees pursuing different activities with the leaves. Some of them would carefully strip the leaves open and eat the soft inner core. Others wadded up the leaves to chew on them. And most of them, in typical orangutan fashion, tried to crawl under the leaves or cover themselves up with them. Then the scene would change, as per my notes at the time.

"Enter the sixth orangutan—Djakarta Jim. He immediately heads for the upper branches in his most dominant fashion. The other orangs scurry. Jim grabs the large banana leaves one by one and tosses them around the exhibit. Eventually they all land on the floor. Jim then descends to ground level, gathers a huge armload of leaves, and walks upright across the exhibit waving the leaves over his head like a flag. He repeats this process until he has piled all of the banana leaves in one corner. He fiddles around in a nest-building type activity, but loses interest after a while. When he ascends into the trees to nibble on primate diet and watch the visitors, the other five orangs then jump in the leaf pile and scatter it all over the floor."

The acquisition of the latest two orangutans (Hill-Da and Maku) was one of the most important events in the history of the zoo. With the addition of two proven breeder females, there were great expectations that a successful propagation program could be established for orangutans at the Topeka Zoo. This did come about and provided an excellent educational exhibit for zoo visitors and enabled the zoo to make a significant contribution to the conservation of this rare and endangered species.

All the expenses incurred in the transportation of Hill-da and Maku from Atlanta to Topeka were met by Hill's Pet Products, with a special grant to the Topeka Friends of the Zoo.

Originally these two orangutans were technically on loan to the Topeka Zoo from Yerkes Regional Primate Research Center at Emory University in Atlanta. But, the zoo made application to the United States Department of the Interior and received an endangered species permit which authorized the zoo to legally own the animals. Yerkes had placed a value of $7500 each on the orangutans, and Hill's Pet Products generously acquired the animals for the zoo as their gift to the community in recognition of their 75th Anniversary.

*****

In November 1984 Jonathan and Rusty, an adult pair of Bornean orangutans, arrived from the Buffalo Zoo, where they had produced young. A year later (November 23, 1985) Rusty gave birth to a female we named Rudy—the first viable orangutan baby to be born in our zoo. Rusty showed good maternal care, but Rudy was not nursing often enough to maintain her strength, and the decision was made to hand-raise her.

In order to minimize any chance of passing along an infection to Rudy, it was decided that her care would be restricted to only a few staff members. (Orangutans are particularly susceptible to human diseases such as upper respiratory infections, which can prove fatal.) Thus, several members of the staff became what was affectionately known around the zoo as the "Orang Gang."

The original Orang Gang members were Alice Miser, Area Supervisor, Discovering Apes building; Piper Kimball, Veterinary Technician; Stan Jensen, DVM, Zoo Veterinarian; Craig Dinsmore, General Curator; and Mike LaRue, Assistant Director. Membership later expanded to include Keepers Kathy Harrison, Ron Ringer, Geoff Creswell, and Mike Ysnaga, and volunteers Susan Chan, Barbara Book and Nancy Cherry. Rudy's pediatrician, Dennis Cooley, MD, was an honorary member. The Orang Gang's responsibilities later extended to hand-rearing Joey, a male orangutan born to Jonathan and Sabtu on February 12, 1986.

Our So-Human Nonhumans

Nancy Cherry, Orangu-Nanny, 1986

Author's Note: Nancy Cherry was an original board member of the Topeka Friends of the Zoo in 1964, and editor of ZOO Magazine from 1969 to 1989. She served as the first chairman of the Topeka Zoo Docents in 1966, and as coordinator for many of the zoo's special events.

Beginning with Easter weekend in 1986 Rudy and Joey, the zoo's two baby orangutans, were on public display every Saturday and Sunday from noon to 3:30. As the babies became accustomed to zoo visitors, their days on exhibit increased.

Normally during the day the baby orangs were cared for in an off-exhibit area of the Discovering Apes building, where they were born. On exhibit days the babies and all their gear were loaded onto an eight passenger electric cart (called the Orangmobile) and transported to the Animals and Man building. There they were on display in the glass fronted nursery unit adjacent to the kitchen (opposite the giraffes). If the weather was especially nice, the babies were taken outside to play on the large lawn exhibiting muntjac deer just west of the Animals and Man building.

During exhibit hours, the babies followed their regular schedule, which included naptime, playtime, and a noon and 3:00 pm feeding.

In addition to selected staff who were members of the Orang Gang, the babies were cared for by volunteer Orangu-Nannies (a term coined by Barbara Book). The Orangu-Nannies helped with daytime feedings and exercising at the zoo, and shared the responsibility of taking the orangs home at night. The Orangu-Nannies were Barbara Book, Carol Brown, Susan Chan, and the author.

The orangs slept in portable playpens, which were toted home, along with diapers, formula, bottles, nipples, baby food, blankets, toys, any medications and miscellaneous baby paraphernalia. A hospital-type chart was kept for each "baby," recording exact amounts of food intake, any vitamins or medicines given, and urine and stool output. In addition, the Nannies kept a notebook on each orang with notations on physical and behavioral progress. In many instances the notebooks read like any baby book. Early entries included: "eyes focusing better," "rolled over and was mad—didn't like being on back," "slept through the night," and *"finally,* first tooth."

Nighttime care of these nonhuman primates was very much like caring for a human baby. In spite of their obvious similarities to humans, one of the most intriguing aspects of caring for orang babies was observing how they differed from humans.

As one would expect from arboreal animals, who are never away from their mothers during their first year, they were incredibly strong. Orangs are born with hands and feet strong enough to hold onto their mothers. Our two had learned to overcome the lack of hair on their Nannies by clinging to clothing or folds of skin (the latter producing ugly bruise marks on the upper arm). And the Nannies learned that necklaces and glasses are fair game for quick strong hands.

In many ways orangs were easier to care for as babies than humans. In the wild with their mothers, they doze on and off regardless of the mothers' activities. Thus, they were good sleepers. At home with their Nannies, they snoozed with lights on, with television or radio on, with human folks moving around and even stepping over them. It wasn't necessary to tiptoe around a sleeping orang.

Another delight was the quietness of orang babies, which was both good and bad. Vocalizing consisted of small squeaks to express unhappiness (usually hunger) or an occasional loud squeal to express anger (*really* hungry). The two sounds they made that most resembled human babies were hiccups and burps. Any parent or baby sitter knows there is nothing more charming than an undemanding baby who sleeps well and doesn't cry. However, just as they seldom expressed displeasure, by human terms, it was difficult to tell when they were happy. They didn't coo, smile, giggle, or laugh—though by their extensive repertoire of facial expressions (both awake and asleep) and with a little experience it soon became apparent when they were unhappy or uncomfortable.

It was a privilege to be one of the Orangu-Nannies, to watch their mobile faces and wonder what they were thinking, and to observe in awe the growth and development of these so-human, nonhuman primates. But I wouldn't trade them for my above average human grandchildren.

After Hours with Rudy and Joey

by Nancy Cherry, Orangu-Nanny, 1986

Many visitors have seen Rudy and Joey, our baby orangutans, on exhibit at the zoo. And many have expressed an interest in what happens to the Kids (as we fondly refer to them) at night. With this in mind we thought it might be of interest to relate what it's like After Hours with Rudy and Joey.

The Kids are not left at the zoo overnight for several reasons. One is their age: Rudy was born in November 1985 and Joey in February 1986 so they are now nine and six months old respectively. They are still young enough to require nighttime care, which is not available at the zoo. The zoo staff leaves at 5:00 pm and reports to work at 8:00 am. Even though both Kids now sleep through the night, until they are on solid food similar to the adult orangs, they require hand feedings. The lucky caretakers were dubbed the Orang Gang soon after Rudy was born. Orang Gang members now consisted of only two staff: Area Supervisor Alice Miser and Veterinary Technician Piper Kimball; and four volunteer Orangu-Nannies: Barbara Book, Susan Chan, Joyce Clarke, and the author. We coordinated through General Curator Craig Dinsmore.

Everyone shared in the daytime feeding and playing schedules, with the night duty divided in such a way as to provide more consistency for the Kids. When you are asked to take one of the Kids home, usually it is for a minimum of three consecutive nights. Occasionally one of the Orangu-Nannies will take both Kids home, but this is the exception.

While I care for both Kids at the Zoo, and have taken both of them home overnight, my main responsibility was to Rudy. For that reason I use her to demonstrate a typical overnight stay of a nine month old orang at our home.

It's 4:30 pm. Pack up Rudy. Tonight she'll need six diapers, one can of formula, two jars of strained vegetables (loves spinach, hates beets), two jars of strained fruit (adores Hawaiian Delight), cereal flakes, her pillow (both Kids have their own), comforter, receiving blanket. Mustn't forget her hospital-type chart and notebook to record her activities. My mental check list sounds an alarm as I realize I've forgotten the baby-wipes. I don't bother with her hot water feeding dish—at home I'll warm her food in the microwave. I may pack a couple of this week's favorite toys, but usually she is quite content to play with my measuring spoons and cups, laundry baskets, our grandsons' outgrown plastic rings and discarded stuffed koala.

The last thing I did before leaving the kitchen at the zoo was check the refrigerator. I take with me any opened jars of baby food and formula concentrate. Rudy and Joey both have shiny new nylon back packs (their second-hand canvas gym bags finally wore out from all the toting) and all of these items must fit into the back pack unless I wanted to make several trips to the parking lot, which I didn't. Both Kids also had their own portable playpens in which they slept. Unless you were lucky enough to have a playpen in the attic, or could borrow one from a friend as I did, these too must be loaded in the car.

And then it's time to pack up Rudy herself. The Kids travel in sky kennels with a beach towel or small blanket to scrunch up with their hands and feet. (Security to an orang baby is holding on tightly to something soft.) The Kids needed some help in climbing through the opening, and I found that putting them in head first on their stomachs, then pushing their bottoms, you usually could latch the door before they're out—after a check for protruding hands and feet.

By now the Kids were used to traveling in the sky kennels and rarely objected since they were still small enough to sit up, and able to look out the mesh sides and window of the car. They don't seem to mind being confined—as long as it doesn't last longer than 15-20 minutes. I never plan to stop for milk on my way home when I have Rudy in the car.

By shortly after 5:00 pm we were home and she was ready for rambunctious playtime (which differs from quiet play). Rudy was familiar with our kitchen and spent the first few minutes checking that everything was as it should be—especially her favorite climbing table and the chairs.

From 5:00 until her dinner at 6:30 Rudy was one busy orang. She would scoot around the floor crab-fashion with remarkable speed, and I learned that silence can be ominous. Orangs do not vocalize much—especially if they are content—and a minute of silence can mean she has crawled somewhere in the house other than where I last saw her. Unlike a human baby, she does not vocalize when I call her name, so I must start searching. I look among the table and chair legs first since orangs are such great climbers. Then I look on top of the tables and chairs. My last resort is under something, like a table, chair or bed. Orangs are nest builders, and true to her species, Rudy often finds happiness in small, compact, secluded nooks around the house. A basket full of laundry (clean or dirty) is especially desirable.

When I first started taking her home she was very like any small baby and was content to lie on her comforter and just look around. But babies grow and get curious—especially orangs. We used a card table in the kitchen as a changing station, and her toys, pillow and comforter were all stashed under it. She liked to grab the legs with her hands, lift up her feet, and swing back and forth.

Another favorite spot was in front of our glass patio doors. She watched the squirrels, birds, and leaves blowing—but when I took her outside she wasn't so sure! As long as she could hold on to me, she was fine. But when I put her down on the patio or grass, that was a whole new strange world.

She did enjoy climbing on our iron patio furniture—but usually with one hand (or foot) touching me. The same was true when I put her hands around a tree limb; swinging from a tree was much better if she was touching a Nanny.

6:30 and it's time for Rudy's dinner. All of the Nannies were fairly rigid in the Kids' feeding schedules because we felt they needed consistency in feeding times since several of us were involved. Rudy was a good eater and always ready for her dinner. She reminded me of a baby bird (without the chirping), as she opened her mouth wide waiting for each bite. She was given a wide variety of baby foods except for meat, since that was not on the diet of the adult orangs at the zoo. In addition to strained food, she received bites of banana, cantaloupe, watermelon, strawberries, cooked green beans, etc. She had a great time mouthing her food when she had 12 teeth, including two molars. After her solids it was time for her bottle or cup—she drank from both. All of this eating only took about 10 minutes—she was fast! By the time she was halfway through her bottle, her eyes began to glaze, the eyelids started drooping, and she sometimes finished it with eyes closed—the only sign of life was her strong jaws sucking on the nipple.

She is in bed in the playpen and asleep by 7:00, and the only noise we might hear from her during the night was the hiccups! Of course, she wasn't always so charming at night—she needed a late night bottle and another about 3:00 am just like a human baby when she was younger.

Once Rudy is in bed it's catch-up time for the Nanny. Recorded in her hospital type chart will be everything she ate and drank since leaving the zoo. In addition, diaper changes are noted and any change in the consistency of stools. After the chart is completed for the day, which includes totaling all solids and formula taken, it's time to record her activities in her notebook. This is a journal of behavioral activities and relates any new or unusual events during the day and evening. Just like a human baby book, it covers everything—her shot record, a new tooth, an illness, a physical accomplishment not done before, even discipline.

Like their human counterparts, baby orangs needed discipline. Rudy had quite a temper when she didn't get her way. I used to wonder if her temper was the result of hand rearing until I read in the literature that even mother-raised orang babies have temper tantrums.

Fear sometimes can be mistaken for temper. She will vocalize with the same high-pitched loud squeal for both, but it's usually evident to the Nanny which emotion she's expressing. One evening she was sitting quietly beside me when I got up to fix her dinner. I put her in my husband's lap, and she was furious! He placed her on the floor and she made a beeline for me, squealing, squeaking, and grunting in anger. I did not pick her up, though it was a little awkward moving from the sink to the fridge with an orang attached to my ankles. Obviously, this was a show of temper.

In contrast, earlier that evening we had showed her two bright red balloons (she loves bright colors) and encouraged her to bat them around the floor. She squealed and moved away from them and came to me for reassurance. It was clear to us that she was afraid. I let her climb up on me and cling for a while before putting her back down. I noticed that from then on when she saw the balloons she hid her head and looked the other way.

At home we encountered difficulties that would not have occurred if she were being raised by her mother. Telephone and lamp cords were a real bugaboo. She loved to chew on them. At one of our Orang Gang meetings when the Kids were quite small, the question arose as to how to discipline an orang baby. It was decided that a firm "No!" coupled with a pinch on loose skin would be the preferred method of discipline. This has been most effective for us at home, and often the pinch isn't necessary—a "No!" with authority does the job.

Visitors often ask if the Kids bite. I have not had much experience with Rudy biting, except for her play bites. I've used the same discipline technique when a bite seemed imminent, and so far it has worked. But with jaws as strong as hers, I was watchful.

One of the fascinating behaviors that my husband and I liked to watch was how Rudy explored with her mouth. I can only imagine how sensitive an orang's lips must be by observing her gently 'mouth' both new and old familiar objects. I know how gentle it feels because she does it to my face, especially my lips. Visitors will interpret it as a kiss, because it looks as if she's puckering her lips. Actually, she extends her lips in a funnel face and 'feels' with them. She will do it to a hard object such as a toy, button, or watchband, as well as my face or neck. I wonder if it is some type of grooming behavior, because grooming is something I had expected to occur naturally with orangs, just like their grasping ability.

I tried to groom her by aping what I've seen the adults do, but only once did I notice her do any grooming—and that was with Joey when she was nearly seven months old and he was three months. I feel confident that once she joins the adult orangs, she will soon learn grooming. Some things Nannies just can't teach.

Rudy sleeps 11 hours and rarely is awake before 7:00 am. She is slow to wake up, and I have about five minutes to lift her out of the playpen and take her to the changing table. Once she comes alive in the morning, she empties a very full bladder (she stays dry all night). Both Kids wear diapers for sanitary reasons, and though disposable ones are great, they weren't made for orangs! Orang thighs are skinny and sometimes the fit of the diaper leg is not quite tight enough. Once she has a clean diaper she is content to play on the floor until breakfast at 7:30. That's fine with me as I like a cup of coffee and a glance at the headlines first thing in the morning.

The time after breakfast is one of my favorites with Rudy. While I am dressing she plays on our antique iron bed. She loves to climb up the head board, which nearly reaches the ceiling. She pats the wallpaper with her hands, and feels it with her lips through the iron bars. Then she will crawl down the bed to the foot, and this is where she occasionally gets into trouble. She sits on the end of the bed holding on to the thin iron bars and looks at herself in my dresser mirror. She attempts to get through the bars, but sometimes gets wedged in and can't squeeze through. After I rescue her she will climb up the outside of the foot board and swing out with one hand, with a glorious expression on her face.

Twice I heard crashes while I was in the bathroom and couldn't see her—once it was the telephone by the bed, and once it was a reading lamp. A few minutes alone can spell disaster with a curious orang. Now I put the telephone on the floor. Even Nannies can be trained.

It's 9:00 am. Time to load the backpack for the return trip to the zoo. As an Orangu-Nanny I can't help but relate to Rudy and Joey as individuals, which means spoiling them to some extent. But I don't think any of us would have been good Nannies if we hadn't had great affection for the Kids, while at the same time recognizing their need to develop and mature as members of their species. For their sake I look forward to the time they will be reintroduced to our social group of orangutans and stay at the zoo permanently to live with orangs, not humans. Who knows, someday Rudy may have a baby of her own—will that make me an Orangu-Granny?

Author's note: Rudy gave birth to her first baby (a female) on April 4, 2005. Named Rayma, she was fathered by Mawas.

24 July 1981

Hi Folks!

Since I am the one that "Jimmied" the dedication schedule for my new
home, the Zoo Staff thought it would be appropriate for me to issue
the invitation for the rescheduled dedication. So here goes:

****
The Topeka Parks and Recreation Department

and the

Topeka Friends of the Zoo

cordially invite you to the dedication of the new

Discovering Apes Building

at the

WORLD FAMOUS TOPEKA ZOO

Friday, July 31, 1981 -- 2:00 p.m.

Please present this invitation at the Admission Booth.
Zoo Phone: 272-5821   Refreshments.
****

The trees have been put back together and they are even stronger than
I am now. Incidentally, if you contributed to the TFOTZ Ape Tree Fund,
I am supposed to tell you that it was not your branch that broke.

See you on Friday.

Your friend,

Djakarta Jim
Male Orangutan

TOPEKA ZOOLOGICAL PARK • 635 GAGE BLVD., TOPEKA, KANSAS 66606 • (913) 272-5821

. . . for a greater understanding and appreciation of animal life . . .

March 1979 $1.00

Topeka
maqazine

*What's right
with left?*

*Confessions of a
reluctant runner*

*Gov. Carlin finds
greener pastures*

**Bridging the
unruly Kaw**

*Artist takes new look
at familiar sights*

Has Topeka Gone Ape?
Ask Max and Tiffany and Gary

This eye-catching cover reflected the controversy surrounding
a much needed home for our growing orangutans and gorillas.

The first of many baby orangutans born in the Topeka Zoo: Rudy (l.) was born November 23, 1985 and Joey (r.) was born February 12, 1986. Both were hand-raised by the Orang Gang and the Orangunannies.
Photo by Nancy Cherry

Joey peers over the playpen. Shortly after this photo was taken he learned how to climb out!

Photo by Gary K. Clarke

Djakarta Jim demonstrated the strength of an adult male orangutan when he twisted this tire like a pretzel.
Photo by The Topeka State Journal

The spectacular Djakarta Jim—just moments before he began demolishing the specially constructed steel-reinforced concrete tree limbs . . . in front of donors, board members, the news media . . . and a flabbergasted zoo director!

Photo by Gary K. Clarke

The glass tunnels in Gorilla Encounter (a first!) proved popular with zoo visitors *and* gorillas. As Max emerged on the left, female M'wasi walked above the crowd. Opening day—May 12, 1985—marked a record crowd: 21,995!
Photo by Gary K. Clarke

Gorillas often shade their eyes to get a better look at zoo visitors in the glass tunnels.
Photo by Gary K. Clarke

Where but the World Famous Topeka Zoo can you look up and see *a gorilla* walking overhead!
Photo (from inside a glass tunnel) by Gary K. Clarke

Adult male gorilla Oscar (l.) climbs on the waterfall while female Tiffany (r.) munches vegetation. The antics of zoo *visitors* in the glass tunnels provide hours of behavioral enrichment for the gorillas!

Photo by Gary K. Clarke

The thrill and enchantment of being nose-to-nose with a magnificent gorilla in the secret garden that is the World Famous Topeka Zoo.

Photo by Gary K. Clarke

Max beckoned from a giant billboard to travelers on the Kansas Turnpike between Wichita and Topeka.

Photo by Craig Dinsmore

Gorilla birthdays were always special occasions, and zoo visitors filled the glass tunnels to greet Max and Tiffany on Max's 20th in 1989.

Photo by Nancy Cherry

The World Famous Topeka Zoo is one of the few places where you can see gorilla knuckle-prints . . . in the snow!

Photo by Nancy Cherry

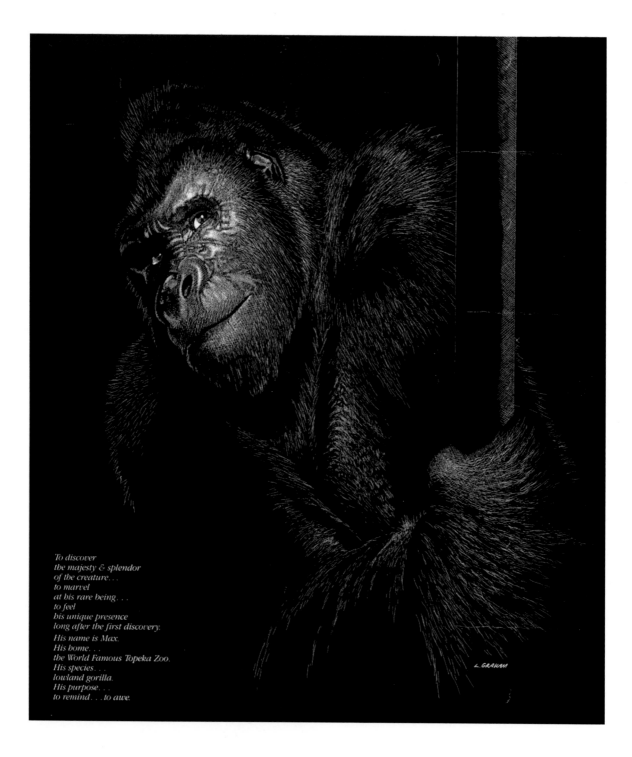

To discover
the majesty & splendor
of the creature...
to marvel
at his rare being...
to feel
his unique presence
long after the first discovery.
His name is Max.
His home...
the World Famous Topeka Zoo.
His species...
lowland gorilla.
His purpose...
to remind...to awe.

L. GRAHAM

This dramatic poster of Max commemorated the opening of Gorilla Encounter, compliments of Hill's Pet Products. The illustrator was Larry Graham of Callahan Creek.

Sunda, the Asian elephant, has smaller ears, a domed head and one "trunk finger" in contrast to the African elephant, Tembo, who has two "trunk fingers," a sloped forehead and larger ears.
Photo by Nancy Cherry

As a "generic" elephant, I promoted the zoo's "Festival of Elephants" throughout the community in 1987.
Photo by Greater Topeka Chamber of Commerce

K'Bluey, the koala on loan from San Diego (that *other* world famous zoo), was weighed daily by his keeper, Elaine Chu (also on loan from San Diego).
Photo by The Topeka Capital-Journal

Caution sign posted by the koala exhibit.
Photo by The Topeka Capital-Journal

Shhh...
K'BLUEY
DOESN'T LIKE
NOISE

The young lioness, Manyara, stalked me while I tried to sneak up on her sister, Arusha, with my camera. This photo ran nationwide on the AP wire, and many people around the country sent inflatable "donuts" for my sore bottom.

Photo by The Topeka Capital-Journal

Our electronic message center always had a special greeting at year's end.
Photo (and message) by Gary K. Clarke

Summer 1987

LIONS
P·R·I·D·E

**WORLD FAMOUS
TOPEKA ZOO**

This appealing scratch board art by Lynn M. Scannell symbolized the essence of our proposed Lions Pride.

Lions Pride features a varied habitat for a family of lions with up-close-and-personal viewing through glass.
Photo by The Topeka Capital-Journal

Lions Pride opened on July 15, 1989 with long lines patiently winding along the Simba Trail.

Photo by Gary K. Clarke

Samburu, the golden-maned pride male, photographed through tension wire at the Adrenalin Grass View.

Photo by Gary K. Clarke

The fabricated kopje rocks at Lions Pride are so realistic that they even fooled my African safari guides.

Photo by Gary K. Clarke

Samburu thrilled visitors inside the Kopje Rock by rearing up on the glass, as photographed from the Bush Camp View.

Photo by Gary K. Clarke

"Genesis," the heroic-sized bronze sculpture of a lion drinking (from a waterhole shaped like Africa), was specifically designed for active participation.

Photo by The Topeka Capital-Journal

At the 1968 zoo director's conference in Los Angeles, I sat at the head table next to the beloved actor Jimmy Stewart, a great zoo supporter. He was the banquet speaker . . . and I presented the Zoo Goof Award to a colleague.

Photo by the Los Angeles Zoo

In your face with my old pal George, the pissed-off tapir who subsequently (and quite unexpectedly) attacked me.

Photo by Henry Gund III

Another mark of distinction: the World Famous Topeka Zoo proudly flying its own flag!
Photo by Nathan Ham Photography

After retiring from the zoo in December 1989, I established Cowabunga Safaris and led photo safaris to Africa. In June 2003 I visited with a crowned pigeon in the Tropical Rain Forest prior to the groundbreaking for the Gary K. Clarke Education Center.

Photo by The Topeka Capital-Journal

Part 7

Nose-to-Nose with Gorilla Giants, Lion Kings and a Koala Rock Star

Giving gorillas glass tunnels, cutting a caper for a koala, and letting lions live lavishly.

With absolutely no qualification or equivocation, the Topeka Zoological Park has to be one of the finest zoological facilities for a city its size anywhere in the world.

—Robert O. Wagner
Executive Director
American Association of
Zoological Parks and Aquariums
Quoted in The Kansas City Star
July 21, 1986, Front Page

Courtesy of the Topeka and Shawnee County Public Library   **Art work by Alice C. Sabatini**

Part 7

Nose-to-Nose with Gorilla Giants,

Lion Kings and a Koala Rock Star

Tuesday, March 5, 1985

4   The Topeka Capital-Journal **Opinion**

Editorials —————————————————— *In God We Trust -*

Zoo spectacular

When the Topeka Zoo's Tropical Rain Forest was erected several years ago, the structure attracted so much national attention that it seemed the zenith of admiration for this medium-sized zoo had been reached. But now the Gorilla Encounter, a unique outdoor exhibit, is nearing completion and promises to be an equal sensation in the zoo world.

It was inevitable that the Topeka Zoo would attempt to design a special kind of exhibit for Max, its 16-year-old star attraction. The gorilla, who arrived here as a baby in diapers and since has grown to 396 pounds, cost $5,000. If the zoo could find another gorilla to buy — which it probably could not — it would cost about $50,000.

But Topeka will have other gorillas. Some other zoos, recognizing the special qualities of Topeka's gorilla exhibit and a need to breed these rare creatures, will lend their gorillas for establishment of two social groups of gorillas here.

Zoo visitors will have a special treat at Gorilla Encounter: The possibility of a nose-to-nose encounter with Max and other gorillas. The exhibit is the only one in the world in which an acrylic-and-glass tunnel for visitors runs through the middle of the outdoor area. The visitors, enclosed in a super-tough environment engineered for twice as much stress as any gorilla might see fit to put on it, may safely observe them. Or, for visitors who don't want to be quite so close, there is an observation post across from a 15-foot-deep moat.

Some tremendous safety factors have been used in building the exhibit. Even if two gorillas were to fall into the moat and one would stand on the shoulders of the other, the top of the moat still would be 3 feet higher than any gorilla has been known to climb.

Gorillas have attained an unfair King Kong reputation as being animals that climb buildings, snatch airplanes out of the sky, roar and beat their chests. Actually they are reserved and cautious creatures. Powerful, yes! But intelligent and interesting. Topeka Zoo visitors, after May 12, will have a better opportunity to observe gorillas more closely and to learn about them.

The new exhibit keeps Topeka prominently featured on the list of who's who among zoos.

Gorillas, Glass Tunnels . . . and You

"You can't put a glass tunnel in a gorilla exhibit!" So said many of my zoo colleagues and scores of other people. But we did, and it was an exciting departure from the standard zoo exhibit.

I must confess, however, that I had toyed with this idea for a long time before I bounced it off my staff, as well as numerous zoo professionals and gorilla experts. Gorilla-proof glass was not the problem; it was in use in various zoos, but only as a vertical front panel. The real challenge was developing the concept for something that had never been done—to create an entire glass tunnel for visitors as part of a gorilla habitat. It was a fascinating process, but you cannot imagine the complexities of the task.

It would be the first animal presentation of its type, anywhere, to feature gorillas. In addition to our imaginative zoo staff, the stellar planning team included Topeka architects Phil Coolidge and Greg Allen as well as Zooplan Associates, zoo design consultants from Wichita. Together we arrived at some ingenious solutions.

Even so, once construction started and the tunnel was taking shape, my excitement was tempered by nagging questions: What if it didn't work? What if the gorillas didn't like it? What if they wouldn't come up to the glass? What if they wouldn't climb on or over the tunnel? What if . . . oh, a thousand other "what ifs"!

Through years of planning, months of agony and the final few days of trepidation—suddenly it was opening day.

AND IT WORKED!

After viewing orangutans at treetop level, you proceeded to Gorilla Encounter and presto—you found yourself literally in the middle of the outdoor gorilla habitat complete with live grass and trees, rock outcrops, fallen tree trunks, earth berms and a sparkling waterfall. Gorillas could be on your right, or on your left, or even directly over your head! In a reversal of zoo roles, gorillas lived in an open environment and *you* were the one in the enclosed area . . . a glass tunnel! Gorillas appeared here as they had never appeared anywhere else—not even in the wild!

Looking to the west from inside the tunnel, you saw the west habitat with natural landscaping that formed several earth berms. Gorillas might visually disappear over the first hill and it looked as if they could easily climb over the second berm as well and explore Gage Park—you might have expected to see them at the Rose Garden or at the tennis courts! In reality, a moat barrier was skillfully hidden between the double berms.

The view to the east from inside the tunnel encompassed the east habitat replete with a cascading waterfall, meandering stream and pool, as well as a view directly across the visible east moat. The moat wall was lined with a fabricated earth bank to provide a natural setting. The ground sloped so that you could easily see the visitors on the public walk as they looked west into the open habitat space with the glass tunnel as a backdrop (where you were). As a result, from the tunnel you were able to see the relationship of the gorillas to the visitors on the outdoor east walk.

One thing that happens when people go to zoos is they like to watch other people almost as much as they enjoy watching the animals. And they particularly like to watch the interaction between animals and people. As far as I know Topeka was the first zoo in the world to purposely incorporate this sociological phenomenon into the design of an exhibit. Here is how it worked.

Proceeding outside to the east walk just viewed from inside the tunnel, you could look back and not only see gorillas but also other visitors in the tunnel reacting to the gorillas. This was the most conventional view of the exhibit, but stepping back from the guardrail revealed yet another dimension. Now it was possible to take in the entire perspective of a unique zoo experience: watching visitors in the foreground as they looked across the moat into the habitat setting to see gorillas who could be looking into the glass tunnel (from the side <u>or</u> from on top) at people who would be looking *back* at the gorillas who might be observing visitors on the sidewalk across the moat—a fantastic multi-dimensional interaction between people and animals in the zoo!!

But the most dynamic encounters occurred from within the tunnel. What could be more thrilling than to watch a 400-pound gorilla deliberately walk up to the glass and position himself just an inch-and-a-half from your face? WOW! Or to see another gorilla climb the rockwork, pause momentarily above the tunnel and then walk on all fours out on the glass directly overhead! WOW again!

With adventures like these word spread about Gorilla Encounter and it grew quickly in popularity. In Topeka it became the "in place" to be, and what fun it was to extend the invitation, "Meet me in the gorilla tunnel at the zoo." People came from all over to see this glass tunnel in the middle of a gorilla habitat, and to say they had been there!

On Sundays it was standing room only in the tunnel, as the gorillas were well known personalities in the community. Max was truly *the* king of the zoo—an adult male silverback lowland gorilla in his prime.

Over the years I had seen many gorillas in zoos around the world, but there was a special, inexplicable quality to Max—one that inspired the following:

To discover the majesty and splendor of the creature . . .
to marvel at his rare being . . .
to feel his unique presence long after the first discovery.
His name is Max.
His home . . . the World Famous Topeka Zoo.
His species . . . lowland gorilla.
His purpose . . . to remind . . . to awe.

To watch Max as visitors oohed and aahed over him was almost as if he were holding forth with his court. It was rather an eerie feeling to see a gorilla as large and ponderous as Max while standing in a *glass* tunnel. You couldn't help but wonder, and even think to yourself, "What would happen . . . if just one time . . . Max were to hit that glass . . . as **hard** as he could?" In a way, you kind of wanted to see him do it; but then again, maybe not—just in case . . .

Max was wise to people. When a huge crowd filled the tunnel, Max would stand in all his glory at a distance, in that characteristic gorilla stance on all fours, and eye the crowd. Gorillas have a peculiar manner of cocking their heads sideways and looking at you out of the corner of one eye. Max was unusual in that he looked at the crowd, not as a group, but individually. His deep-set, unblinking eyes, with their penetrating gaze, would meet *your* eyes and bore into your soul.

It made the hair on the back of your neck bristle and sent a shiver down your spine. After Max had scanned everyone, the suspense mounted and you wondered, "What is he going to do next?" Then, without warning—
BAMM!

Max had launched himself and hit the glass with all his strength!

It is impossible to imagine the hideous unnerving noise that glass makes when impacted by a 400-pound gorilla—it sounded as if the entire tunnel had collapsed.

What a fright! Everyone grabbed his/her heart and knees buckled a bit. Some people immediately reported to the restroom.

The tunnel was intact. Max had hit the glass hundreds of times and knew it would not break. So why did he hit it? Max hit the glass because he liked to watch the people jump, and he knew they would jump every time. After that crowd moved on amid excited chatter and nervous laughter, a new crowd would fill the tunnel and, yes, Max would set them up and repeat the routine.

The gorillas had access to a variety of textures: live grasses and trees, natural soil and fallen logs, as well as the rockwork, vertical earth banks, waterfall, stream and pool. Grade levels varied so that the gorillas could stand on hills or in the low area adjacent to the pool. All live landscape materials were chosen for their hardiness in the four-season Kansas climate and for their decorative qualities. Included were green ash, sycamore, cherry, white pine, honey locust, southern magnolia, asparagus, clump bamboo, miniature roses (why shouldn't gorillas smell the roses, too?), weeping mulberry and birch. Perennial rye grass was planted along with native grasses including big blue stem, little blue stem and Indian grass, which grew in bunches in the exhibit. To provide climbing possibilities for the gorillas, a group of "fallen trees" reaching more than 15 feet in height was fabricated by bolting together fresh-cut mulberry logs. The gorillas had access to three areas that crossed over the tunnel, or they could actually be on top of the tunnel and walk its length. From this vantage, they enjoyed looking down through the glass at the visitors below, a unique situation that provided them with the possibility for some interesting people watching!

The exhibit space was oriented toward the sun to allow maximum opportunity for gorillas to remain on exhibit during winter weather. An all-weather grotto occupied the northwest corner to protect them from winter winds and provide an overhang to maintain a dry space. The grotto contained radiant heating elements. During warm weather the grotto provided a cool, shady oasis for the apes to escape the heat. One of the two gorilla access doors was provided with a double set of heavy duty rubber weather flaps to enable the gorillas to exercise their option to go out or stay inside during inclement weather.

In itself Gorilla Encounter was an impressive exhibit—but with the presence of living gorillas, it became an electrifying experience that could never be forgotten. You gained an entirely new perspective on these remarkable apes, their physical capabilities, their behaviors and activities. Gorilla Encounter truly stood in the forefront of sophisticated zoo exhibits and provided both gorillas and visitors a multi-dimensional experience.

The World Famous Topeka Zoo strikes again!

A Distinctive Dedication

As you might expect with an incredible exhibit such as Gorilla Encounter, we wanted the official dedication (prior to the public grand opening) to be memorable and colorful. Here is what we did.

Inside the tunnel we covered all the glass panels with white paper and invited school children to paint murals on them. Then, on the day of dedication, we brought all the dignitaries out—the Mayor, Chamber of Commerce officials, City Council, Friends of the Zoo Board, etc.

The tunnel was packed with VIP's, TV crews and reporters. None of them had seen the exhibit. All they could see were the children's paintings. Each one of the murals had a string attached at the top with a banana hanging on it. The banana was yellow plastic and inscribed, "Gorilla Encounter Dedication. World Famous Topeka Zoo. May 8, 1985."

There were 18 panels so 18 dignitaries were designated to man their stations. We gave the Mayor a T-shirt that said, "Top Banana at the World Famous Topeka Zoo."

At a signal from the Mayor, everybody pulled their banana. The murals literally dropped down and unveiled the exhibit on both sides. Then the gorillas started climbing all over the rocks and the glass tunnel. I never heard so many "oohs and aahs" in all my life!

I still have my yellow plastic banana.

A Preeminent Preview

Prior to our grand opening we held another special event. It was customary in the zoo world to host a preview of any major new exhibit for professional associates from other zoos across the country. Not only could you extend hospitality to your colleagues, but also it gave you a chance to share your accomplishments with those who could truly appreciate all of the necessary blood, sweat and tears. Just about everyone who had received an invitation said they would be there, as they all had heard of Gorilla Encounter.

We were surprised and humbled by the response—zoo directors and associated staff came from all over. After touring our zoo, they assembled at Discovering Apes. Many had not seen the orangutan exhibit (completed in 1981) and enjoyed tropical sundowners in the visitors' bamboo tree house while the orangs entertained with a watermelon party of their own at tree-top level.

Proceeding to the glass tunnel, the guests found a stunning scene: dinner tables the full length with festive decorations and candlelight.

The surrounding ambiance was a natural habitat with grass, trees, rockwork, waterfall and pool. As they sat down to a gourmet meal, gorillas appeared in front of them, in back of them . . . even overhead! What fun to see these prominent professionals of the zoo world, all of whom had created spectacular exhibits of their own, reacting excitedly like children in this never-before experience—the Gorilla Encounter at the World Famous Topeka Zoo!

The highlight of the evening, however, was something that even I could have never anticipated. One of our best-known and well-loved colleagues (world-wide) was Clayton F. Freiheit, L.H.D., President and CEO of the Denver Zoological Foundation. He was a distinguished zoologist, a well traveled zoo historian, a ranking officer in our professional organizations, and director of one of the world's great zoos. He was always well groomed and impeccably dressed, a sophisticated conversationalist and a connoisseur of fine wine and dining. Just prior to dessert one of the gorillas (who shall forever remain nameless to protect the innocent) climbed to the top of the tunnel, proceeded out onto the glass directly over Dr. Freiheit's head, and . . . yes . . . urinated! The tunnel exploded with laughter as Dr. Freiheit continued unabated with his meal. To this day that incident is remembered by colleagues and I must say that Clayton, always the good sport, also found it humorous.

Such were some of the adventures and unexpected eventualities of the glass tunnel in a gorilla exhibit.

The following page features the full-page ad in *The Topeka Capital-Journal*, Sunday, May 5, 1985. The ad was sponsored by Hill's Pet Products, Inc. Art work by Alice C. Sabatini.

GRAND OPENING

AT THE WORLD FAMOUS TOPEKA ZOO

SUNDAY, MAY 12, 1985 9 a.m. to 6 p.m.

KS

GORILLA ENCOUNTER

Free Shuttle bus from Gage Shopping Center and Hayden High School every 15 minutes — 10 a.m. to 5:30 p.m.

- Free "Max" Posters
- Free Gorilla Fact Sheet
- Free "Max and Me" Comparison

DRAWING FOR ONE THOUSAND GORILLA ENCOUNTER TOTE BAGS

GRAND PRIZE: TRIP TO CHICAGO

Visit Brookfield Zoo and Lincoln Park Zoo
4 days, 3 nights, Family of 4

FREE ADMISSION

SPONSORED BY **Hill's** PET PRODUCTS, INC.

What To Do When a 400-Pound Gorilla Won't

The stage was set . . . or I should say, the zoo was set.

There was an atmosphere in the air, rather like the calm before the storm, although the weather was perfect.

It was just before 9:00 am on Sunday, May 12, 1985—the scheduled time for the Grand Opening of our new Gorilla Encounter. Dozens of volunteers—actually hundreds—had been working for days—actually months—in preparation for the day. I personally had been waiting for this very moment for over ten years! And now it was here.

We anticipated a large crowd—14,000 or more. That would equal or surpass our one-day attendance record set in May 1983 on the occasion of our Zoo's 50th Anniversary celebration. But that was then and this was now. We were **ready!**

A long line of visitors had already formed outside the main gate, all the way across the zoo parking lot to the miniature train station.

The Topeka community was excited (and so were we), not just because our long-awaited gorilla exhibit was finally opening, but because this event heralded the return of the zoo's singular star attraction—Max, our male gorilla.

He had arrived as a baby in 1969 and had grown up in our zoo. In 1983, when construction began on the Gorilla Encounter, Max was transferred to the Denver Zoo on loan as part of the national cooperative conservation program. Now he was back, a beautiful adult silverback tipping the scales at 400 pounds. This would be his debut in the new exhibit.

Transmissions on the zoo's walkie-talkie radios were fast and furious. Area supervisors were adjusting barricades on the switchback system that had been set up to channel the large crowds into a structured traffic pattern. The general curator was checking with various animal keepers, since all exhibits and buildings were opening an hour earlier for the occasion. The concessions staff was scurrying around the zoo setting up extra portable stands in remote locations, and volunteers were asking staff members with radios to communicate last minute messages.

The assistant director radioed me and advised that it was precisely 9:00 am. He asked, "Should we open?" I replied, "Yes!"

The gates opened and the initial wave of visitors flooded into the zoo. As they were snaking through the switchback system on their way to Discovering Apes and Gorilla Encounter, I radioed the lead keeper to go ahead and let Max out from the night quarters into the outdoor exhibit. The timing would be ideal, as Max should emerge into this fabulous new habitat setting in perfect weather just as the initial visitors walked into the glass tunnel in the middle of the exhibit.

I watched the crowd on its way and waited for the keeper's response. And waited . . . and waited. Just as I was about to inquire again, the keeper radioed with four words that are now indelibly imprinted upon my mind:

"*Max won't come out.*"

What to do now?

To be continued . . .

Well, obviously—as the saying goes—a 400-pound gorilla can do anything he wants, so if Max didn't want to come out now, that's it.

Fortunately, there was another gorilla waiting in the wings—Oscar, who had been residing in the Omaha Zoo and was now on loan to us from the Jackson, Mississippi Zoo.

"Send Oscar out," I replied.

And out he went.

Oscar was also an adult silverback male, weighing nearly the same as Max. And while they had totally different facial characteristics, both were equally impressive in appearance. In fact, many visitors often confused Oscar with Max. It became the prime duty of our volunteers in the glass tunnel that day to identify gorilla personalities and direct zoo visitors to the portraits that assisted in recognizing the individual gorillas.

In retrospect, Max not coming out at 9:00 am may have been a good thing. We had already anticipated that with extended hours on opening day we would probably not have the same gorillas on exhibit the entire day. We thought it best for their sakes to rotate them out in shifts. And while Max had been scheduled to be in the first shift, we simply substituted Oscar and he did beautifully.

Oscar readily climbed the rockwork in the central section of the tunnel on the west side. If you were lucky enough to be standing on the east walk looking at the waterfall, you would see this massive head emerge over the rocks and this giant form assume the characteristic four-point stance of a gorilla. It was spectacular! After Oscar investigated the area and sized up the crowd, he would then proceed to climb headfirst down the waterfall, descending to ground level and exploring the east yard, frequently tearing up trees. He related well to water and would crouch at the edge of the pool, dip his massive hand into the water and lift it to his lips for a drink.

Oscar was out until about 1:30 pm, at which time the signal was given (we rang a bell) for him to come back in. He did so, and Max was then introduced into the exhibit. This time he walked right out.

While the crowd was pretty well dispersed throughout the day, the bulk of our visitors came in the afternoon and thus the majority of the people on Grand Opening day were able to see Max. After that we alternated gorillas on exhibit so that on a given day visitors had the opportunity to see different personalities.

When you anticipate a crowd of 14,000 people or more in a zoo that normally considers 3,000-5,000 people a very busy day, you had better be prepared. We had planned accordingly, and as the day progressed we felt very good about how well things seemed to be going. When we reached the 14,000 mark and still had a good portion of the day to go, we knew we were in for another record-setting crowd. Periodically we would monitor visitors to see how long it took, from the moment they entered the front gate until they were able to exit the glass tunnel at Gorilla Encounter. The maximum time seemed to be about 45 minutes. During that time they were generally on the move through our switch-back system and, fortunately, we had a variety of other animals in the zoo to view while waiting to enter Gorilla Encounter.

By the end of the day, when we closed our gates at precisely 6:00 pm, we had registered 21,995 visitors! Several people said, "Gee, round up another five people real quick so we can make it an even 22,000!" While that certainly was a temptation, I felt it was important to record exactly how many visitors we had from 9:00 am until 6:00 pm. In reality, we had well over 22,000 people in the zoo that day if you consider the multitude of volunteers that were present in a variety of capacities.

Many factors fell into place to insure the success of our biggest day ever. The weather was excellent, the pre-publicity and marketing strategies for the event were superb, and the planning was precise. But, the response of staff and volunteers alike throughout the day was the key to making for a smooth event.

In the days following this event many people asked me: "Well, how are you going to top that?" I replied that I was not so sure that we wanted to. Yes, it was great to have such significant numbers; and yes, we were pleased that everything went so well. But our goal was not to see how many people we could get through the zoo in a single day. Rather, our goal was to provide quality environments for animals that resulted in memorable experiences for zoo visitors. If we could achieve that and still generate record-setting crowds, so be it. If not, then the numbers would be secondary.

Besides, I had a number of other things that demanded my attention, including dealing on a daily basis with *two* 400-pound gorillas!

Wednesday, May 15, 1985

The Topeka Capital·Journal **Opinion**

Editorials ———————— *In God We Trust*

It was a real zoo

The Topeka Zoo was, in every sense of the word, a zoo Sunday as 22,000 people thronged to the new Gorilla Encounter.

It could have been even more frantic, but a preview Friday night for Topeka Friends of the Zoo helped alleviate some of the Sunday rush.

There is no doubt about it. The unique new gorilla exhibit is indeed a drawing card for the zoo. Nowhere in the world except Topeka, Kansas, can one experience the entertaining and massive primates in such a clear, close-up view. Encounter is the perfect description for the exhibit.

Of course, weekends are always popular at the zoo — particularly when the weather is as cooperative as it was Sunday. But Sunday's attendance broke the previous record by nearly 8,000 visitors.

Credit Max, the resident gorilla, who was back home after two and a half years. Credit curiosity over the new exhibit. And credit Hill's Pet Products Inc. and its parent company, Colgate-Palmolive, for picking up the gate charge for all 22,000 visitors.

It was a memorable day in zoo history. It was a marvelous welcome back party for Max.

But the best part is that the Gorilla Encounter is still there today. It will be there tomorrow and a year from tomorrow. Those who missed it Sunday can go out any day of the week and see it themselves.

It is a one-of-a-kind exhibit — and it is right in our own back yard.

Awesome Angels and Unsung Heroes

"Every zoo needs an angel when planning a special event, particularly one such as the opening of Gorilla Encounter," declared Nancy Cherry.

Fortunately, Hill's Pet Products was an exemplary community angel and an awesome angel to the zoo. When Hill's took on this role, it encompassed much more than just being a financial benefactor—it included people in the form of volunteers. And much of their support was behind-the-scenes.

During the planning of the Gorilla Encounter opening day, we were asked to contribute ideas to make the day a memorable event for the community. Each time we suggested an idea that we thought was too wild, Bob Wheeler, President of Hill's, said, "Go for it!" He then would turn to Ginny Trygg of his staff, and say, "Do it!" While Ginny's official title at Hill's was Personnel Supervisor, her assignment in this case was to coordinate the project between Hill's and the zoo. Part of her job was to stay within a budget, and her lament was, "How can I keep expenses down when Bob wants everything?"

And "everything" included much more than free zoo admission sponsored by Hill's, 20,000 free Max posters, 1,200 free gorilla tote bags, Max-sized neckband giveaways, gorilla fact sheets and a grand prize trip to Chicago for four days and three nights with tours of the Brookfield and Lincoln Park Zoos. It also included Hill's employees volunteering in three-hour shifts all day at the zoo.

Long before the Grand Opening, Hill's had played a major role in assisting the zoo with the transportation of gorillas (and orangutans, too). Moving primates between zoos was a complicated affair, and required enormous planning. The welfare of the animal was paramount, and consideration had to be given to weather, length of the trip, and method of transportation.

Max was on loan to the Denver Zoo during the construction of Gorilla Encounter, and ground transportation was deemed advisable for him as he was relatively close. This mode of travel entailed renting a truck, courtesy of Hill's.

Hill's also paid for M'wasi, a female gorilla, and her keeper's transportation from the National Zoo in Washington, DC, via Flying Tigers Air Cargo. In planning for the future of a species such as gorillas, it is essential that the animals be loaned between zoos—which incurs shipping costs. This is typical of the generous though unglamorous support that Hill's provided.

But back to planning for the grand opening. We had numerous factors to consider, ranging from the unpredictable Kansas weather to how many portable restrooms we should rent. Other dilemmas we faced were those common to any large zoo gathering: traffic jams and parking, long lines of people, how to service auxiliary concession stands, first aid, trash and litter control, communications with a limited number of walkie-talkies, and all the little things that go into making a very special day at the zoo a pleasant experience for visitors.

Our solution to the parking problem was to "leave the driving to us"— with "us" meaning shuttle buses. From past experience we knew that traffic jams and parking would be a problem. The zoo's parking lot only held 213 cars, which would not begin to be enough space, even with Hill's and Friends of the Zoo volunteers parking in the service area. Shuttle buses were chartered to service two nearby parking lots—Gage Shopping Center and Hayden High School. Each bus was dubbed the "Gorilla Express" and large signs were put on the sides of the buses. They ran continuously every 15 minutes all day.

Among our volunteers that day were members of two Explorer Scout Posts. The Police Department Explorers assisted in directing traffic in the parking lot, while the Zoo Explorers aided staff and volunteers on the zoo grounds. A Medevac ambulance was parked inside the zoo to provide any needed first aid by corpsmen who were volunteering their time.

Susan Chan, 1985 Vice President of Topeka Friends of the Zoo and volunteer events coordinator for the opening of Gorilla Encounter, called volunteers "the vital link." I fully agree. She expressed volunteer involvement in Gorilla Encounter so well that I'd like to share some of her observations with you:

"Planning for this particular event had begun a year and a half earlier as a one-day event sponsored by Hill's Pet Products. As momentum began to build and the exhibit took shape, this single event escalated into a week's worth of activities! The week evolved after long hours of planning by volunteers and zoo staff. It began on the Sunday prior to the Grand Opening with a special preview for all the volunteers who would work on the 'Big' day. This was followed on Monday by a preview and picnic for the staff and their families. This was a week of no vacations and no days off for the staff. Tuesday saw zoo colleagues from across the U.S. converge on Topeka for a professional preview. Public officials and media attended a preview and participated in a dedication on Wednesday. Friday evening was a sneak preview for Friends of the Zoo. On Saturday night a black tie, fundraising dinner dance was held at the zoo. And, of course, the Grand Opening on Sunday was an event beyond our wildest imaginations, both in terms of number of visitors and overall success.

"Behind the scenes of these events were the volunteers—planning programs, coordinating press releases and publicity, working with caterers, printers, community sponsors and those who would actually provide enough people-power to make the events successful. Some of the work was exciting and some was mundane. Trivial yet important items like providing the right number of extension cords, enough toilet paper for the portable toilets, and working out a parking lot strategy, took countless hours but certainly never made the front page of the local newspaper. While these things may not seem glamorous, they are the types of details which cannot be overlooked and which go a long way in making any special event successful.

"You may wonder why anyone would want to spend his or her free time in such labor-intensive pursuits. The answers are probably as many and as individual as the volunteers behind them. Speaking personally, the zoo is something that gets into your blood. It becomes family and like any close-knit family, you work towards the ultimate success of the unit. You ride a high tide of elation at the birth of a new animal and mourn the loss of one you had come to know as an individual. The rewards of seeing a successful event come off without any major hitches make the long hours seem worthwhile. You're tired, dead tired, when it's over but it doesn't take long before the adrenaline begins pumping as you anticipate the next event and mull over new plans and innovative prospects for the future. It's an intangible kind of reward in a way, but one that leaves a glow."

So many unsung heroes and heroines volunteered during my tenure at the World Famous Topeka Zoo that I could never suitably thank them all. May I take this opportunity to express my deep appreciation to each and every one! And once again hats off to the zoo's awesome angel, Hill's Pet Products, with a humble "thank you" to Bob, Ginny, and their entire staff.

Gorillas in the . . . Snow?

The phrase "Gorillas in the Mist" is a familiar one as a result of the popular book and film of that title. But to read or hear "Gorillas in the Snow" seems out of place.

And to actually find gorillas in snow is highly unusual. Certainly the elevated habitat of mountain gorillas gets quite cold at times, but there's no snow.

Special features in Gorilla Encounter were designed to enable our gorillas to enjoy the habitat even in winter: high north walls for wind protection, plus a heated grotto facing south to maximize solar energy. Weather flaps allowed the gorillas easy access in and out.

Keepers would daily consult the National Weather Service, and gorillas were permitted outside if the wind-chill factor was 25 degrees F or above. (The inside thermostat was set at 50 degrees F in winter.) The gorillas all grew thick winter coats even though they were of the lowland variety. Extra hay was provided outside and gorillas would make nests and cover themselves with hay.

Max, our star adult male, readily adapted to cold weather and would forage throughout the exhibit for raisins, peanuts and seeds, returning inside now and then to warm up.

Our gorillas encountered snow (in the Gorilla Encounter, of all places) for the first time on December 5, 1985. Area Supervisor Alice J. Miser astutely observed that, ". . . each gorilla has its own unique personality and each reacts to new things in a different manner." Hence, it would seem apropos to quote Alice on how our gorillas initially reacted to snow.

"M'wasi (a female) went out first and took the snow right in stride. She climbed the ice-covered log climber, crossed over the snowy bridges, and continually looked for food items in the snow. Oscar, also, didn't seem bothered by this cold white blanket. I did notice he climbed up and down the snow-covered waterfall slower than he had during the summer.

"Max seemed a little more apprehensive about the white stuff. (This could have been due to the glare as the sun was shining brightly on the snow.) He walked to the edge of the concrete in front of the cave, then reached out and raked the snow with his hand. He looked at this cold, wet material, smelled it, then licked his hands clean. This was all the investigating Max was going to do that day. He moved into the grotto area to look for food items in the hay—and stayed there."

We now knew that, without hesitation, our gorillas would go out in the snow. And the World Famous Topeka Zoo was one of the few places on the planet where you could see gorilla footprints—and gorilla *knuckleprints*—in the snow!

Breakfast at Tiffany's

Merely having the *only* glass tunnel in the world set in the middle of a gorilla habitat was not enough for the World Famous Topeka Zoo. Oh, no. We simply *had* to utilize this unique venue in special ways to create lasting memories for our visitors . . . and our gorillas. And when you have imaginative individuals on your foundation board like Randy Austin, Attorney and Managing Trustee of Fairlawn Plaza Shopping Center in Topeka . . . watch out!

With all the festivities of the grand opening of Gorilla Encounter in May 1985, "Someone missed the party," as Assistant Zoo Director Mike LaRue said. It wasn't just a "someone." More correctly, it was Tiffany, our female lowland gorilla, and one of the main reasons for the ideas, plans and construction of Gorilla Encounter. Mike said that, "Where's Tiffany?" was one of the most asked questions at the party!

Mike had the answer, and I'll quote, "Tiffany had a prior engagement: species survival, which meant Tiffany was at the Buffalo Zoo being a gorilla. We sent her there in January 1983, under the auspices of the Gorilla Species Survival Plan of the American Association of Zoological Parks and Aquariums."

Mike went on to explain that Tiffany had been placed with a group of gorillas to gain social experience and, hopefully, breed and produce offspring. We had the option to bring her back for the opening, but felt it was important to leave her in Buffalo as part of the Species Survival Plan. Meanwhile, our zoo had received M'wasi, a female gorilla on loan from the Bronx Zoo in New York, as well as Oscar, a male on loan from the Henry Doorly Zoo in Omaha.

In time, however, it was determined that Tiffany should be returned home, and that was when Randy Austin sprang into action. You may recall that back in 1969, when we first put Max and Tiffany together, I had made a feeble attempt to capitalize on Tiffany's name and the popular film "Breakfast at Tiffany's," based on the book by Truman Capote. Randy was not impressed, and wanted to do it in a proper manner.

This meant a full fledged, early morning breakfast in the tunnel, with guests served by Randy and myself in tuxedos, and Tiffany herself in attendance. Guests would be selected via a competition sponsored by Fairlawn Plaza, and the breakfast itself would be "eggstra" special with omelets personally prepared by Howard Helmer, the world record holder for the number of omelets prepared per minute—fourteen! Other menu items included cinnamon rolls, a fresh fruit salad (which Tiffany enjoyed), juice and coffee. The date was September 5, 1987.

It was fabulous! The guests raved and Tiffany was so intrigued that she was all over the tunnel! Those of you reading this who may have been a participant, consider yourself among the privileged few! Breakfast at Tiffany's at the World Famous Topeka Zoo was a one-time-affair, never to be repeated. Thank you, Randy.

Koala Connection '86

The idea was so preposterous that I labeled my file folder OPERATION LONGSHOT.

The San Diego Zoo had announced they would allow some of their koalas to be available for a one-month loan to select zoos across the country. I requested the necessary forms, completed the application and returned it. Weeks passed, months passed, and finally a year.

Then word came that the San Diego Zoo had accepted our application *if* we could meet qualifications. And that was a big "if." By all things logical, there was no way a modest zoo like ours in Topeka could expect to pull off such an ambitious undertaking as "Operation Longshot."

The San Diego Zoo had 13 (yes, *thirteen*) pages of detailed requirements, all necessary and reasonable, but: we were the smallest zoo, with the least resources, ever to attempt a koala loan.

We had to be an accredited zoo (we were) with a fulltime staff veterinarian (we had one). And, we had to provide *everything*: specialized housing for the koala with controlled temperature, humidity and lighting; direct air transportation for the koala—and its keeper—from San Diego to Topeka (and return); twice weekly shipments of fresh cut eucalyptus browse (that's all a koala eats) direct from the San Diego Zoo; insurance coverage ($20,000) for the koala while it was in Topeka and for two weeks after its return to San Diego; salary for the San Diego koala keeper, plus housing, meals, and daily transportation; local staff for 24-hour-a-day behavior observations of the koala the first five days, with daily monitoring after that with volunteers during exhibit hours; a $2,000 contribution to the Conservation Fund of the American Association of Zoological Parks and Aquariums; and the list went on.

Have you ever booked a rock star? Probably not, but that is the only way I know to compare what we were in for. A rock star might demand dressing room walls painted fuschia with yellow stripes, but that's only a paint job—we had to build a whole new indoor exhibit to specifications, including climate and lighting. A rock star might insist on eight pizzas and a six-pack after his performance, but there are lots of pizza parlors around the country. We had to provide fresh cut eucalyptus leaves, flown in twice weekly, from San Diego. I use the analogy between the rock star's dressing room and food with the koala's exhibit space and food, not to put either of them down, but to demonstrate that what we see up front often is only a small part of the whole picture.

It never occurred to us to tell San Diego that we simply did not have the wherewithal for such a major undertaking. After all, we *were* the World Famous Topeka Zoo.

My first approach was to Hill's Pet Products, for several reasons. The folks at Hill's had been incredibly supportive of the zoo over the years, particularly with much behind the scenes assistance that most people never knew about. And Hill's had been a good barometer with reference to what the citizens of our community wanted from their zoo. In other words, we didn't just rely on their financial support, but also on their wisdom and experience. With their blessing and support, we proceeded with the project and what I called the "K-Team."

The K-Team would consist of anyone and everyone in our community who could contribute in some way to help our zoo in bringing a koala to Topeka on loan from the San Diego Zoo.

It wasn't just a question of money—thousands upon thousands of dollars, and not a penny from the city—but also everything else necessary for us to qualify.

One of my biggest concerns was the number of people that would be needed above and beyond the staff—**dozens** of volunteers willing to commit **hundreds** of hours! This would be an enormous task requiring a super-duper experienced volunteer coordinator familiar with both our zoo *and* complex special events. We had such a person in Friends of the Zoo Past President Susan Chan.

A notice ran in the April 1986 issue of the *Bear Facts* newsletter under the headline, "Calling on Friends." It advised of the need for volunteers to work two-hour shifts to assist visitors viewing the koala during exhibition hours. In addition, the San Diego Zoo required 24-hour observation of the koala the first five days it was in our zoo. FOTZ members responded—overwhelmingly! They considered it a privilege to be part of zoo history.

A different set of volunteers assisted the zoo staff and park department crew in converting the old Animal Kingdom Building into a koala exhibit that met the exacting standards of the San Diego Zoo. The entire structure was gutted, the alligator pool was overlaid, surfaces were scrubbed and repainted, and a visitors' traffic pattern was established. Walls were covered with graphics about koalas and related subjects, special lighting and television monitors were installed, a distinctive koala tree-perch (with holders for eucalyptus leaves) from the San Diego Zoo was positioned just so, and a small office was fashioned for the koala keeper.

It cost a pretty penny to do all of this—actually many pretty pennies. Major funding came from Hill's Pet Products, Friends of the Zoo, Fairlawn Plaza Merchants Association, Topeka Dairy Queens and Shawnee Federal Savings. But funding wasn't just from businesses and organizations. A significant donation was provided by the Fowler family—Nile, Kate, Garrett and Kylie—all longtime, enthusiastic supporters of the zoo. Ray Beers Clothing Company, American Linen Supply and Country Day Pre-School gave additional funding. The specialized glass and climate controls for the koala enclosure were contributed by the Independent Insurance Agents of Topeka, with assistance from City Glass and Mirror.

What a community! No wonder we had such a great zoo!

It was an amazing metamorphosis . . . so much so that I renamed the building the "Koala Day Inn." (We also used that term for the Holiday Inn that provided daily lodging and breakfast for the koala keeper).

We felt very good about the entire project, but—would it pass the test? On June 5, 1986 an official from the San Diego Zoo made a special trip to Topeka for the final inspection. It was detailed, and we were on pins and needles, as the saying goes. I held my breath for so long that my normal ruddy complexion had a bluish cast.

Finally . . . the decision . . .

Yes!

Now we could tell all of those folks who had been calling from as far away as Denver to, "Come on down!"

When I learned that the koala assigned to us would be the one and only K'Bluey, I was ecstatic! He was known to be a character, and what a fantastic name!

K'Bluey's keeper, Elaine Chu (who had a degree in Animal Sciences from the University of Massachusetts at Amherst), explained that K'Bluey's name had a double meaning. "Bluey" is Australian slang for a red-haired man (when he emerged from his mother's pouch, he had a red tinge on the top of his head). And "K'Bluey" was for the imagined sound of the population growth of the San Diego Zoo's koala facility. Seven koalas were added in 1983, the same year K'Bluey was born.

San Diego described K'Bluey as good-natured and noted he liked to climb as high as possible and sit on crossbeams. He was entering koala puberty and seemed to be "feeling his oats." He was reportedly camera shy, and hence, we had to prohibit the use of flash pictures in the exhibit.

It was very important that everything was just right for the visit by K'Bluey the koala. Not only was this a significant event for the entire community, but I certainly did not want K'Bluey to go "kablooey" while he was at the World Famous Topeka Zoo.

In anticipation of Koala Connection '86, I started wearing my various koala neckties every day for several months before the event. All over town we distributed calling cards (I liked to call them "ko-al-ing cards") with K'Bluey's photo and the headline: **The Koala Is Coming!**

Zoo Artist Alice Sabatini created a wonderful logo. It was utilized to promote the event on grocery bags in supermarkets from Topeka to Denver, and on placemats in McDonald's restaurants in Topeka, Lawrence, Manhattan and Junction City, complete with Koala Footnotes (facts about koalas).

The Greater Topeka Chamber of Commerce Convention and Visitors Bureau distributed Koala Connection '86 brochures at 157 locations along Interstate 70 from Denver, Colorado to St. Louis, Missouri.

The local media were simply fantastic in their coverage of preparations for our big event. But so was the out-of-town press. A week before our public opening, STAR Magazine in *The Sunday Kansas City Star* featured a color photo and an article under the headline KOALA CONNECTION that began:

First Gary Clarke had to arrange transportation: by air, direct. Then he had to build a special home. And provide lodging, and meals, and a car, and a paycheck, and spending money for a month for a chaperone.

Then there was the matter of the eucalyptus . . .

And all for a 14-pound guest named K'Bluey. He's an Australian koala.

The article continued with details about K'Bluey coming to Topeka Zoo on loan from San Diego Zoo "courtesy of donors all over Topeka." And it mentioned Hill's Pet Products by name as the major sponsor.

It is interesting to note that when *The Kansas City Times* did a follow-up article in their Mid-America section of June 23, 1986 the lead sentence was: "This summer's celebrated visitor to the World Famous Topeka Zoo hasn't lost any sleep as a result of his star status." Please note WORLD FAMOUS TOPEKA ZOO! (Oh, how I loved it!)

Another preliminary activity, this one by a K-Team member, was the "Koala Khallenge" by Shawnee Federal Savings. A very clever three panel foldout brochure had koala facts and several challenges: connect the dots, maze puzzle, hidden word brain teasers, and a logo mystery comparison.

Incidentally, Nancy Cherry deserves much credit for providing facts, information and ideas for all the materials mentioned previously.

K'Bluey and his keeper, Elaine Chu, arrived from San Diego (courtesy of United Airlines) on Wednesday, June 11, 1986. The Metropolitan Topeka Airport Authority made their conference room at Forbes Field available for a press conference. Laird Noller Ford provided a luxury car to transport K'Bluey and Elaine to the zoo, complete with motorcycle escort by the Topeka Police Department.

By the next day K'Bluey was settling into his home quite nicely, but remained in isolation with only Elaine in attendance. This period of adjustment was for both koala and keeper to establish their routine in a new environment. Although our public opening was not until Sunday, June 15, we did have special functions scheduled for Friday and Saturday.

Perchance the most significant social event ever at our zoo was the Koala Kaper, a black tie fund-raising gala on June 13, 1986 sponsored by Friends of the Zoo. Chairman Bette Martin (now Bette Felker) and her committee pulled out all stops. The weather was perfect, the atmosphere was festive, a costumed koala mascot mingled with guests, and the Australian flag was flying. To her everlasting credit, Bette engaged some notable special guests for the occasion: the Honorable Terence B. McCarthy, Australian Consul-General in Chicago, Illinois, the Honorable Edwin J.L. Ride, Australian Consul-General in Houston, Texas and Sue Atkins, traditional folk singer and guitarist from Brisbane, Australia. Ms. Atkins and Mr. Ride performed a number of Australian ballads, followed by a soliloquy in verse by Mr. Ride from "The Sentimental Bloke" by the Australian poet C.J. Dennis. The performance was concluded by a rousing rendition with the audience of "Waltzing Matilda."

The printed program for the evening had an entire page devoted to "Koolewongs and Bangaroos." It contained factual information on koalas, and the first paragraph was particularly interesting:

Koolewongs you may call them; bangaroos you may call them; or you *may call them New Holland sloths. But <u>please</u> don't call them bears. Koalas are not related to bears but are marsupials, which means pouched animals. The most commonly known marsupials are the kangaroos of Australia.*

Both Australian Consuls-General commented on the excitement caused by the arrival of the koala, and Mr. McCarthy said: "It is an absolute thrill to come to see a city that has gone to the preparation Topeka has gone to."

Statements like that from an honored V.I.P. made us all puff with pride.

As with other special events in the past, our loyal Friends of the Zoo (FOTZ) members were rewarded with a special preview of K'Bluey the day before the koala exhibit opened to the public. A line started forming outside the zoo an hour before scheduled opening time. I was concerned, but everyone assured me they did not mind the wait. Once we did open the line stretched from the koala exhibit, in the center of the zoo, out past the zoo entrance. Traffic patterns were arranged to keep people out of the summer sun and in the shade as much as possible, and the Capital City Dixieland Jazz Band played Australian tunes to entertain the crowd.

FOTZ previews (for any event) also served as a trial run for zoo staff and volunteers alike before the big opening to the general public. It was a blessing to have a limited number of close zoo supporters view the exhibit first to see if everything worked as planned. If not, we could make adjustments and "fine tune" with folks who were understanding and supportive.

I was anxious for feedback from FOTZ members. One lady at the midway point in line said the wait, no matter how long, would be worth it, even if the koala was sleeping, as this would probably be the only chance she would ever have to see one. Much to my surprise and delight, K'Bluey was visible most of the day. Credit FOTZ members for this! We had hung a prominent sign at the exhibit entrance that read: Shhh . . . K'BLUEY DOESN'T LIKE NOISE. And everyone was observant!

Reaction to K'Bluey was tremendous. People were grateful just to get a glimpse of this ball of fur in the eucalyptus leaves. Those who saw him with his head up felt doubly privileged, and rightly so. Others, who only got a glimpse, were philosophical, with such comments as, "He was asleep, but at least I got to see him."

K'Bluey's behavior was laid back. I was relieved he was taking things in stride. And I was very pleased to report to the San Diego Zoo that the people of Topeka were very cooperative and so appreciative. Their trust in us was validated.

So much had happened leading up to the public premiere of our visiting koala that, when the day finally arrived, we all breathed a collective sigh of relief. The long-awaited K'Bluey D'Buey (as we called it) went extremely well as a result of our extensive planning and legion of volunteers. Hill's Pet Products, our prime sponsor, provided free admission to the zoo. Our attendance of 7,356 was not a record (probably a blessing), but was three times that of a normal Sunday crowd at the zoo. Little did we realize at the time that *daily* attendance for the next month would equal that of our routine Sundays.

We wanted the visit by K'Bluey the koala from the San Diego Zoo to be more than just a unique animal temporarily on exhibit at our zoo. We felt this was an occasion for a festival of Australian wildlife and culture involving the entire community.

At the zoo we highlighted a variety of other species from the "land down under," including Australian black swan, Matschie's tree kangaroo, dama wallaby, sulphur crested cockatoo, emu, carpet python, shingleback skink, and kookaburra (the bird with such a strange vocalization that it is also known as the laughing jackass).

Marshall's Civic Band performed a concert in the Gage Park amphitheater featuring Australian tunes. The Topeka Public Library presented an Australian Aboriginal Art Exhibit, sponsored a "Koala Tea" in the Children's Department, and provided Australian book exhibits and reading lists in the Adult Services Department. The art exhibit featured religious bark paintings, coiled palm baskets, musical instruments, totem carvings, ceremonial regalia and weapons—including boomerangs and spears. The Australian Consul General from Chicago, while in Topeka to see K'Bluey the koala, made a special point to visit the library as well.

"My boomerang won't come back!" This was the humorous title some years ago of a popular novelty song. As part of Koala Connection '86, we *wanted* the boomerang to make a comeback! It did! On June 27-28, 1986 Topekans learned the art of boomerang throwing and construction through a series of demonstrations and workshops sponsored by Parks and Recreation of Topeka, and offered free to the public with no age limit.

To do this they brought to Topeka the 1985 boomerang World Champion and International Masters Trophy Holder, Chet Snouffer. He thrilled crowds in Gage Park with a bag full of brightly colored, different shaped boomerangs he personally had designed, built and painted. He had been making and throwing boomerangs for 19 years, from the time he was ten years old. Chet would rummage through his bag, select a favorite boomerang, then send it spinning into the sky. The crowd followed its journey as it arched through the air and anxiously anticipated its return. Chet acknowledged that Kansas presented some difficult wind problems but, yes, his boomerang always came back!

But back to K'Bluey. Koalas are almost mythical—like a unicorn or a mermaid. There is a mystery and magic about them that captivates the hearts of people. I knew K'Bluey's visit would create excitement in the community, but I never dreamed there would be such koala mania. My colleagues around the country said they had never known a comparable response, and even the San Diego Zoo was impressed!

Koala collectibles suddenly became very popular—not just stuffed koalas, but cookie jars, planters, towels and pictures as well.

Everyone wanted to be part of Koala Connection '86. Even those who were not officially on the K-Team jumped on the bandwagon. Restaurants had "K'Bluey Buffets," stores featured koala themed items, and radio disc jockeys came up with every koala joke and pun imaginable.

But the real heroes of Koala Connection '86 (and I mean this sincerely) were the members of the K-Team—so much so that they deserve special recognition. As I reflect now on their contribution then, I wish I could do more as an acknowledgement of my appreciation. At this point, however, the best I can do is devote a chapter to them. (It follows this one.)

The consequence of K'Bluey's appearance was that a record number of people visited our zoo during his engagement. As of closing time on his last day, officially 90,717 people had been to the zoo during his one-month stay. Of course, this did not count all the volunteers, which probably pushed the number to over 100,000!

Our average monthly attendance was 35,000. A previous monthly attendance record of 50,000 was set in 1983 with the appearance of a visiting white tiger during our 50th Anniversary celebration. Then, in 1985, the opening of Gorilla Encounter attracted 74,299 during its first month.

K'Bluey's visit was *not* intended to set a new one month (or one year) attendance record (although that was a gratifying happenstance). Rather, it was to enable the people of our community and region to see a very special animal they might not experience otherwise, and to raise awareness of our zoo as an educational resource and an integral part of the fabric of our community.

The most interesting thing to me was that, as fulfilling (and exhausting) as Koala Connection '86 was, the community was eager and curious for "next year's big activity!" When I was asked about our forthcoming plans, I responded that "we are thinking about something that is unique and different and would be a mammoth (hint, hint) special event for 1987." (Dear reader, see a subsequent chapter, "Have Trunk, Will Travel.")

*****

The K-Team

Do you remember the A-Team from the old TV series?

Well, as heroes go, they were *nothing* by comparison to the K-Team, headquartered at the World Famous Topeka Zoo.

The K-Team was responsible for the impossible—bringing a *live koala* to the people of Kansas, and the Midwest, for a special visit in the summer of 1986.

Topeka was one of only three zoos in America that year (and the smallest zoo ever) to receive a koala on limited loan from the San Diego Zoo. Koalas are unique and appealing, but delicate, specialized animals. The San Diego Zoo had rigid specifications and requirements that had to be met in order to receive a koala.

The K-Team provided the necessary time, talent, materials, services, and funding for Koala Connection '86 at the World Famous Topeka Zoo. It didn't stop there: one of the prime needs of the K-Team was volunteers, lots of them. This need resulted in the following want ad: *Require someone with a chauffeur's license to drive a refrigerated beer truck to Kansas City International Airport to pick up a 55 lb. shipment of fresh cut eucalyptus browse twice a week for a month to feed K'Bluey, the Koala, from the San Diego Zoo. And the pay? We'll make you a member of the K-Team and give you a free T-shirt!*

Without the K-Team there would not have been a koala in Topeka!

And now we proudly present . . . (drum roll please):

The K-Team

HILL'S PET PRODUCTS
- Sponsor of Free Day at the Zoo for K'Bluey D'Buey on Sunday, June 15, 1986
- Koala Trolleys to shuttle visitors from auxiliary parking lots during K'Bluey D'Buey
- Free Koala Connection buttons on Sunday, June 15, 1986
- Principal funding for Koala exhibit building renovation
- Wages and benefits for the San Diego Zoo Koala Keeper
- Replacement labor costs for the San Diego Zoo
- Contribution to the AAZPA Conservation Fund

UNITED AIRLINES
- Round trip air transportation San Diego/Topeka for the Koala and the Koala Keeper

METROPOLITAN TOPEKA AIRPORT AUTHORITY
- Special assistance for Koala arrival and departure at Forbes Field

TOPEKA POLICE DEPARTMENT
- Motorcycle escort for the Koala from Forbes Field to the Zoo

BRANIFF, INC.
- Twice weekly air shipments of fresh cut eucalyptus browse from San Diego to the Kansas City International Airport

LAPEKA, INC. (Eldon Dananhaeur)
- A refrigerated Coors truck for ground transportation of the eucalyptus shipments from Kansas City to Topeka

KANSAS MOTOR CARRIERS ASSOCIATION

RYDER TRUCK RENTAL
- Coordination of qualified drivers for eucalyptus ground transportation from Kansas City International Airport to Topeka Zoo

LEO STONE

BOB LASTER

DON BOWER

LOWELL KOELLING
- Volunteer drivers to transport eucalyptus from Kansas City to Topeka

U.S. INSURANCE GROUP, a Crum & Forster Corporation
- Required insurance on the Koala

LANDMARK HOTEL CORPORATION
- Daily lodging and breakfast for the Koala Keeper at the downtown Holiday Inn (or the Koaladay Inn, if you wish)

LAIRD NOLLER FORD
- Vehicle for daily transportation for the Koala Keeper

KSNT-TV CHANNEL 27
- Television monitors and technical assistance for Koala video tapes
- Ten dinners at The Loft Restaurant for the Koala Keeper
- Live remote broadcast from the Zoo during K'Bluey D'Buey on Sunday, June 15, 1986

MCDONALD'S RESTAURANTS
- A daily meal for the Koala Keeper

CASA DEL SOL
- Ten meals for the Koala Keeper

MRS. WINNER'S CHICKEN & BISCUITS
- A daily meal for the Koala Keeper

MCFARLAND'S RESTAURANT
- Four meals for the Koala Keeper

DAIRY QUEEN NO. 6
- A daily dessert for the Koala Keeper

LONG JOHN SILVER'S NORTH
- Two meals for the Koala Keeper

DAIRY QUEEN NO. 2
DAIRY QUEEN NO. 3
DAIRY QUEEN NO. 6
DAIRY QUEEN NO. 8
TOPEKA DAIRY QUEEN BRAZIER
- Major funding for Koala exhibit building renovation

TOPEKA FRIENDS OF THE ZOO
- Major funding for Koala exhibit building renovation
- Australian horticultural materials for landscaping
- Funding for signs and graphics

SHAWNEE FEDERAL SAVINGS
- Major funding for Koala exhibit building renovation
- Special promotion for additional funding

INDEPENDENT INSURANCE AGENTS OF TOPEKA
- Specialized glass for Koala exhibit
- Climate control for Koala exhibit

CITY GLASS AND MIRROR
- Specialized glass for Koala exhibit

THE FOWLER FAMILY: NILE, KATE, GARRETT, KYLIE
- Significant funding for Koala exhibit building renovation

FAIRLAWN PLAZA MERCHANTS ASSOCIATION
- Significant funding for Koala exhibit building renovation

RAY BEERS CLOTHING COMPANY
- Support funding for Koala exhibit building renovation

VOLUME SHOE CORPORATION
- Major funding for Koala exhibit building renovation

GARY CHAN
LARRY SHANKLES
LOREN RISCH
STEVE BURNETT
- Cleaning and painting of Koala exhibit and interior public space

COUNTRY DAY PRE-SCHOOL
- Support funding for Koala exhibit building renovation

KANSAS NEA
- Significant funding for educational graphics and teaching materials

KARLAN'S FURNITURE
- Security draperies for the Koala exhibit

AMERICAN LINEN SUPPLY COMPANY
- Support funding for Koala exhibit building renovation

ALICE C. SABATINI
- Koala Connection logo artwork

GREATER TOPEKA CHAMBER OF COMMERCE
CONVENTION AND VISITORS BUREAU
- Koala Connection brochures at 157 locations along Interstate 70 from Denver to St. Louis
- Koala billboard on Kansas Turnpike between Kansas City and Lawrence

PARKS AND RECREATION OF TOPEKA
- Koala Connection promos in various travel publications
- Sponsorship of Champion Boomerang Thrower Chet Snouffer for workshops and demonstrations

RAMADA INN DOWNTOWN
- Lodging and breakfast for Champion Boomerang Thrower

MARTIN OUTDOOR OF KANSAS
- Double-sided promotional billboard featuring K'Bluey

IGA SUPERMARKETS
- Koala logo on grocery bags

HARRY'S IGAs
- Koala logo on grocery bags

JM BAUERSFELD'S
- Koala logo on grocery bags

H.M. IVES & SONS, INC.
- Design and printing of four color poster of K'Bluey

MCDONALD'S RESTAURANTS
- Place mats featuring the Koala at McDonald's Restaurants in Topeka, Lawrence, Manhattan, Junction City

BRYAN WORLD TOURS
- Round trip air transportation Topeka/San Diego for K'Bluey D'Buey day Grand Prize trip to the San Diego Zoo

KANSAS EXPOCENTRE
- Koala announcement on their electronic message center

MEDEVAC MIDAMERICA
- Emergency medical stand-by during the K'Bluey D'Buey free day

HAYDEN HIGH SCHOOL
- Auxiliary parking during K'Bluey D'Buey

GAGE SHOPPING CENTER
- Auxiliary parking during K'Bluey D'Buey

CAPITAL CITY DIXIELAND JAZZ BAND
- Live music during special preview of Koala for Friends of the Zoo

TOPEKA PUBLIC LIBRARY
- Aboriginal Art Exhibit at the Library
- Koala Tea in the Children's Department
- Australian Book Exhibits

MARSHALLS BAND
- Free concert in Gage Park featuring selections of Australian music on Sunday evening, June 15, 1986

MEMPHIS ZOOLOGICAL GARDEN
- Educational graphics on koalas

AUSTRALIAN CONSULATE-GENERAL'S OFFICE, CHICAGO
- Technical and diplomatic assistance

ST. LOUIS ZOOLOGICAL PARK
- Educational graphics on marsupials and Australian animals

MALCOM KING
- General support

BARNETT'S RESTAURANT AND BUFFET
- Significant funding through a special K'Bluey Buffet all day Sunday, June 15, 1986

KTPK COUNTRY 107
- Special promotion of K'Bluey Buffet at Barnett's Restaurant and Buffet
- Live remote broadcast from the Zoo during Friends of the Zoo preview

KLDH-TV CHANNEL 49
- Live remote broadcast from the Zoo on Sunday, June 29, 1986
- Special Koala promos

HYGIENIC DRY CLEANERS
- Dry cleaning for Koala Keeper during her stay in Topeka

THE KOZY KITCHEN
- Two dinners for the Koala Keeper

WIBW-TV CHANNEL 13
- Six meals for the Koala Keeper at Ramada Inn restaurants
- Live remote broadcast from the Zoo on Monday, June 16, 1986

TOPEKA JAYCEES
- Special activities at GO 4th to assist in Koala exhibit building renovation

WOLFE'S CAMERA & VIDEO
- Donation of VHS video recorder to the Topeka Jaycees for K-TEAM fund-raising event

HURST COFFMAN
- General support

FLEMING PLACE MERCHANTS ASSOCIATION
- Sponsor of free children's passes to the Zoo during Koala Connection

STANLEY'S FLOWERS
- Special floral arrangements

THE FIDELITY BANKS
- Support funding for Koala exhibit

TOM ROOT
- General support

What an honor to be a Member of the most prestigious club in town!

A distinguished visitor

Today marks what Gary Clarke, director of the Topeka Zoo, affectionately calls the K'Bluey Debuey. The small, shy koala, which arrived in Topeka from San Diego last week, is scheduled to go on public display today. Admission to the zoo will be free to the public to mark the occasion, with Hills Pet Products reimbursing the zoo for gate receipts.

Koalas are not bears, although they remind most observers of live teddies. They in actuality belong to the same family as kangaroos — marsupials — and carry their newborn in a pouch. They live in trees, sleep as much as 20 hours a day and subsist on a diet consisting exclusively of several eucalyptus leaf varieties — and they expect a change in variety every few days.

K'Bluey's month-long visit to Topeka is a triumph for the local zoo. Koalas are native only to Australia, and even in captivity can only be permanently maintained in zoos where the climate permits year-round production of eucalyptus. The San Diego Zoo maintains a 16-acre eucalyptus grove solely for the benefit of the koala.

Because of this strict requirement, only three U.S. zoos house koalas, and only renowned, major city zoos have received the creatures on temporary loan.

This is largely because preparations for the animals, even on the short term, are extremely expensive and time-consuming. Topeka, the smallest zoo to receive a koala, did not have money or resources for the project. But Hills officials and a group of more than 60 supporters called the "K-Team," including individuals, groups and businesses, banded together to raise the needed funds, cooperation and volunteers.

Preparations and shipments alone would have cost at least $50,000, Clarke said. Braniff Airlines will fly in the needed eucalyptus leaves twice weekly (they must come from the grove K'Bluey is accustomed to). They will then be transported from Kansas City in a refrigerated beer truck furnished by Lapeka. Holiday Inn is providing housing for the koala's keeper. Restaurants have provided meals. The list of donations and volunteers is lengthy.

It is exciting to see a project of this scope undertaken in Topeka and even more interesting to know it is only possible through the widespread enthusiasm and cooperation of northeast Kansans.

K'Bluey K'nnects with Kansas

By Merle Bird
The Topeka Capital-Journal
Sunday, June 29, 1986

A koala named K'Bluey was an Aussie through and throughy
Who decided on a life in San Diego.
Then he took a short vacation near the center of the nation
Where so many of the nation's zoo goers may go.

So K'Bluey used his noodle, and packed up kit and k'boodle,
Headed east to visit friends in the midwest.
With him came Ms. Elaine Chu, from the San Diego Zoo,
Who knows what koalas always like the best.

Yes, K'Bluey is an Aussie (he is almost never bossy)
Who may drink a Foster's when he gets too dry.
He k'vorts with great good pleasure and at times just for good measure
Will add koala mode to apple pie.

If you know K'Bluey's diet you would never want to try it
For it's yew k'lyptus leaves of many kinds.
They are filled with people toxins, even worse than chicken poxins,
But they're how a keyed up koala unwinds.

K'Bluey gets his provender from a San Diego sender
Flown to Kansas City I by Braniff Air.
Volunteers from Ryder truckus without any bit of ruckus
Drive Coor's beer trucks to the zoo's own Frigidaire.

A koala looks sedated but they're rarely medicated
Though it happens sometimes, someone has explained.
One hospital out west is the one that serves them best —
The koala tea of Mercy's never strained.

Now, a koala's a sleeper, REM and even deeper,
Who is soporific 20 hours a day.
He awakens for a snack, eats a bit then settles back,
Shuts an eye or two and hits koala hay.

A koala has no use for a railroad train k'boose
Or for going marching with West Point k'dets
It couldn't sing k'denzas if threatened with influenzas
Or with being made into k'bobs for pets.

In a koala's k'llection of the world's best k'nfections
Would be eucalyptus, me tarzan sweet meats —-
They don't care much for k'nfetti or for k'mquats with spaghetti
It's k'nfusing when you're planning home room treats.

It would be no use k'joling a koala bent on strolling
Into staying in his tree to take a nap.
Although usually lethargic, if they become taking chargic
They will never mind the marsupial flap.

Yes, koalas although pouchy are just never, ever grouchy.
They do make lethargy an active term.
When it's time to get to work, no koala's known to shirk,
But they never, ever get the early worm.

But K'Bluey's been a draw like nothing you ever saw,
Folks come from afar to see him doze away.
For K'Bluey cutting *zzzz*'s in his eucalyptus trees
Is worth the watch before he goes away.

Letter From K'Bluey's Mom

Elaine Chu, Koala Keeper, San Diego Zoo

Author's Note: We were privileged to have Elaine at the World Famous Topeka Zoo for a month in the summer of 1986 as Koala Keeper on loan from the San Diego Zoo. We asked her then to record some of her impressions since this was her first visit to Kansas.

Here I am in Topeka, Kansas, land of tornadoes and home of Dorothy and Toto . . .

I'd heard a great deal about Gary Clarke and the Topeka Zoo and was looking forward to the koala loan trip scheduled for June and July. This was the first time I'd been in the Midwest and so I expected to see very open, flat land, plenty of roaming cattle and tumbling, tumbling, tumbleweeds. But what I saw instead was a growing community made up of the nicest people, who treated me like one of the family.

From the moment I arrived in town I was showered with invitations to home-cooked meals, Jacuzzi parties, barbecues, the theater, and *more* parties. Of course, it was impossible to accept them all, unless I planned on joining a health spa or going on a diet during my stay.

My first week was devoted to my charge, K'Bluey. He required my full attention and it was not until after K'Bluey's Debuey that I was able to take a deep breath and relax a bit. With some free time available, I began socializing with the keepers, absorbing information on the care and feeding of the various animals at the zoo. One day I was given the opportunity to go behind the scenes and feed fresh strawberries, cherry tomatoes, honeydew and melon balls to Oscar, Max, and M'Wasi, the adult gorillas. Just the sweet aroma of gorilla was enough to make me feel right at home.

It was baby season, too, and I was allowed to interact with Rudy and Joey, two hand-raised Bornean orangutans. I was present for the birth of a giraffe, and observed the baby two-toed sloth shortly after it was born in the Tropical Rain Forest. So my time was filled with interesting events right at the zoo.

Some of the more amusing incidents dealt with K'Bluey and myself, as the koala keeper. I guess people considered me a celebrity after seeing me on television or in the newspaper. Wherever I went people started to poke one another and whisper, "There's K'Bluey's keeper" or "K'Bluey's mom!" I can imagine what goes through a child's mind when the parent states I'm K'Bluey's mother. Personally, I don't think we look anything alike!

Other people are a bit bolder and will come up and shake my hand, yell "Hello!" out the car window, or just politely stare. It was times like this when I couldn't even buy a certain personal hygiene product in privacy.

To top it off, some of the zoo staff were considering graphing my daily weight for the month to see how it correlated with K'Bluey's daily weight gains and losses. You see, I have a tendency to be anorexic when K'Bluey's not eating well, and just the opposite when things are going splendidly. They felt it was an interesting phenomenon worth studying.

There were quite a number of newspaper, television, and radio reporters stopping at the zoo to catch a glimpse of K'Bluey or to interview me. Most of the questions were aimed towards the care of the koala but it was during a telephone interview for a radio station that I was asked, "Is the Topeka Zoo as world famous as they say they are?" Well, at that time I had been in town less than a week, so I could not answer that question satisfactorily, but now near the end of my visit I believe I can. Yes, the Topeka Zoo *is* known for such things as the first successful hatching and rearing of golden eagles, the breeding program of Przewalski's horses, the Tropical Rain Forest, and the Gorilla Encounter. But it's the dedicated staff, docents, and volunteers plus the community response and support shown by Hill's Pet Products, the Rotary Club, the K-Team, Friends of the Zoo, the Topeka Zoo Foundation, etc. It's people like this who make the World Famous Topeka Zoo what it is!

I've had a wonderful time this past month. Thank you to all those folks who made K'Bluey's and my stay so enjoyable.

Marsupially,
Elaine Chu
"K'Bluey's Mom"

Thursday, July 10, 1986

4   The Topeka Capital·Journal

Opinion

—Editorials——————————— *In God We Trust*——

The koala factor

For director Gary Clarke and the staff at the Topeka Zoo, it has been the proverbial month of Sundays.

The monthlong visit of K'Bluey, the koala, has spurred Monday through Friday crowds equal to the size of average summer Sunday attendance at the zoo. Weekend gate receipts have doubled.

K'Bluey has adjusted well to his Topeka habitat, Clarke reports. The small marsupial has established a routine, eats well and gets adequate sleep, even by koala standards. Topeka crowds have been cooperative, responding to guidelines and keeping all noise to a minimum near the koala display. The easy transition has kept the zoo's atmosphere relaxed — after all, it's a big responsibility to play host to a koala.

By closing time Sunday, 64,521 visitors had passed through Topeka Zoo gates during the three weeks since K'Bluey's arrival. That figure already surpasses the monthlong attendance in 1983 when the zoo hosted a rare white tiger.

The new Gorilla Encounter exhibit led to record breaking attendance during the first six months of 1985. But that record was broken during the first six months of this year, and the koala's popularity, even though it reflected only two weeks of the period, contributed greatly to the 167,814 attendance figure.

Not only children have been drawn to the zoo. A greater number of extended families and senior citizens have visited, Clarke said. Organized community groups from throughout Kansas have arrived in chartered school buses. Many first-time visitors are among them, as well as those who haven't come to the zoo for years.

And what they find, of course, is that there's much more to see at the Topeka Zoo than a koala, interesting as he might be. There's the Gorilla Encounter, Rain Forest, a baby giraffe and many other exhibits set within well-planned and spotless grounds. Those who visit will undoubtedly be back.

Despite strong attendance, lines are minimal, Clarke said. K'Bluey's last day will be Monday. It's a great time to visit the zoo.

Front Page: The Kansas City Star—Twice!

Yes! The World Famous Topeka Zoo was featured on the front page of *The Kansas City Star* twice—in one month! Credit the koala.

The first article was Tuesday, July 8, 1986 on the front page of The STAR TECH section under the headline, "K'Bluey big hit at Topeka Zoo." It was by staff writer Elaine Adams, and following are a few excerpts.

Each Tuesday and Friday about 12:30 p.m., a 55-pound crate arrives at Kansas City International Airport aboard Braniff Flight 596 from San Diego.

It's quickly loaded into a refrigerated Coors beer truck. Ninety minutes later the cargo is in Topeka, ready for consumption by a visiting celebrity who is exceedingly selective about what he eats.

Nothing but eucalyptus leaves will pass the lips of K'Bluey, a 3-year-old koala on display through Monday at the Topeka Zoo. So it's eucalyptus he gets, courtesy of Braniff, Coors and volunteer truckers.

. . . K'Bluey has been a smash hit in Topeka where attendance on some days has more than tripled normal, said Zoo Director Gary K. Clarke.

The zoo converted an entire building for the koala, complete with controlled temperature and humidity. A legion of Topekans, known as the K-TEAM, was marshaled to contribute the money and volunteer help to bring K'Bluey from San Diego.

The second article was even more impressive. It appeared on the front page of the main section on Monday, July 21, 1986 complete with color photographs and a map showing directions to our zoo! Also written by Elaine Adams, accurate but clever in presentation, it no doubt stimulated residents of the Kansas City metropolitan area to visit Topeka and the zoo. It was always gratifying to me that our zoo could serve as a catalyst for people to journey to the Capital City of Kansas, and that the fame of our community spread because of the zoo.

Despite the uncomfortable emphasis placed on me, this story did reflect the team effort and community spirit responsible for the success of our zoo. And it served as a profile of our zoo at that point in time by an objective outsider, as well as expressing the vitality of our zoo to those who had never visited. It read as follows and is reproduced with permission of *The Kansas City Star*.

Topeka Zoo reflects one man's dedication

Topeka—Some callers just chuckle when they phone the Topeka Zoo for the first time. A few are taken aback.

"World Famous Topeka Zoo," the operator answers.

World famous? In Topeka?

As a matter of fact, it may be.

At one time the zoo was famous mostly because the guy who ran the place, Gary K. Clarke, said it was. But through creativity, humor and personal charisma, Mr. Clarke and his staff have made the zoo worthy of respect by national zoological experts and beloved by Topekans.

"With absolutely no qualification or equivocation, the Topeka Zoological Park has to be one of the finest zoological facilities for a city its size anywhere in the world," said Robert Wagner, executive director of the American Association of Zoological Parks and Aquariums.

But in 1963, when a 24-year-old Mr. Clarke took it over, the zoo was dismal, said Topeka research veterinarian Mark Morris.

"It was bad. It was a mangy old lion and a couple of prairie dogs," Dr. Morris said. "What you see has been basically his creation in the last 20 years."

The zoo, squeezed into 20 acres in Gage Park, now boasts a domed building housing a tropical rain forest with birds and bats in free flight; a lagoon full of water birds; an island where gibbons perform acrobatics; and a gorilla exhibit where ape and man can stare at each other just inches apart, separated only by glass.

K'Bluey the koala, who just completed a monthlong stay on loan from the San Diego Zoo, was only the latest animal celebrity at the Topeka Zoo.

In 1971, an orangutan won a statewide children's art contest. That same year the zoo oversaw the first birth of golden eagles in captivity in the Western Hemisphere, with more born since.

The way the zoo has been promoted also has caught the public's attention. The main walkway isn't called Madison Avenue, but perhaps it should be.

Mr. Clarke, for example, dubbed the koala's arrival as the K'Bluey Dubuey and got the koala's picture on grocery sacks from Topeka to Denver. When the Holiday Inn offered a free room to the visiting koala keeper, the zoo called the hostelry the Koala Day Inn.

Other clever animal names have made folks remember the zoo: Submarie the hippo, Julius Squeezer the boa constrictor and the dynamic duo known as the Gnus: Weather and Sports.

As a result, the zoo has endeared itself to the city and its residents.

"It's a beautiful relationship," Mr. Wagner said.

In Australia, the name K'Bluey means "an old, red-haired man," Mr. Clarke said. The zoo director acknowledges it probably fits him as well as it does the koala.

Beads of sweat and freckles are more predominant than hair on Mr. Clarke's scalp, but gray hasn't completely erased the red in his beard.

Wearing a navy blue koala tie and clutching a hand-held radio, Mr. Clarke roams the zoo at a brisk pace. He jovially greets keepers and returns the salutation of visitors who say, "Hi, Gary." He knows he has met them at a talk somewhere.

When special visitors arrive, he motions them back through the gates so they can enter the zoo on a short piece of carpet. "I just wanted to roll out the red carpet to the World Famous Topeka Zoo," he says with the sweep of an arm.

With 450 animals on its 20 acres, the Topeka Zoo is compact. By contrast, Kansas City has more than 700 animals in its 80-acre zoo.

"Ah-whoop, Ah-whoop," Mr. Clarke calls to the gibbons after picking up a flattened paper cup and throwing it away.

His enthusiasm is infectious.

"There's Oscar," he says of the gorilla roaming outside the glass tunnel where humans come face to face with the apes. "Look at him looking around casing the joint."

When a companion gorilla turns human heads skyward by climbing over the glass tunnel, Mr. Clarke doesn't have to feign delight at both the ape and the spectators.

"I tell you," he says, "no matter how many times I see 'em do this, it gives me goose pimples."

Mr. Clarke, formerly a keeper at the Kansas City Zoo, said he was working at the Fort Worth Zoo in Texas when Topeka officials approached him about taking over the city zoo.

He visited mainly as a courtesy but wrote a memo outlining what the zoo needed: everything from a better diet for the animals to professional management.

"I just figured Topeka would say, 'Ah, that's too much trouble.' They didn't," he said. "They wrote back and said, 'That's great. That's just what we want to do.' How could I say no?"

Now he works in a mobile unit that doesn't even have a flushing toilet. It does have a library, however, with books arranged according to the "Zooey Decimal System."

The cramped office is filled with mementos from African safaris as well as gag gifts he has collected from zoo people across the country—like the mounted kazoo from Wichita with two peas hanging from it by a string. Two-Pea Kazoo. Get it?

He's a delightful character," said William Conway, general director of the society that runs the Bronx Zoo in New York City. "Among other things he has the second-best collection of animal neckties there is. He might say he has the best, but that's not right. I do."

Behind Gary Clarke's banter, however, is a man who cares very much about Topeka and his zoo.

"Gary likes people and animals in equal amounts," Mr. Conway said. "I think that comes across."

Mr. Clarke has tried to create exhibits that immerse people in animal habitats. In the rain forest, for example, plants and animals are all around. He considers the visitors as much a part of any exhibit as the animals.

And he believes in getting the public involved in other ways.

Fifteen years before Peter Ueberroth nudged corporate sponsors into bankrolling the 1984 Olympics, Gary Clarke launched Operation Noah's Ark, in which 10 businesses bought animals for the zoo after consumers turned in a certain number of promotional coupons on company products.

In 1969 Topekans needed only one week to raise $5,000 to buy a gorilla named Tiffany from Kansas City. On billboards, Tiffany was promoted as a companion for Max the gorilla.

"The first day she was here at the zoo we kept her and Max separate all night long so that the next morning—are you ready for this?—Max could go into Tiffany's exhibit and . . . have breakfast at Tiffany's," Mr. Clarke said.

Peter Crowcroft, director of a zoo in Maryland, fondly calls Mr. Clarke a "con man" because of his salesmanship, and Topeka Mayor Douglas S. Wright says Mr. Clarke makes more speeches than anybody else in Topeka.

The key, Mr. Clarke said, is personally taking the message to the public. More than once, he said, he's given speeches at breakfast, lunch and dinner.

The effort has paid off because increased gate receipts have financed capital improvements, and private interests have donated time as well as money for animals and other items like signs and exhibits.

Attendance last year was almost 274,000 in a metropolitan area of 159,000. That's up significantly from the 197,903 who visited in 1970. The Kansas City Zoo, which must compete with sporting events and other entertainment, drew 535,000 last year in a metropolitan area of more than 1.4 million.

Last year the Topeka Friends of the Zoo raised nearly $130,000 with about 3,600 members. The Kansas City Friends of the Zoo, with 10,220 members, raised more than $422,000, a spokesman said.

Mr. Clarke has had opportunities to leave Topeka, including a substantial offer a few years ago to take over the Minnesota state zoo. He's chosen to remain, partly because he likes the area.

He acknowledges bigger zoos may offer more space, bigger budgets and rarer animals. "But I don't think I would be able to express myself professionally in some other places as I have been able to here," he said. "I guess that's an important thing to me."

A Month of Sundays

A month of Sundays!

I had always heard that expression, but never totally understood what it meant. On the surface, it sounds like fun. I guess in the usual context Sunday is a day off, devoted to relaxed activities centered around the family. In fact, Sunday is a great day to go to the zoo.

But, if you're in zoobiz, it means something entirely different.

It means your largest crowds of the week. It means additional staff devoting extra time and attention to the visitors: more admission gate services, more food and drink stands, more trash pick-ups, a busier gift shop, an overflowing parking lot, more lost children (or lost parents), more phone calls from out-of-town folks on how to get to the zoo, and coordinating more volunteers who assist the zoo with special events. Sundays also mean that daily office work is not done (reports, correspondence), that major maintenance is postponed (welding, electrical work, plumbing), that elective veterinary procedures are not scheduled (surgery, hoof trimming, root canals) nor are animal transfers and shipments. There are simply too many people at the zoo on a Sunday to do anything but the basic animal care, exhibit cleaning, and respond to the crowds.

That's all well and good on a once-a-week basis, but—*every day* for one solid month? You've got to be kidding!

Well, dear reader, it happened to us at the World Famous Topeka Zoo, thanks to K'Bluey the koala. Our weekday crowds were like Sunday crowds and Sundays were two or three times the normal attendance. And it was GREAT . . . now that it is over. It was somewhat like walking across the Sahara; fun to say you have done it once, but no sense in ever doing it again.

We learned several things: that a well planned special event elicits a tremendous response for our zoo; that the community can join together to make something happen; that our staff is the greatest in the world and can really put forth the extra effort when needed; that our volunteers are a super fantastic army of unsung heroes; and that if we had to do it for more than a month, we would have to completely re-gear our daily operations.

Once again I'd like to express my sincere thanks to everyone who helped with Koala Connection '86. The continued interest and support of the zoo was most gratifying. Having K'Bluey in our zoo for one month *was* a special event.

We will long remember K'Bluey, and for generations to come we will talk at the zoo about our Month of Sundays.

When Your Koala Has Gone

Now, dear reader, another confession. To make Koala Connection '86 happen, we had to—among a myriad of other things—convert the oldest structure in our zoo to the high and exacting standards of the San Diego Zoo in order to be certified for a koala loan. Hill's Pet Products, in addition to *everything* else they had done, covered the major expenses. It was not an easy task, and took the talent and skills of many people on the zoo staff and from Parks and Recreation of Topeka.

But—we did it!

Harkening back to my arrival in Topeka in the mid-1960's, I was elated then to refurbish the 1907 greenhouse/monkey house/snake house into an acceptable zoo exhibit building (see the chapter "The Hand-me-down Animal Kingdom" in this book). Now this same facility, after much struggle, qualified to house K'Bluey, our honored visiting koala, for one spectacular month.

But once K'Bluey had returned to the San Diego Zoo in mid-July 1986, what to do with an empty specialized koala exhibit?

We proposed developing an even more sophisticated exhibit for those significant species not represented elsewhere in our zoo: reptiles, amphibians, fish and invertebrates. Once again, Hill's came to the rescue! They agreed to fund the project.

Work progressed through the winter of 1986-1987. A miraculous transformation took place: from the home for one animal to specialized habitats for a variety of colorful and unique species. Many of the exhibits utilized the "jewel box" technique with interior back lighting in a darkened space.

And the specific exhibit that housed the koala, an Australian marsupial, now served well as the domicile for another Australian marsupial—the Matshie's tree kangaroo. Our pair had produced a baby in November 1986, so it was active outside the mother's pouch by the spring of 1987—perfect timing for the dedication of the "new" Hill's Animal Kingdom on May 16, 1987.

It was exciting for our zoo to once again be able to exhibit some of the lesser known, but significant, members of the animal kingdom, and I issued the following press release:

Where can you see a fire-bellied toad? Or a Puerto Rican anole? Or an Argentinean horned frog (also known as the Pac-Man frog)? These and other fascinating creatures will be on display in Hill's Animal Kingdom at the World Famous Topeka Zoo.

Many Topekans will remember Hill's Animal Kingdom as the old "Snake House," and last summer as the home for K'Bluey, the visiting koala. The building, which was the first structure in the zoo, has been closed since K'Bluey left and the interior has been completely refurbished and renovated. Dedication of the new Hill's Animal Kingdom will take place on Saturday, May 16, and the building will be open to the public at 10:30 am.

Hill's Animal Kingdom is the new home for small animals with emphasis on reptiles, fish, amphibians and invertebrates. Included in the building will be jewel box displays incorporating themes such as Snakes of Shawnee County, Kansas Fish Pond, Chorus of Color, Invertebrates (animals without backbones), Kansas Amphibians, and Tropical Fish. The building is also home to the zoo's family of tree kangaroos, with a baby who is just out of the pouch.

Additional animals on exhibit include ornate box turtles and mata-mata turtles, giant marine toads, Emperor scorpions, the brightly colored arrow poison frogs and emerald tree boas, Gila monsters and desert iguanas, Cuban burrowing cockroaches, as well as salamanders and newts.

Development of Hill's Animal Kingdom was completed by the Zoo Staff, particularly Education Coordinator Ron Kaufman, Area Supervisor Mike Coker and Lead Keeper Kitty Shipman. Assisting the Zoo Staff with the renovation was Roy Baughman, a volunteer who spent many hours with a tape measure, saw and hammer in the construction of the new exhibits. Ten large aquarium tanks were donated by Mr. and Mrs. Ray Hollis, and a variety of tropical fish was provided by Bart's Pet and Hobby Mart in Seabrook Center.

The zoo received a major grant from Hill's Pet Products for the renovation. Topeka Friends of the Zoo provided special project funding. Volume Shoe Corporation, Shawnee Federal Savings and the Independent Insurance Agents of Topeka made significant contributions.

Supporting contributors were: City Glass and Mirror, the Fowler Family—Nile, Kate, Garrett and Kylie, Fairlawn Plaza Merchants Association, Ray Beers Clothing Company, The Fidelity Banks, Topeka Jaycees, American Linen Supply Company, Karlan's Furniture and Country Day Pre-School.

It was fitting that the building be named for Hill's, since they not only enabled our zoo to have a spectacular one month special event, but also served in a leadership role to provide a variety of interesting and educational exhibits on a permanent basis for the benefit of the community.

Although Lions Pride was still in the development stage, anticipation ran high in the community, as evidenced by this editorial

4   Friday, May 1, 1987

The Topeka Capital-Journal **OPINION**

Editorials ———————————— *In God We Trust*

The Pride of Topeka

An African safari may be a dream vacation for many animal-loving Topekans, but for most it remains exactly that, a dream. But soon the Topeka Zoo will be able to satisfy some of the curiosity about jungle animals in their natural habitat.

With the Lions Pride project, the zoo has launched its first major improvement effort since the completion of the wonderful gorilla exhibit. So next summer, when the grand opening is planned, zoo visitors will get to observe lions as they would live in the wild — in a pride.

Just hearing Gary Clarke, zoo director, describe the new exhibit arouses anticipation among those who have learned to expect great things from Topeka Zoo. Visitors will have three viewing stations from which to observe the lions. The approach to one will be through tall grass, another will be on rocks and the third will be a wilderness area.

Like the Gorilla Encounter, the Lions Pride exhibit will hold the audience more captive than the lions. For both the lions and the people, it will be a much more satisfactory and more natural arrangement than the traditional cage.

The exhibit will be outdoors, with no buildings to be constructed. The Topeka Zoological Foundation hopes to raise $400,000 to fund the project. Contributions, of course, are always welcome.

Topeka Zoo has a long history in Topeka and has earned a reputation for innovation and significant contributions to the zoo science. The unique gorilla exhibit is only the most recent.

Topeka Zoo claims the distinction of being the first zoo in the world to successfully hatch and raise the American golden eagle. It also has helped with the preservation of other endangered and threatened species. And the Tropical Rain Forest won the Exhibit Achievement Award from the American Association of Zoological Parks and Aquariums.

Lions Pride will expand that list of accomplishments. It deserves our wholehearted support.

Have Trunk, Will Travel

There is an old adage that an elephant is always ready to travel since it carries its trunk with it. Certainly this is true for certain individual elephants, and how fortuitous that we knew *two* elephants in this category, as they provided a "first" for our zoo—elephant rides.

It was all part of our Festival of Elephants from June 14 to 21, 1987 sponsored by our ever-generous benefactor, Hill's Pet Products. The purpose was to focus attention on the world's largest land mammal. Elephants are among the best known of animals (I've always chuckled at the description in a field guide to African mammals that read: "Large, gray, unmistakable"). Still, much fascinating information about them is little known to the general public.

How many muscles are in their trunk? (At least 40,000). How much water do they drink each day? (50 gallons or more). What are tusks? (Modified upper incisor teeth). What is their gestation period? (18 to 22 months, depending on species). How can you tell Asian elephants from African elephants? (See the chapter "Of Olifonts and Loxodonts" in this book).

While our resident elephants—Sunda the Asian and Tembo the African—had been ridden by staff in the course of routine management, we had never been able to offer rides to the public. Hence, our visiting ride elephants would be a unique opportunity and special treat for our Festival visitors.

For this mammoth event, our elephant population doubled for more than a week with the addition of two visiting female Asian elephants, C.C. and Suki, from the Dickerson Park Zoo in Springfield, Missouri. Both were experienced ride elephants who had traveled around the country. Our primary responsibility was to garner and train volunteers to assist visitors to get on and off the elephants safely. Once again Friends of the Zoo Past President Susan Chan coordinated this event.

The special events were launched on June 12 with a Friends of the Zoo dinner-dance fund-raiser entitled, "On Safari." Participants were asked to wear safari clothes and ride an elephant in the course of the evening.

The next day, June 13, was Friends Family Night with free elephant rides. Public activities ran from Sunday, June 14 to Sunday, June 21. While rides were offered all week, none were available on the two Sundays due to the normal larger crowds. On those Sundays we had a series of related continuous activities: elephant films; dances and foods of India; face painting and storytelling; free posters by Alice Sabatini; Docent Discovery Carts; an elephant weight guessing contest; touching and photographing elephants; keeper demonstrations with elephant shower baths;

and . . . with predictable results . . . a tug of war between "Hill's Hunks" and C.C. the elephant!

Thousands of visitors to the World Famous Topeka Zoo gained new understanding and appreciation of these wonderful creatures during the Festival of Elephants (as noted in *The Topeka Capital-Journal* Editorial of June 20, 1987).

And, it was a trunk full of fun!

4   Saturday, June 20, 1987

The Topeka Capital-Journal   OPINION

Editorials ——————————————— *In God We Trust* —

An elephantine festival

The Topeka community has come to expect a special event at the zoo each summer, says director Gary Clarke.

It began in 1984 with the visit of a rare white tiger. The next year marked the opening of the permanent Gorilla Encounter exhibit. Last year attendance records were continually broken during the visit of K'Bluey the Koala. Clarke was repeatedly asked how he was going to top that showing.

The answer is the Festival of Elephants, in full swing at the Topeka Zoo this week.

Topeka's resident pachyderms, Tembo (Swahili for elephant) and Sunda, the local Asian elephant, have been joined by C.C. and Suki, Indian elephants from Dickerson Park Zoo in Springfield, Mo., for the event.

Included are a number of educational opportunities (an elephant has 40,000 muscles in its trunk) and displays (such as 51 plastic gallon-containers of water to illustrate what an elephant drinks in a day), free posters and children's activities.

But the hands down favorites are the elephant rides, which appeal to all ages. Adults ride for $2 and children for $1. The youngest rider during the first half of this week was 11 days old. Holding the senior honor was a 93-year-old rider.

Today is the last day for elephant rides. The festival concludes Sunday, but Clarke said Sunday crowds are expected to be too large to accommodate for rides. The elephants will be available that day for touching and photographing, a shower bath will be demonstrated and keepers will give talks on the world's largest land animal.

Clarke says both the size and enthusiasm of crowds have been phenomenal. The Springfield elephants' handlers, who have traveled across the country helping with such events, say they've never seen such response from a community. Attendance has been unhampered by unseasonably high heat and humidity.

Zoo officials, Friends of the Zoo and sponsor Hill's Pet Foods all deserve a round of thanks from the community for undertaking this "mammoth" event.

Cheetah Spotted at Topeka Zoo

Who spotted the cheetah?

There are two answers to this single question.

The first answer: nature, who provided the beautiful mottled pattern on this most unusual of cats.

The second answer: visitors who had a first sighting of this rare animal at the World Famous Topeka Zoo.

This was all part of a grand nine-day Conservation Festival at the zoo from July 16 to 24, 1988.

Conservation education and awareness are prime functions of any zoo. And while they were practiced every day at our zoo, we felt that a Conservation Festival would focus attention on specific issues.

It was a SUPER event! Although it involved myriad activities, many volunteers, and a complex set of circumstances, it went extremely well and received a tremendous response from the public. Proclamations were issued by both the Governor and the Mayor. The weekly shopper, *Pennypower,* published a special supplement outlining a schedule of events.

The Festival was staged by Friends of the Topeka Zoo and enhanced by the Saturday, July 16 visit from Jim Fowler, well-known conservationist and formerly co-star of Mutual of Omaha's Spirit of Adventure television specials. KSNT-TV 27 cosponsored Jim's visit which began with him signing autographs at 10:30 am. Afterwards he gave demonstrations with snakes, tortoises, elephants and macaws. At noon Jim led a walk down "Conservation Avenue," the sidewalk by the Rain Forest that Maria Henderson's 5th and 6th grade Zoo Schoolers had painted with conservation scenes.

Jim also led zoo visitors in reciting the "Declaration of Dependence," which emphasized human interdependence with animals in the struggle to survive and to perpetuate our natural environment.

On Sunday, July 17 Maure Weigel of the Prairie Raptor Rehabilitation Project (and a Kansas native son), hosted a series of demonstrations with raptors (birds of prey). He only possessed the birds because they could not survive in the wild for one reason or another.

During the week various conservation themes were featured, including recycling, habitat destruction, vanishing animals, wildlife trade, and Species Survival Plans. The Kansas Beverage Industry Recycling Program sponsored a recycling collecting station at the zoo.

All aspects of the zoo's Conservation Festival were splendid, but the culminating highlight on July 23-24 was the special appearance of Damara, an adult female cheetah from Wildlife Safari in Winston, Oregon. Damara was accompanied by her trainer, Laurie Marker, who had earned recognition by raising a cheetah in captivity and teaching it to hunt successfully in

Africa. (Laurie later moved to Namibia in Africa to establish and manage the Cheetah Conservation Fund.)

Sometimes known as the "greyhound of the cats," cheetahs have canine characteristics, and unlike other cats, have no sheaths into which their claws can be retracted. The coat pattern of the cheetah consists of solid black dots as opposed to the leopard and jaguar, which have rosettes (a spot in a fragmented circle). Cheetahs are the swiftest mammal, with speeds of over 70 mph for a short distance.

As they had on so many occasions, Hill's Pet Products played a major role in the success of the Conservation Festival. They sponsored the cheetah and her trainer, commissioned original artwork by Galen "Duke" Senogles for a commemorative cheetah poster that was given away, and contributed a grand prize drawing for four to visit Disney World, Orlando.

The cheetah spotted at Topeka Zoo was more than a rare sighting; it was a memorable and noteworthy event.

The weekly shopper, *Pennypower*, featured zoo activities and special events in each issue.

The "One Minute Manager" Visits the Zoo

Really? Yes, it was true! Here's how it happened.

During my years as a zoo director, I did not consider myself to be in "sales" or "marketing," and certainly never put myself in the "executive" category. I was just an animal keeper with the gift of gab.

Nevertheless, the Topeka Chapter of Sales and Marketing Executives (SME) asked me to speak at one of their monthly dinner meetings. I did. What an appreciative and receptive audience! Then they invited me to join the organization. I did. What a fascinating group of people! I learned so much at every meeting.

Each year SME Topeka would sponsor a regional seminar, open to the public, and featuring a prominent national speaker. In 1986 they headlined Dr. Kenneth Blanchard, of San Diego, The One Minute Manager himself! He was an internationally renowned management consultant, as well as a best-selling author (his books were in *every* bookstore and international airport). What a coup for SME Topeka. And I was selected to meet him at our airport and provide transport to his downtown hotel.

Having flown regularly in and out of Forbes Field I knew the staff and made arrangements to meet Dr. Blanchard on the ramp as he stepped off the plane (the airport had no jetways and security was much less stringent in those days). His flight landed, and as our special guest descended the stairs from the aircraft, I rolled out a section of red carpet and said, "Welcome to Topeka, the Capital City of Kansas." Although surprised by this unexpected greeting, he beamed and said, "Thank you."

After introducing myself and claiming his luggage, we proceeded to my Jeep. Then I popped the question: "Since we have a little time, would you like to see the World Famous Topeka Zoo?" Since he *was* from *San Diego,* I thought he might scoff at this. Instead, with a generous grin he replied, "Sure."

Such a response immediately told me something very important about Ken Blanchard (he requested that I skip the "Dr." prefix): he was *sincerely* interested in people. He had never been to Topeka, had never met me, and had never heard of our "world famous" zoo. No matter; he was *genuinely* eager to see the zoo (and probably try to figure out what made me tick as well).

For more than two decades I had conducted personalized tours of our zoo for a medley of people: students, donors, politicians, news media, board members, professional colleagues, beauty queens, all-star athletic teams, safari guides, travel writers, foreign guests of the mayor, and VIPs of all ilk. But—never had there been a tour for anyone even close to this

Ken Blanchard guy. He was interested in *everything*: animals, behavior, exhibit techniques, zoo history and philosophy, the business end of the zoo, and yes, management—how *Topeka* could have a zoo of "World Famous" caliber.

Ken was extremely perceptive! Without me saying so in specific words, he understood my foremost belief: that a zoo should be for people, not just animals, and their experience should be memorable and rewarding. He also appreciated the great team we had in our qualified, dedicated staff, and recognized the importance of community support, which resulted in pride and volunteerism. Ken was particularly impressed with our zoo's focus on the multidimensional interaction between visitors and animals, especially as evidenced by the Tropical Rain Forest, Gorilla Encounter, and the concept for Lions Pride.

At the end of our tour I was *charged up*! Ken Blanchard's numerous books, tapes and videos certainly are enlightening, but to be one-on-one with him was *inspiring . . .* and a privilege. To my good fortune, this serendipitous meeting developed into a lasting personal friendship that I greatly treasure.

My association with Ken gave me a new perspective on the principles of effective management, and increased my respect for the values of motivational leadership.

My association with SME Topeka continued to broaden my horizons. In 1988 I was surprised and humbled when they honored me as Sales and Marketing Executive of the Year.

After I changed careers and established Cowabunga Safaris, Ken Blanchard, together with his family and friends, traveled to Africa with me on numerous safaris. In fact, his group holds the record for the most people to participate in a mud bath on the Zambezi River.

He's quite a guy!

SUNDAY, NOVEMBER 12, 1988

The Topeka Capital-Journal *OPINION*

Editorials ———————————————— *In God We Trust—*

A special zoo director

"People think being the director of a zoo is fun and interesting," Gary Clarke once wrote in The Capital-Journal. "They're right."

Clarke has been director of the Topeka Zoo for 25 years. When he accepted the position in 1963, other zoo directors told him he was committing professional suicide. Today, they may be envying him. Unknown then, the Topeka Zoo today frequently carries the preface "world famous."

Thanks to Clarke's dynamic leadership, the zoo has progressed to one of the finest small zoos in the country. And it keeps getting better. The Lion's Pride exhibit will be the latest improvement.

No wonder the zoo is a favorite for family outings in northeast Kansas.

Clarke credits much of the success of the zoo to Topeka. The community has been supportive of the zoo, not just in revenue, but in volunteer work. Clarke admits that he has had offers from bigger zoos with bigger budgets and more challenges. But they didn't have "the responsiveness of this community."

Topekans are grateful for Clarke's loyalty and leadership. And they get a chance to show it today. Clarke will be the guest of honor at an open house from 1 to 4 p.m. at Fairlawn Plaza.

In that article he wrote in 1967, Clarke also said, "As a child I viewed the zoo as an animal wonderland; I still do."

Thanks to Gary Clarke, so do many Topekans.

"25 Years is a Long Stretch"

So proclaimed the headline of an eye-catching display ad (featuring a very long necked giraffe) in *The Topeka Capital-Journal* on November 10, 1988. Sponsored by the Fairlawn Plaza Mall and Shopping Center, the display was an invitation to the community to celebrate my Silver Anniversary as zoo director in Topeka. It read as follows:

Gary K. Clarke will be honored on Sunday, Nov.13, to acknowledge his 25 years as Director of the World Famous Topeka Zoo. The Merchants Association of Fairlawn Plaza, on behalf of the Topeka community, will host an Open House to recognize his achievements. The entire community is invited to stop by during the afternoon and congratulate Gary. Children are encouraged to bring home-made cards for Gary, which will be displayed on the wall of the Mall.

A unique lion cake, sculpted and decorated under the supervision of Dorothy Dalton, will be the featured centerpiece. In addition to free cake and punch, visitors will be offered yogurt from I Can't Believe It's Yogurt.

The occasion inspired a unique rendition of a popular song.

GARY COWABUNGA!
(Puff the Magic Dragon)

Gary, Cowabunga lives at TZP
And frolics in the tall grasses
Since 1963

A Kansas City Keeper, respect for all wildlife
From Ft. Worth to Topeka
Four children and a wife!
From Keeper to Director, with a visionary mind
Watched DA grow, and boilers blow
Ideas of all kinds

Gary, Cowabunga lives at TZP
And frolics in the tall grasses
Since 1963

Gary, Zoo Director, loves to go downtown
And deals with lots of paperwork with all the city clowns
A jungle in Topeka? And lions roaming free?
Sometimes they thought that Gary's mind was
Still on safariiiiiiii

Managed to convince them World Famous we could be
Up there with San Diegoooo and Washington D.C.

At feeding time for Gary, here's how you can't go wrong
Just toss him fruits and vegetables
Some tuskers and biltong!

Oh Gary Cowabunga, lives at TZP
And frolics in the tall grasses
Since 1963

His friends are in the 1,000's
They're local they're worldwide
They're human and they're animal
The source of all pride

Last Verse
A more kind and caring person
You shall never see
That's GKC at TZP since 1963333333333333

HAPPY 25ᵀᴴ ANNIVERSARY!!!

K&C

The Open House was both humbling and gratifying. The next day *The Topeka Capital-Journal* gave an excellent account in a front page article by staff writer John Boyette, Jr. Following is an abridged version.

City Thanks Clarke for 25 Years

Sitting in the middle of Fairlawn Mall on Sunday was a large lion-shaped cake.

A steady flow of people looked in awe at the cake, about a square yard in size, and some couldn't resist plucking off a nibble of brown icing to satisfy their sweet tooth.

"That's good, mommy," a toddler said, with icing around his lips.

That lion-shaped cake was the perfect symbol of what was taking place in the mall, for Sunday was the day Topekans helped Gary Clarke celebrate his 25ᵗʰ anniversary as director of the Topeka Zoo.

About 500 people turned out at the reception to chat or reminisce with Clarke, or to just say "thanks" to the zoo director, according to Randy Austin, president of the Fairlawn Plaza Merchants Association, which sponsored the three-hour reception.

"I am overwhelmed," said Clarke, as he watched well-wishers munch on cake—not the lion-shaped one—yogurt and punch. "It's been fun. I see a lot of people I haven't seen in a long time, and people who have supported the zoo since I've been there."

If you ask him to nail down one or two of his most memorable moments at the zoo, well, Clarke just couldn't do it.

"I think overall that the progress at the zoo has been very good," Clarke said. "I give credit to the community, the city and to the Friends of the Topeka Zoo."

"A lot of my colleagues tell me that it is remarkable how our zoo continues to progress."

But Clarke, a hard-working and determined man who is not one to rest on his laurels, said more can be done at the zoo and that more will be done.

"Sometimes I get frustrated because we haven't been able to move faster than I think we could," he said. "But that's typical with anything."

As Clarke spoke, he clutched a fistful of homemade cards given to him by area children. More cards were on display on a mall wall.

"The most satisfying thing for me is to see the thousands of youngsters who come to the zoo," the zoo director said.

"I was in the grocery store the other day, and there was this young man, about 18 years old, sacking groceries. He asked me if I remembered him. I told him I did not, and he said that when he was 6 years old he was in Zoo School (a Topeka Zoo program that teaches children about animals).

"That really impressed me, because he remembered (the Zoo School) and the experience was so significant to him," Clarke said.

Clarke also remembered the time he was at the Grand Canyon when a National Park Service official recognized and approached him.

"He said he had lived in Topeka and had gone on the zoo tour," Clarke said. "He said (the tour) encouraged him to go into the Park Service."

The lion-shaped cake that drew a lot of attention Sunday was "sculpted" by Topekan Dorothy Dalton. Cake and Candy Supply Shoppe of Topeka supplied the ingredients, which included 108 eggs and 90 pounds of icing.

Dalton said it took her and helpers about 150 hours to plan, sculpt and bake the cake. The cake was not cut during the reception.

But cake aside, Clarke was the hit of the day. One woman best summed up the feelings of those who attended the reception.

"We're lucky to have you," she said to Clarke. "You've been here for 25 years, and we hope it will be 25 more."

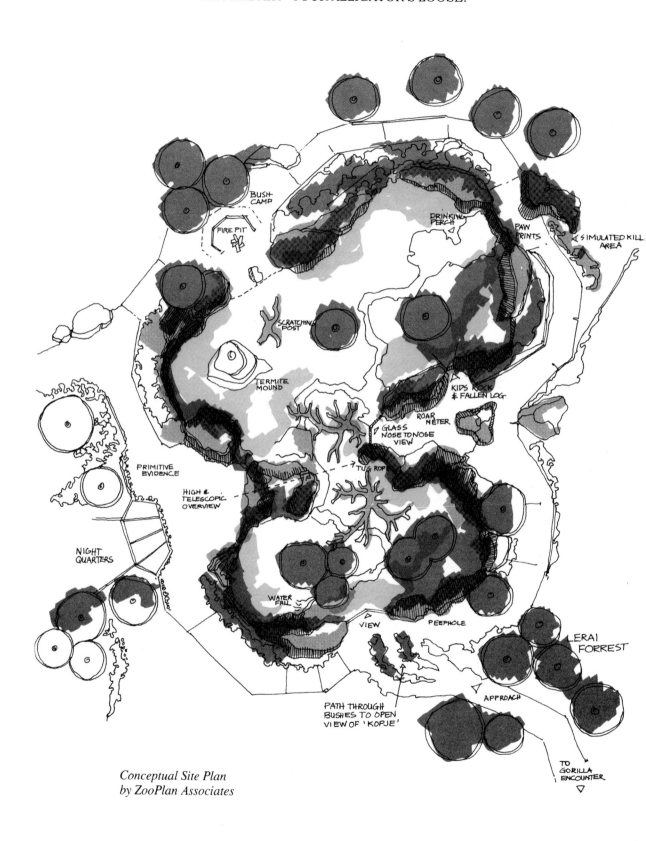

BUSH CAMP

FIRE PIT

DRINKING PERCH

PAW PRINTS

SIMULATED KILL AREA

SCRATCHING POST

TERMITE MOUND

KIDS ROCK & FALLEN LOG

ROAR METER

GLASS NOSE TO NOSE VIEW

TUG ROPE

PRIMITIVE EVIDENCE

HIGH & TELESCOPIC OVERVIEW

NIGHT QUARTERS

WATER FALL

VIEW

PEEPHOLE

LERAI FORREST

APPROACH

PATH THROUGH BUSHES TO OPEN VIEW OF 'KOPJE'

TO GORILLA ENCOUNTER

*Conceptual Site Plan
by ZooPlan Associates*

Lions Pride: The Vision and Foundation for a Roaring Success

The lion: symbol of power, strength and courage.

The lion: subject of legend, fable and folklore.

The lion: present in heraldic emblems, Egyptian tombs and antiquarian maps.

The lion is the largest predator on the African continent. The unforgettable sight of a lion in the wild is much written of, though not a very universal experience. Those who have witnessed it are taken with the big cat's raw beauty and awed by the almost contradictory embodiment of power and grace that serves as a constant reminder that theirs is one of the few remaining worlds so vastly different from our own. It's a feast for the senses, not to be understood, but to be experienced.

The lion is found in the Bible (with the lamb), in the sky (the constellation Leo), in books (The Man-Eaters of Tsavo), in movies (MGM), even at the library—two reclining stone lions named Patience and Fortitude guard the 5th Avenue entrance of the New York Public Library.

And the lion is found in the zoo!

After the successful completion of Gorilla Encounter in 1985, attention focused on our next major project: Lions Pride. Following are the thoughts I had at the time on the concept for Lions Pride.

Zoo-goers have become sophisticated because of travel to other zoos and eco-tourism destinations, and because of the wealth of natural history and animal-oriented films, books, and television programs. Hence, they now expect their own community zoo to maintain national and international standards of exhibit technique. Many zoos show the same species of animals—lions are a prime example. So . . . what is it that makes *one* zoo exhibit stand out over the others in the visitor's mind?

In my opinion it is the *perspective* presented to the visitor, and the way the visitor *experiences* the animal in its setting, that makes it memorable.

In Lions Pride at the World Famous Topeka Zoo you will experience lions as you have never experienced them anywhere!

Lions will be shown in a naturalistic environment, but not restricted to the standard open grassy plains frequently depicted. Rather, the exhibit will feature that aspect of lion habitat that incorporates scrub forest, boulder outcroppings, and a strong bush element—such as an area in Zimbabwe that is subject to seasonal changes, with some vegetation similar to Kansas.

Glass will be utilized as an element to allow the closest of interactions between lions and visitors in a completely safe manner. You can be nose to nose with the pride male, or watch a mother lion caring for her cubs just inches away. Visitors may follow lion pug marks (footprints) on the trail, or possibly put their hands on the same log the lion is resting on—what a thrill!

As with the Tropical Rain Forest and Gorilla Encounter, visitors will not simply look at an exhibit, but will actually be a part of the animal's environment in an unforgettable experience.

Imagine walking down a true African bush path—an irregular trail that curves and meanders, with vegetation so tall that you cannot see anything on either side. You are now on the Simba Trail, and although you are in the middle of the zoo, you are completely swallowed by this microhabitat. Your anticipation is keen when you are abruptly startled by a lion's roar. From the loudness of the roar, it is obvious you are only yards away from a lion. The trail winds around a corner and suddenly you're there at Lions Pride—as close as you would ever want to be to the King of Beasts!

The sight in front of you is an African bush setting, and you are immersed in a different habitat—the lion's, not yours. It features a varied terrain with huge fallen trees, rocky outcrops, termite mounds and natural plantings.

The exhibit will not be moated, since a safe moat for lions is at least 25 feet wide with an added six feet for a buffer zone to the public guardrail. Coupled with the fact that lions may be at the back of the exhibit, this means that the visitors could be as far as 75 feet from the lions. Instead, at Lions Pride, visitors will be just a few feet away from the lions—actually able to count the whiskers on their muzzles!

The exhibit will have three themed view stations. The first is the Adrenaline Grass view. The zoo visitor will follow a bush path (the Simba Trail) through tall stands of adrenaline grass (so named because if you unexpectedly encounter a lion in Africa your adrenaline shoots everywhere). This initial view will be through tension wire, which resembles harp wire.

Only a quarter of an inch thick, stretched taut it presents a minimal visual barrier—a very dramatic way to see a lion!

The visitor then follows the Simba Trail to the Kopje Rock view. Kopjes (pronounced copies) are huge boulder outcroppings found in many areas of Africa, and a favorite resting place for lions (which are then called "kopje cats"). Zoo visitors will actually proceed inside the kopje rocks for a spectacular glass-fronted view of the Lions Pride habitat. The only source of drinking water in the entire exhibit will be located right in front of the glass, so each time a lion takes a drink, zoo visitors will be just inches away, eye-to-eye.

At the exit from the Kopje Rocks the visitor comes face to face with a heroic size bronze sculpture of a male lion crouched and drinking. Titled "Genesis," it has been commissioned especially for Lions Pride by Randy Austin and Eva Bennett of Fairlawn Plaza Development Inc., and sculpted by wildlife artist Dennis Anderson.

From there the visitor continues down the Simba Trail to the third view, Bush Camp. Visitors enter under a safari tent canopy and approach a "hide." This consists of a stockade fence with holes cut at various levels (adult size, child size, wheelchair size) and canvas flaps hanging over the holes. It is a participatory view station, and visitors lift the flaps in order to peer into Lions Pride to see lion activity. A separate enclosed hide at Bush Camp will enable study projects on lion behavior.

An important key to the success of the Lions Pride experience will be the horticultural dimension. How fortunate to have Park Naturalist Bob Foster on our team. Just as he and his staff created an instant jungle for the Tropical Rain Forest, I foresee an instant savannah for Lions Pride. Bob anticipates using a wide variety of plants, nearly 200 in all, in an attempt to, as he says, "Try to create a Readers' Digest version of African lion country." Thornless honey locust trees will be pruned to give the impression of flat-top acacias. Gourds will be planted for fast growing vines, and the large leaves of rhubarb plants among the grasses will give a tropical appearance to the site. Africa in Kansas.

Although not open to the public, a sophisticated night quarters and off-exhibit building will be adjacent to the exhibit and utilized in the management and husbandry of the animals.

Lions Pride will emphasize the natural social order of a pride of lions and allow observation of their seldom-seen behavior as it is in the wild. In this multi-dimensional exhibit, visitors can study a lion intimately, from maternal care to lions sleeping regally overhead in trees or on rock outcroppings.

Lions Pride will truly be a unique experience.

*****

"The Little Zoo That Could" had been chugging full steam ahead for over two decades with spectacular results. Community response was overwhelming, support from Topeka Friends of the Zoo was extraordinary, and backing by the City of Topeka (particularly through the Parks and Recreation Department) was tremendous.

Major capital improvements—Animals and Man Building, Tropical Rain Forest, Discovering Apes (including Gorilla Encounter)—had all been financed through general obligation bonds, with admission revenues being used to retire the bonds. But now, with the vision set for our next unique exhibit—Lions Pride—the zoo was at its limit for financing another major development through admission fees.

UH-OH!

With the opening of Gorilla Encounter in 1985, the zoo experienced record-breaking attendance. We had our largest one day attendance—21,995—our largest one month attendance—74,299 (surpassed in 1986 with the "Koala" month attendance of 90,717)—and our largest single year ever—273,921. The previous record of 232,634 visitors had stood for more than a decade, and occurred in 1974, the year the zoo opened the Tropical Rain Forest.

The records set in 1985 were particularly significant. For a zoo with our parameters—tax-supported by a modest municipality, located in a four-season climate, charging an admission, and not situated in a terminal tourist destination—the average attendance was comparable to the population of the city in which the zoo was located. Census figures at the time listed the population of Topeka, Kansas at 119,000 people. Hence, the zoo should have expected about that many visitors each year. Our 1985 attendance was truly exceptional: the equivalent of *230 percent* of the city's population!

In fact, over the years attendance at the zoo had consistently exceeded normal expectations, with the average number of visitors each year at 150 percent of the city's population.

Somehow we had to keep the momentum going, and Lions Pride would be a critical factor. It made me think back to 1965 when the bridge over the Kansas River collapsed, which halted all capital improvements in the city and threatened the development of our first major exhibit, as well as the zoo's momentum at that time. Our answer then was the admission charge.

Now, thanks to a study funded by the Topeka Friends of the Zoo (TFOTZ), a new organization emerged under the leadership of Robert Wheeler, President of Hill's Pet Products, together with Charles Henson and Dr. Mark Morris, Jr. In early 1986 Bob Wheeler announced the formation of a non-profit corporation, the Topeka Zoological Foundation. The Foundation was not intended to replace or substitute any of the activities of TFOTZ. Rather, it was organized to assist the zoo in raising capital funds for major exhibits in the long-range development of the master plan. The

President of TFOTZ would serve as a Trustee on the Foundation Board to insure that both organizations worked in concert to achieve the common goals and objectives of the zoo.

Lions Pride was the next major phase of the zoo master plan, and the Foundation's Board of Trustees officially adopted it as their initial project, with an established goal of $400,000. It was the first time in the zoo's history that the majority of capital funds came from the private sector: corporations, businesses, and many, many individuals. The City of Topeka contributed $150,000 (including in-kind services) to the project for a total construction budget of $550,000. In addition, the Topeka Friends of the Zoo had already funded a preliminary concept design study for $12,000, and later provided $10,000 for landscaping and $32,000 for graphics and interpretive materials for Lions Pride. In March 1987 the Junior League of Topeka contributed nearly $16,000 to the Lions Pride project in celebration of their 50 years of community service. The Junior League had long supported the zoo. In 1966 they established the Zoo Docent program under the direction of Nancy Cherry, who was a member of both the League and Topeka Friends of the Zoo Board.

Topeka artist Galen Senogles was commissioned to do an original painting symbolic of Lions Pride, with 50 signed and numbered prints given to major contributors.

The Foundation needed initial promotional materials, and Hinkle/ Frye/Scannell Advertising offered to contribute their creative services for layout and design. Lynn Scannell produced a striking black-and-white scratch-board illustration of a mother lion carrying a small cub in her mouth. It served as a dramatic cover for a Lions Pride brochure containing the conceptual site plan, and an acknowledgement of donors. Ives Printing provided paper and printing services.

In 1989 Foundation President, Betty S. Cleland, wrote: "The Topeka Zoological Foundation has just completed its third year of activity. As its first project the Foundation established Lions Pride and all gifts and pledges were earmarked for the exhibit's development. It is the first example of private/public funding for a major capital improvement at the Zoo.

"The Trustees of the Topeka Zoological Foundation take great pride in their support of the Zoo. The World Famous Topeka Zoo, and others like it, are protecting our animals and preserving the wondrous species that inhabit this Earth. Lions Pride was also dedicated to the greatest animal right of all—the right of survival." With the combined efforts of the Topeka Zoological Foundation, the Topeka Friends of the Zoo, the city and the community at large, a wonderful team was formed, providing the foundation for a roaring success.

The success of Lions Pride was due to many donors as listed in our 1989 brochure.

Lions Pride is made possible by The Topeka Zoological Foundation and the generosity of the following:

City of Topeka
Parks and Recreation of Topeka

Eva Bennett
Randy Austin

Hill's Pet Products
Dr. Mark L. & Bette Morris
BANK IV Topeka, N.A.
Junior League of Topeka, Inc.
James & Marilyn Nellis
Volume Shoe Corporation
Frank & Alice Sabatini
Laird Noller Dealerships
Security Benefit Group of Companies
Friends of the Topeka Zoo
Merchants National Bank
Columbian Nat'l. Bank & Trust Co.
Topeka Bank & Trust Company
Mark Morris Associates

Capitol Federal Savings & Loan
Fleming Companies
Nile, Kate, Garrett & Kylie Fowler
James & Bonnie Garrett
Murray & Sandy Hardesty
Highland Park Bank & Trust Co.
Hypermart USA Associates
KPL Gas Service Co.
Southwestern Bell Foundation
Stauffer Communications Foundation
Gerald Stoltenberg &
    Linda Wahl-Stoltenberg
Vincent Roofing Co.
Wal-Mart Foundation
Vic Yarrington Oldsmobile
Dennis Anderson
Eidson, Lewis, Porter & Haynes
Gault-Hussey Charitable Trust
Harry Turner & Associates, Inc.
Hinkle/Frye/Scannell Advertising
H.M. Ives & Sons, Inc.
Kansas Sand & Concrete Inc.
Martin Tractor Company
Alan & Ann Rolley
Santa Fe Foundation
Galen Senogles
Shawnee Federal Savings
Lee & Liz Stratton
Touche Ross & Co.
William Trahan
Jere & Harry Turner, Jr.
Wolfe's Camera & Video
Adams Business Forms
Ken, Pam & S.K. Alexander
Guy Almeling & Linda Sebastian
John and Jan Benson
Bryan World Tours
Anderson and Patricia Chandler
Dr. Art & Nancy Cherry

Sally Searle Clark
Gary K. & Margaret Clarke
John & Betty Cleland
Commerce Bank & Trust Company
Phil & Collette Coolidge
Dr. & Mrs. Robert Cotton
Harry & Karen Craig
John B. & Brenda Dicus
Robert E. & Renie Edmonds
Fink Foundation (C-G-F)
Bob Foster
Ron & Vicki Francis
Everett & Sally Gille
Dr. Hall & Joanne Harrison
Danton & Jenny Hejtmanek
Dr. Harry & Jane Kroll
Lardner Monument Co.
May Dept. Stores Foundation
Will McElroy
Penwell-Gabel Funeral Directors
Quaker Oats Company
Dr. & Mrs. Ralph Reymond
Fred & Jeanne Reynolds
Don Roepke
Eleanore Rost in Memory of F.J. Rost
L. William & Saundra Rudnick
Salisbury Supply Company
Turtlenest
Dr. & Mrs. Kirk Wanless & Family
Robert & Opal Wheeler
Fairlawn Plaza Shopping Center
    The Ad Shop Agency, Inc.
    AMOCO Food Store
    Ben Franklin Arts & Crafts
    Byers Optical
    Cake & Candy Supply
    Cards & Such
    Cat's Meow
    Classique Boutique
    The Copper Oven
    Diamonds 1st
    Eagle Auto Wash
    ERA Simnitt Auction Service
    Footlights
    Frame Shop & Gallery
    G.G.'s Beauty & Barber
    Kansas City Saloon
    Kitchen Gallery
    Kobe's Japanese Steak House
    Langer Floral
    Petland
    Rabbit Hollow
    Reuters Boots, Shoes & Repair
    Rusty's Outdoor Sports
    Shimer's Store West
    Swan Tours
    T-Shirts Etc.
    Topeka Business Computers
    Topeka Lions Club
    Venture
    Walgreens
Bill Kobach Buick Dealership
Blackburn Nursery
Fidelity State Bank & Trust Co.

Webb Garlinghouse
Goodell, Stratton, Edmonds,
    & Palmer
Hartmarx Foundation
    (Ray Beers Clothing Co.)
Kaw Valley State Bank & Trust Co.
Lanny & Jacque Kimbrough
Charles & Bette Martin
North Plaza State Bank
Dr. & Mrs. Dennis Petterson
Ringling Bros Barnum & Bailey
    Circus
Ronald L. & Jane Robb
Doane & Marjorie Smith
Charles M. Springer
Dr. Ernest Swisher Memorial Gifts
    Gene & Vera Clatterbuck
    Patrick Dickey & Jane Schlicher
    Carol Emert & Family
    Friend from Erie, KS.
    Evelynn Heidepriem
    Ms. Cindy Horn
    William & Carol Hunt
    Eva & Leroy Sebring
    Burl & Helen Sparks
    Barbara Sund
    Charles Swisher
    Harry & Virginia Wade
    Robert & Margaret Waugh
    Shirley Weideman
    Sharyl & Robert Whitehead
Dr. & Mrs. Henry Blake
Jerome & Barbara Fink
Mr. & Mrs. H. Bernerd Fink
John & Harriet Green
William Humenczuk
Dr. & Mrs. William Leifer
J.F. McGivern
Dr. & Mrs. James Owen
Super D Drugs
Dr. Byron Ashley
Dr. & Mrs. Stuart Averill
Beta Sigma Phi, Laureate Alpha
    Gamma Chapter
Dr. & Mrs. Russ Bridwell
John & Marcella Briery
Bryan, Lykins, Hejtmanek
    & Wulz, PA
Capital City Bank & Trust
Maurice & Naomi Cashman
Don & Evelyn Chappell
Coldwell, Banker, Griffith & Blair
Dr. Jeffrey & Connie Curtis
Degginger Foundry
Dr. Ronald Evans & Dr. Sara Tucker
Dr. & Mrs. Richard Fields
Richard & Julie Friedstrom
Dr. & Mrs. S.K. Gandhi
Janet R. Gasch
Nancy Goodall
Harold & Bev Goodman
Goodyear Women's Club
Charles & Sally Henson
Dr. & Mrs. Robert N. Hill

Lynn Hinkle & Lynn Scannell
Stanley & Lois Hornbaker
Richard Hunsinger
G. Lester Jordan
Judith Clark Kerr
Kirk & Cobb, Inc. Realtors
KMAJ-Radio
Marjorie Konopaska
Kroh Brothers
KSNT-TV
KTPK Radio
KTWU-TV
WIBW-TV
KTKA-TV
Dr. & Mrs. Song Ping Lee
Dr. Chester & Edith Lessenden
Mr. & Mrs. Bob Mackey & Jeff
Drs. Brad Marples &
    Aileen McCarthy
Mrs. F.B.W. McCollum
McDonalds Restaurants
Robt. Menninger, M.D.
Donna Rae & Laird Noller
Dr. & Mrs. Robert O'Neil
Pauline South Middle School
Pennypower
Mr. Lee Porter
Mr. & Mrs. Pat Powers
Dr. & Mrs. Brad Prokop
Charles Reynolds
Dr. William & Jane Roy
Don & Marjorie Schnacke
Dana Schroeder
Mary Shortman
St. Francis Employees
Monte L. Stiles
Dr. & Mrs. David Thurston
Topeka Capital Journal
Dr. & Mrs. Jack Travis
Dr. & Mrs. Nate Uhr
John Vestal
Ron Vine
Kelly Waldo
Dr. & Mrs. William Walker
Donald & Sue Wester
Douglas Wright
Dr. Craig Yorke & Mary Powell
Tim & Sue Benaka
Lee M. Benson
Marshall Clark
Janelda A. Gill
Thelma H. Neal
Daniel & Roxanne Ortiz
Steven & Marsha L. Ralston
Roy A. Reese
Cristy & Scott D. Reichert
Dale & Dorothy Richardson
Gary & Carmella Roth
Roger & Lanette Scurlock
Mr. & Mrs. Don Tilton
Jean L. Turner
Lloyd W. Woodburn
James W. Woods, Jr.
Mark Young

Super Cubs

Acquiring new animals for the zoo was always a challenging task. In most cases, we preferred captive born specimens as we then had a history of their parents, an accurate date of birth, and other pertinent information. Zoos are more successful today than at any time in history in the propagation and husbandry of wild animals, and thus fewer are being imported from the wild. When you acquired a specimen from its country of origin you did not know the exact age of the animal, its history or nutritional status. You could encounter unexpected veterinary problems and transportation costs would be greater. Even with captive-born animals there are many unknown factors. Obviously, you deal with reputable organizations and professional colleagues in whom you have confidence and trust. They, in turn, want to provide healthy specimens. With all of these good intentions it is still possible to acquire young animals that at the time appear to be in excellent condition but later develop problems.

Our two female lion cubs, a gift of Hill's Pet Products, were from a private breeder in New York state and hand reared until they were transferred to our zoo in late October 1987 at eight weeks of age. When they were a little more than six months old, it seemed an appropriate time to assess their development and status. Both had progressed remarkably well and each now weighed over 60 pounds. Their curiosity and alertness were all that we could hope for. They were so vibrant and responsive to life. They related to each other well and showed the sibling social relationship that was important to the future development of the pride.

It was wonderful to see them as they were exercised outdoors by the keepers. They would stalk and run, wrestle and play, sit in an alert posture and study anything that caught their eye. The keepers had done a wonderful job of developing their responses and stimulating behaviors that would be appropriate for the new Lions Pride exhibit. They were beautiful animals and, if we opened Lions Pride on schedule in 1989, they would be just perfect for our new exhibit.

On Friday, March 4, 1988 in order to document their progress, I scheduled a photo session for the lion sisters Arusha and Manyara. The day was brisk but full of sunshine. The local news media were invited, and I had asked well-known Topeka photographer Nathan Ham to take photos of the cubs for a postcard. I had my camera as well, since this would be a good opportunity to update my photo file of "the girls."

The expansive west lawn of the Animals and Man building was an ideal setting, with abundant space and an infinity background. The cubs were in a festive mood and wanted to play rather than pose, a bit frustrating for us photographers.

At one point Arusha struck a "picture-perfect" stance and I quickly crouched to sneak up on her to get the shot. Unbeknownst to me, my posture apparently was a visual signal to Manyara, Arusha's sister, to stalk. Suddenly I felt sharp claws and fangs on my buttocks! Manyara had ambushed me from behind in a playful attack! And at that very instant, photographer Earl Richardson of *The Topeka Capital-Journal* snapped his shutter and captured the image!

Immediately Nathan Ham said, "That's the photo that will be in the paper." He was right. It was featured again at the end of the year as one of the favorite "Lasting Images" of 1988. The caption read, "Most Topekans know how much Gary Clarke loves animals. What isn't often seen is just how much the zoo's animals love Clarke. But when one lion cub playfully toyed with Clarke, Earl Richardson was there."

When the photo was first published in *The Topeka Capital-Journal* in March, it was also picked up by the Associated Press and ran in newspapers nationwide. Over the next few weeks I received clippings in the mail from all over the country—as well as several dozen of those inflatable donut pillows frequently used when one has a sore bottom!

The Mane Event x 7

From the moment of inception I knew Lions Pride would be something special. Accordingly, I felt everything we did with respect to Lions Pride—from groundbreaking to grand opening—should be distinctive and unique. Originally I thought it would be appropriate to designate the public debut of the exhibit as "The Mane Event." As it turned out, however, we had numerous occasions that qualified as a "Mane Event." Hence, the name of this chapter, together with a summary of each event.

GROUNDBREAKING. This would *not* be the usual groundbreaking, so we needed a better name for it. Ah-ha! What do lions do? With their powerful paws and sharp claws, they tear the turf. So, why not a Turf Tearing? Great, but a bit of background first.

At the zoo we needed some unglamorous site preparation before we could initiate our new spectacular attraction. To clear the area, the old carnivore units had to be demolished, a feat accomplished by the Parks and Recreation Department as part of their in-kind contribution. Also, a maze of unsightly utility poles and overhead power lines had to be removed and rerouted. This seemed to take forever, but at last we were ready.

Two creative members of the Zoo Foundation Board—Betty Cleland and Donna Rae Noller—co-chaired the Turf Tearing and came up with some very clever touches. One was a commemorative folding camp stool, complete with the Lions Pride logo, as a fun souvenir for participants.

Another special touch was to hand deliver invitations to the doorstep of each invitee. But—these were *not* the standard engraved invitations. Oh, no! The invitation consisted of a small green bottle of champagne, to which was attached (with a gold thread) a card with the pertinent information.

Before I share the text of the card with you, permit me to explain a little known bit of geographical reference in the zoo at that time. When the specialist contractors had fabricated the elaborate rockwork as part of Gorilla Encounter in 1985, they had some excess material. They used this to develop a small "mountain" adjacent to the public walk for children to climb. Someone on the zoo staff dubbed this "Mt. Kilimanclarkeo" in deference to my regard for the highest mountain in Africa.

Knowing that, here is how the invitation read:

A Happening Near Mt. Kilimanclarkeo
LIONS PRIDE Turf Tearing.
Wed, October 14, 1987. 5:30-6:30 P.M.
World Famous Topeka Zoo—Gage Park
Topeka Zoological Foundation

I still have my invitation and champagne bottle, but the champagne is long gone!

I felt it would be appropriate for a big cat to actually tear the turf, so I contacted Zoo Foundation Board Member Harry Craig, who happened to be president of Martin Tractor Co., our local Caterpillar Diesel dealer, and a long time zoo supporter. He pounced on my idea (like a predator after prey) and happily provided a piece of heavy equipment to do the honors. Decorated with a smiling face and named, "Martin the Big Cat," it was christened (with one of the small bottles of champagne) by Zoo Foundation President Bob Wheeler. He commented, "Raising money for Lions Pride gave each of our Trustees pride in our community as each of our donors was pleased to be part of continuing the reputation of the World Famous Topeka Zoo."

He also noted that $364,000 had been raised toward the foundation's goal of $400,000.

Lion paw prints (or pug marks) led from the zoo entrance to the construction site. Among the 70 or so invited guests attending the Turf Tearing was Topeka Mayor Doug Wright. During the ceremony he said, "I thank you from the City of Topeka for making the pride exhibit a reality. The private sector has really expressed its pride in the zoo."

Originally I had hoped to open the exhibit in 1988. But the planning by Phil Coolidge and Greg Allen of Coolidge Architectural Services of Topeka was detailed and exact (as it should have been) and the completion was rescheduled for the spring of 1989. Even so, with this official beginning, we knew that Lions Pride would be a catalyst for our zoo.

GENESIS PRESS PARTY. On June 16, 1988 donors Eva F. Bennett and Randolph G. Austin of Fairlawn Plaza Development Company hosted a Press Party and Preview Showing of the heroic-sized bronze sculpture "Genesis."

Depicting an adult male lion crouched and drinking, it was commissioned especially for the Lions Pride exhibit and sculpted by artist Dennis Anderson. The preview was held in the Fairlawn Plaza Mall, complete with champagne and hors d'oeuvres.

After an exhibition period at Fairlawn Plaza, Genesis was on a nationwide tour prior to being permanently placed in the World Famous Topeka Zoo as part of the Lions Pride complex.

LUAU FOR LIONS PRIDE. This was the theme for the fund-raising gala sponsored by Friends of the Topeka Zoo on June 24, 1988. Supported by more than four dozen Topeka businesses and individuals, the evening included cocktails, dinner and the band Crusin' for guests' dancing pleasure.

Hawaiian dancers were the featured entertainment, followed by a drawing for a trip to Hawaii. The grand prize was given by Mark I Travel of Topeka.

Proceeds from the gala were pledged to the educational dimensions of Lions Pride.

LIONS FIRST! During the period of construction, the trio of lion cubs we had acquired for the new exhibit had GROWN! Suddenly they were strapping young adults! The male, Samburu, now had a beautiful full mane and tipped the scales at 437 pounds—all muscle! *That* is a BIG lion. Unrelated to Samburu were the two females—Arusha, 276 pounds, and Manyara, 268 pounds, who were sisters. This was important since the social structure of a pride of lions is based on the relationship of the females.

By early July 1989 we were putting the finishing touches on the exhibit. Final preparations were made to introduce the lions into their new habitat for the first time—an exciting, but scary, situation. (If we had made any mistakes, the lions would let us know.)

Normally only zoo staff are present for such an occasion, but in this instance, we invited major contributors as well. We called it "Lions First!" and extended the invitation featured on the following page.

It was SPECTACULAR! The lions ran and chased and played with each other. They jumped on the rocks and tried out all of the special features we had contrived for them—the scratching post, termite mound, water hole, den. Some people commented that we had *trained* the lions to do all of this! No, they were simply responding to an environment designed to stimulate various behaviors, and they responded much more than even I had anticipated.

But we couldn't rest on our laurels. We had to immediately prepare for the next Mane Event.

FOTZ PREVIEW. Friends of the Topeka Zoo Members Night on July 12, 1989 was a splendid event! Friends members wholeheartedly endorsed the picnic idea introduced the previous year, when 500 members made reservations. This year 1,300 reservations were received, with more arriving after the cut-off date. (An additional 400 came to the zoo for the evening's activities, but did not eat.) A great fried chicken picnic supper was provided at a nominal price.

The Capital City Jazz Band greeted members as they came in the front gate of the zoo. We kept most of the buildings open after hours, including the Tropical Rain Forest, Animals and Man, and Discovering Apes. But the highlight of the evening was the sneak preview of Lions Pride for FOTZ members only.

After winding down the Simba Trail they were greeted by their first sighting (through tension wire) of the lions from the Adrenaline Grass View. The lions were spectacular! One FOTZ member accused Samburu, the male lion, of hotdogging for the crowd. At the second view, inside the kopje rocks with only glass for a barrier, FOTZ members had a marvelous close-up look at lions only inches away. The Kopje Rock View overlooked the only waterhole

Lions First!

The Board of Trustees
of
The Topeka Zoological Foundation
extend a special invitation
to you and a guest
to be present when the lions are
introduced for the first time into

LIONS PRIDE

Procedures such as this are normally witnessed by professional Zoo Staff only. The behavior of wild animals in a completely new environment is totally unpredictable. It could be the most exciting thing in the history of our Zoo, or it could be dull. The Zoo Staff will have emergency and veterinary equipment at the scene in case of an unexpected eventuality.

The event will take place at 6:15 am (yes, 6:15 AM!) on Tuesday, July 11, 1989. Please be prompt. The main entrance to the Zoo will be open from 5:30 am and a Trustee will greet you. The front gate will be closed and locked at 6:30 am for security reasons, so don't be late.

You are requested to wear earth-tone colors (tan, beige, olive, brown, dark green). Bring your binoculars. Photos will be permitted, but no flash please. A Safari breakfast of coffee, juice, bran muffins and fruit cups will be provided, courtesy of Hill's Pet Products. You may leave at any time.

This is a once-in-a-lifetime event, and our special way of thanking you for your support.

Please RSVP to Nancy Cherry at the Zoo, 272-5821 by Friday, July 7, 1989.

in the entire exhibit—which meant the lions drank just inches away. The females, Arusha and Manyara, seemed as curious about their evening visitors as the visitors were about them.

Genesis, the 4,000 pound bronze lion sculpture just outside the kopje rocks next to the Simba Trail, was a hit with everyone. It was the perfect place for a snapshot of the kids—where else could you sit on top of a larger than life lion?

After leaving Genesis, the Simba Trail split, with the main path for adults and a Cub Adventure Path for children. Along the Cub Path were trees, boulders and bridges to climb over (or under). Real lions close by helped youngsters imagine they were on a jungle trail as a lion cub, an explorer, or nature photographer.

The final view, Bush Camp, was a great success, much to the delight of zoo staff members who had worked hard to make it a participatory experience. It was clear this would be a popular area with children, with all the peepholes to look through at various heights, and built-in telescopes to zero in on areas that could only be seen from this view.

One of the nicest things about opening the zoo in the evening for FOTZ was the responsiveness of members. As they left the zoo a number of Friends members thanked the volunteers for the picnic and sneak preview and praised the staff for their work. That made it all worthwhile.

Staff and volunteers were not the only ones to be praised. The morning after the picnic several keepers commented on how considerate and tidy Friends members were—there was very little litter on the grounds. With 1,700 people picnicking and walking through the zoo for three hours, the potential is great for one big, fine mess. But FOTZ people were not like that, and the staff was grateful, particularly since we had to get ready for the next Mane Event.

OFFICIAL DEDICATION. Before we get to the dedication itself, I must share something with you. There was so much interest in Lions Pride that, well before it was finished, we had a constant stream of people eager to tour the construction site—from donors to public officials to celebrities to news media. One such incident stands out in my mind, because the reporter was ill-prepared for what she experienced—but she was such a good sport about it. The lady in question was Roberta J. Peterson of *The Topeka-Capital Journal*, and excerpts from her article convey her acquiescence to the unexpected quandary she encountered in July 1989. She wrote:

I should have known better than to wear a silk dress and 4-inch heels to an interview with Gary Clarke . . . . to take a look at the . . . Lions Pride exhibit before its feline occupants took up residence.

It was 94 degrees on this humid Kansas afternoon, and we were crouching in the dirt on our hands and knees inside the exhibit atop the highest berm, peering out through jungle grass and tension wire at a few curious zoo visitors.

"This is the way lions will see the exhibit," said Clarke, his enthusiasm infectious.

Clarke explained that the new facility offered many advantages to the big cats that visitors will never see.

"See the glass beneath us here? These are skylights for the lions' den, to let in more light.

"And it is important to lions to be able to identify their territory visually. This mound gives them a 360-degree view of their habitat. From the lions' point of view, that's marvelous."

We continued on an exhaustive tour of Lions Pride, from both the lion's *and* the visitor's perspective. Roberta, to her credit, kept pace every step of the way, and produced an extensive article that appeared (complete with Bern Ketchum's superb color photos) on the front page of the Accent section of *The Topeka Capital-Journal* on Sunday, July 16, 1989, our Grand Opening day.

But, back to the dedication. This occurred just a day before our Grand Opening. Our invitations read:

Ready or Not . . . We are going to dedicate Lions Pride and you are invited. Saturday, July 15, 1989, 9:00 A.M. World Famous Topeka Zoo. Come out for coffee in a Pug Mug. Wear casual clothes and comfortable shoes. The ceremony will be short and sweet.

The ceremony was also symbolic. In the course of my safaris, I had collected samples of soil of three significant lion habitats: the Serengeti in Tanzania, the Zambezi Valley in Zimbabwe, and the Maasai Mara in Kenya. These samples were mixed into the soil of Lions Pride by the officiating dignitaries: Betty S. Cleland, President of the Topeka Zoological Foundation; Marshall Clark, President of the Friends of the Topeka Zoo; and Butch Felker, Mayor of the City of Topeka. Africa will forever be a part of the habitat for lions in Topeka.

GRAND OPENING. (*The* main Mane Event)

During my tenure at the World Famous Topeka Zoo, we had had some truly phenomenal special events, but: the Grand Opening for Lions Pride was really the cats' pajamas!

The prelude alone was almost a Mane Event in itself. The community had been following the development of the Lions Pride project, the arrival of the lions to form the pride, the fund raising efforts, and the construction progress. Interest—and anticipation—were at fever pitch.

All of the media were heralding the event, and *Pennypower* produced a special 12-page supplement, complete with color cover of the commemorative poster by Galen Senogles. Articles covered personality profiles of the lions by lead keeper Cindy Bjork, the plants of Lions Pride by Park Naturalist Bob Foster, the role of the Friends of Topeka Zoo by FOTZ President Marshall Clark, a "Did You Know . . ." about lions by FOTZ Past President Susan Chan, the Genesis sculpture by Nancy Cherry, lions in

Africa by me, a FOTZ membership application, and information on the Zoo Foundation.

Finally the big day arrived: Sunday, July 16, 1989. The Grand Opening was sponsored by Hill's Pet Products. Ginny Trygg and her energetic team of volunteers had spent weeks in preparation, and their efforts showed.

Visitors took home a variety of free mementos: a tote bag imprinted with a life-sized lion pug mark (paw print), posters, key chains, buttons, pencils. Activities included face painting, a scent trail, Discovery Carts, lion films, and a lion roar contest for kids 12 and under. Special drawings were held for stuffed plush lions, a battery operated Safari Jeep for ages 6 and under, and 25 FOTZ memberships. The grand prize drawing was for a complete camping outfit: large domed tent, sleeping bags, lantern, flashlight/radio, cooler. And all of this was provided by Hill's!

From the entrance visitors followed the zoo's version of the Oz yellow brick road—yellow paw prints led to Lions Pride! People were four or five deep along the Simba Trail as it wound through the tall grass. The glass-fronted view inside the Kopje Rock was the most popular. Visitors got an unexpected thrill when the pride male, Samburu, sauntered over to the glass, reared up on his hind legs to his full height, and struck the glass with his massive front paws! Everyone stood in awe and fascination. None had ever experienced a lion in such dramatic fashion!

Just outside the Kopje Rock, kids clambered all over Genesis, the large bronze sculpture, as well as the surrounding "Kiddie Kopjes" provided by a grant from the Nile Fowler family.

Youngsters thoroughly enjoyed the lion roar contest. FOTZ Board Member Bill Trahan served as a judge and observed that the smaller the child, the louder the roar. Bill was quoted the next day in *The Topeka Capital-Journal* as saying, "We had this one kid who could barely see over the table, and his roar about knocked us off our chairs."

The Duncan Movie Magic double decker bus shuttled visitors to outlying parking areas, KSNT-TV 27 had personalities on the scene, and KTKA-TV 49 distributed Lions Pride guide maps.

It was an event fit for a king!

The 1988 Topeka Regional Telephone Directory featured Lions Pride on the cover, with a four-page spread (and map) inside.

And to top off everything, the lioness Arusha delivered four cubs in late September 1988. Suddenly our lion population had gone from three to seven! General Curator Craig Dinsmore called it "instant pride."

Sunday, July16, 1989

Opinion

The Topeka Capital-Journal

Editorials —————————— In God We Trust

Roaring with pride ...

Today marks an important event in the life of the Topeka Zoo. The new Lions Pride exhibit makes its official public opening at 9 a.m.

The exhibit continues the transformation begun with the new gorilla facility. It frees the animals from the usual caged environment and allows viewers to see them in their natural habitat.

It is a more humane approach from the animal's perspective, and it is more educational and esthetically pleasing to the human viewer.

It is a tribute to Topeka's dedication to the zoo that it has been able to provide such quality exhibits that normally one would expect to find only in much larger zoos.

That dedication comes from the expertise and leadership of Gary Clarke and his staff, a supportive city government and an active and involved community both on the individual and corporate level. The new exhibit cost about $500,000. Much of that came from private and corporate contributions, not from tax money.

In addition, Eva Bennett and Fairlawn Plaza State Bank commissioned a beautiful bronze sculpture for the exhibit. It features a lion drinking from a pool shaped like the continent of Africa.

Visitors on this opening day also will be provided special mementoes by Hill's Pet Products. The local company is sponsoring today's activities.

Lions Pride gives Topekans another reason to be justifiably proud of their zoo.

GENESIS

by Randy Austin, President
Fairlawn Plaza Development, Inc.

In 1984, it was my great pleasure and good fortune to meet Dennis Anderson, an extremely talented artist from El Dorado Springs, Missouri. Dennis and his award-winning wildlife works came highly recommended by mutual friends. Fairlawn Plaza Development, Inc. in Topeka acquired two of Dennis' bronze bears, which we display in Fairlawn Plaza Mall. It was soon discovered that Dennis and I shared an admiration for the World Famous Topeka Zoo and also shared an interest in the upcoming opening of Lions Pride. Zoo Director Gary K. Clarke and Dennis had for some time been discussing a piece of sculpture to "set off" the exhibit. Because both the late Eva Bennett, Chairman of the Board of Fairlawn Plaza Development, Inc., and I had previously discussed possible ways to assist Lions Pride, it was a natural progression that Dennis, Gary, Eva and I began to discuss seriously the feasibility of commissioning the piece Gary and Dennis had been discussing.

After preliminary commitments were made, Dennis prepared a small beeswax and clay model of a drinking lion which was brought to Topeka on October 10, 1987 for approval. Phil Coolidge (the architect for Lions Pride), Gary, Eva and I were all very pleased, so Dennis began work to complete the project by a June 1988 deadline. It was the hope of everyone concerned to have a period of time to exhibit the sculpture before placing it at the World Famous Topeka Zoo in order to build excitement, interest and anticipation for our unique Lions Pride exhibit.

Because the model of the sculpture measured slightly over five feet in length and the finished sculpture measures over twelve and one-half feet, the task of converting the smaller model to the larger piece was the first order of business. Frameworks were erected and complicated conversion systems were utilized in the transfer, which took several months to complete. Under Dennis' direction, Garland Weeks and a highly skilled crew recruited from several states completed the process of enlarging during the winter. The model of the actual sculpture was presented to Gary, to the architect and to the donors for approval. Our approval was unanimous and loud!

Work then began again. A master mold was prepared (a three month process), then shipped by truck to Oklahoma City. In Oklahoma City, master fiberglass molds were poured, which then were trucked to Topeka's Degginger Foundry.

In Topeka, Dennis, Tim Degginger and an experienced and dedicated group of casters, grinders, braisers and other foundry personnel molded, poured, braised, chased, brushed and coated over 100 pieces of high quality silicon bronze to form "Genesis." Days were long and nights even longer, as over 4,000 pounds of metal were lovingly coaxed into place. Late one night (or was it early one morning?) Tim confided to us that the lion had taken on a life of its own: "Everyone involved has become consumed by the lion . . . and we all feel the majesty of the piece justifies our dedication." Those most closely affiliated with the project spent weeks working in Topeka without contact with their families other than by telephone.

Today "Genesis" is an accomplished reality, and during June and July (1988) sat proudly in the center of the mall at Fairlawn Plaza Shopping Center, waiting to go on exhibit in August in Colorado at the Society of Sculpture in the Park show in Loveland, and in the Animal Artists Annual Exhibition in Rochester, New York in the fall.

Genesis is not just a lovely sculpture to admire. When you see him, if you are so inclined, feel free to rub his nose, feel his rough tongue, and even climb on him. He's a very friendly lion.

A Feel for Lions Pride

Mary Jo Hobbs, Zoo Docent, 1989
National Editor, Association of Zoo and Aquarium Docents

"I'm sure I'll learn from you today as much as you'll learn from me."
I often have this attitude when I'm giving a tour of the zoo, but on this day
I voiced it because I'd never meant it more.

You see, the people in this group were blind and it was a new experience for me to share the zoo with those who couldn't see. We had prepared
special "touch" opportunities in anticipation of the group's visit: our lovely
speckled king snake was on hand, skulls were available for investigation
and the keepers had been asked to bring the elephants to the fence for
what we hoped would be a more enlightened encounter than in John Godfrey
Saxe's famous poem.

But what turned out to be the high point of the afternoon was an
area of the zoo where the residents couldn't be trotted up to the fence for an
inquiring pat—Lions Pride. These two hundred-pound carnivores seemed
to be inaccessible to this group who couldn't see them—or so I thought.

The plantings of Lions Pride have been planned to simulate lion habitat
in the wild and to immerse the visitor in that habitat. I learned this is never
more evident than when you get to experience it with a consciousness at-
tuned to *every* aspect of your surroundings, not just to what you see.

Hands dragged the rough swells of the kopje rocks as we entered the
cool earth-scented interior. Our voices echoed as we conjured images of
lions sleeping in the shade of these islands in a sea of grass.

Noses shared flowers with butterflies as we searched for the source
of a distinctive "spicy-sweet smell you pick up right here," to quote one of
the blind participants.

Fingers sought the myriad of textures from fuzzy to tasseled to ropey
to beaded to lacy to spiked—all *grass*—all parts of that mosaic that is the
lion's source of life—the savannah. The smooth fullness of the gourds suggested calabashes for holding liquids as they are used in Africa.

And the sounds—the hum of bees amid the "shushing" of the grasses
in the wind with a counterpoint of katydid song—are enchanting. We felt a
splendid isolation from the rest of the zoo in this world of the lion. But what
of the lion itself?

Genesis—the heroic-sized sculpture of a lion drinking—made the lions of this habitat "real." What a powerful lesson for sensitive fingers to
explore! A bronze "description" of a lion, articulate from its barbed tongue
to its tufted tail. The group listened with their hands to the story of muscled
strength told by this eloquent sculpture.

Small details like the African mask in the "mud" and the furrows in
the face were all taken in. Hands spanned the massive paws and traced the

retracted claws. The notched ear, the animal footprints all around, delighted and instructed in ways I could never have done with descriptions.

Facial expressions told it all as each visitor in turn was helped to sit upon the back of the sculpture. Awe was there and I saw respect, too, as each person felt the expanse of that bronze body below them.

Though we had no "real"' contact with the lions of Lions Pride that afternoon, I stepped away from Simba Trail feeling that, in a unique way, I'd *really seen* them and their exhibit for the first time.

Look at Those Lions!

During my lifetime, I have had the privilege of seeing hundreds of lions in a variety of situations and environments. I have visited nearly two hundred and fifty zoos worldwide and have been to Africa dozens of times. But never have I seen lions do the things our lions do in Lions Pride here in Topeka in the year 1989.

Our lions run and chase and play and wrestle. They pick up good-sized *logs* and carry them around in their mouths. They rub against the young thornless honeylocust trees and play with the branches. Samburu, the male, has jumped vertically more than 10 feet into the air to rip green leaves and branches off the catalpa tree on the east side of the berm. They also make good use of the fallen tree just inside the first viewing area, the Adrenalin Grass View. They lie under its limbs, drape themselves over the limbs, and even climb out to the ends of the upper branches.

The simple act of drinking water is an interesting behavior in lions. Sometimes zoos put the drinking water in the back of the exhibit where it is convenient for keepers but out of sight of visitors. Or, if it is in view, water is in a large container elevated off the ground. This makes the lions stand and drink like domestic animals. But, in Lions Pride we have located the only source of water directly at the base of the glass-viewing window of the Kopje Rock. Hence, visitors have an up-close-and-personal view—just an inch away! Since the water is in a depression simulating a natural waterhole, our lions crouch to drink in a normal posture.

Thus, we have showcased what is an everyday natural behavior for lions. It is fantastic to see them crouching and drinking water from ground level—just as they would in Africa. You are so close to the lions that you can actually see how they lap water with their rough tongues. And when you leave the Kopje Rock View you can go over and feel the tongue of the sculpture Genesis, which vividly illustrates the lapping motion of lions when they drink.

One of our lions' most engaging behaviors is the "stalk." As I walk down the Simba Trail through the adrenalin grass and around the corner for my first view through the tension wire, the lions frequently sense my presence. As soon as we make visual contact, I will stop and crouch. While I stay there motionless, I note their ears thrust forward and their eyes intently watching me. As I then take slow steps in my crouch position, I notice how they tense and assume their crouch-alert position. If I make exaggerated slow steps, they will take several slow steps with their bellies close to the ground. If I break into a run down the trail towards the kopje rock they will bolt across the habitat and run parallel to the path. As I rush inside the kopje, they burst around the corner and jump onto the rocks by the glass. I will place my bald head next to the glass and the female Manyara will attempt to lick it. Frequently the lions stand on their hind legs and paw at the glass with their front legs, or playfully try to touch my arm or shoulder through the glass. It is a delight to see our lions and their rapport with the visitors, particularly at the large glass window.

Although it may not be obvious to the casual visitor, there are many subtle aspects to the habitat setting in Lions Pride. And our lions seem to have discovered, investigated, and responded to all of them. First and foremost is the fact that the terrain varies greatly in elevation. Lions identify their territories visually; they like to be up high where they can survey their domains. The large earth dome in the center of the habitat enables them to do so. Frequently you will see them standing or lying on top of this hill.

Initially, the hill (or berm) was literally overgrown with vegetation nearly four feet tall; in fact, our lions could easily disappear in it. They had so much fun romping through the vegetation that they virtually destroyed all of it. As the seasons have changed from summer to fall and air temperatures have grown cooler, I have seen our lions basking in the sun on the rocky outcrop over their south-facing den.

In contrast to the berm, there are a variety of low-lying areas in the habitat that are often frequented by our lions. The den was planned specifically as a place where the lions could cool off during warm weather and have a hide-away even though they still can be seen by visitors standing at the window inside the kopje. In addition, you can always see the lions from at least one of the three viewing stations, no matter where they are in the exhibit.

Near the Bush Camp View is a tall dead tree, put there for the lions to use as a scratching post. And that's exactly what they do! They rise up on hind legs, reaching with their front paws as high as they can on the scratching post. This benefits the lions in two ways. First, it acts as a stretching exercise to keep their muscles in good shape. Second, it enables the lions to "file" their claws. Many people think that lions are sharpening their claws when they dig into the rough bark on a tree. Actually they are smoothing their claws much as humans do with an emery board on their fingernails. They also use the scratching post as a rubbing post. It almost seems as if they're saying "Aaah" when they rub their chins on it.

There are a number of theories as to why our lions have demonstrated such an unusual range of behaviors. Yes, they are young animals and prone to be more active than older adults. Still, I believe that the main stimulus has been the rich multi-faceted environment of their new habitat. While I expect some of this activity will decrease over the years, I feel confident that our lions will always demonstrate a greater degree of activity than most other lions you will see in zoos—or even in Africa!

And It Could Have Been Better

There was no doubt that Lions Pride was a dazzling success, particularly from the perspective of the lions: they were flourishing!

And the public was responding. People were flocking to Lions Pride, many loaded down with camera gear. Visitors not only liked the activity of the lions, but the extensive landscaping as well. With the exception of the Tropical Rain Forest, it was the richest horticulture exhibit in the zoo.

Attendance for the first week after Lions Pride opened (July 17-23, 1989) was 15,985. Attendance for the same week the previous year was 8,252.

Yet, as good as all of this was, I have a confession: it could have been a much better experience for zoo visitors. While we had achieved a great deal of what we envisioned for the exhibit, there was so much that did not come to fruition for a variety of reasons: lack of funds, failure on my part to sell the concept, or (in some cases) the dreaded bureaucratic red tape. But before I delve any further, permit me to review what *was* special about Lions Pride from the visitors' perspective.

The Simba Trail was magnificent. An irregular path winding out of sight, in a sea of adrenaline grass stretching upward to the sky, created an atmosphere of anticipation. And if an unseen lion roared, loud and close, your adrenaline would shoot everywhere (just like in Africa). Then, suddenly, you visually encountered a lion . . . or two, or three, in a habitat area separated only by nearly invisible tension wire.

Proceeding into the semi-darkened and cave-like atmosphere of the kopje rocks provided an entirely different experience. Who would think of *lions* in such a situation? It is common in Africa, especially when pregnant females isolate themselves to deliver their cubs. Other creatures—animal and human—inhabit kopjes. In our kopje there is evidence of both. Bat droppings, or guano, indicate they used to live here, and Bushman rock paintings show the importance of animals to indigenous peoples. Protected in Africa from the elements, the paintings are still used today in some parts of lion country as a form of art and communication.

Bao (Swahili for board) is an ancient game played all over Africa on linear boards with two rows of parallel holes. It is played when seeds or pebbles (called kete) are placed in the finger holes and dexterously moved from hole to hole according to some mysterious, unfathomable principle in order to capture your opponents kete. Traditionally played at a fast pace (it takes a quick eye, a quick mind and a quick hand), the game represents bartering for cattle or goats between tribesmen.

Inside our kopje we replicated a bao game (accessible to visitors) etched in stone. I personally have seen two such timeworn examples in Africa: one elevated in the middle of an island in the middle of Lake Baringo in the middle of the Great Rift Valley in the middle of present day Kenya; the other is underwater at Ngoitokitok Springs on the floor of the Ngorongoro Crater in what is now Tanzania.

The prime feature inside the kopje rock is the dramatic glass-fronted view into the habitat of the lions. To insure that visitors would see the lions up-close-and-personal, we intentionally located Maji Springs (Maji is Swahili for water), the only source of water in the exhibit, at the base of the viewing window. Hence, visitors were nose-to-nose with a lion as it crouched and lapped water using the reverse curl of its tongue!

And the kopje rocks themselves were one of the outstanding features of the exhibit—and the zoo!

Fabricated kopje rocks (constructed of sprayed concrete called gunite) in many zoos frequently have an unrealistic sameness, and I wanted to make sure ours were not of that mold. The specialist contractor was most receptive to our input, and used actual photos I had taken of kopjes in southern Zimbabwe to sculpt the shape and texture of ours, and then perfect the color. Once the plantings flourished on and around them, the kopjes looked like they had always been there! I used to drive my jeep back to the zoo on summer evenings at sunset to watch the changing color hues and dancing shadows on our kopjes—the closest thing to Africa, and right here in Topeka!

Certainly I was pleased, but could these kopjes *really* be that good? Yes! This was confirmed in the U.S.A. *and* Africa. We had zoo visitors ask (not just once, but regularly): "How in the world did you move all those big rocks here?" While on safari I showed photos of our kopjes and asked Africa's most experienced guides, "Where are these?" After considerable study they would cite a general area, or even refer to a specific location in Africa. Never once did they deduce that they were at the World Famous Topeka Zoo, even though they knew of my association!

To accent our kopjes, visitors could look through a viewing scope focused on two hyrax (actually concrete but *so* realistic) among the rocks and another scope focused on top of the kopjes to see a simulated Verreaux's eagle nest, a frequent scene in Africa.

Adjacent to the kopjes, the magnificent sculpture Genesis fulfilled every expectation. Glinting in the sunlight, this beautiful bronze lion inspired awe and invited participation—children (of all ages) could not wait to touch and climb on it.

As we had anticipated, the Bush Camp View was an instant success, especially with kids. An authentic hide, designed so that one could observe animals without them knowing you were there (*if* you were quiet!), it was a wonderful setting for imaginations to run rampant.

Constructed with natural wood poles and covered with khaki colored canvas, it was accessible by pushing aside mosquito netting as per a safari camp. Small observation windows were covered with lift-up flaps, and safari supply boxes were available for the smallest viewers to stand on. It was a perfect place to visually stalk lions and dream of exploring Africa.

This completes the visitor circuit along the Simba Trail. Undoubtedly Lions Pride was one of the best exhibits of its type to date. So how could it have been better?

Let me count the ways.

First: more animals. No, not more lions, but additional smaller species that are found in lion country, such as rock hyrax (live, not concrete), African crested porcupine, mongoose, guinea fowl, even meerkat, or possibly suni, the smallest of the antelopes. Yes, these were considered in the original concept but, each time we had to reduce costs, another species was eliminated. Kopje rocks are often called "islands of life in a sea of grass." Kopjes provide pockets of water and shelter for many small species we could have exhibited inside our kopje: brilliantly colored agama lizards, industrious dung beetles (we had a ready supply of fresh African elephant dung), unbelievably flat pancake tortoises, and the incredible African egg-eating snake! It could have been so cool . . .

Second: a waterfall. Not large, but a focal point that would provide natural sound and motion, and introduce an interactive element into the habitat for the lions.

Third: more interpretative elements. Yes, our graphics were excellent, but how about a simulated "kill site"? Just off the Simba Trail could be the remains of a Cape buffalo—skull, horns, rib cage, hooves—complete with hyena teeth marks to reflect scavengers as well as predators. Further along, how about a scratching log actually clawed by a lion? Or a ground nest of several dozen ostrich eggs? All it takes is money.

Fourth: INTERACTION! Getting the visitors (especially children) involved with lions as we had planned *could have been* SENSATIONAL! To my knowledge no zoo had ever (or has yet as of this writing) offered such participatory engagement between lions and visitors as we had envisioned!

Example: the roar of a lion is probably the best known animal sound in the world. Every time I hear a lion roar in Africa or in a zoo, I stop and savor it, as though it were for the first time. In Africa you can hear a lion roar from five miles away—yet it will often sound like it is just outside your tent. (Sometimes it is scarier to *hear* a lion than to see one.)

In Topeka, Kansas you can hear a lion roar up to two and one-half miles away—if it is in winter with no leaves to muffle the sound, and between midnight and 6:00 am when traffic noise is minimal. I know, because as zoo director I would frequently arrive in the morning and my secretary would already have a stack of those pink telephone messages (long before voice mail) for me to return calls to various residents. When I did so, it was the same question: "Are the lions still in the zoo? I heard them roaring last night and could've sworn they were outside my window!" After I assured each caller that the lions were secure I asked what time they heard the roar and where they lived. Then, I pinpointed the location on a map of the city and noted the time in a record book. The data were consistent over many years.

To get visitors involved with this most iconic sound of the animal kingdom, at Lions Pride we planned a "roar meter" that would compare the level of a lion's roar to other sounds, natural and manmade. Next to it would be an device enabling visitors to roar and see how they matched up with a lion.

Example: lions sleep up to 18 hours each day—in Africa or in the zoo. Not a very exciting behavior for zoo visitors . . . but it could be!

Visualize the large fallen trunk of an ancient baobab tree (fabricated from fiberglass, but extremely realistic). It so happens that half of the hollow trunk fell in the lion exhibit, and the other half on the visitor's path. Both ends are open, and a circular piece of glass divides the trunk in the center. While a lion sleeps in one side of this hollow tree trunk, a visitor could safely crawl into the other side for an unprecedented experience!

Example: the strength of a lion is legendary. How would you like to test it? Imagine a section of pipe extending into the lion exhibit as well as out to the visitor's area. In the pipe is a long, thick rope, half on the lion's side and half on the visitor's side. Strong knots on both sides allow for back-and-forth play, but prohibit the rope from going completely in or out. Even bigger knots are on the lions' side, periodically sprinkled with catnip to encourage the lions to play with them. When visitors pull on the rope, the lions chase the knots like a domestic cat chasing a ball. When the lions grasp the knotted rope with their teeth or claws, visitors could have a tug-of-war with the King of Beasts!

Alas, this was nixed by the City Safety Department. So was the Cubs Adventure Path. Just off the Simba Trail we had developed a bush path for human youngsters where they could climb over logs and rocks, cross a log bridge, even crawl through a fallen hollow log. Intrepid would-be safarists could take this path to the Bush Camp View. It was very popular, stimulated the imagination of the kids, and provided great photo opportunities for parents. We honestly never thought of having to seek approval from the City Safety Department, but once they learned of it we had to abandon it.

And now we come to my greatest disappointment of what could have been: the Lions Pride Bush Camp. It remains truly a dream unfulfilled. I have only myself to blame, as I simply did not sell the project properly to potential donors in order to make it happen. Even today, if you know where to look, you can see how we had incorporated design elements for Bush Camp activities that would have gone far beyond the perfunctory view by everyday zoo visitors.

It could have been *very* special—the flagship element that would have made Lions Pride a field study experience in the social behavior of the King of beasts-right here in Topeka, Kansas! The possibilities were as boundless as the energy of a litter of lion cubs! Over and above educational qualities, it could have also served a social function (*and* generated revenue) as a rental area for group events such as "campfire sundowners" or safari dinners, as well as the setting for overnight campouts for school age children, or Friends of the Zoo members and families.

But the prime function of Bush Camp—and the most significant to me—would be twofold: as an interpretive area to teach visitors about the African lion's world, using participation in basic activities and interaction with low-tech displays; *and,* as a bush setting, with authentic ambiance and observation hides, where students could utilize actual equipment and participate in techniques used by field researchers.

Students would be challenged to identify individual lions; observe and categorize behaviors, social interactions and facial expressions (especially with cubs); examine and discriminate between signs of various animals (tracks, dung, shed whiskers, claw marks, teeth marks); and recognize vocalizations (roar, growl, snarl, grunt) of individual lions.

Alas, this represents just preliminary thoughts—there was *so much* potential: association with area universities, seminars by guest field researchers, parallel studies with lion prides in Africa . . .

Oh, what could have been!

Noble reader, when it comes to living life on this earth, I have always been (or tried to be) an optimist. True, the world is far from perfect, and everyone experiences failure to fulfill expectations in life's journey. Still, I count my blessings and have appreciated even the smallest of accomplishments, especially in my zoo career. Yet—to be perfectly candid and brutally honest—I must confess frustration with what could have been, but what we did not accomplish, with Lions Pride. It was a great disappointment to me. (Sorry to vent on the negative; thanks for listening.)

Even so, I will share with you that my thoughts were positive within a few short weeks after the opening of Lions Pride. I wanted to see the zoo's continued development while retaining the personal touch as part of the visitors' experience. Once again we were revising and updating the Zoo Master Plan. The 1989 version would provide guidance and direction until the year 2000.

Certainly there was a focus on animals. We needed to provide additional outdoor space for existing species (such as elephants and giraffes), as well as return bears to the zoo and develop a Kansas exhibit.

Just as essential was the need to improve the people dimension of the zoo. Not just better walks and more benches, but additional landscaping, a new entrance, and a **proper education facility.** The latter would enable the zoo to more properly realize its function as a learning resource. The new plan placed emphasis on service to the community and the expanded role of our zoo as a focal point.

A zoo is never finished . . . and it could always be better.

Part 8

The Way We Were: Untold Tails

An insider's look at the people and animals behind the scenes involved in frequently humorous, but sometimes serious, adventures and misadventures in the zoo.

A Zoo is a place devised for animals to study the habits of human beings.

—Oliver Herford
English writer
and illustrator,
1863-1935.

Courtesy of the Topeka and Shawnee County Public Library   **Art work by Alice C. Sabatini**

Part 8

The Way We Were: Untold Tails

The Impossible Somersaulting Giraffe

"TWIGA IS OUT!"

In a panic, head keeper Bill Gage shouted those daunting words as he stomped up the stairs to my second floor office.

Twiga, our male reticulated giraffe, was the first giraffe in Kansas. He and the female Jan were both sub-adults. They had adjusted well in their new home—built specifically for giraffes, hippos, and elephants—at the Topeka Zoo.

"TWIGA IS OUT," Bill yelled again. How could this be? I glanced out the window—and my heart sank. There he was, standing in the grass area between the outdoor giraffe yard and the visitors' guardrail.

I felt queasy. Of *all* the most unthinkable things that could ever happen at our zoo—at *any* zoo—this one was beyond belief. The barrier around the giraffe enclosure was continuous, and Jan was still in there, munching hay. By what means could this be possible?

"How did it happen?" I asked.

"He did a somersault," Bill replied.

"A somersault? A SOMERSAULT?" IMPOSSIBLE!

I dare say that of all the giraffes that have ever lived, nary a one had even contemplated, let alone attempted, a somersault! With their long, gangly body, they simply could not do such a noteworthy trick without breaking one or more legs . . . or their neck!

I stared at Bill incredulously. He answered my obvious disbelief with an emphatic, "YES!"

Impossible as it may have been, Twiga *was* out, and we had to respond immediately, for his well-being as well as the safety of visitors.

With great reluctance, dear reader, I interrupt this crisis to explain exactly *how* Twiga got out in order to help you understand what followed. It was my fault, not his. I had made an error in design calculations, which reflected my naiveté about animal behavior. It was most humiliating at the time . . . which is why I have not told this story until now—some 40 years after the fact.

Giraffes are such lovely creatures, and I wanted our visitors to gain a full appreciation and experience them up-close-and-personal. Hence, in 1967 I proposed—instead of the standard high fence, or even a moat—an outside exhibit with a minimal barrier of just two horizontal cables stretched taut between posts set 12-feet apart. To match the inside fence dimensions (which the giraffes were used to), one cable would be eight feet above the ground, the other four feet, with nothing in between! To zoo visitors, the cables would be practically invisible. How spectacular!

So that the giraffes would comprehend the barrier and visually recognize its established boundary, we initially defined the full eight-foot height visually. To accomplish this we draped sections of burlap from the 8-foot cable to the 4-foot cable and snow fence filled the space from the 4-foot cable to the ground. When we first introduced the giraffes to the outside yard in June, they were cautious and kept their distance. But giraffes are such curious animals they were soon patrolling the cable line and even chewing on the burlap (giraffes chew on anything!).

Once the giraffes became comfortable with the cables and familiar with the territory they defined, an involved process would follow, one step at a time. We would gradually remove alternate panels of burlap to reveal the open space between the 8-foot and 4-foot cables, and then sections of snow fence from the 4-foot cable to the ground. Eventually all visual panels would be down and—TAH-DAH! Giraffes, here and now, with virtually no barriers! Everything was fine until . . .

Keep in mind that it is awkward and strenuous for a giraffe to straddle its legs and bend its neck downward far enough to get its mouth to the ground. In the wild they have to in order to drink. In the zoo water pans are elevated, and leafy hay is conveniently available in high mangers. Yet, that old adage "the grass is greener on the other side of the fence" would apply here if "fence" were changed to "cable." Succulent green grass grew in the area between the cable perimeter and the visitors' guard rail.

Twiga was tempted.

On the third of August he carefully ducked his head under the eight-foot high cable and slowly walked forward until his legs were touching the lower four-foot cable, with his head and neck extending over the grass area. Then he positioned his front legs, stretched his neck toward the ground and leaned his weight forward on the lower cable. As he did so, the cable probably wavered a bit. Twiga's center of gravity shifted, he lost his balance and *somersaulted* head over hooves, landing on the outside of the cable barrier! I cannot imagine a more bewildered giraffe.

Immediately he was on his feet, unscathed. Not only was this entire scenario "impossible," it had now become miraculous!

This was the point at which Bill Gage had shouted, "TWIGA IS OUT," and the following transpired.

An emergency call was transmitted to all radio units and the First Response Team assembled near the giraffe exhibit. The zoo entrance was closed, as well as all perimeter service gates, and visitors were secured in buildings.

I was thankful that Twiga was still inside the three-foot high public barrier, and quietly eating leaves. Then, inside the yard, Jan began to run back and forth along the cable line. On his side Twiga followed suit and gaining momentum, he unexpectedly jumped the three-foot high visitor's guardrail—an unimaginable feat for a giraffe! Now he *truly was* out, and calmly eating leaves from the trees on the west lawn of the Large Mammal Building. Jan was quickly moved inside the building.

A wave of dread and dismay swept over me. It seemed a hopeless task to get this delicate, high-strung, sensitive creature safely back into his quarters. In the mid-1960's chemical immobilization (the "tranquilizer gun" as it is commonly called) was still in its infancy, and even today is a risky procedure with a giraffe.

The most important thing was not to stress Twiga and unintentionally cause a panic reaction. He seemed content to feed on leaves; so keeping our distance, we formed a large circle with outstretched arms to establish a comfortable, but visible, perimeter around him. Before he had jumped the guardrail we had already planned to drop the cables so he could return through the yard and back into the building. Now, however, the guardrail was an obstacle, and I certainly did not want Twiga to have to jump it again!

An urgent call to the Park Department brought Woody the Welder to the zoo, and he cut out a large section of the rail. We then dropped the cable. Now a smooth route had been cleared, and we needed to patiently and gently encourage Twiga to enter the yard.

Unless you use physical or chemical restraint, you cannot make a giraffe do what it does not want to do. You have to wait until, on its own accord, it does what *it* wants, and then you respond accordingly. In this case whenever Twiga would move—even just a step or two—toward the giraffe yard, all of us forming the circle would "take up the slack" and close the same distance. From his perspective it should seem that nothing had changed.

Slowly but surely, step-by-step, Twiga walked to the edge of the yard, and then stepped into familiar territory. Trucks were then positioned to form a barrier around the outside yard. We quickly closed ranks in a tight circle and Twiga calmly walked through the open door of the building and into an empty stall next to Jan. A waiting keeper rolled the door shut. Twiga was safe, secure and calm. I could feel the nervous tension draining out my toes. It was such a relief that Twiga was in, not out.

At the end of the day our admissions clerk told me a cute story. An out-of-town family had entered the zoo just before the clerk received word to close. As she was securing the gate she overheard the mother say, "Oh, what a neat zoo; they have giraffes on the lawn."

My great giraffe exhibit design had failed. I can just hear today's generation of zoo professionals muttering something like, "Well, it should have been obvious to *anyone* that it wouldn't work." The cables were replaced with a standard chain-link fence. I didn't like the aesthetic appearance, but it was a safe and proven barrier.

In the good ole days of zoobiz we certainly took our responsibilities seriously, yet we could laugh at ourselves. A highlight of the annual national conference was the formal recognition of various accomplishments during the past year and presentation of coveted awards. The most eagerly anticipated (or most dreaded, in some cases) was the Zoo Goof Award of Excellence.

The 1967 Annual Conference of the American Association of Zoological Parks and Aquariums was held in Tampa, Florida. Although still a comparatively new zoo director, I had been honored to chair several committees and to be elected to my first term on the board.

I took pride in the professional recognition our modest zoo in Topeka, Kansas had received. Additionally, I was privileged (and thrilled) to meet the special guest speaker—the most respected zoo professional in the world: Dr. Heini Hediger from Switzerland. He was the author of numerous scientific papers and books, including *The Psychology and Behavior of Animals in Zoos and Circuses*. Such a wonderful aura for me at this conference . . . all soon to be shattered.

Imagine my chagrin at the final banquet when the presenter of the Zoo Goof Award—Don G. Davis, Director of the Cheyenne Mountain Zoo in Colorado Springs—called me to the podium. With great humility I was forced to stand in the spotlight before all of my colleagues (and the esteemed Dr. Hediger himself) while Don read—slowly and distinctly—the following text (these are his exact words):

THIRD ANNUAL ZOO GOOF AWARD OF EXCELLENCE

Giraffes is dangerous animals. They can bang you with their horns, swing their neck in an arc and strike you with their head, kick you with their powerful legs, switch you with their tail, and they bite.

Giraffes is also difficult to restrain in captivity. Some zoos have found it necessary to place strong steel bars on the front of the cage and a top overhead to prevent the giraffe from leaping out. Other zoos have found it possible to restrain giraffes through the use of shallow moats or low walls but are obviously taking a considerable risk. One zoo in particular (we will not mention the name) maintains an outdoor yard which is slightly elevated where giraffes are separated from the visitors by only a shallow depression or moat. These giraffes in San Diego are obviously being fooled, for due to their lofty elevation, the moat appears to be twenty feet deep. This is a perfect example of zoo psychology.

The giraffes at the Topeka Zoological Park are not so fortunate however. Their staff is composed of a dynamic young zoologist who in the true modern sense of progression attempts to develop radical exhibition and restraint techniques. Not satisfied with stockade or chain-link fences which the giraffes could crash into, or low walls which the giraffes could bang their legs on, or moats which the giraffes could fall into, this ingenuous young zoo administrator designed a giraffe barrier consisting of eight-foot vertical posts placed at twelve-foot intervals, and an intricate system of horizontal cables. The barrier was intended to trip a giraffe which attempted to escape, and it works. On August 3rd, Twiga, the male giraffe at the Topeka Zoological Park, fell over the tripping device but unfortunately landed on the wrong side of the barrier. Easily clearing the three-foot guard-rail he proceeded to stroll around the confines of his new exhibit, the zoo proper. Needless to say our industrious and capable zoologist returned Twiga to his pen and proceeded to install an eight-foot chain-link fence.

For experimentation in the field of animal exhibition, for extensive and untiring research in the area of giraffe restraint, and for clever interpretation of giraffe psychology, we hereby award Gary Clarke, Director of the Topeka Zoological Park, the 1967 Zoo Goof Award of Excellence.

*****

It was all in good fun, and for years afterwards (even to this day) my colleagues in the zoo world have found great joy reminiscing about my ingenious giraffe-tripping device.

At the 1968 zoo conference in Los Angeles, I had to present the Zoo Goof Award to the next recipient. The banquet speaker that evening was the revered movie star Jimmy Stewart. I sat next to him at the head table during dinner. He told me of his wonderful life, and was intrigued with my stories of our zoo in Topeka (or maybe he was a good actor).

Tornado at the Zoo

As I write this, it is 40 years to the day of Topeka's darkest hour—the deadly tornado of June 8, 1966.

Anyone living in Topeka then will never forget that evil wind. It burns in memory like the day President John F. Kennedy was shot, or when man first walked on the moon, or 9/11 . . .

The tornado swept over Burnett's Mound from the southwest cutting a swath one-half mile wide across the city to the northeast. It stayed on the ground for 27 minutes, leaving a wound that disfigured the earth for 22 miles.

Sixteen lives were lost, and more than 500 people were injured. With winds in excess of 250 mph, the tornado was a rare "supertwister" in the F5 category. It was the most destructive tornado on record to that date—over $100 million of damage. Adjusting for inflation, today that would be equivalent to $494 million, and still near the top of storm damage lists.

The 1966 tornado is a significant part of Topeka's history, and has had a lasting impact on the community psyche.

But back on June 8, 1966 in the shadow of impending disaster, who would think of the zoo? I would. As zoo director, the zoo was my responsibility.

What seemed so strange, as I reflect on that day, is that things were ordinary—no hint of what was to come. Crowds at the zoo were thrilled to see our only two residents in the newly-opened Large Mammal Building—'Peka-Sue, the infamous hesitant hippo, and Twiga, the first giraffe in Kansas. That evening, at home after dinner, I was ready to relax with my wife and four pre-school age children.

Topeka was under a tornado watch, which was not unusual. But by 6:00 pm there were reports of severe storms (and funnel cloud sightings) in the Manhattan area west of Topeka. Our home had no basement or tornado shelter, so as was our usual practice, we quickly put the family in our station wagon and drove to the zoo. I did not know, of course, how bad things might be, but the family would be safer in the basement of the zoo service building.

In addition, there were certain severe weather procedures I needed to perform at the zoo. I removed the poisonous snakes from their exhibits in the Animal Kingdom Building (the old converted greenhouse) and placed them in sturdy metal containers with heavy-duty locks, and then secured these in the basement.

At 7:02 pm a tornado warning was issued and the sirens wailed. The sky was ominous and I knew the situation was serious. My concern, of course, was the possibility of a direct hit on the zoo that might result in a dangerous animal escape. Leaving my family safe and secure, I took the zoo's only weapon, a .22 caliber rifle, and patrolled the zoo grounds. I was on the alert not just for direct damage to animal facilities, but also the possibility of trees and heavy limbs falling, downed power lines, and blowing debris.

I know this sounds risky on my part, but I was closely monitoring reports of the tornado's progress on a small battery-powered radio, and ready to dash for safety if necessary.

The winds howled and the rain pelted, but the twister itself missed the zoo. It's path veered to the east of Gage Park and ripped across the Washburn University campus and then through downtown Topeka striking the dome of the State Capitol. While the zoo did suffer tree damage, no animals were injured and facilities survived intact.

Much of Topeka, of course, was not so fortunate. The next day I offered my services to the Red Cross, and used my station wagon to deliver food and supplies to victims. With an official placard in my windshield, emergency personnel directed me to devastated areas of town. When I personally saw the destructive force of the tornado, it was beyond belief, and difficult to comprehend. So many people had lost their homes and possessions; their lives were shattered. What courage it would take to face such hardship! My heart went out to them.

A natural disaster like this certainly puts things in perspective. As important as the zoo was to me—next to family, my life *revolved* around the zoo—its relevance seemed diminished in light of the tornado. Or so I thought.

With Topeka immersed in the aftermath of the catastrophe, I expected little attendance at the zoo. Surprisingly, the days immediately after the tornado were very busy. Many visitors were tornado victims, seeking refuge from adversity. The zoo provided solace, a place of family togetherness and happy memories. The zoo was a continuum in the lives of many Topekans, and served as a source of renewal in the community, something I had not anticipated. I am constantly amazed at the roles zoos play in our society.

The tornado also provided an unusual opportunity to observe animal behavior under extraordinary circumstances. I had always heard that animals could tell when severe weather was approaching, and thus would become excited. I have no doubt that many animal senses are developed far beyond those of humans, and that animals have a keen awareness of climatic changes. Whether or not this causes excitable behavior is, at least in my mind, questionable. Let's take the Topeka tornado as an example.

On that evening a man in the Capital City is watching television as is his custom every night, and his dog is asleep at his feet. The weather outside is clear and calm. The tornado is not here yet, but when the weather bulletin interrupts programming with a tornado alert, the man's heart beats faster, his chemistry alters, fear grips his system and his body language is different. The family pet senses these changes in the behavior and physiology of its master and responds. The dog sits up and barks, and the man says to his wife, "It *must* be a tornado. Look! Even the dog knows it's coming!"

Certainly the dog is aware of changes in the weather, as well as changes in its master. But the dog has experienced severe weather previously, and probably would not demonstrate great excitement *until* the noise and violent force of the tornado itself were apparent. It is more likely that the dog is reacting to its master's demeanor than to the impending tornado. There are exceptions, of course, but it is so easy to misinterpret and read into the dog's behavior something other than what it may actually represent.

Now let's go back to the zoo. As the twister roared through Topeka and I was patrolling the zoo on the alert for damage, I also observed the animals and their behavior. I was afraid that the strong winds, heavy rain and emphatic noise would frighten the animals to the extent they would run into fences and injure themselves, or they would be in a frenzy, desperate to flee or hide from the storm. They weren't.

If anything, it was just the opposite. The tigers were not pacing back and forth, but in their den with chins resting on the threshold, calmly watching the rain. The eagles were not frantically flying around, but perched in their shelter, calmly watching the rain. The bison were not running along the fence line, but resting on a mound, calmly watching the rain. Deer were standing motionless, ignoring the rain; llamas were chewing their cud, ignoring the rain; polar bears were playing with a log in their pool, ignoring the rain.

If you stop and think about it, these behaviors make perfect sense. Wild animals *regularly* experience extremes in weather. It is part of their existence. Nature has prepared them to cope with the elements. It would be implausible for animals to go berserk every time the weather was drastic.

Once again, it is so easy to misinterpret. Since we are humans, we think like humans, and sometimes assume animals do, too. No, they think like animals, whatever species they may be. Since we do not have protective fur or feathers, our skin is quite sensitive to sun, wind and rain. We are taught to "Come in out of the rain." Some animals *like* the rain!

Granted, my one-time observations of the animals in the Topeka Zoo in this situation were quite limited, and do not provide enough information for a scientific conclusion. But they do make me question some of the long standing folklore about animal behavior in severe weather conditions.

The Topeka tornado of June 8, 1966 changed our community forever, and it also defined a special dimension of our zoo.

Monkeyless Island *Déjà vu*

"Poppycock!"

That silly word instantly jumped into my mind one summer morning in 1966 when, as zoo director, I arrived at the Topeka Zoo to discover there were no monkeys on Monkey Island . . . and there was no water in the moat!

I had the illusory feeling of having already experienced this very moment!

As an animal keeper at the Kansas City Zoo in 1962, I had arrived one summer morning to discover there were no monkeys (except one lone female) on Monkey Island . . . and there was no water in the moat!

A reporter from *The Kansas City Star* had asked me then about the awkward catching bags we were using and I had replied that the bags were "Poppycock!" Now that word came to haunt me as I faced another monkeyless island, a nightmare I had lived before.

At the Kansas City Zoo the drain valve had broken in the water-filled moat. Guess what? In the Topeka Zoo, the drain valve broke in the water-filled moat!

The Topeka Monkey Island dated back to 1933, when the Works Progress Administration (WPA) began work on the first facility in Gage Park to be specifically designed for exotic animals (hence, the founding date of the Topeka Zoo). The Monkey Island officially opened in 1934 and was known as "Monkey City." On the island the stone shelter was designed like a miniature city. Monkey-sized doors and windows touted signs that proclaimed "city hall, fire department, grocery store, café, drugstore, and dance hall" among others. (Lloyd Zimmer Books and Maps, in downtown Topeka, often has old post cards depicting this.) It was quite popular in its day, but over time the structure deteriorated.

In 1962 (prior to my arrival at the zoo), the island was renovated and the "old city" became a mound-like shelter for the monkeys while sea lions swam in the moat. In May 1964 I had the steel climbing poles removed and replaced with trees supplied by the forestry department to provide a more natural exhibit for both the monkeys and zoo visitors.

Before I return to the plight of monkeyless island *déjà vu*, I must tell you of some other specimens we *intentionally* wanted to release—but they refused to go. In one of our bird flight units we were exhibiting several crows, which are among the most clever of all birds. To make room for a pair of South American king vultures recently donated to the zoo, we decided to turn the crows loose, since they were indigenous to Kansas. We opened the keeper access gate and stood back. The crows did *not* fly the coop! We went inside to encourage them to fly out, but they fluttered around and refused to leave. Finally we had to catch them in nets, take them out and turn them loose! The crows lingered around the zoo for several days before giving up and flying away to a more difficult life. I realize that some people feel sorry for zoo animals because they are "cooped up," but in many cases they feel so secure they are reluctant to leave. (This incident was reported nationwide, and an article appeared in the *National Observer* newspaper.)

And now back to 1966. The ten spider monkeys who crossed the dry moat and fled the island did not go far. They stayed together as a group and climbed to the top of a nearby tree where we could not reach them. However, Paul Linger, our newly appointed zoo curator, devised a scheme to catch them. We started by placing their favorite foods at the base of the tree. The monkeys got used to coming down, grabbing some food, and scampering back up.

Paul's idea was to slip the monkeys a "Mickey Finn." But rather than use a strong alcoholic drink, we would inject oranges with a sleep-inducing drug. We would then position ourselves around the base of the tree with a large circular net and catch the monkeys, one-by-one, as they fell asleep and dropped out of the tree. Ingenious!

Plans were set and the laced oranges placed accordingly. The monkeys immediately swooped down, seized *all* of them, and returned to their high perch to savor their unexpected delicacy. Quickly we took up the huge net (it was **heavy**) and stood under the monkeys.

We watched them eagerly devour the oranges, and stood ready for the first monkey to fall into the net. We waited. Their chattering subsided. We waited. They showed signs of drowsiness. We waited. We were getting tired and impatient. We waited. Finally the monkeys were asleep. We waited.

The monkeys were *not* dropping! Why?

Then it dawned on us, and we looked at each other with embarrassment, because we *knew* this fact. When an arboreal monkey goes to sleep in a tree, it has a reflex-grip to hold on to limbs and branches so it won't fall! Spider monkeys also cling with their prehensile tail, which serves as a "fifth" hand. Boy, did we feel dumb!

Our next plan was more practical. Each day we moved the food offerings on the ground a short distance closer to Monkey Island, and eventually onto the island. The monkeys would cross the dry moat, snatch food, cross back over and then quickly climb a nearby tree. The food was then placed *inside* the shelter, and one-by-one, we caught them.

But the facility was aging and becoming very difficult to maintain. Even after being repaired, the valve leaked. The sewer line was full of roots and the walls were starting to crack. The monkey exhibit was discontinued, and in 1967 the island was converted to "Aoudad Mountain" to exhibit a sheep-like animal from the Atlas mountains adjacent to the Barbary Coast in North Africa. After a few years structural failures were beyond repair and the old WPA island was phased out and replaced with an extensive landscaped area.

Unfortunately that was not the last of our monkey escapes. In 1969 we had a standard outdoor exhibit with seven rhesus monkeys. On the morning of June 1, the lock was found on the floor, the access door was open, and all seven monkeys were in nearby trees. This became local news, and we had reports from all over town that the monkeys "are in my backyard," even though they never left the area and we monitored them daily until we got them back using the "food trick."

Not long after that they were out . . . again! What was going on? Apparently one of the monkeys had learned how to pick the lock! This, of course, made *international* news.

In response to the situation, our colleague and neighbor down the Kansas Turnpike—Ron Blakely, Director of the Sedgwick County Zoo in Wichita—sent me a new lock with a note saying, "Just give the monkeys their own key and tell them to come back each morning."

A Dire Rhea Quandary

The answer: ostrich from Africa, emu from Australia, cassowary from Australia and New Guinea, and rhea from South America.

The question: what are the four giant flightless birds, and where are they from?

Collectively they are known as ratites as they all have a flat rather than raised, or keeled, breastbone for attachment of flight muscles. Their wings are comparatively small but their legs are strong for running. There is a fifth ratite, the kiwi of New Zealand, which is much smaller than the other four "giants." The Topeka Zoo has exhibited all but the kiwi and has successfully reproduced ostrich, emu and rhea.

Adult rheas are four to five feet tall and weigh about 50 lbs. Their feathers are gray (they lack tail plumes) and males have a darker neck. They have three toes and can run up to 30 mph.

We started with a pair of rheas (their names were Dire and Gono). In the spring of 1969 several rhea eggs were laid during a two-week period. The eggs were placed in an incubator by Associate Curator Frank Kish and hatched in 37-45 days, another first for our zoo! More eggs were laid and hatched the following year and husbandry procedures established.

We maintained a rhea flock of three males and four females in a large yard. In 1971 our rheas gained fame, as Zoologist Mike LaRue said, by "being ridiculously prolific." That year the first egg was laid on April 12. By the time it had hatched, 72 more eggs had been laid and no end was in sight! Mike became guardian and protector of the rhea realm at the Topeka Zoo, and he experienced quite a reign.

Rhea eggs were removed from the yard as they were laid and placed in artificial incubators where temperature and humidity were strictly controlled. Each egg was dated and maintained in an incubator at a dry bulb temperature of 98 degrees F. and wet bulb of 86 degrees F. Each egg was turned one third of a turn three times a day. Usually eggs remained in the trays for 37 days, and then were transferred to a hatching tray, which allowed the chicks to stand after hatching.

Hatching usually occurred in groups; that is, when one bird hatched, most others in the tray hatched with it, irrespective of the incubation time. Just prior to hatching the chicks emitted a whistle resembling a dive bomb. Eggs hatched after incubating for as little as 35 days, or up to 45 days and more. Birds remained in the hatching tray for 24 hours, after which they were moved to a brooder and the incubator trays were then thoroughly cleaned and fumigated.

The chicks were brooded in a small enclosure approximately 36 inches by 60 inches in size with a heat lamp. The young rheas remained in the enclosure for two days or until they could walk well. They were not offered food these first two days because they were still absorbing their yolk sacs.

Then the birds were put into a larger enclosure, with either older rheas or turkey chicks, whichever were available. Mike felt that the older birds were most instrumental in teaching the hatchlings to eat. For the next two weeks the hatchlings were fed small balls of ZuPreem Bird of Prey diet rolled in ZuPreem Ratite diet. Young birds seemed to watch older ones chase these balls, and eventually they did the same. ZuPreem Ratite diet (a pellet) was available at all times and the birds ate it as they wandered around pecking. After two weeks they were eating the pelleted ratite diet exclusively.

At the end of the laying season the four females had laid 197 eggs. After carefully making 20,685 egg turns, 116 rheas hatched. Fifty-nine percent of the eggs laid hatched, and an average of 74% of the chicks survived.

Mike called it the "Year of the Rhea." The following year was even better! More than 134 rheas hatched at our zoo in 1972!

At first this was a bonanza. Rheas had a sale or trade value of $100 apiece, and this helped our meager animal acquisition budget immensely. We supplied rheas to nearly every zoo in the country. I dare say, dear reader, that if you saw rheas at any zoo you visited in the mid-1970's, no doubt they had been hatched in Topeka. But in a few short years we had flooded the market and still had rhea chicks in every nook and cranny of the zoo. Visitors frequently asked, "What are those funny little birds everywhere?"

What were we going to do with all those rheas? We dropped the $100 value and made them cheaper by the dozen. Then it was, "Please take our rheas." It truly was a dire rhea dilemma.

One day, during our weekly Animal Management Committee meeting, I was interrupted by a long distance phone call from Kentucky. It was Col. Sanders, and he wanted to feature a giant rhea drumstick at his . . .

No, we wouldn't do that with our rheas.

Instead, I told Mike LaRue to pull the plug on the incubators.

Pissed-Off Tapir

What the heck *is* a tapir?

It is an innocuous animal that is difficult to describe, and even when you see one you're not quite sure what it is. In that classic film *2001: A Space Odyssey*, the extended opening scene depicts the dawn of creation and first life on earth, featuring some really bizarre creatures walking around—and they were **real tapirs,** not computerized. Tapirs! How ingenious. I recognized them immediately and was so impressed with this brilliant casting.

The trustworthy pocket-sized *Golden Nature Guide to Zoo Animals* defines tapirs as odd-toed hoofed mammals related to rhinos and horses. It goes on to say that there are several species and some may reach 8 feet in length and weigh over 500 lbs., that their nose extends beyond the mouth in a short proboscis, and that in zoos they are fed hay, grains and vegetables. The nature guide also states, "Keepers find they usually are docile."

While a keeper at the Kansas City Zoo I cared for a pair of Brazilian tapirs named Maggie and Jiggs and grew quite fond of them. Imagine my surprise and delight to find a tapir at the zoo in Topeka on my arrival in the fall of 1963. Not that they were uncommon in zoos, just unexpected here. The single male named George was an adult with a thick muscular body.

When tapirs walk they often hesitate before taking the next step, then proceed carefully, although they can run surprisingly fast for their size. Their eyes appear rudimentary and they frequently hold their head high with the proboscis stabbing the air in all directions to pick up scents. The Kansas City pair always seemed rather placid and I worked directly with them in the outdoor area and in the barn, petting or brushing them, hand feeding them, etc.

George lived in a large yard next to the old monkey house (later the Animal Kingdom Building) with a small pool, shade trees, and a heated wooden shelter for winter. The only barrier was a tall wire field fence with four-inch square openings. Since there was no guardrail, visitors would reach through the fence and scratch George behind the ears or under the chin, and he would squeak with pleasure. I was appalled at this, but both George and the visitors loved it, and there never had been an incident.

Male tapirs are well endowed and have a unique talent called retromicturition, which means they can urinate backwards. And, instead of relaxing the sphincter muscle to allow urine to flow by gravity, they constrict it to produce a series of squirts that can be aimed accurately up to six feet away. Many times George would lure people to the fence to scratch him, then turn around and squirt them! Squeals of shock and peals of laughter erupted from the spectators. At this, George would run around the perimeter of the yard, squeaking and squirting, somewhat in a victory lap!

Several such occasions were more than humorous. One Sunday morning a father and his young son (5 or 6 years old) were visiting George. To share this strange animal more intimately the father squatted beside his son. George let fly right on target and the little boy observed, "Daddy, he baptized you!"

One of my many VIP tours was for a beautiful Miss Kansas contestant. Accompanied by her chaperone and pageant officials, she looked the all-American wholesome girl you would expect. As we passed by George he retromicturated all over her festive white dress. Outraged, she exclaimed, "That damn thing pissed on me!" Sorta shattered her image.

In spite of these incidents, George was a likeable character with as much charisma as any tapir could muster. As a zoo director I had no favorite animal, but George was one of my favorites, and I made it a point to spend time with him whenever possible.

The routine procedures in our daily care for George were rather straightforward. We simply went into the enclosure with him, raked the yard, changed the bedding, cleaned the pool and provided fresh daily rations. Sometimes he'd follow us around and sometimes he'd ignore us. He wasn't trained but he wasn't a problem. He was just there, a nonchalant tapir. *Until one day.*

It was a warm afternoon in August 1967. I was making the rounds of the zoo and had just unlocked the gate and stepped into George's exhibit when suddenly, unexpectedly, he charged me at astonishing speed in an unprovoked attack. He knocked me to the ground and fortunately I fell back against the gate which pushed it shut. It all happened so fast I'm not sure I understood the ramifications of my position.

George was lunging at me on the ground so I drew my knees to my chest and delivered a powerful jolt to his jaw full force with both feet. It didn't faze him. Now I was scared and knew I was in deep dung (a serious situation).

George was savagely biting my legs. I could not believe the pain, especially through heavy, tough jeans. A tapir's incisors are chisel-shaped and the third upper incisor is canine-like and actually larger than the canines.

Then George did the most unexpected thing: he seized my right knee in his jaws (which surprised me as I had never seen a tapir open its mouth very wide) and lifted my lower body off the ground. I was completely helpless. As I attempted to struggle he violently shook his head from side to side, as though I were a rag doll. Incredible!

Lucky for me a zoo visitor had witnessed all of this and ran into the building for help. Paul Linger, our general curator, responded and rushed to my aid. Paul was a big guy—6' 4" tall, over 200 lbs and very strong. He immediately straddled George's back and with doubled fists rained Herculean blows to his head and face. George would not let go of my leg. Paul kept hitting him and finally he dropped me. The visitor immediately stepped in and dragged me out of the yard. I thought George would turn on Paul, but instead he ran around the yard squealing and urinating, and Paul quickly escaped and locked the gate. Paul acted in a fearless manner and I am forever grateful for his courage.

At the hospital x-rays showed no broken bones, just flesh wounds, missing skin and blood everywhere. After treatment I was sent home to rest and recuperate, but it was some time before I could walk normally.

I never figured out why George acted as he did, but nonetheless I felt no animosity and he remained one of my favorites. Wild animals are unpredictable (I knew that) and I may have unintentionally done something to provoke George. Certainly this experience increased my respect for him as an individual and tapirs as a species—and, we changed our daily routine.

Since I'd not heard of aggressive tapir behavior in other zoos, I conducted a nation-wide survey. To my surprise there had been a number of other incidents around the country, but most were just a single bite as opposed to an attack. I wrote a serious paper of my findings to help inform my colleagues.

My good friend Charlie Hoessle, then director of the St. Louis Zoo, who was always trying one-upmanship on me, followed up with a survey to all zoos on the occurrence of *snail* attacks at their institutions.

How the World Famous Topeka Zoo *became*

The WORLD FAMOUS TOPEKA ZOO

It was the people and their love of the zoo. Yes, community support was the prime reason that the municipal menagerie long known as the Gage Park Zoo emerged as the World Famous Topeka Zoo. One day I simply requested our secretary to modestly and unpretentiously answer the telephone with, "World Famous Topeka Zoo." Lo and behold, the first time she did the caller on the line responded, "You're right! My cousin lives in Denver and he has heard about us!"

That did it. From then on (the early 1970's) we answered the phone with that assertion. It was not a hollow, boastful claim by a small, nondescript zoo—we had earned it and we deserved it. We knew it was valid as everyone in our community puffed up with pride whenever they heard or said the phrase. But there were a few outsiders who doubted our status and asked, "What makes *your* zoo world famous? San Diego, maybe; but Topeka?"

I had the answers.

It had not happened overnight. It was not a single event or occurrence. It was a combination of achievements and milestones over a period of years. And as things happened, we began to hear of our notoriety from around the world. People sent us newspaper clippings from overseas, or called to say they had seen our zoo on network television, or heard news about the zoo on an out-of-town radio station. It was more of a tortoise race than a horse race, but once the zoo was on the move there was no stopping it!

Many of these happenings have already been chronicled in this book. Operation Noah's Ark became known beyond Kansas when I presented a paper on it at the Ibero-American Zoo Federation International Conference in Mexico City in March 1967. In attendance were zoo officials from the United States, Mexico, Central America, South America, Spain, Portugal and Germany. One of the animals received through Operation Noah's Ark was the hippo who was dubbed the "Hesitant Hippo" when she refused to enter her crate at the Kansas City Zoo to be transported to Topeka. That story captured the attention of people all over the world and was carried on the Associated Press and United Press International wire services.

Another international story was that of our orangutan artist, Djakarta Jim. He would sit at a table with a brush and poster board, and paint. Several of his paintings were entered in a statewide children's art contest under the name "D. James Orang." A week later we were informed that Jim had won first prize for his painting "Train from Tokyo." As soon as the local news media broke the story, a chain reaction was initiated that became more incredible each day. Jim's story was on television and radio, and carried in newspapers around the world including the *Bangkok World, Pacific Stars and Stripes, International Herald Tribune, Japan Times* and the *Miyazaki Nichinichi Daily* in Japan.

Jim's popularity resulted in a call from the producers of the nationally syndicated television show "What's My Line?" asking me to come to New York City in 1971 to try to stump the panel—which I did! The following week in Washington, DC, I presented one of Jim's paintings to the White House. The painting, appropriately enough, was titled "Fourth of July." If the zoo wasn't world famous by this time, certainly Djakarta Jim was!

Many people feel our zoo truly became world famous in 1971 when our pair of American golden eagles successfully hatched and parent-raised a chick, which was a first for any zoo in the world. Another first for our zoo occurred when our female Bengal tiger gave birth to six cubs in one litter. Not only was this a world record at the time, but the parents raised all six cubs. Over the years our zoo has sent tiger cubs to zoos across the United States, as well as to the Netherlands, Germany and South America. Some zoos even named their tigers "Topeka."

There have been wire service stories in which our zoo would have preferred not to have been featured, though in a sense they contributed to the zoo becoming world famous. One incident was the escape of a Bengal tiger, much to the embarrassment of the keeper who left the exhibit unlocked. The tiger went to a nearby bush, laid down beneath it and dozed off. He was darted with a tranquilizer and safely moved back into his exhibit.

Mike LaRue, long-time staff member, heard about our zoo while serving in Vietnam. He had started his career in Topeka as a keeper taking care of, among other animals, rhesus monkeys. He was surprised one day to read in the "Pacific Stars and Stripes" about the escape and challenging recapture of those very same monkeys.

One of our more humorous zoo escapes involved our European white storks. For several months they flew around the southwest area of Topeka. One day a local veterinarian called to say they were near his clinic and his office girls wondered if they would become pregnant! We received daily calls from people who had spotted the storks, which enabled us to keep track of their wanderings. Eventually they flew to a farm near the zoo and were lured into a barn with food. The storks were in fine shape, but the zoo staff soon tired of the wisecracks.

Our zoo acquired a reputation for hospitality and may have been the only one in the world to provide the "Red Carpet" treatment. We kept a strip of red carpet at the entrance, and whenever we had a VIP visit, we would literally "roll out the red carpet." We also distributed ZOO POWER buttons, and the last week of December each year mailed cards around the world that exclaimed, "Happy Zoo Year!"

In 1983 I received an inquiry from a Mr. Glen D. Willbern of San Antonio, Texas. He wanted to know the official name of our zoo. In my response I asked why he made such a request. The following was his answer:

Dear Mr. Clarke:

Thank you for your courtesy in responding to my request for the official name of your Zoo. Why did I make the request? I had recently read an article in the New York Times on great Zoos of the world, an article in which "the Zoo in Topeka" was described as "modern and innovative;" particular mention was made of the Zoo's Rain Forest. Now, to the point: In my spare time, I construct word puzzles for the Dell Publishing Company, which insists upon strict accuracy in the word lists, so that we list the Omaha and Seattle Zoos, for example, as Doorly and Woodland Park. I decided to do a puzzle, inspired by the Times article, on Great Modern Zoos of the World. The World Famous Topeka Zoo is one of the 23 listed in the puzzle submitted to Dell. I hope that the puzzle, when it appears in print a few months hence in the Dell Word Search Puzzle Magazine, will help to spread the fame of the already famous Topeka Zoo.

I was glad to receive the information on the Zoo; I read it with great interest and with admiration for all that you have accomplished.

Sincerely, Glen D. Willbern

And if all of this were not enough, I knew we had "arrived" when San Diego would telephone and say, "This is the *other* world famous zoo calling!"

*****

Addendum. Reporter Mike Hall wrote an article published April 24, 1988 in *The Topeka Capital-Journal* about persons who stay in Topeka and those who move on. It contained the following story:

"And by the way, it isn't really 'The World Famous Topeka Zoo' as Gary would have you believe. It is the Topeka Zoo under the management of The World Famous Gary Clarke. A friend of mine was once involved in a traffic accident on the streets of Dallas. As he was standing on the sidewalk waiting for the police to arrive, one of the witnesses asked him where he was from. When he said he was from Topeka, the man said 'Oh, do you know Gary Clarke?' "

4 The Topeka Capital-Journal # Opinion Saturday, August 7,

1982

Editorials

In God we trust

World Famous Gary Clarke

Did you ever wonder why Topeka's zoo can claim to be "The World Famous Topeka Zoo"? Mostly it's because of the World Famous Gary Clarke, the zoo's director.

In his 19 years here, Clarke has not only worked hard to upgrade the displays and the variety of animals there, but he also has shown a genius for attracting national attention to the zoo.

When two new gnus were born at the zoo, Clarke named them "the gnus, Weather and Sports." That sort of imagination gets Topeka mentioned on newscasts and in publications all over the world. CBS commentator Charles Osgood penned a poem on the event, which he read over the air and which now is immortalized in Osgood's book.

Who else but Gary Clarke would name a hippopotamus, which spends a lot of time under the water, "Submarie." Or a boa constrictor "Julius Squeezer." And then there was "Gregory Peccary." A peccary is a piglike animal.

After Clarke gave the zoo's orangutans some paint and turned them into abstract artists, the national publicity led to an appearance on the nationally televised quiz show "What's My Line" — for Clarke, not for the orangutans.

To show its appreciation for all that Clarke has done for the zoo, the Topeka Friends of the Zoo has scheduled some events later this month to commemorate Clarke's 25 years in the zoo business.

Clarke will stand in a receiving line at the zoo from 2 to 4 p.m. on Sunday, August 29. That will be open to the public. Then at 6 p.m. the TFOTZ will have a cocktail party and dinner for Clarke at the Holiday Inn West.

Meanwhile Clarke will not be sitting around waiting for his honors. Today he is leaving on his 10th safari trip, leading a group this time to south central and east Africa.

V.I.P. at a Mythical Zoo

I love zoos and everything about them.

I collect zoos . . . by way of visiting as many as possible.

And I collect anything and everything about zoos: books, articles, guide books, newsletters, periodicals, annual reports, animal inventories, letterheads, business cards, posters, master plans, maps, brochures, postcards, lapel pins, logo mugs, pennants, neckties, patches, buttons—buttons?

Yes, buttons. Over the years I amassed a huge collection, and every zoo and aquarium wanted to make sure *their* button was in my collection. In my humble opinion, the greatest of all zoo buttons was issued by none other than the World Famous Topeka Zoo! It simply read: ZOO POWER. I wore one all the time. It was extremely popular, and I distributed thousands across the nation to flight attendants, salesclerks, waitresses, receptionists, and anyone else who admired mine. I was proudly wearing a ZOO POWER button when I met President Jimmy Carter at a White House reception in 1977. He couldn't help seeing it (bright white on my dark suit lapel), and I was crushed when neither the President nor the First Lady said one word about it.

My button collection went far beyond zoos. I had a propensity for buttons of every description, and the more humorous (or ridiculous) the better. I never bought buttons; friends and associates took great pleasure in adding to my collection. When the stack of mail would arrive each day at the zoo, I could tell at a glance if any of the envelopes contained buttons. I'd grab the letter opener and delight in what new gems had been sent to me. The rest of the mail could wait.

At zoo conferences I would wear five different buttons at a time (one on each lapel, one *inside* each lapel, and one on my tie), and change them three times a day. Delegates were always eager to check out the newest set. What fun!

On one occasion a lady came up to me and said, "I don't read the morning paper, I just read your buttons." She then turned to her friends and asked, "Have you read Gary today?"

The button that *always* got a reaction was the one that read, "Too Much Sex Is Hard On Your Eyes." It had very fuzzy letters and was difficult to read. I remember the time I was surrounded by several ladies, all reading my various buttons. One of them couldn't read the "Too Much Sex" button, so she put on her glasses. Was she ever embarrassed! And the subject of many chuckles the rest of the conference.

My favorite button was one that simply said, "Belly."

And, of course, I wore my belly button *under* my tie.

But now to continue—from collecting buttons to collecting zoos. I've always found zoos fascinating, and my window into the world of animals. My colleagues used to explain that my parents had taken me to a different zoo each weekend . . . but I always managed to find my way back home!

Seriously, I have visited almost every zoo in the United States, as well as many in Canada, Mexico, Europe and some other foreign countries, for a total of nearly 250. And if I had not visited a particular zoo in the USA, I at least *knew* about it—or so I thought. And this is where collecting buttons and collecting zoos came together for me.

In late 1973 a mysterious brown envelope arrived. It was from the Flossmoor Zoo, in Flossmoor, Illinois. What?—Flossmoor! It sounded like a slogan for the American Dental Association.

Even if I had never heard of the Flossmoor Zoo, maybe it *was* real. I checked the *International Zoo Yearbook* (published annually by the Zoological Society of London) and the Directory of the American Association of Zoological Parks and Aquariums (AAZPA). No listing there. I then searched other official sources, as well as any and every reference to obscure and little-known zoos in my extensive library of literature on zoological parks. Nothing.

There was, however, a letter enclosed, on what appeared to be official notepaper that read:

Flossmoor Zoo
745 Park Drive
Flossmoor, Ill. 60422
November 21, 1973

Mr. Gary Clarke, Director
Topeka Zoo
Topeka, Kansas 66606

Dear Mr. Clarke:

The Flossmoor Zoo is interested in acquiring a breeding pair of Lapel Buttons and imagine our utter amazement and joy to find in the most recent AAZPA Newsletter that you have a surplus at the Topeka Zoo. We are a small, non-profit organization and feel that 50 cents each is a bit steep for our budget. Would you consider 25 cents each? You would receive a lot more than 50 cents worth of publicity and good will in return. We are a do-it-yourself zoo.

Hoping to hear from you in the near future, I remain

Cordially yours,
Beauregard Beanblossom
Director

True, I had placed an ad in the AAZPA Newsletter but only as a joke. The apparent tongue-in-cheek tone of this letter, as well as the obviously phony name of the director, led me to believe this was a joke in return—no doubt from my buddies at the Lincoln Park Zoo in Chicago. They may have been big shots in a big shot zoo, but I was not about to let them get ahead of little old Topeka. So I fired off the following on Topeka Zoo letterhead:

21 December 1973

Saul or Dennis or Mark . . .
c/o Lincoln Park Zoo
100 West Webster Avenue
Chicago, Illinois 60614

Gentlemen?

I have a problem (well, I really have many problems) but one with which I feel you may be of help.

I have received an overwhelming response to my Ad in the AAZPA Newsletter about surplus lapel buttons. In addition to inquiries from such leading institutions as London, Frankfort, and Bisbee, Arizona, I have also received a letter from the Flossmoor Zoo in Flossmoor, Illinois. I do want to respond but am having trouble tracking down the details on this Zoo. It is not in the AAZPA Directory or the International Zoo Year Book. Roger Caras never heard of it, and Marlin says there are no Mutual of Omaha policies issued to that city. There is a Flossmoor, but the universal information operator can find no phone number for the Zoo and despite an accurate zip code the postal service returned my Christmas card. The Director, Beauregard Beanblossom, is not listed in "Who's Who in America," or even in "Who's Not Who in America."

Our ZOO POWER buttons are in short supply, and all we have left are blatant, cheap imitations of the real thing.

Sincerely,

Gary K. Clarke,
Director

That would teach those guys!
Oops! Next thing I knew I received a packet with a letter dated January 23, 1974 on truly "official" letterhead from the VILLAGE OF FLOSSMOOR, Flossmoor, Illinois 60422. At the top this letterhead listed

the Mayor, Trustees, Manager, Clerk, Attorney, Treasurer, and various Commissioners and Inspectors. This was **real!** Here is what it said:

January 23, 1974

Mr. Gary K. Clarke, Director
Topeka Zoological Park
635 Gage Blvd.
Topeka, Kansas 66606

Dear Mr. Clarke:

I recently received a copy of a letter you wrote to Lincoln Park Zoo saying that you could not find out anything about the Flossmoor Zoo. From the tone of your letter I guess you don't think there actually is a Flossmoor Zoo. Rest assured, there definitely is a Flossmoor Zoo.

I must admit that we are not listed in the International Zoo Yearbook nor are we members of the AAZPA. We are a small city Zoo and don't have much contact with other Zoos. We do have good relations with both Brookfield and Lincoln Park, however, and they help us out a lot.

I am enclosing a picture of a part of our Zoo. You can see that it is not new. We have been here for some time and kind of resent your letter saying no one's ever heard of us. Incidentally, my name is not Beauregard Beanblossom, either. Mayor Reed is kind of annoyed, too.

Mr. Kitchener of Lincoln Park Zoo tells me that you like to collect various items such as buttons, banners, etc. We don't really have much, but I am enclosing a banner and some buttons. I know they're not very professional, but our youth group, the "Zoo-Doers," make them to sell for the Zoo's benefit. They sell for 50 cents each and we have cleared a nice piece of change selling them this past summer.

Well, Mr. Clarke, I would like to invite you to visit us at the Flossmoor Zoo and see our small facility. If you ever have occasion to write us all our mail goes to City Hall.

I hope this letter has clarified the situation for you.

Sincerely yours,
Mike Rogale
Zoo Supervisor

The packet contained not one, not two, but *three* handmade buttons promoting the Flossmoor Zoo. The Flossmoor Zoo banner was also handmade. It was on felt material of putrid green color with gaudy red letters.

Well, they were certainly unique additions to my vast collection, but were they valid?

Now I *was* confused. Maybe the Flossmoor Zoo *did* exist. The photo enclosed was an 8"x10" black-and-white print. It showed a rather old-fashioned exhibit with a standard three-foot high guard rail, and beyond that an eight-foot high chain-link fence topped with three strands of barbed wire. The exhibit contained—get this—several dozen domestic geese!

Even if I had not visited a particular zoo, I usually could identify it in a photograph, but not this one. I must confess I was mystified. Regardless of the evidence, I still felt this was all a hoax about a mythical zoo. I put everything in an envelope and filed it away.

Fast forward six years to the 1980 AAZPA Annual Conference in Chicago, hosted by the Brookfield Zoo, the Shedd Aquarium, and the Lincoln Park Zoo. In addition to the technical sessions and committee meetings, delegates were bussed on successive days to each of the three host institutions for study visits.

On my arrival at the Lincoln Park Zoo, I was intercepted by Assistant Director Dennis Meritt and Curator of Mammals Mark Rosenthal. They whisked me to a waiting limousine with a private chauffeur. I felt like I was being kidnapped, but my captors (oops, I mean hosts) assured me I was a V.I.P. and we were on our way to . . . the Flossmoor Zoo!

Sure enough, on the north side of Chicago there was a zoo! And I was given an extensive behind-the-scenes tour. So, was it real, or mythical? Actually, I'd say a bit of both.

For many years the Lincoln Park Zoo had operated a little-known "neighborhood" zoo in Indian Boundary Park, which happened to be on the far north side of the city. One of the Lincoln Park Zoo staff members had a relative who worked at the Village of Flossmoor City Hall, and that's how they had obtained official letterhead for the initial correspondence back in 1973-1974. The zoo was actually known as Indian Boundary Park Zoo and it was *not* located in Flossmoor, IL.

In any case I added another zoo to my life list. It was a wonderful surprise and the highlight of the conference for me. I know my zoo pals had great fun plotting this scheme, but I had more fun as the recipient. Actually, I was honored that they had put forth so much effort on my behalf. After all, who else has ever been a V.I.P. at a mythical zoo?

And I still have those three unique buttons.

Coke and Buns and Elephant Dung

GARTH THOMPSON MEMORIAL DUNG PILE!

So read a large sign (complete with an illustration of fresh, steaming elephant dung) made for a special guest scheduled to visit the World Famous Topeka Zoo in June 1987.

Earlier I had met with our elephant keepers and asked them to save *all* of the dung from Tembo, our African elephant, for a week prior to Garth's arrival. No problem, they said. It could be stockpiled on the compost trailer in the off-exhibit service area adjacent to the elephants. But who *was* this guy? And why were we saving *dung* for him?

Garth Thompson, born and raised in Zimbabwe, was one of only six licensed wildlife safari guides in that country in 1987. As a guide, Garth concentrated on fulfilling the dreams and expectations of his clients on their once-in-a-lifetime experience of an African safari. Garth is the individual who introduced me to the term "adrenaline grass" which we used in Lions Pride. He says it is "grass so thick that when it suddenly begins to move, you experience a rush of adrenaline."

Garth and I had met serendipitously some years earlier on one of my Zimbabwe safaris. He was a young guide with great exuberance and spirit. I was immediately impressed with his knowledge of mammals, birds, trees, plants, insects—all aspects of the ecosystem. But what really struck me was his *passion* for the African bush—his sensitivity to the cycles of life. In his words, "While canoeing down the Zambezi in silence, floating on nature, using the energy of the river for motion, you become aware of the sounds, the smells, and the touch of the wind and sun."

One of the reasons we hit it off so well, however, was that we both had a weird sense of humor and shared a propensity for practical jokes. Some of the funniest moments of my life have been on safari with Garth.

One of Garth's favorite activities is a walk in the bush. As he says, "We designed walking trails into wilderness areas, devoid of any road but abundant in flora, fauna, and scenery. The paths that you will walk are clean and covered only with the tracks of life. It is here that you will smell dust and dung, drink in the songs of birds, encounter animals at close quarters, sit silently at waterholes and watch nature in its quest for survival."

Safarists benefit from his wealth of information and zest for teaching. Sometimes, though, he becomes so absorbed in the wonders of nature—from the track of a mammal to the bark of a tree—that he forgets about those with him. Oh, he is *always* conscious of their safety, but not necessarily of their comfort. Usually his walks depart at dawn after a quick cup of coffee or tea. By noon, when the sun is high in the sky and his walkers are hot, tired, and thirsty, they begin to ask how far it is back to camp. Only then does he lead them back for nourishment and rest.

My normal safari attire included a T-shirt with a "Cowabunga Safaris" logo. But on one occasion I had a special surprise for Garth. At the end of the bush walk I lagged behind, then staggered into camp moaning, dirty and disheveled. My custom made T-shirt read, "I survived the Garth Thompson Death March," and it was complete with drops of blood scattered on it.

While safari guides strive to make their clients comfortable in even the most remote camps, they pride themselves on personally being able to survive under the most rugged conditions. So, when a camp provides cold beverages (beer, Coke) and warm dinner rolls (buns), it is disdained with the nickname "Coke and Buns." Hence, I prepared another T-shirt to wear on a Garth safari that read on the front: "This is a Coke and Buns Camp." On the back it read: "Warm Beer and Biltong," which was the counterpart to Coke and Buns (biltong is dried meat like jerky). When Garth saw me wearing this T-shirt he laughed—and then instructed the camp staff to serve me nothing but warm beer and biltong for the duration of my stay. At every meal I drank and ate as though I really enjoyed it! Garth was puzzled that I seemed none the worse for wear. Unbeknownst to him, his camp staff was regularly supplying me with decent food behind his back, and even a cold beer now and then.

While Garth loves and appreciates *all* of nature, his forte is elephants. He is a recognized expert, and it is so rewarding to be with Garth and glide silently by elephants at arm's length in a canoe, or track them on foot. I've sat with Garth at numerous waterholes adjacent to the Zambezi, surrounded by elephants at trunk's length, observing their behavior, listening to their stomachs grumble, marveling at their majesty. Many times we have watched elephants churn and wallow in mud, and when they departed, we have stripped down and luxuriated belly deep in that same oozy mud.

Garth had done so many special things for me in Africa that I was eager to return the favor. That opportunity came to pass when Garth visited Mike and Joyce Basel of Fun Safaris in Bloomingdale, Illinois. I invited the three of them to Topeka for the weekend of June 12-14, 1987. And I asked Garth to present a lecture to our staff and volunteers while he was here.

Just like in Africa, I prepared an official itinerary for their Topeka Safari. The day they arrived I drove them in my open Jeep (the "Blue Dung Beetle") on a highlight tour of the Capital City of Kansas. That evening they attended the "On Safari" Gala sponsored by the Friends of the Topeka Zoo.

The next day at the zoo a standing room only crowd filled the Education Room in the Animals and Man Building, eagerly awaiting Garth's program. He beamed as he walked to the podium. Little did he know that this group of friendly faces had an unconventional welcome ready for him. I gave Garth a glowing introduction, building him up as the rugged guide who thrived on minimal conditions in the remote African bush.

Then I stepped aside and said, "Please welcome Garth Thompson of the Zambezi." Instead of thunderous applause, the audience was dead silent. In unison, each person held up a bright red can of Coke . . . and a bun.

Momentarily Garth was nonplussed, but quickly regained his composure and broke into a big grin as he realized he'd been had. His lecture was well received and everyone kept their Coke and bun as a souvenir.

Garth was impressed with the zoo, especially the Tropical Rain Forest and Gorilla Encounter. He was particularly excited to meet Tembo, our female African elephant. And while he had seen thousands of elephants in Africa, Garth had a first time experience at the World Famous Topeka Zoo: he rode one! Elephant keeper Ron Ringer gave him a few pointers, and up he went. With great excitement Garth tossed his camera to me and said, "Take a picture; take *lots* of pictures!" What a pleasure it was for me to be able to provide Garth with a special thrill in the world of nature—and with his favorite species, no less.

But the best was yet to come. On the pretense of showing Garth "behind the scenes," we took him into the elephant service area. As soon as he saw the compost trailer and personalized sign from a distance, he ran at full speed and made a flying leap into the midst of the GARTH THOMPSON MEMORIAL DUNG PILE! He may have been on the other side of the world, but he felt at home.

Headhunters Come Calling

I suppose when you are at the top of your game (as they say) you attract the attention of others in your field searching for qualified candidates to fill vacant positions.

Here I was, director of a modest zoo in a mid-western municipality, quite content and not looking to go anywhere—but opportunity kept knocking on the door.

Sometimes the governing authority itself from another zoo would make direct contact with me. More often than not, however, one of those "Executive Search Firms" with a fancy name would discreetly advise me that I was "under serious consideration" for the top administrative post at the "greatest zoo in the world" (their client). This, of course, would be "kept in complete confidence." I replied that was not necessary, as I always told my superiors whenever this happened to simply be candid and up front. The firm would ask me to complete a detailed application and submit extensive documentation on my career. Again, having neither the time nor desire to do so, I would instead send my standard one-page bio sketch used in speaking engagement introductions, hoping that would deter them. It didn't.

Next thing I knew they would be sending representatives from the firm and the zoo in question to Topeka to meet with me. That was fine and we would extend gracious hospitality. But it didn't end there.

The final step was an invitation to visit their zoo and city to see firsthand this "great opportunity"—all expenses paid, of course. I would reply that was not necessary as I had already seen their zoo (true), and really was not that interested (true), even if it was a bigger zoo, larger salary, etc. But they would insist, adding, "Bring your family along as well."

Close friends who knew of these situations would always encourage me to "check it out" in fairness to me, my career, and my family. I felt a bit awkward going at the expense of the host zoo when I was rather certain my decision would be no. But they kept insisting, so we often went, the kids had a blast, and my decision was still no.

This happened with some really neat zoos—zoos I liked and admired: Pittsburgh, Colorado Springs, Milwaukee, Dallas, even my old alma mater Kansas City. But I was happy in Topeka and, just as important, so was my family. Probably the closest I ever came to jumping ship was in response to the offer from the Minnesota State Zoo in Minneapolis. Somehow the *Minneapolis Star-Tribune* got wind of this, and in turn *The Topeka Capital-Journal*, which resulted in unwanted front page headlines. No, I didn't blame the media, but I must admit I was a bit perturbed that the Minnesota Zoo board apparently made assumptions, and then announcements, before I had made any decision—or even discussed it thoroughly with my family.

The front page of *The Topeka Capital-Journal* on Friday, November 12, 1982 carried the following story under the headline, **"Zoo Chief considers job offer."**

Gary K. Clarke, director of the Topeka Zoo for 19 years, acknowledged Thursday that he has been offered the job of general director at the new multi-million dollar Minnesota Zoological Garden at Apple Valley, Minn.

The state-owned zoo is south of the twin cities of Minneapolis and St. Paul.

Clarke said he has not made a decision but "I would hope that certainly by the first of next week, if not sooner, I would need to get this resolved."

Clarke said the Minnesota zoo board, in its search for a general director, contacted him and some of the other zoo directors it felt might qualify for the job.

"I am really very happy here in Topeka," Clarke said. "This is a tremendous zoo. We're able to do so much because the people are so responsive."

Clarke said "frequently people in search of a zoo director invite us to look around their zoo and to visit with them. They (the Minnesota zoo board) invited me last Monday, which was a vacation day.

"There were some other very competent, qualified people there, some of whom I knew.

"When I got back to Topeka, the zoo board representatives called me and said they would like me to come back up there again and meet with their board and, in essence, were offering me the job."

Clarke said he has talked with his two Topeka supervisors, City Park and Recreation Director Ron Vine and Park Commissioner Harry Felker, and told them the offer was made and that he was considering it.

"I haven't even had time to visit with my family about this whole thing," Clarke said. "It is a very important decision that can't be reached immediately. I need to think about it. And there are some unanswered questions.

"In my heart I really don't want to leave Topeka. The new job is a unique opportunity and undoubtedly would be a tremendous challenge. But we still have a lot to do here in Topeka, as far as that goes."

On that same date the *Minneapolis Star-Tribune* carried the following story with the headline, **"Topeka Zoo chief is panel's choice for Minnesota Job."**

Gary Clarke, director of the Topeka Zoo in Kansas, will be recommended for the job as head of the Minnesota Zoological Garden.

Patricia Davies, who heads the zoo board committee evaluating candidates, said Thursday that Clarke was the clear choice of board members who interviewed him and three other applicants in private sessions earlier this week.

"I think that he'll bring a very steady hand to the zoo," she said. "He's done tremendous things with the Topeka Zoo on a very limited budget. We hope he'll be able to make our zoo as attractive to the general public as he has with the zoo down there."

Davies's recommendation is expected to be endorsed by at least seven of the 10 zoo board members who already have met Clarke and who unanimously agreed that he was the leading candidate for the job.

"The reason we don't have more finalists (to be interviewed by the zoo board) is because we were so unanimous about Clarke," she said. Although none of the Minnesota Zoo board members visited the Topeka Zoo, Davies said they were impressed with Clarke's credentials and with reports they received on his zoo. It is billed as the "World Famous Topeka Zoo," is supported with city tax dollars and has numerous public-appeal programs, such as free days, she said.

"Clarke is very good at stimulating interest among the general public by making the zoo a more active, exciting place to visit," she said.

The Minnesota Zoo, the newest zoo in the nation and one of two state-owned zoos, is best known in the international zoo world for its emphasis on natural-habitat displays and for its strong scientific work in the fields of endangered species reproduction. It has focused on displays that include a large number of animals from the same species, especially animals that are native to northern climates, such as moose, Bactrian camels, Siberian tigers and Przewalski horses.

In most situations the spotlight does not faze me, but I felt very uncomfortable being the focus of this kind of attention. Things seemed to be already decided from the other end, which prompted my decision to stay at this end. I called Minnesota and told them, and then advised the media in Topeka. This prompted the following story on the front page of *The Topeka Capital-Journal* on Sunday, November 14, 1982 under the headline, **"Zoo director rejects offer from Minnesota."**

Gary K. Clarke, Topeka Zoo director, said Saturday he has turned down an offer to become general director of the new multimillion dollar Minnesota Zoological Garden.

"A part of me wants to accept that challenge" he said, "but more of me feels that we really have a lot of very positive things here in Topeka, especially with the new gorilla exhibit coming up and the tremendous support we've received from everybody. Our roots are pretty deep here."

Clarke said he called a representative of the Minnesota zoo's board Saturday to "decline their very generous offer."

Clarke had acknowledged late Thursday that the offer included a "considerable increase in salary" and that he was considering it.

The Minnesota zoo is state-owned, has a more than $5 million annual operating budget, and has about a million visitors each year. It is situated on a 480-acre site, as opposed to the Topeka Zoo's 30 acres in Gage Park.

Clarke said, however, "I think we've been able to accomplish things with our zoo that some bigger zoos haven't been able to do, so size isn't everything."

He said he had time to give the offer a lot of thought, to weigh the aspects and to talk it over with his family before making the decision.

"This particular opportunity really did make me think very hard and very seriously," he said. " But actually things are going very well at Topeka Zoo, and I'm very happy there."

He said he feels the zoo has excellent support from the Topeka Parks and Recreation Department and from Topeka Friends of the Zoo "and we've got a good staff."

He emphasized, however, it was not just the zoo alone that led to his decision to reject the Minnesota offer.

"It's the Topeka community itself that has had a lot to do with it." Clarke said. "It's a great place to raise a family. It may be a little reserved about making progress at times, but it eventually moves ahead."

I don't know how the Minneapolis paper treated it, and frankly I didn't care. I was just glad it was all over. The community was very reassuring about my decision, and my big boss at the time, Park Commissioner Harry L. "Butch" Felker, III, sent the following handwritten note:

Gary,

Just a note to tell you how happy I am that you decided to stay with us. It's a compliment to the City and all its folks that someone of your caliber would decide to pass up a super opportunity to continue your work here.
Butch

The headhunters increased my appreciation for everything. And I have never regretted my decision.

Marsupial Masquerade

It would be *such* a dirty trick. And the people intended as victims were *so* nice. Should I really do this? Would it reflect negatively on our zoo? Or damage my professional reputation?

I must confess I debated the issue back-and-forth in my own mind . . . for about two seconds. Heck yes, I *would* do it! What other choice did I have?

The marsupial in question was none other than K'Bluey, the koala that had been on loan to Topeka from the San Diego Zoo, June 15-July 14, 1986. And the guests at the masquerade would be delegates to the first National Docent Conference, to be held in Kansas City, Missouri, July 19-21, 1986. There would be nearly 200 docents and zoo educators, from 47 zoos and aquariums in more than 30 states and Canada. On July 22, 1986 the entire group would travel to Topeka to "converge on the World Famous Topeka Zoo" (as Susan Chan put it in her news release) for a post-conference tour.

Our fabulous Topeka Zoo docents were quite active on a national level (I was so proud of them), and Mary Jo Hobbs was serving as editor of the National Docent Newsletter. Between our enthusiastic docents and creative staff, we had quite a day planned.

Delegates would arrive by chartered buses and have a breakfast of home-baked muffins and champagne punch in the Gorilla Encounter glass tunnel. This would be followed by an elephant training session and behind the scenes tours throughout the zoo. Lunch would be on the future site for Lions Pride, the zoo's next major exhibit. In the afternoon Topeka Trolleys would transport delegates to the zoo's Conservation and Propagation Center at Forbes Field to see the Przewalski wild horses. The day's activities would finish back at the zoo with a wine-and-cheese social gathering in the Tropical Rain Forest.

The day would truly be perfect if *only* we could showcase K'Bluey, the koala (*everyone* knew of his visit to Topeka). K'Bluey was scheduled to return to the San Diego Zoo on July 15. I contacted them, explained about the national conference, and requested that K'Bluey's visit be extended. They declined. I was disappointed, but fully understood and respected their decision. And to be quite honest, we could not afford to keep K'Bluey another week anyway.

Still, I did not want to deny our special guests a "koala experience."

I was honored to open the conference in Kansas City as the keynote speaker. My biographical sketch in the program had the usual litany, but (to my surprise) concluded with: "His latest accomplishment for the Topeka Zoo has been the month-long visit of K'Bluey, the San Diego Zoo's famous koala!"

At the close of my presentation I expressed to the delegates how excited we were about their upcoming post-conference tour to the World Famous Topeka Zoo. I outlined the activities planned and mentioned, "We will have a special surprise for you."

This prompted squeals of delight from the audience. I suspect they *assumed* we had somehow arranged to keep the koala a bit longer, and they would get to see K'Bluey. But that is *not* what I said. Once again, my exact words were, "We will have a special surprise for you."

K'Bluey *had* departed our zoo as scheduled, but we kept everything in place, just as though he was still there: all of the graphics, the videos, the exhibit itself, even the "Shhh . . ." sign.

On the morning of July 22, 1986 as our guests were en route from Kansas City to Topeka, we made final preparations for their "special surprise." The remaining eucalyptus leaves were removed from the cooler and properly positioned in the exhibit. So were the actual samples of K'Bluey's droppings, meticulously collected on his final days with us. As a finishing touch we carefully placed a stuffed koala (in sleeping posture), the size and likeness of K'Bluey, in his favorite spot among the eucalyptus.

PERFECT!

Then I proceeded to the main entrance and awaited the busses. When the visiting docents arrived a huge sign welcomed them, the red carpet was rolled out, and I handed each docent a long stemmed carnation. The weather was ideal, our staff had the zoo sparkling, and our docents greeted delegates with warm and gracious hospitality.

Despite the polite interest shown by everyone in our planned activities, anticipation of the "special surprise" was building, and I knew we could not wait any longer. As the group assembled outside the koala building, I heard comments like, "Oh, thank you, Gary; thank you," and "This is so exciting," and "I just can't believe it," and "Oh, Gary—you were so sweet to arrange this."

OH, NO! What was I doing? My mind flashed back to my initial thoughts: that this was a dirty trick, and that these were truly nice people. Had I gone too far?

But there was no turning back. The crowd flowed quietly through the traffic pattern and respectfully into the koala exhibit. They stretched and strained to get a glimpse of fur within the green leaves, and when they did they oohed and aawed. One woman even exclaimed, "Oh! He moved!"

I did not know how to feel. Thrilled that it was so successful? Ashamed that it was so successful? Or both?

It had been my intention all along to fess up, and now was the moment of truth. As the group exited the building, I stood on a park bench and asked them to gather around. I looked into a sea of happy faces and said: "And now, the special surprise I told you about . . . that was not K'Bluey, but a stuffed koala."

I half expected to be thrown into the nearby Water Bird Lagoon, but to my relief laughter erupted from the crowd! There were some friendly boos and hisses amid shouts of "We should have known better," and "I suspected something," and "It was fun, anyway," even "We still love you, Gary."

Thank heavens zoo people have a great sense of humor, so this "surprise" did not spoil their day at our zoo. In fact, they could not wait to return to their own zoo and tell the story of the "phony K'Bluey."

After the post-conference tour we received dozens of letters. I'll share two.

TULSA ZOO DOCENT COUNCIL

July 26, 1986

Dear Gary,

Thank you very much for a delightful visit to your zoo. The carnations were a wonderful touch.

I had been looking forward to visiting the World Famous Topeka Zoo ever since you spoke at my docent graduation, and I was not disappointed. The Rain Forest is my idea of a perfect hideaway. I could sit in that peaceful place all day long.

A couple of messages from T-town – Carolyn Dewberry wants to know if you received your Cowabunga pins and Barbara says you are still not forgiven for the "Koala caper."

Thanks for a great time from all of us in Tulsa.

Sincerely,

Robyn Bohls

GREATER LOS ANGELES ZOO ASSOCIATION

July 25, 1986

Dear Gary,

What a delightful host you are. You and the Docents made us feel so welcome and pampered and we had a marvelous time. From the carnation when we arrived to the home baked muffins and champagne punch to you spending the entire day with us—everything was so special. The extra effort you put in to keep the Koala exhibit was great. I don't think there are many zoo directors who would refrigerate Eucalyptus leaves and save feces to put on the "fun show" you put on.

Max pounding on the glass (in our face) gave us a real gorilla encounter and will never be forgotten.

The trip to Forbes Field and seeing the Asian Horses was a special memory and we will remember your thoughtfulness in arranging it.

Sincerely,

Jeannie Collier

So, despite my pangs of conscience, the marsupial masquerade was a success . . . and maybe *not* such a dirty trick after all.

Why God Made Madagascar

"During your time at the Topeka Zoo, which was your favorite project?"

Back when I was still the zoo director, a similar question always focused on my favorite *animal*. But after retirement, the subject had changed to my favorite *project*. And that was good.

My tenure spanned a quarter-century (1963-1989), and thanks to a great staff, a supportive governing authority and an especially responsive community, the zoo was fortunate to be involved in numerous projects.

Some were not glamorous, but certainly necessary: filling in the old abandoned Gage swimming pool to build the zoo parking lot; developing service areas, staff quarters, maintenance and storage facilities; and providing improved amenities for zoo visitors, such as walkways, benches, guardrails, rest rooms, food service, and landscaping.

Many projects were "in-house," accomplished with Park Department and zoo labor (with support funding from Topeka Friends of the Zoo). Examples were converting the old greenhouse into the Animal Kingdom Building, the old concession stand into a nocturnal exhibit, and an abandoned power station into quarters for a cassowary, as well as building the zebra-camel barn, and constructing moats for zebra, greater kudu and gemsbok antelope.

Probably the most amazing project was the Australian Building, an **all-volunteer** effort through the Topeka Friends of the Zoo in 1966. It was designed by architect Bob Jones; nearly three dozen donors contributed materials; labor and construction were provided by eleven members of the Topeka Trades Council, and thirteen members of the Topeka Division, Kansas Builders' Chapter, Associated General Contractors. It was *more* than amazing, and reflective of the surging community spirit in support of the zoo.

HEY! Already we have some worthy nominees for a favorite project, and we haven't mentioned the Water Bird Lagoon and Gibbon Islands, the off-exhibit Conservation and Propagation Center, or any of the major capital improvements that have made a lasting impact on our zoo.

The Animals and Man Building, opened in 1966, enabled the zoo to exhibit elephants, giraffes, hippos and great apes for the first time. For over four decades it served the zoo and community well, and in 2007 was doubled in size to provide expanded and improved facilities for the pachyderms.

The first-of-its-kind Tropical Rain Forest opened in 1974 and won a national zoo exhibit award. Discovering Apes opened in two phases; the unique orangutan treetops forest in 1981, and Gorilla Encounter with its one-of-a-kind glass tunnel in 1985.

Each and every project has been special, with its own challenges (from design to financing), its own rewards, and a sense of accomplishment.

Hence, it is *very* difficult, if not impossible, to pick my favorite zoo project. But if forced to do so, I would have to say . . . oh, geeze. . . Lions Pride, dedicated in 1989.

Why? *Not* because it was my last project, and *not* because it features the "King of Beasts," and *not* because of the dynamic lion/visitor relationship. Certainly all of the above are true and no doubt influence my choice.

Lions Pride edged out the other projects *because* it was the first major project in the history of our zoo to be funded almost entirely by the community. Truly a team effort, success was achieved by the combined forces of the Topeka Zoological Foundation, Friends of the Topeka Zoo and private contributions . . . many, *many* private contributions.

It was a list of over 300 names! Yes, we had companies and organizations, professional associations and foundations, memorial gifts and even the Ringling Brothers Barnum & Bailey Circus! But we had sooo many families, couples and individuals, too. It was most impressive, and we thanked *all* who had been involved in the project in a separate edition of the Lions Pride brochure.

For major donors, I felt it would be appropriate to give them permanent recognition at the zoo. Certainly it was deserved, and hopefully would serve as a stimulus for others to support the zoo.

I thought of the many ways I had seen donors acknowledged at various institutions: museums, hospitals, libraries, universities . . . even other zoos. Some were innovative, but most were disappointingly dull and routine. Whatever we did had to be distinctive, unique and memorable. After all, this was for *Lions Pride* at the WORLD FAMOUS TOPEKA ZOO, and these donors were **very special!**

It should be prominently located in relation to the exhibit, where everyone would see it. Since it would be outside, it should be of a material that could withstand the punishing elements of our four-season climate. And it should require little, if any, maintenance.

Bronze! That was the answer.

But, something other than the standard plaque. What could we do? Lions were from Africa . . . hmmm . . . that's it! The African continent cast in bronze, with donors' names in raised letters. SUPER! I had never seen anything like *that!*

Fortunately Topeka is home to the Degginger Foundry, with three generations of craftsmanship, an international reputation, and work represented around the world.

I had spent a lot of time at Degginger Foundry during the casting of the heroic-sized lion sculpture, "GENESIS." It was an involved and detailed process, but oh, so fascinating!

Donor Randy Austin had such an appreciation for fine art, especially sculpture. Sculptor Dennis Anderson was cognizant of portraying the lion realistically. And foundry artist Tim Degginger never ceased to amaze me with the breadth and depth of his insight and knowledge—from the chemistry of bronze to the poetry of Robert Frost to the philosophical assessment of artistic expression in society.

Tim said the African continent concept was feasible, but to include so many names, the finished work would be over five feet tall! We did a mock-up to lay out the names. There were *dozens* of names: individuals, couples, families, companies, firms, organizations—and what a complicated procedure to make them all fit. It was worse than an intricate jig-saw puzzle. We'd switch some from the Okavango Delta to the Sahara Desert, or move others from Uganda to Namibia. Once they were all placed we had the critical task of proofreading them, again and again, to check spellings, placement and type of punctuation, etc. It was so important that the donors' personal and business names were correct, especially when they were to be cast in bronze.

Satisfied at last, work proceeded. As soon as it was ready Randy, Dennis and I met Tim at the foundry to see the finished product. It was stunning! The raised names stood out against a green background over the entire continent. It was a work of art in its own right, and without question would be the most striking and beautiful of any form of donor recognition.

Even though there would be no way to change a misspelling at this juncture, while the other guys gazed in admiration I could not help but read each and every name one more time.

WHEW! They were all correct.

But wait a minute. Where was the law firm of Goodell, Stratton, Edmonds, & Palmer? They were significant donors, involved with Lions Pride from the beginning, and one of their partners was a member of the Board of Trustees of the Topeka Zoological Foundation (who were paying for this bronze African continent). I knew they were on there . . . they *had* to be on there . . . but where?

"Don't panic," I told myself, and started one more careful and deliberate read of each and every name. I went from Cairo to Cape Town and all points between. This firm simply was *not* on the continent! How could I have possibly missed them? It was *my* responsibility, and I had been *so* careful, lying awake at nights dreading such a possibility.

A pall befell me. I felt faint and sat down, horrified. By now Randy, Dennis and Tim were celebrating, beers in hand. They noticed my dazed condition and sensed something was wrong . . . terribly wrong. "What is it?" they asked in unison.

As if in a bad dream, I replied, "Goodell, Stratton, Edmonds, & Palmer are not listed."

Immediately Randy and Tim recognized the gravity of the situation. Dennis, however, with artistic aplomb, took a swig and simply said, "Madagascar."

MADAGASCAR? Of course! We (I) were (was) saved! That *wonderful* island, just across the Mozambique Channel in the Indian Ocean, is *almost* **always** depicted on maps of Africa. YES! Those four names of this important donor law firm *would* fit on Madagascar.

Tim had his staff cast Madagascar, and when the bronze African continent was erected at Lions Pride, there it was, as though it had been part of the original plan all along.

The Topeka Zoological Foundation hosted a reception at the zoo for the unveiling and dedication of this magnificent plaque honoring major donors to Lions Pride. All the partners of Goodell, Stratton, Edmonds, & Palmer were there. They thanked me for featuring their firm on Madagascar, since this off-set island caught everyone's eye, and would be read first. They assumed this was intentional and not an afterthought.

I smiled and observed, "That is why God made Madagascar."

The Way We Were

I am blessed to have had a career in the world of zoos. It was both my chosen vocation and my avocation. I am particularly fortunate to have been associated with so many remarkable zoo personalities—professional colleagues as well as staff teammates—during the golden age of zoos.

It was a time of spirit and energy, of dedication and sincerity. It was a time of camaraderie and jocosity—while we took seriously our responsibilities for the animals and our visitors, we did not take *ourselves* seriously. Shared humor and inside jokes strengthened our bonds. You have already read several examples—the Zoo Goof Award and my visit to a Mythical Zoo among them.

Faithful reader, thank you for remaining with me up to this juncture. Your reward now is an insight into the weird and wonderful sense of humor that prevailed in zoobiz circa 1960-1990.

*****

While Topeka is the capital of Kansas, Wichita is the largest city in the state. The two communities are about 127 miles apart and connected by a lovely drive through the scenic Flint Hills under a huge expanse of prairie sky. In Wichita the old Central Riverside Park Zoo was a municipal operation. In 1963 the Junior League and Junior Chamber of Commerce formed the Wichita Zoological Society, which started a campaign for a new zoo with the slogan, "Boo Hoo! We Need a New Zoo!" A bond issue passed in 1966 and the county of Sedgwick committed to develop a regional zoo. The sponsoring group was then called the Sedgwick County Zoological Society. In 1967 Ron Blakely, then Associate Director of Brookfield Zoo in Chicago, came to Kansas to build and direct the Sedgwick County Zoo for the Wichita metro area. I knew Ron as a competent zoo professional, and was delighted he would be our neighbor. I also considered him a sage with great wisdom and a sharp wit. One of his favorite expressions was, "Zoos are a window to the world of wildlife."

Over the years I had fun teasing Ron, and his successor Mark Reed, about the parallel development of our zoos. Every time we developed a major exhibit in Topeka, they would build a similar one in Sedgwick County, but theirs was always bigger and better! We built the Large Mammal Building, they built an African Savannah; we built the Tropical Rain Forest, they built a Jungle Building; we built Lions Pride, they built a Pride of the Plains; we built the Gorilla Encounter, they built a Downing Gorilla Forest. And every time I attempted a practical joke on Ron Blakely, he would come back with one that was, yes, bigger and better. (Remember, Ron was the one who sent me a key for our escaped monkeys so they could return to their exhibit each morning!)

To build the Sedgwick County Zoo from scratch, Ron started with 212 acres of bare land, and for a number of years he was a zoo man without a zoo. To satisfy his need to associate with animals he would visit us in Topeka on a regular basis. If something special was happening at our zoo, I'd let him know.

Topeka was one of the first zoos to breed trumpeter swans. They nested on the bank of our Water Bird Lagoon, not far from the visitors' path. When they laid their first egg, I was impressed (and surprised) by its size—it was huge! Not as big as an ostrich egg, but so much larger than I expected. I called Ron and told him he had to see this egg to believe it.

A few days later he popped into my office and said, "I want to see that *big* trumpeter swan egg you've raved about." So off we went to the lagoon. As we approached, I noticed that instead of a swan *on* the nest, there was what appeared to be a GIGANTIC egg *in* the nest. What the___? Ron casually observed, "Wow, Gary; that *is* a big egg."

It was not an egg . . . it was a watermelon painted white! Ron had safely placed the real egg in an incubator at the proper temperature and substituted his version! After a good laugh we put the real egg back in the nest, the swans continued incubation, and the egg hatched on schedule. That was not, however, the end of the story. A few days later Ron sneaked into my office and left on my desk . . . a hard-boiled chicken egg—painted like a watermelon!

When the Sedgwick County Zoo opened, one of the bird species that Ron exhibited was the ground hornbill. A turkey-sized bird from Africa, it has a large, pointed beak and is one of the few birds with *eyelashes*. I knew Ron had surplus specimens, so I dropped him a line that simply read, "Send me a ground hornbill."

No answer. Sometime later I sent another note that read, "Send me a ground hornbill." Still no answer. And again, "Send me a ground hornbill."

Not long after the last message was sent I returned to the zoo from a meeting at the Park Department to learn that Ron had stopped by and left something for me. On my desk was a note that stated, "Here is your *ground* hornbill," and next to it a plastic bag full of raw hamburger meat . . . and a set of false eyelashes!

In a related incident, Ron and his staff successfully reproduced Siamese crocodiles in their Jungle Building. On a visit to the Sedgwick County Zoo I saw the hatchlings. They were exquisite little creatures that I thought would be ideal for our Tropical Rain Forest. On my return to Topeka I wrote to Ron and requested that he send us a pair of Siamese crocs.

Sure enough within a month a live animal shipping crate arrived marked "Siamese crocs." Inside I found two earthenware crocks conjoined by their handles! I should have expected it.

As Ron continued development of the Sedgwick County Zoo, unexpected construction delays sometimes resulted in facilities not quite ready when new animals were scheduled to arrive. In one instance he was to receive a tiger from the zoo in Erie, Pennsylvania and asked if we could house it for awhile. We had space available and were happy to assist.

When Ron's new exhibit was ready we started preparing the tiger for shipment. The procedure to condition her would take about a week. First, we connected the shipping crate from Erie adjacent to our exhibit so the tiger could freely move from one to the other. Next we fed the tiger in the crate to condition her to go in and out. Then we placed bedding in the crate so the tiger would feel comfortable resting or sleeping in it.

The scheduled day of shipment arrived and a crew from the Sedgwick County Zoo was at our zoo early in the morning. Our staff placed food in the crate and when the tiger stepped in, they gently dropped the door behind her and locked it. Everything worked beautifully, just as planned.

The crate was then placed securely in the bed of the Sedgwick County Zoo's heavy-duty truck, ready to go. As their crew prepared to depart, one of our keepers exclaimed, "Look! There's an opossum in the crate!" Sure enough, a wild opossum from Gage Park had slipped through the bars into the shipping crate during the night and was lying on its back, mouth agape, in the bedding. Was it dead? No—it was just "playing possum." And the tiger was completely ignoring it!

What to do? The only way to get the opossum out of the crate was to uncrate the tiger back into the exhibit. If the tiger moved out of the crate we'd *never* get her back in that day . . . or the next. We would have to start the conditioning procedure all over again, which would take another week or more. The Sedgwick County Zoo team was eager to get on the road, and their zoo staff in Wichita was expecting the tiger *today*. All of the necessary paperwork was dated *today.* Oh, geeze!

Everyone looked at me. I looked at the tiger, oblivious to the opossum. I looked at the opossum, feigning death. (I wished at that moment that *I* could feign death.) I knew this was a survival trait that occurred, not just with opossums, but among some other mammals as well as birds, snakes and insects. Zoologists seem to think it is comparable to fainting or temporary paralysis, a reaction controlled by the nervous system.

Everyone was looking at me for a decision. I gave the situation **very serious** consideration. Trusting to my instincts and the ways of nature, I made a decision . . . to proceed. My judgement was sound. Both the tiger *and* the opossum made the trip in great shape.

The Sedgwick County Zoo returned the opossum to Topeka. The accompanying letter I received from Ron was "classic Blakely," and I can't help but chuckle every time I read it. His letter follows on the next page.

SEDGWICK COUNTY ZOOLOGICAL SOCIETY

March 11, 1982

Gary K. Clarke
Topeka Zoological Park
635 Gage Boulevard
Topeka KS 66606

Dear Gary:

You guys never cease to amaze me with your thoughtful
consideration of animals. I thought that providing
ice cubes for the polar bears to cool their sweltering
buns on was the epitome but then you all come along with
the ultra humane concept of providing a traveling companion for our tiger. Fantastic!!! and it really works!!

The opposum that your staff put in the crate with our
tiger made all the difference in the world. That tiger
did not look even the least bit lonely when she arrived
here.

I know so little about such matters that I guess, if the
idea had occurred to me, I would have worried that the
tiger might have eaten the opossum. Obviously you
folks realized that a tiger has more sophisticated
taste buds than some Georgians do.

We are returning herewith your opossum. I wanted to get
him right back to you because I have no way of telling
but what you have another trip scheduled for him in the
immediate future.

I hope that everything is satisfactory anent arrangements
to repay you for your care of the tiger. If not, please
do not hesitate to let me know right away.

And thanks again for another illuminating lesson in the
proper handling of our four-footed friends. If we keep
our eyes open for these little clues to proper animal
husbandry perhaps, someday, we too can become "world
famous."

Sincerely yours,

R.L. Blakely
Director

P.S. We didn't know the opposum's
name. We've nicknamed him
"Lucky."

Area Code 316 942-2212 • Wichita, Kansas 67212 • 5555 Zoo Boulevard

The huge Great Plains Grizzly reigned supreme in this area before the coming of white man. Capable of preying upon full grown bison, this magnificent creature and his fellow plains dwellers, the Indian, treated each other with respect. The fearlessness of the bear made him vulnerable to the white man's guns and he was probably the first wild animal to be exterminated in Kansas. We have used his footprint to remind us that he is no more, and that the bear family is an endangered group the world over. The outline of the Sedgwick County Zoo encloses the print to indicate that zoos are often the last refuge that an ever-increasing human population will allow the vanishing wildlife of the world.

But I could not let it stand at that . . .
I had to respond, and did so with the following letter:

18 March 1982

R.L. Blakely, Director
Sedgwick County Zoo
5555 Zoo Blvd.
Wichita, KS 67212

Dear Ron:

Oh my gosh!

I can't believe it!

Your crew was good enough to return the opossum last Sunday, but
you sent the wrong animal back!

As I understood it, you folks picked up an opossum from the Erie
Zoo which we held on deposit for you until your new Marsupium
Exhibit was ready. Last week when your people came up we prepared
one of our heavy duty shipping crates and carefully loaded your
opossum for the trip to Sedgwick County. Based on our extensive
experience with captive wild animals and our in depth knowledge
of animal behavior during shipment, we thought it would be good to
provide a traveling companion for the opossum during the trip--
thusly we sent the tiger along, expecting full well that you would
return the tiger to us at first opportunity.

Well, what's done is done, and since you seem so happy with the
tiger, why don't you folks just go ahead and keep it. We appreciate
your assigning a nickname to "Lucky"; that he may be but I suspect
that he's just good at playing 'possum.

Sincerely,

Gary K. Clarke
Director

GKC/dlb

We released Lucky back into the wilds of Gage Park. But three years later we had another opossum incident. Our new Gorilla Encounter exhibit was nearly ready to open and we had just put the finishing touches on the landscaping in the spacious outdoor moated yard. As we stood on the public path to get the "zoo visitors' perspective," lo and behold there was an opossum in the exhibit! Could it be Lucky? Maybe, but no way of telling for sure. Probably it was another wild specimen from Gage Park. But—we quickly grabbed a camera and took a picture of this little teeny-weeny opossum in this GREAT BIG EXHIBIT. We sent a copy to Ron Blakely and said this was Lucky's new home, and invited him to see our spectacular new exhibit, "The World of the Opossum."

*****

When the zoo profession was much smaller and every zoo director in North America knew every *other* zoo director by first name, there was strong rapport among colleagues, especially when it came to helping each other acquire the necessary and appropriate animals. A monthly "Animal Exchange List" was circulated to all zoos and aquariums listing surplus animals each institution had available as well as those animals sought. Baby animals born in your zoo grew up and frequently would be relocated to another zoo. If one member of a pair was lost an effort was made to acquire a new mate. The exchange list was extremely helpful.

While there was a dollar value assigned to each animal, and sometimes they were bought and sold, most zoos preferred to trade (or loan) for two reasons. First, many zoos had limited or non-existent purchase budgets. Second, if an animal was sold, the proceeds usually did *not* go to the zoo, but rather to the city general fund or some such thing.

Once again, while this was serious business, it sometimes generated a laugh. A good example would be that of one monkey with a distinguishing characteristic that we had at Topeka Zoo, and wanted to make available on the list. It was an adult male Moor macaque, an Old World species from Celebes and adjacent islands in Indonesia. They have thick-set sturdy bodies that approach baboons in form. Primarily black in color, Moor macaques are noted to be active and mischievous. This particular specimen had a non-flexible digit on his right hand—I really don't know how or why this was so. In any case, he would show off to visitors by jumping to the front panel of his enclosure and grabbing the mesh tightly with clenched fists (except, of course, for the non-flexible digit, his *digitus impudicus*).

As always, I wanted to be forthright with my colleagues, so when I enumerated the qualities of this individual monkey as surplus for the Animal Exchange List I noted: "Moor macaque, adult male, good health, perfect specimen except for stiff middle finger on right hand. Draws big crowds on Sunday afternoon." The response was overwhelming! And since every other zoo seemed to want this unique character, we decided to keep him!

*****

Prior to the public opening of a major new exhibit, it was customary in the zoo world to host a preview for professional colleagues. They wanted to see it, you wanted to show it off, and it was a chance to poke fun at yourself and each other. Here's how the invitation read for our Tropical Rain Forest preview.

Wanna drink? Wanna look at Gary Clarke's
new plumbing? Wanna see how the largest
waterfall in Kansas makes it impossible
to hear a Docent lecture?

Wanna come and share our joy and pride
(and a few mistakes) by being among the
first persons to preview the World Famous
Topeka Zoo's new

TROPICAL RAIN FOREST

Join other Zoo folks on a special preview
of the new facility. Then pick it apart
and harass Gary.

We'll booze and food 'ya . . . but we need
to know if you'll join us on Tuesday, 21
May 1974. Just so we'll buy enough cheap
liquor and celery, please write or call

Nancy Cherry
no later than Friday, 10 May 1974.

The R.S.V.P.'s were often humorous. Bill Conway, General Director of the New York Zoological Society simply wrote: "I wanna but I canna."

Then there was Steve Clarke (yes, my brother), who wrote the following:

FORT WORTH ZOOLOGICAL PARK
Fort Worth, TX 76110

Dear Nancy:

Yes, I wanna drink. No, I don't wanna look at Gary's plumbing. Yes, I wanna see the largest waterfall in Kansas and try to hear a Docent.

Yes, I wanna share your joy and pride (but not your mistakes, I have enough). No, I don't wanna pick it apart but I wanna harass Gary. Why don't you buy good liquor and cheap celery?

I'm sorry but I won't be able to join you for the Tropical Rain Forest celebration. I do plan on seeing it later in the summer.

Sincerely,
Steven L. Clarke
Mammal Supervisor

As might be expected, Ron Blakely's response was . . .well . . . Ron Blakely.

SEDGWICK COUNTY ZOOLOGICAL SOCIETY
Wichita, KS 67212

Dear Nancy:

Do I wish to come to the Grand Opening of Topeka's Rain Forest? Aren't rain forests where one contracts jungle rot, elephantiasis and malaria? Isn't one apt to be molested by a tanager with the blood lust?

May I bring some other Wichitans with me? When should I get there? Will you accept, as a donation, a breeding pair of Tsetse flies? Can I have some Cheez-whiz on my celery? Can I sit up front to watch John Wortman streak from waterfall to baobab tree during the height of the ceremonies? Is this the Topeka in Kansas? Isn't zoo business just a real groovy kick?

My advice to you is that you don't answer the above questions because if you do I'll be there and if I am there I'll naturally feel it incumbent upon me to foul up the proceedings in every way possible. After all, I owe Gary that much!

Sincerely,
R. L. Blakely
Director

To celebrate the success of the Tropical Rain Forest, editor Nancy Cherry and I prepared a special double issue of *ZOO Magazine*—the first issue to use full color photographs (thanks to the Topeka Friends of the Zoo). We extolled the virtues of the exhibit, and mentioned how unique it would be for visitors during a Kansas winter to step into a tropical paradise. In addition to being mailed to TFOTZ members, the magazine went to zoos and aquariums around the world. This prompted compliments, usually with requests for additional copies, and sometimes a tongue-in-cheek tribute to the exhibit itself. For example, the following letter from Jack Throp, the zoo director in Honolulu, Hawaii.

HONOLULU ZOO – KAPIOLANI PARK
Honolulu HI 96815

Dear Gary and Nancy:

You have done a superb job on the Rain Forest special issue, really superb! I would like to keep the copy you have sent me for my own library. Could I have two additional copies, one for the Zoo library and one for our Curator?

I have a great deal of admiration for the skill and enterprise that you have shown in creating a Rain Forest in Topeka.

On the other hand, I must admit to not much sympathy with the endeavor. If your zoo wasn't so badly situated in the first place, you wouldn't have to be creating artificial environments. If one would only think of these things first. For instance, my great ambition is to capsulate a Kansas winter . . . showing groundhogs and squirrels struggling for survival, eating up meager stores of soggy popcorn and salted peanuts, the wind howling, snow swirling, blue-nosed keepers, and frozen water lines. Unfortunately, I haven't yet figured out a means of keeping the exit doors from freezing solidly closed or for getting people to want to go in in the first place.

Still, I suppose simply because a thing is totally impractical, like Rain Forests in a Kansas winter, there is no reason why somebody shouldn't prove that it can be done.

Sincere Aloha,

J. L. Throp
Director of Zoo

We had so many humorous happenings associated with the opening of Gorilla Encounter that the newspaper featured them in a column entitled " . . . and that's life."

The Topeka Capital-Journal
Tuesday, May 28, 1985

Gorilla gag gifts for zoo director

By Kathy Flanders
Capital-Journal staff intern

The opening of the Gorilla Encounter at the Topeka Zoo thrilled Gary Clarke, zoo director, but that's not what he's been smiling about recently.

The exhibit caused excitement not only in Topeka, but all through the zoo world, and zoo directors and Topeka zoo staff showed Clarke their enthusiasm through unusual gifts.

The staff prepared for the opening day of the exhibit with a breakfast at 6 a.m.

They also prepared a veterinary card for Clarke as a joke, and gave him a prescription bottle with an aspirin about two inches long for the headache he would get that day.

One of the staff also took a picture of the empty parking lot at 6 a.m. and gave it to Clarke with the caption: "The calm before the storm."

"Nearly 22,000 people came that day," Clarke said. "That's not only a record for our zoo, but for any zoo our size."

Directors from other zoos joined in with gag gifts.

Dave Zucconi, director of the Tulsa Zoo, searched until he found an out-of-date gorilla joke book to give Clarke.

"In the zoo world I'm known for my corny jokes," Clarke said.

Clarke collects zoo and animal neckties from all over the world. One gift was given to Clarke early—about six years ago. But he put it away until the opening of the exhibit.

Warren Thomas, director of the Los Angeles Zoo, gave him the tie.

"It's a hand painted gorilla tie," Clarke said. "I vowed never to wear it unless the exhibit opened."

The original concept for the exhibit came 10 years ago. When the exhibit opened recently, Clarke pulled the tie out, and put it on.

Clarke's favorite gift came from Ron Blakely, director of the Sedgwick County Zoo in Wichita.

"We call ourselves the world famous Topeka Zoo," Clarke said. "He gave me an award—a kazoo with two peas hanging from it. The front of the

trophy had the phrase: 'The World Famous Two Pea Kazoo.' It's probably the only one like it in the world."

Clarke said the response from the community to the exhibit has been gratifying, but the gifts and thought behind them mean a lot to him.

"Part of the fun of opening the exhibit is the response from our staff and the zoo world.

"It has really brightened our day."

*****

After the triumphant opening of the Gorilla Encounter, I became absorbed in the concept and design of Lions Pride. I wanted it to be innovative, particularly with respect to the interaction between lions and visitors. I had shared some of my ideas with various colleagues, including Peter Karsten, Executive Director of the Calgary Zoo, Botanical Garden & Prehistoric Park in Alberta, Canada. Peter was not only an eminent zoo director, he was an accomplished artist as well . . . and he had an engaging sense of humor. The following was his suggestion for the Ultimate Lion Exhibit.

CALGARY ZOOLOGICAL SOCIETY

P. O. Box 3036, Station "B"
Calgary, Alberta, Canada T2M 4R8
Telephone (403) 265-9310

CALGARY ZOO, BOTANICAL GARDEN & PREHISTORIC PARK

27 January 1986

Gary K. Clarke
Director
Topeka Zoological Park
635 Gage Blvd.
Topeka, Kansas 66606

Dear Gary:

Enclosed is a design illustration of interactive events of the ultimate lion exhibit.

When I started at our Zoo, we had a fabulous display which really involved people, keepers and the cats. The carnivores had an extraordinary repertoire of entertainment besides reaching out through the bars trying to grab the keepers as they pushed the wheelbarrel along. It was indisputedly one of the greatest thrills we could ever offer to zoo visitors. I believe that the lions were totally in control. They would make the keepers jump and squirm and the visitors laugh and then make the visitors jump and squirm and the keepers laugh, while the lions were smiling all the time.

Our present exhibit does not offer these wonderful elements and, if interaction is what you want, I suggest you build one of these outdated lion cages, as we destroyed them a decade ago.

There will be no charge for this consultant service.

Sincerely,

Peter Karsten
Executive Director

PK:jeh

 Accredited by the American Association of Zoological Parks and Aquariums

The Ultimate Interactive Lion Exhibit

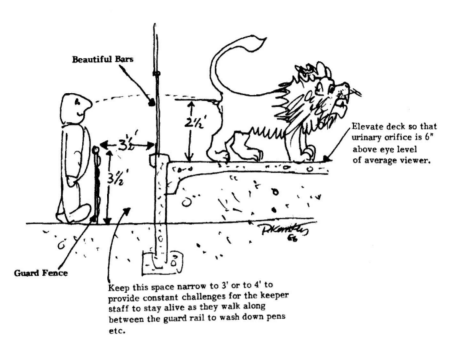

Beautiful Bars

Elevate deck so that urinary orifice is 6" above eye level of average viewer.

Guard Fence

Keep this space narrow to 3' or to 4' to provide constant challenges for the keeper staff to stay alive as they walk along between the guard rail to wash down pens etc.

The old fashioned lion cage offered such wonderful 'participaction' involving the lion, the keepers and, most importantly, the visitor.

Fig. 1

Male lion roars and roars.

Fig. 2

People stream to the site and squish up against the guard fence to see the roaring beast.

Fig. 3

Male lion marks his territory.

Keeper runs away as fast as he/she can.

People behave totally disorganized.

Lion has big smile on face.

*****

Richard Naegeli—from his early days in St. Louis to a principal developer of Busch Gardens in Tampa, Florida to Director of the Division of Zoological Gardens in Boston, Massachusetts—was a dear friend and colleague. However, noble reader, please carefully note that in the following correspondence he addressed me *not* as Gary Clarke, but as "Hairy Cluck." And in his signature block he arrogantly claimed to be Director of the "*Universally Famous* Franklin Park Zoo," obviously a direct slam on our affirmed predicated birthright as the "World Famous Topeka Zoo." Oh, such hollow, deceitful, insidious boastfulness on his part!

Also note that my press release referred to Richard Naegeli as "Retched Nakedly." I might add, in all sincerity, that his visiting staff member was a most honorable individual, despite having Retched Nakedly as a boss. The complete written exchange follows (fortunately I had some "Boston Zoological Society" Press Release forms in my blackmail file).

OFFICE OF THE
DIRECTOR

The Commonwealth of Massachusetts
Metropolitan District Commission
Division of Zoological Gardens
Boston 02121

July 1, 1980

Mr. Hairy Cluck
Director
Topeka Zoological Park
635 Gage Boulevard
Topeka, Kansas

Dear Hairy:

This letter will introduce Mr. Charlie Bailey, a member of our supervisory
staff at Franklin Park Zoo. Charlie has worked at Franklin Park for more
than 14 years, is the Zookeeper in charge of our mammal collection, and
will probably try to talk you out of anything he finds appealing in your
zoo.

Should you happen to have a red carpet in Topeka, I should appreciate
your rolling it out for Charlie.

Yours zooly,

Richard G. Naegeli
Director of the Universally Famous
Franklin Park Zoo

BOSTON ZOOLOGICAL SOCIETY
Franklin Park • Dorchester, Mass. 02121 (617) 442-2002

For Release: Immediately

Subject: V.I.P. Visit

For Further Information Contact: Frank Buck

The World Famous Topeka Zoo was recently honored by a visit from Mr. Charlie Bailey, the Keeper-in-Charge of the mammal collection at the Franklin Park Zoo in Boston.

Mr. Bailey was most impressed with the Topeka Zoo and said it was the only one that he had seen that ranked above Franklin Park.

Retched Nakedly, the Director of the Franklin Zoo, had instructed Mr. Bailey to swindle the Topeka Zoo out of anything he could, but Mr. Bailey's high moral principles and professional character would not permit him to do that. In fact, he was appalled that Mr. Nakedly had jokingly referred to the World Famous Gary Clarke as Hairy Cluck.

Mr. Bailey invited Mr. Clarke to Franklin Park once the new Tropical Forest Pavilion is completed. Mr. Clarke said he would do so as he was anxious to see the New England Patriots play a football game in the building.

-30-

While I never received a direct written response from Retched (oops, I mean Richard), I did find a telephone message on my desk that read: "... some guy named 'Nakedly' called from Boston and said he has a press release he's gonna 'shove up your ...' at the next zoo directors conference."

Like I said, such a dear friend and colleague.

*****

Almost daily I would receive requests to present programs—most were local, some were from out-of-town, and quite a few would be from other zoos. The Kansas City Zoo was developing a Speakers' Bureau and asked that I come over to conduct a training session. We agreed on a date. In my confirmation letter to the Kansas City zoo director I made my usual attempt at *in jest* humor, with a ridiculous list of what I would need. Here's my letter.

TOPEKA ZOOLOGICAL PARK
Topeka, KS 66606

26 January 1982

Ernest Hagler, Director
Kansas City Zoological Park
Kansas City, MO 64132

Dear Ernest:

This will confirm my program for your Speakers' Bureau on Thursday evening, 25 March 1982, at 7:00 p.m. in the Loose Park Garden Center.

I don't know that you need a title, but if you do, how about "Zoo Your Thing" or "A Pep Talk on How to Give a Pep Talk" or "Sloth Dung is an Endangered Feces" or whatever.

I will come prepared, but will need some equipment. Could you provide 17 slide projectors, 6 movie projectors, 12 tape decks, 3 P.A. systems, thunder, lightning, and the Kansas City Philharmonic? If, on the other hand, you just cannot provide all of the above, a simple podium will suffice.

Please advise your group that this will be a very serious session and, as a result, I expect you to be on your very best behavior (you so often embarrass me at public gatherings).

Sincerely,

Gary K. Clarke
Director

Ernest responded as follows:

KANSAS CITY ZOOLOGICAL PARK
Kansas City, MO 64132

1 February 1982

Gary K. Clarke, Director
Topeka Zoological Park
Topeka, KS 66606

Dear Gary,

Thanks for your letter confirming 25 March at 7:00 p.m. for your talk to our Speakers' Bureau.

Don't think we need a title – it's been my experience that you rarely stick to the subject anyway!

We have the equipment – we are assuming you can use 16mm projectors (you didn't indicate which type). And, since we didn't have one, we are building a podium. Even though that takes us away from vitally needed maintenance work, you are worth it, Gary.

And, don't worry, I won't embarrass you. In fact, I will take <u>sincere</u> pleasure in introducing you to the audience. I think they ought to know the kind of professional that will be speaking to them – don't you?

Best regards,

Ernest Hagler, Director
Kansas City Zoological Gardens

In all of the time I had known Ernest he impressed me as polite and respectable and not prone to some of the craziness of many of our other colleagues. Boy, did he ever fool me! What he did was so out of character for Ernest.

When I arrived at the venue he *did* have 17 slide projectors, 6 movie projectors, 12 tape decks, 3 P.A. systems, thunder, lightning, as well as an elaborate new podium! And—to top it off—three actual musicians from the Kansas City Philharmonic! Seldom am I at a loss for words, but I must confess, Ernest got me! The audience loved every minute of it.

*****

I know this may sound corny (to use a Kansas phrase), but the staff at the World Famous Topeka Zoo had some of the characteristics of a family. We had sincere concern and regard for each other, and were kindred spirits associated with the stewardship and safekeeping of the animals under our care. I was very pleased with such an ambiance. There was a willingness to put forth extra effort for the zoo, even when the budget would not allow overtime pay, and we were not authorized to grant compensatory time off (this was before bureaucracy stifled such *esprit de corps*).

In my early days at the zoo I would frequently ask for volunteers to stay after the end of the workday to help with a special project. Sometimes it would be mundane—like modifying an old facility; sometimes exciting—like developing a new exhibit; and sometimes unexpected—like unloading an animal because the transporter was delayed and would be late.

A surprising number of people would stay and help. Afterwards, we would adjourn across the street to the Gage Tavern for a cold beer and snacks, with June (the owner/hostess) in attendance. These were great sessions, convivial and informal. Regardless of rank or title, we were all just "zoo people." We'd discuss the day's activities, recent events or accomplishments at our zoo, future projects, or general zoo philosophy.

Before continuing, I must comment on our Zoo Docents. Remember, these were the volunteer ladies (and later, a few gentlemen as well) who had *already* spent countless hours at the zoo in training and conducting tours, not to mention the outreach programs in schools throughout the community. Yet, year in and year out they hosted a Christmas party and a summer picnic for the zoo staff—complete with scrumptious homemade goodies. I always felt that *we* should be hosting a party or picnic for *them!*

From time to time we had staff-only functions. Prior to the public opening (or even the professional preview) of each major exhibit, we would hold after-hours parties just for staff, so we could experience the exhibit *once* as we would never be able to again.

Hence, a fortunate few were able to do such things as swim in the hippo pool before the hippos did, be the first to have sundowners in the Rain Forest, climb in and swing on the orangutan trees, and picnic in the Gorilla Encounter—*not* in the glass tunnel, but in the outdoor habitat area developed for the gorillas. Maybe the most unique activity was in the orangutan exhibit *before* the fabricated trees were installed. It was such a cavernous space with high vertical walls that Mike LaRue and Roger Wilcox used it as a racquetball court.

The hippo pool played an intermittent central role in staff celebrations for many years (always, of course, when the hippos were safely *off* exhibit). On special occasions—be it a birthday, an anniversary, or whatever reason was appropriate—individuals would be swept off their feet and unceremoniously tossed into the hippo pool—fully clothed! Sometimes we even cleaned the pool first.

The best hippo pool incident involved not hippos, but sea lions . . . and Zoo Curator Paul Linger. It was early May 1966. The new Large Mammal Building was not yet open to the public. 'Peka-Sue, the hippo, was the only resident.

Unknown to Paul, two sea lions had arrived late the previous night. Since we did not want to unload them into the Monkey Island moat in the dark, we shifted 'Peka-Sue into her transfer stall and put the sea lions in the hippo pool for just that night.

Each morning at 8:00 am we had a brief staff meeting in the service building for announcements and to advise everyone of the day's activities. On this particular morning I asked Paul to check on 'Peka-Sue. As soon as he left we all gathered around the window to watch him walk across the mall and disappear into the Large Mammal Building. We could just imagine his initial reaction when he looked into 'Peka-Sue's pool and saw two sea lions rather than a hippo.

It did not take long. Paul literally exploded through the front doors and raced back to the service building! We had just resumed our meeting stance when Paul burst into our midst exclaiming: "YOU WON'T BELIEVE IT! YOU WON'T BELIEVE IT!"

The staff all kept a straight face while I quizzically asked Paul, "Believe what?"

"YOU WON'T BELIEVE IT," he repeated in the height of his excitement. "There are *two* **sea lions in the hippo pool!**"

In all seriousness I replied, "I don't believe it."

Then we all broke into peals of laughter while I explained what had happened.

*****

Ken Kawata was born in Japan and entered the zoo world on an internship at the Ueno Zoo in Tokyo. After serving as periodicals editor for the Tokyo Zoological Park Society, he followed his dream and came to America to pursue a zoo career. We first met in 1969 at the national zoo conference in Oklahoma City. I liked his determination and enthusiasm, and offered him a position as a keeper. Ken jumped at the chance. With perseverance he earned his U.S. citizenship, furthered his education, and moved on to curatorial positions in a number of prominent zoos. A recognized zoo historian with many publications to his credit, Ken is most proud of his American zoo career.

During his time in Topeka, Ken was well liked and made many contributions to our zoo. Yet, there was an annual practical joke that we came to expect. On December 7th (Pearl Harbor Day) every year, Ken would let the air out of the tires of all the cars in the zoo staff parking lot. Until . . .

One January day we had a severe winter storm with an exceptionally heavy snowfall. When the Park Department snow plow operator showed up to clean the zoo staff parking lot, a plot formed. Very carefully he dumped load after load of snow on Ken's compact car. At the end of the day Ken stepped out of the service building to discover that his car was nowhere in sight! He knew the general area where he had parked and suspected it was buried under a huge pile of snow, but—there were *many* huge piles of snow! I'll never forget Ken, with a long wooden pole, poking into heaps of snow, trying to locate his car. When I took his picture he smiled and gave me half a peace sign.

It was all in the family.

*****

As youngsters, gorillas Max and Tiffany lived in the primate area of our new Large Mammal Building (my small office was upstairs, above the diet kitchen). Keeper Bill Gage had a great rapport with the gorillas, and while Max was an agreeable individual, Tiffany would try to get away with whatever she could.

During the morning cleaning routine Tiffany would often slip past Bill into the service aisle, dart past the diet kitchen, and silently zoom up the stairs to hide in my office. Since I usually did not hear her ascend the stairs, the first I would know about it was when I heard Bill yelling, "TIFFANY! TIFFANY! Come down here!" I'd look under my desk and sure enough, there was a gorilla. When Bill clomped-clomped up the stairs in his rubber boots, Tiffany would jump into my lap—almost in defiance.

One time she hopped into the empty secretary's chair and sat looking at the typewriter. When Bill popped into my office looking for her, I said: "Oh, that's O.K., Bill. Tiffany's taking a letter."

As Tiffany grew she seemed to become more proficient at eluding Bill. She gradually reached the size where she was too big to fit under my desk or sit on my lap. Eventually, there was a reversal of roles: Bill would come running up the stairs to hide in my office, and Tiffany would be in hot pursuit behind him! Those were the days!

*****

At the World Famous Topeka Zoo we had a great time with names for our animals. Some had a special significance: Max, the gorilla, named after the President of Rotary Club; the hippo, 'Peka-Sue, to rhyme with Topeka Zoo; and Sunflower, the first giraffe born in Kansas, after the state flower. Others had appropriate meanings: "Tembo" was Swahili for elephant; "Twiga" was Swahili for giraffe; and the "Djakarta" in Djakarta Jim, the orangutan, was the capital of Indonesia.

Some animal names were just for fun. You've already met the gnus, Weather and Sports. We also had an otter named Splash Gordon, a ferret named Farahet Fawcett-Majors, a boa constrictor named Julius Squeezer, a jaguar named XKE, a llama named Dalai and another female hippo (born in the Milan, Italy Zoo) named Submarie. And there was Spot, the zebra, and Speed, the giant tortoise. We must not forget the pair of Central American pig-like mammals called the peccary or javelina. Our male was named Gregory Peccary, and the female Olivia de Javelina.

*****

The busiest day in most American zoos was probably the Fourth of July. The most dreaded day in most American zoos was probably April Fool's Day. Why? Primarily, because of the crank telephone calls.

Dear reader, visualize this: you arrive at your place of business on April 1st and on your desk is a phone message to return a call to a Mr. Lyon or Mr. Bayer or Mrs. Fox or even Mr. L.E. Phant. So you innocently call the number. To your surprise (or embarrassment), it is the zoo! And the prankster at the next desk can't stop laughing.

From the zoo's point of view this was no joke. The calls tied up our telephone lines that were needed to conduct daily business, or possibly for an emergency. It was a problem . . . but I had a solution.

Prior to April Fool's Day we lined up volunteers to help us out. I explained that the person calling would *not* be the guilty party. When the call came in, the volunteer would explain to the caller that they were the innocent victim of an April Fool's joke. Invariably the caller knew who did it, and our volunteer asked for the *prankster's* name and address. We would then send to *them* a Topeka Friends of the Zoo membership application and a letter from Mr. Lion or Mr. Bear, stating that since they had so much fun at the zoo's expense, it was only fair that they should support us. And they did!

The World Famous Topeka Zoo strikes again!

*****

Zoos and Aquariums in the U.S.A. are among the most regulated and inspected of institutions. This oversight rains down from the United States Department of Interior, the Convention on International Trade in Endangered Species, our own professional accreditation standards and Species Survival Programs, the United States Department of Agriculture—and all points in between. All zoos are *inspected* and *licensed* by the USDA, and a veterinary inspector can show up unannounced at any time. That was fine with us, as we daily strived to meet and exceed *every* standard, since our self-imposed goals were higher.

Imagine our chagrin at *this* scenario, which is true, as even *I* could not make it up. The USDA inspector unexpectedly appears in the zoo office. Assistant Director Mike LaRue instantly abandons his critical work of the moment to escort the USDA inspector around the zoo. As they emerge from the Tropical Rain Forest, the USDA inspector casts a glance up the mall and observes our adult male greater kudu antelope majestically strolling on the visitors' walk just inside the main entrance. He calls this to Mike's attention and casually inquires, "Do you always have greater kudu bulls free-ranging on the zoo grounds?" To which Mike replies, "Only when a USDA inspection is in process."

Somehow the kudu had overcome our foolproof moat and was exploring the rest of the zoo. And this day of all days! With gentle encouragement the kudu returned safely to his exhibit . . . and we modified the moat.

*****

Hiring the best individuals for our zoo staff was not easy. We had a steady stream of interested and qualified people coming to the zoo every week, as well as applications in the mail from all over the country. But—since we were operated by the City of Topeka, we could not hire directly. *Everyone* had to apply through the personnel department at City Hall. After a screening process, they would select certain candidates to be sent to the zoo for an interview. This was true not just for animal care staff, but for all other positions as well—maintenance, horticulture, even a secretary.

For a number of years I had to depend on secretaries in the Park Department at City Hall *(extremely inconvenient)* and also on my wife Margaret, who was unpaid, but typed correspondence and reports for me at home. When we eventually were able to budget a secretarial position at the zoo, I scheduled interviews in my cramped upstairs office in the Large Mammal Building. This was in the days before computers, but we did have an early model electric typewriter that was pretty snazzy. After I reviewed a candidate's application and explained the duties, we would prepare for the obligatory typing test. One young lady named Sandy sat at the small desk in the little office chair ready to start, then hesitated and said, "This chair is too low." Ever the gallant nobleman to a damsel in distress, I sprang to the rescue and said, "Oh, please, let me adjust that for you."

Sandy stepped aside and I scrambled to my hands and knees under the chair, fumbling heroically with all the unfamiliar mechanisms while making lots of noise. I must confess that I am *not* mechanically inclined at all, even for something as simple as an office chair. At last I stood up, embarrassed (but with macho grease on my hands) and said, "Sorry, I can't seem to fix it." Sandy gave me a polite, consoling smile, but must have been wondering if she would want to work for such an inept boss.

All was not lost, however, as we had in the office a very thick international dictionary. I suggested to Sandy that—just for the typing test—maybe she could sit on the dictionary. She agreed.

As Sandy proceeded with the typing test, I could not help but come up with one of my witty and clever remarks (even though we had just met). So, I said: "Well, I guess this puts you on the seat of knowledge." Without pausing Sandy replied, "Either that, or it makes me a smart ass."

To which I responded, "Forget the test. You're hired!"

*****

When I arrived in Topeka in October 1963 there were four employees to care for the animal menagerie in Gage Park. By August 1966 that number had doubled and a valid zoo had emerged. A professional staff was developing and I felt it was important to document this with an official staff photo. This became an annual event, which evolved into a tradition. And just as you have some funny instances when taking a family photo, we had our share with the "zoo family" pictures as well.

The first photo (in black-and-white) was taken by Henry Gund III, a local photographer who also worked part-time as a reporter/photographer for the *Pictorial-Times,* a local weekly newspaper. Henry loved the zoo and was always seeking "human interest" stories and pictures. When I asked if he would take a staff photo he was thrilled and made a print for each of us.

Since the Large Mammal Building was new, and the elephants were among our first charismatic megavertebrates, we took them outside and grouped ourselves around them. Toka, the smaller elephant, is mostly hidden behind Sunda, the larger elephant. And, yes, that clean-shaven skinny kid squatting beside Sunda is . . . yours truly.

In successive years a zoo staff member served as the photographer: Paul Linger, Mike LaRue, Ron Kaufman among them. Once everyone was in position ("tall ones in back, shorter ones in front") the photographer would fix his camera on a tripod, set the focus, activate the self-timer, and then run to join the group before the shutter clicked. Often he would not make it in time and his backside would appear on one edge of the frame.

In order not to disrupt the daily schedule, we started taking the photo in early morning, before starting time, often with coffee and doughnuts as a "thank you" for everyone coming in early. Invariably staff photo day would be a day off for some people. They were not obligated to come in, but did. Our only real problem was John Wortman, who would sometimes be late. We'd wait as long as practical, but then felt obligated to proceed. On more than one occasion we took a uniform shirt of John's and held it up on a hanger to represent his absence.

The black-and-white images eventually became color, and we tried different locations for our photo from year to year. A favorite setting was the Tropical Rain Forest, especially in cold weather. Due to the high humidity, it was always a challenge to keep the camera lens clear of condensation.

As our annual staff photos accumulated, Mike LaRue displayed them in the zoo administration building under the heading "The Way We Were." It was fun to see the changes from year to year in hairstyles, staff uniforms, zoo logo patches, and personnel.

Many staff started their professional careers in Topeka and advanced to other zoos, while others changed occupations. Whenever one of our alumni would return for a visit, they always paid homage to the wall of staff photos. It was rather like looking at your class picture, and always generated laughter, memories and the inevitable question: "Whatever happened to so-and-so?"

I honestly don't know if Topeka was the only zoo to do an annual staff photo, but we must have been one of the few to have a Zoo Flag. On a white background it featured large black letters that spelled ZOO in our distinctive logo style, and below that the words "World Famous Topeka Zoo." We proudly flew that flag each day just inside the main entrance.

*****

Dear Reader—I must be candid with you. Putting this book together has been a Herculean task for me, and has taken years because of my safari schedule and a desire to spend time with my family. Writing is *work*, and I am *not* truly a writer. Hopefully, as you have read this tome, it has made sense, and the prose seemed to flow effortlessly. If so, don't credit me; credit *everyone* else (and there were many) who had a hand, a finger, an eye, or even an opinion, in the final effort.

I mention all of this only because this section on "Untold Tails" and especially this chapter—"The Way We Were"—flooded my spirit with *so many* wonderful and gratifying memories.

As I reflect on my years in the zoo profession—especially those at the World Famous Topeka Zoo—it not only seems a lifetime ago, but also a dreamlike illusion as well. When you are living "the good old days" you don't realize it. It is only when you reflect decades later that you fully appreciate the events, *and people*, in your life. I am grateful for such wonderful memories . . . and for the way we were.

Part 9

A Zoetic Zoologist Changes Camps

From the dynamic World of Zoos and the astonishing afterglow to Life on Safari and sharing the majesty that is Africa.

Eat Dessert First . . . Life is so Uncertain

—Bumper sticker on
Gary Clarke's Jeep

Courtesy of the Topeka and Shawnee County Public Library   **Art work by Alice C. Sabatini**

Part 9

A Zoetic* Zoologist Changes Camps

The Mountain
The Decision
The Memo
The Response
The Sequel

*Zoetic (adj.-Greek) of or relating to life; living; vital.

The Mountain

As far as one can see,
as far as the entire world,
high and inconceivably white in the snow,
shines the summit of Kilimanjaro!

—Ernest Hemingway

The first time I saw Kilimanjaro, on my initial safari in 1974, I couldn't believe it. We had been in the area for three days, and Kili was always shrouded in clouds. We were in the last hour of our last game drive on the last day of the safari. I was so disappointed and had given up hope. Suddenly the guide shouted, "There it is!" I looked in the direction of the mountain and saw nothing but clouds. Frantic that I would miss it I asked, "Where?"

He answered, "There." I looked again—just clouds. "Where?" I yelled in frustration.

"Not there," he said, pointing to where I was looking across the plains. "But *there*," he exclaimed as he raised his arm to an almost vertical position towards the sky.

OHMIGOD! YES!

I gasped as I saw that huge flat-topped volcanic cone. With a necklace of stratus clouds concealing its base and a halo of cumulus floating above its "wedding cake" peak, the snow covered summit of Kilimanjaro seemed disjointed from the earth and suspended from the heavens, magically floating in the African sky at 19,340 ft. And I knew then that someday I must climb the highest mountain on the continent. Not "because it was there" (an oft stated reason), but because I wanted to stand on the roof of Africa at least once in my life.

Hans Meyer, a German mountaineer, was the first person known to successfully scale Kilimanjaro, and he did so in 1889. To climb Kilimanjaro is to pass through five life zones, from tropical rain forest to permanent snowcap; from the equator to the Arctic Circle, all on a single mountain.

Though the main route is not a "technical" climb, it is rugged. Narrow trails, huge boulders, deep mud, marshland, slick rocks, exposed tree roots, mountain streams, loose scree, and ice present a diverse challenge.

And the weather gods test you to the limit: heat and humidity, heavy rain, pelting hail, burning sun, freezing cold—sometimes all in one day. Crossing the Saddle, or High Desert Zone between Mawenzi and Kibo Peaks, equates to intense solitude and desolation.

I was never very athletic, had never climbed a mountain of any kind, and probably was the least likely candidate to even consider such an endeavor. But I was determined to give it my best shot and had initiated a demanding fitness and training program. For two years (and nearly every day) I had walked several miles carrying a 35-pound backpack in good weather and bad. Since there aren't many hills in Topeka, I climbed steps, backpack and all—sometimes at the State Capitol, but usually in parking garages. I reached a point where I could climb enough steps to equal half the height of the Empire State Building. I felt rather smug until I figured out that Kilimanjaro was about as high as sixteen Empire State Buildings!

In January 1989, at age 49, I fulfilled my goal by attempting to climb Kilimanjaro. The climb took six days and was the most glorious and the most horrible experience of my life—both at the same time! I fell numerous times, was battered and bruised, damaged my toenails to the extent that they later fell off, and lost 12 pounds while consuming 4,000 calories a day.

During our climb we learned of the deaths of two other climbers and watched in silence and reverence as one of them was carried in a body bag down the mountain past us. The other had fallen in the crater.

At the 15,000 ft. rest hut my body was nearly beyond its capabilities, primarily because of lack of oxygen and high altitude sickness. As I attempted the final ascent in the midnight darkness I felt like my shoestrings were tied together and I was breathing with half a lung with a plastic bag over my head. Every few steps I had to stop and rest, sometimes passing out momentarily while leaning on my walking stick.

Eventually I made it to the summit, much to the relief of my guides and climbing companions. But on the descent I collapsed from sheer and utter exhaustion, and had to be carried the rest of the way by the rescue team. Still, I felt a great sense of accomplishment.

I turned 50 on the mountain and although I stood on the roof of Africa, I did not conquer Kilimanjaro.

I conquered myself.

The Decision

A decision weighed heavily on my mind. And I felt miserable. I'd not slept well for several nights. My head was throbbing, my muscles ached, my bones were weary. I was nauseous. There was a terrible pain in my bladder. No, I was not at a stressful city council meeting, fighting for the zoo. I was on Mt. Kilimanjaro in the final throes of my climb.

During my time on the mountain I had a lot of time to think. My first thought was, "Why am I doing this? I'm about to die . . ." My other thoughts rambled on the philosophical, and turned to life itself, and where I was on that journey. Thoughts of family and anticipation of grandchildren; thoughts about the zoo and the increasing frustration of accomplishing hopes and plans; thoughts on Africa and the realization that it was becoming more and more a part of my essential existence. My decision would be of immense importance, and would impact the rest of my life.

Funny how the human mind works sometimes. In these most bizarre circumstances I made the decision to change my life's emphasis from zoos to safaris. Despite feeling so bad physically, I felt so good spiritually.

I always had thought that if/when I eventually "retired" from the zoo I would devote full time to sharing Africa with others. Now the bumper sticker on my Jeep popped into my mind: *Eat dessert first — Life is so uncertain.* That did it!

Certainly I wanted to complete current projects at the zoo, and once off the mountain I needed to do a careful evaluation of my decision. To give up established success and job security was a daring risk for me as I had never been in business for myself. Besides, I really loved the zoo.

Yet, zoos were changing—drastically. The American mind-set on entertainment over learning experiences, competition from shopping malls and self-centered video games, the preponderance of sugar-coated theme parks—all contributed to zoos acting out of character. People visited zoos to see costumed, cartoon personalities instead of live animals, to see Spider Man rather than a real spider, to see robotic dinosaurs as opposed to living prehistoric crocodiles. Why throw this artificiality to the public when zoos were already fascinating and enjoyable?

And the nature of my function as zoo director had undergone a complete metamorphosis. Far beyond being zoologist, exhibit designer and manager, I now dealt with capital campaigns, labor relations, governmental affairs, and a burgeoning bureaucracy. A greater percentage of my time was increasingly devoted to petty policies and procedures, ridiculous rules and regulations, filling out formidable forms, etc. UGH!

At the same time my sentiment for Africa was developing into an all-consuming passion. With each safari I would relinquish a fragment of my soul to this magnificent continent and return home with the spirit of Africa flourishing in my heart.

But two-thirds of my life had been spent as part of the zoo profession. Could I live without this active involvement? Would there be too large a void in my life?

On my return I sat down and did one of those list exercises: you know, where you list all the things you like, and don't like, about a given situation; and then list all of the things you like, and don't like, about an alternate situation. Here's what I found.

List #1
What I liked about zoobiz

> Animals
> Being in the presence of animals
> Watching, studying and learning about animals
> Photographing animals
> Haunting secondhand bookstores for books on wildlife
> People
> Being with people who like animals
> Sharing animals with people
> Helping people learn about animals
> Creating memorable experiences for people
> Working with volunteers
> Interacting with students
> Presenting classroom programs
> Laughing
> Public speaking (about animals)
> Camaraderie with colleagues
> Being able to express myself professionally

List #2.
What I didn't like about zoobiz

> Politics
> Bureaucracy
> Bullshit
> Monthly reports, weekly meetings, daily hassles
> Budget preparation
> Unfair budget cuts
> Hidden agendas
> Petty personality conflicts
> Bids that were over budget
> Construction delays

The Dr. Seuss Syndrome
Being held responsible for things beyond my control
Not being my own boss
Lack of time for family, especially grandchildren

List #3
<u>What I liked about leading safaris</u>

Animals
Being in the presence of animals
Watching, studying and learning about animals
Photographing animals
Haunting bookstores in Africa for books on wildlife
People
Being with people who like animals
Sharing animals with people
Helping people learn about animals
Creating memorable experiences for people
Working with volunteers
Interacting with students
Presenting classroom programs
Laughing
Public Speaking (about animals)
Camaraderie with colleagues
Being able to express myself professionally
Being my own boss
Implementing my own agenda
Working on my own schedule
More time for travel, speaking, consulting and photo exhibits
Lots of time for grandchildren

List #4.
<u>What I didn't like about leading safaris</u>

THIS SPACE INTENTIONALLY LEFT BLANK

So . . . my decision on the mountain was verified. And I have been so fortunate to maintain an association with zoos and colleagues while pursuing life on safari.

They say that climbing Kilimanjaro can be a life-changing experience, and certainly it changed mine. (Actually I climbed Kilimanjaro *twice*—the first and the last time.) Zoos are still a major element in my life and always will be. But there IS life after zoobiz.

The Memo

Date: 11 September 1989

To: Dave Graverson, Acting Director of Parks & Recreation
             Harry "Butch" Felker, Mayor

From: Gary K. Clarke, Zoo Director

Subject: My Retirement

On 1 October 1989 I will complete 26 years (more than half my life) as the Director of the World Famous Topeka Zoo. It has been an honor and a privilege to serve my community in this capacity. Now that Lions Pride is complete and the new Zoo Master Plan is in place, I plan to retire from my position on 31 December 1989. I'm making the announcement now to allow the City to have ample time for a smooth transition in Zoo Administration. I will honor all of my program commitments and community activities between now and the end of the year.

Animals have always been a central focus in my life. The two things I love most (outside of my family) are the Zoo and Africa. I've been so fortunate to have been a part of the Zoo profession for the past 32 years. Now, I want to devote my time to leading safaris, speaking, consulting, writing, photography and other pursuits. My first two grandchildren are expected in October, and I am eagerly anticipating their arrival.

Topeka is a warm and responsive community. I will be forever grateful to the thousands who have shown so much support over the years. The Zoo stands as a tribute to these wonderful people, and I extend my humble thank you.

My home is Topeka and I plan to remain active in community affairs. I will continue my love and support for the World Famous Topeka Zoo, the Friends of the Topeka Zoo, and the Topeka Zoological Foundation. Our Zoo has a bright future, and I am so pleased with the success of Lions Pride, Gorilla Encounter and the Tropical Rain Forest, as well as the Zoo's education and conservation programs.

Yes, I will miss the animals (especially Max, and 'Peka-Sue, and Tembo, and Samburu...). But I will miss the children just as much. I hope, in some capacity, to maintain a continuing communication with the youth of Topeka.

The Response

4-A Wednesday, September 13, 1989

The Topeka Capital-Journal

Opinion

In God We Trust

New safaris for Clarke

After more than a quarter of a century at its helm, Gary Clarke says he has never considered the Topeka Zoo as "my zoo." But in a very real sense, it is his zoo.

The Topeka Zoo is what it is today because of Clarke's vision and leadership. Clarke can say all he wants about the support of the city, the Friends of the Zoo, the Topeka Zoological Foundation and local businesses. But the projects and improvements they made possible originated in Clarke's fine mind.

The Lions Pride exhibit is only the most recent example of Clarke's innovative planning. Before that it was the Gorilla Encounter and the Rain Forest. The lagoon also has been redesigned. And more innovations are being formulated, possibly including an education center.

The zoo population increased since Clarke came in 1963. He introduced elephants, hippopotamuses, giraffes, gorillas and orangutans to the zoo.

Special emphasis has been placed on endangered species. The zoo claims the distinction of being the first in the world to hatch, raise and release into the wild American Golden Eagles. It also has earned acclaim as one of the prime zoos in the nation for the propagation of Asian wild horses.

One testament to the respect that Clarke and the Topeka Zoo have earned is that Topeka was selected to host the koala exhibit a couple of years ago. Only a few zoos were so honored, and most were in big cities.

Topeka Zoo, though small when compared with the famous zoos of San Diego, Chicago and New York, must be the envy of many. It has adapted to the new concept of exhibiting animals, not in cages, but in areas that exemplify their natural habitats. It is a treat for both the animals and the humans who like to watch them.

The credit for that goes to Clarke.

Topekans cannot help but be saddened by the announcement that Clarke will be leaving his post at the end of the year. Although he will be staying in Topeka, he wants to devote more time to other interests, including a safari business.

At the same time, Topekans are thankful that Clarke has stayed as long as he has. The opportunities for Clarke certainly came knocking often enough in the form of more lucrative offers from bigger zoos.

Fortunately, Clarke chose to stay in Topeka. It will be difficult replacing him.

Clarke has earned a special tribute from the city. How about naming a street in Gage Park for him? And the community owes him thanks for his dedicated loyalty all these years. We wish him well.

Both *The Topeka Capital-Journal* and *The Topeka Metro News* carried front page stories about my resignation, as well as follow-up editorials. I was surprised, however, when the *Lawrence Journal-World* carried the following editorial entitled "Appreciated Effort" on January 3, 1990.

Appreciated Effort

Lawrence Journal-World/EDITORIAL

Gary Clarke didn't live or work in Lawrence, but he did have a hand in many hours of enjoyment for residents of Lawrence and Douglas County.

Clarke retired over the weekend as the director of The World Famous Topeka Zoo. The "World Famous" isn't just an adjective; it's part of the zoo's actual name. And even though the Topeka Zoo may not be known around the world, it has, under the direction of Clarke become a popular and appreciated attraction across much of the region.

After 26 years as director, Clarke has stepped down to pursue another passion: Africa. In his zoo work, Clarke, 50, has traveled to Africa many times and now plans to make a living by leading four to six safaris there each year.

Looking back on his years in Topeka, Clarke recalled that when he became director in 1963, the Topeka Zoo was "at a point where it either needed to be closed down or operated at a professional level." Obviously, it wasn't closed down, and Clarke's professional management has brought the zoo back to life. Since he took over, the zoo underwent an expansion that included a large mammal building in the 1960s, a tropical rain forest in 1974, a new gorilla exhibit in 1985 and a new lion facility last year. The zoo had more than 279,000 visitors last year, making it one of the state's top tourist attractions.

Topeka is proud of the zoo and the job Clarke has done. But the zoo is appreciated by residents far beyond Topeka's borders. As Clarke leaves for his adventures in Africa, he should know that Lawrence residents also are grateful for the work he did in Topeka and wish him success in his future adventures.

*****

One of the Topekans I most admired and emulated was Jim Marvin, Director of the Topeka Public Library (an exceptional community institution). Imagine my thrill at his kind remarks.

Friends of the Topeka Public Library
Newsletter – Fall 1989

From the Director's Desk

When I came to the Topeka Public Library to interview for my present job, nearly 23 years ago, the proper dignity of the Library's Fine Arts department was interrupted by the shill cry of a caged bird. I was assured that the bird was legitimately on loan to the Library from the Topeka Zoo and that I must get to know its young director, Gary Clarke.

I did get to know him, and have seen our Library and the Zoo involved in a number of cooperative projects since that time. One of the more unusual undertakings was a bibliography of Australian books and animals contained by both institutions, in proper classified form. On countless occasions, animals have been brought to the Library, to delight and inform our young story hour audiences.

Gary Clarke asserts in the quotes accompanying his retirement coverage, that the completion of planning for the future Zoo encouraged him to make his decision. More incisive, and Zen-like, I thought, was his successful climb of Mt. Kilimanjaro, in his 50th year and the thinking it unleashed in him regarding his life and what his future should be.

For me, and many of us, Kilimanjaro is in Topeka and the problem is to know, or have sense enough to know, where it is, what it is and if we have scaled it. I'm not certain, but somehow I see a shadowy figure coming up that looks like a mountain, one I'd like to climb. It would be a thrill to make it, to rejoice as Gary has done, in a task completed.

Thanks, Gary, for your wonderful work in improving the quality of life in Topeka. We are pleased to know you plan to remain here, where your enthusiasm and inspiration are going to be needed.

—Jim Marvin

*****

Many of the responses were extremely humbling, but none more so than this one.

The Bear Facts Newsletter
Friends of the Topeka Zoo
December 1989

From the editor—Zoo Director Gary Clarke announced Monday, September 11 that he will retire from his post to pursue personal ventures at the end of this year. The news was surprising, since for many of us, Gary Clarke and the Topeka Zoo are synonymous. It's hard to imagine one without the other.

It's like peanut butter without the strawberry jam, or a day without sunshine. A certain zip will be gone, something important will be missing.

Sure life goes on, but what will it be like without Gary to champion our zoo—not only here, but wherever he goes all over the world?

It's interesting to realize that, to many other people in many other places, Gary Clarke **is** Topeka. They associate Topeka with Gary, and vice-versa. That's a wonderful thing. He's really an ambassador, the very best kind.

His delight in everything having to do with wildlife is infectious. Travel brokers would love to have Tour Directors as enthusiastic as he. His laughter and ability to have fun with what he knows spreads to all the people he meets and teaches as our zoo director.

When he gets that gleam in his eye and people know he's about to let them in on a special wild animal joke or story, he makes them feel that the greatest adventure in the world lies just around the next bend in the path at the zoo. Suddenly they find themselves becoming co-conspirators in the race with him to preserve wildlife, not just because it may be the right or good thing to do, but because it matters to them when viewed from Gary's perspective.

Although he doesn't shout his views from the rooftops, still, a person doesn't have to spend much time with him before coming to understand clearly what his beliefs are. He doesn't need to shout about anything, anyway, because the Topeka Zoo stands as a testament to his vision and beliefs about man and animals and how they can live together.

So, just from me, Gary, "It's been a pleasure and a privilege to have seen some of life through your eyes. I can't remember a time since living in Topeka that I haven't known you. Since taking the job as *Bear Facts'* volunteer editor, your wisdom, your support and encouragement have come to mean even more. Your presence has been a special gift."

—Mary Van Petten, Editor

*****

On December 28, 1989 Mayor Harry "Butch" Felker issued two PROCLAMATIONS. One was humorous with such "Whereas-es" like…"Gary K. Clarke has developed finely-honed marketing and fund-raising skills, enabling him to educate you, tell a joke and pick your pocket all at the same time." The other was more customary and cited the growth and development of the zoo. Both proclamations, however, conferred upon me the title of "Zoo Director Emeritus" of the World Famous Topeka Zoo.

*****

It is one thing to receive a proclamation, and quite another to have an ode composed in your honor (and a very clever one, I might add).

Ode to Gary Clarke

Our days before us are somewhat dark,
Our zoo without its Gary Clarke.
For his decision has got us down,

He's sometimes teacher, mostly clown.
As Safari as I can see,
Our zoo's future will always be
Influenced by that one man
Bringing forth his master plan.
Someday they may name a park,
For lion-hearted Gary Clarke.
Topeka's proud of its dear zoo,
From all of us, our thanks to you.

Truly Yours,

Jeff Imparato (Staff member, Topeka Public Library)

P.S.
It wouldn't be lion to say that you left ostrich.
It's a parrot that other zoos will ape us to the Max.
It otter be said of Gary Clarke that he camel and went.
I s-hippos they'll say you were always Arusha-n around,
"He'll be back either today or Manyara," they'd say. – I tigress.
I'm sure it's not gnus to you, bat no one can kopje you.

*****

I was surprised to receive so many gratifying letters. Among them was a handwritten note from Nancy Landon Kassebaum, on official United States Senate letterhead. She wrote:

Dear Gary,

The zoo will just not seem the same without you. Over 25 years you have built a very special contribution to our community and state which will continue to be enjoyed by future generations.
That is a priceless gift. Thank you, thank you.
With appreciation and warmest regards,

Nancy

*****

And on official State of Kansas letterhead:

Dear Gary:

You are one dynamite individual. I have always marveled at your accomplishments and appreciate what you have done for the City of Topeka and for our great state. The "World Famous Topeka Zoo" is not just a place where animals are kept, but is an innovative and realistic portrayal of animals throughout the world that not only entertains, but teaches. You have left an indelible mark and many thousands for years to come will benefit from your brilliance.

I extend to you every good wish in your future endeavors.

Sincerely,

Robert T. Stephan
Attorney General

*****

And even a letter from San Francisco, California:

Dear Gary,

My mom sent me the article about your "Retirement." I can't imagine . . .
Hey—You're the guy with energy that reached beyond the city limits of Topeka, beyond the state lines of Kansas—in fact beyond anything anyone expected 25 years ago! How can you RETIRE!
Congratulations on the achievement of your vision, and your direction of a cause for the future, and your tomorrows.
You're one of a kind, and I'm happy to have been there at the beginning.

Best Wishes,

George Olson
(Former Photographer,
Topeka Capital-Journal)

*****

Then another surprise.

The 1990 calendar issued by Shawnee Federal Savings was a salute to the World Famous Topeka Zoo. The cover photo showed the electronic message center donated to the zoo by Shawnee Federal Savings and located at 10th and Gage (the message read HAPPY ZOO YEAR). Each month featured a photo of an animal or activity at the zoo.

The text inside the calendar read as follows:

This calendar is dedicated to **Gary K. Clarke**, *director of the Topeka Zoo for twenty-six years. Clarke became director at the age of twenty-four, and through his visiion and master plan development has seen the Zoo earn national recognition and rise to the title of "World Famous." He is the first to acknowledge that much of what has been accomplished would not have been possible without the support of the city and groups such as Friends of the Zoo and the Topeka Zoological Foundation.*

On December 31, 1989, Gary Clarke retired from the Topeka Zoo, but his accomplishments will live on for years to come. We join with all of Topeka in wishing him well in his new endeavors.

*****

Perhaps the most unexpected eventuality resulting from my retirement was the announcement about a new McDonald's restaurant. Following are excerpts from an article in *The Sunday Topeka Capital-Journal* dated October 15, 1989.

New McDonald's will honor Clarke
Restaurant to feature jungle theme
By Nancy Tompkins
Capital-Journal business writer

A jungle safari theme to honor retiring Topeka Zoo director Gary Clarke will be incorporated into a new McDonald's Restaurant at 12th and Gage, owner Bonnie Garrett said this week.

The building will have a mansard roof with wood shake shingles and khaki-tan colored bricks toward the rear of the building, appropriate to the safari theme, she said.

"It will be the first McDonald's ever to have a safari theme," she said. "It has been chosen to compliment the wonderful job that Gary Clarke has done at the zoo. I'm delighted to have a store close enough to the zoo to pick up that theme and to complement the neighborhood."

The interior decor will complement the safari theme with a waterfall, large murals depicting the jungle animals in their native habitat and there will probably be some three-dimensional replicas of jungle animals, she said. Employees will dress in safari uniforms, she said.

Plans currently are to include some indoor tropical trees. Garrett said she hopes to have simulated clouds on the ceiling and lighting that simulated sunrise and ending with a simulated sunset.

"This will give a real feeling of the jungle, within the limits of a restaurant," she said.

Other thematic effects will include the occasional sounds of elephants, hyenas and other jungle animals and animal footprints that track through the store and possibly over the counter.

Garrett said Clarke has volunteered to help create "authentic reproductions and safari images from his experiences in his travels to Africa."

Author's note: The world's only Safari McDonald's opened in early 1990 with great fanfare. At my request, they even featured banana milkshakes—a McDonald's first.

The Sequel

Less than a week after my last day at the zoo I was on Safari. The Associated Press ran a feature article in various newspapers across the country. Following is the story that appeared in *The Kansas City Star* on June 12, 1990.

Yearning for a safari?
You can start in Kansas
Retired director of Topeka Zoo likes sharing
the African continent with Midwestern visitors.

By Matt Truell
The Associated Press

TOPEKA—He calls his office, situated in the wilds of Topeka's Fairlawn Plaza shopping complex, his Main Camp.

Over a cup of Kenyan coffee, Gary Clarke, sometimes known as Mzee Shetani—Swahili for Old Devil—plans his next safari.

Clarke is unabashed about his sojourns to Africa—they are the stuff of dreams, of romance and adventure, of savanna and rain forests.

"I not only love Africa, I love sharing Africa," said Clarke, the only safari operator in Kansas, perhaps the only one in the Midwest. "It's like taking kids to Disneyland."

Clarke, who retired as director of the Topeka Zoo six months ago, took his first trip to Africa in 1974. Since then he has logged 26 trips and escorted almost 500 people to Africa, while starting Cowabunga Safaris.

The word "cowabunga" comes from the old Howdy Doody show, an exclamation used by Buffalo Bob whenever Clarabelle the Clown snuck up and honked his bicycle horn.

The word "safari" is Swahili for journey.

"It has come to mean going out to the African bush to see animals," Clarke said. He has seen most of them in the wild. Elephants, giraffe, cheetah, hippo, lion, gorillas.

Hunters can leave their rifles at home; this is photography only. Clarke figures he has at least 60,000 slides of African trips. But game animals are only part of a trip to the African bush.

"It's not just the animals," he said. "It's the sky and the rivers, the moutains and the valleys, the trees and the lakes. It is also the people and the cultures."

Clarke said he decided to give up his job as zoo director to become a safari operator when he climbed the highest mountain in Africa—Mount

Kilimanjaro in Tanzania—in January 1989.

"I wanted to stand on the roof of Africa," he said.

The six-day climb, which started in tropical rain forests and ended on a snow-covered peak, was both glorious and grueling for the intrepid zoo director.

"You don't conquer Kilimanjaro, you conquer yourself," he said.

He turned 50 on Kilimanjaro, thought about how his four children were grown and married, and how he really wanted to show others the beauty of the continent.

One year later he had left the zoo and set up his Main Camp near a discount store in Topeka.

A Cowabunga safari lasts two to four weeks. Clarke has taken people as young as 12 and as old as 85 on these jaunts through the rain forests and across savanna.

Most people think a trip to African bush is dangerous, Clarke said. That is a common misconception.

"We've had elephants go right through camp," he said. "The most dangerous part is getting through the airports."

"Snakes, poisonous or otherwise, are rare, and Kansas has more mosquitoes than central Africa," he said.

Clarke's trips into the bush might not be as physically demanding as some people might think. Some tours provide indoor accommodations during the entire safari, with hot and cold running water and three meals a day. Hardier travelers can canoe and camp along the banks of the Zambezi River, which runs through west-central Africa.

Still others have stayed in tree houses in the Hwange National Park in Zimbabwe and climbed aboard a hot air balloon operated by a man known as "the baboon pilot" in the Maasai Mara Game Reserve in Kenya.

Clarke said he does not dwell on the political problems in Africa and the emergence of a Westernized culture. He said his groups have never been caught in a coup or run into any roving bands of guerrillas.

But he said the Africa he has come to love is disappearing. Poachers are taking their awful toll in the animal preserves, especially in Kenya, Clarke said, although that problem appears to be under control.

"It's not just the animals," he said. "It's the people, the cultures, the flavor, the romance."

*****

And now, dear reader, I ask you in all seriousness: where, but Topeka, Kansas, could a "has been" zoo director be honored with a U.S. Postal Service special cancellation featuring his Swahili name, of all things? Read on from a article in . . .

The Topeka Capital-Journal, Thursday, March 29, 1990.

Philatelic thank-you to honor Gary Clarke

Gary Clarke, former director of the Topeka Zoo, will be honored with a special philatelic "thank you" arranged by the Topeka Zoological Foundation.

The event will be 10 a.m. to noon on April 7, when the U.S. Postal Service will provide a special cancellation to honor Clarke at the "Mzee Shetani Station" to be set up at the zoo. Mzee Shetani is Swahili for "Revered Old Man With a Devilish Nature."

The cancellation will be provided on a cacheted envelope that will be available for purchase at the station, and all purchasers will receive free admission to the zoo during the two hours.

The envelope's cachet is a drawing featuring significant additions to the zoo during Clarke's tenure as director, said Marjorie C. Schnacke, representing the Topeka Zoological Foundation. The envelope will bear an animal-related stamp that will be cancelled by the device with Clarke's likeness and appropriate wording.

Alice Sabatini, Topeka artist, did the artwork.

*****

Well over a decade after I retired from the zoo, a truly unexpected—and certainly most humbling—occurrence happened. It prompted the following editorial on June 30, 2003.

THE TOPEKA CAPITAL-JOURNAL

Volume 129, No. 242 • Monday, June 30, 2003

E D I T·O R I A L S

GARY CLARKE

World famous

Naming zoo education building after director who put it on the map is fitting

You'd almost need the memory of an elephant to remember what the Topeka Zoo was like when Gary Clarke was named director.

The year was 1963, and the zoo Clarke walked into that October morning was little more than a neighborhood pet collection. The zoo had one building, no fence around the perimeter and no reason to charge admission.

By the time he resigned 28 years later, that modest little zoo had become world famous, largely because of Clarke. He was the zoo's first professional director, but he was so much more — ambassador, promoter, entertainer, teacher.

It is entirely fitting, therefore, that the zoo's new education center will carry his name. Ground was broken Friday on the $850,000 Gary K. Clarke Education Center. In addition to housing the zoo's education programs, the building will house the gift shop and zoo offices and serve as the main entry the zoo.

No other person is so closely linked to the Topeka Zoo as Clarke, whose love affair and work with animals began when he was an 18-year-old animal keeper at the Kansas City Zoo. Six years later, Topeka contacted him, and at the age of 24, he became the youngest zoo director in the country.

One of the most innovative, too.

Clarke helped place Topeka in the zoological spotlight. After the Topeka Zoo won a national award and national attention in 1971 when the first golden eagle chick born in a zoo was born here, he quickly added the phrase "World Famous" to the zoo's unofficial title.

More important were his tangible accomplishments. During his 28 years as director, Clarke coordinated construction of most of the zoo's current buildings — Animals and Man, the Tropical Rain Forest, the Waterbird Lagoons, Discovering Apes and the Lions Pride — before he resigned in 1989 to concentrate full-time on his African safari business.

While it was Clarke who coined the phrase "World Famous Topeka Zoo," perhaps a more appropriate nickname would be "The Topeka Zoo Gary Clarke Made World Famous."

Groundbreaking took place on June 27, 2003. The Gary K. Clarke Education Center was dedicated on April 28, 2004. I was deeply honored to have this new building named after me—particularly since it provided much-needed educational facilities, and I've always felt education is the primary function of the zoo. As I have said, my concern is not that children remember how many bones are in a giraffe's neck, but that they gain a new appreciation of living animals, and develop an understanding of our natural world and responsibility for its stewardship. How gratifying to know that our zoo will be a resource for this to happen for future generations.

*****

And now, faithful reader, my last confession as I draft these final words in January of 2009.

It is more than half a century since my first day at the Kansas City Zoo in 1957, and nearly twenty years since I retired as zoo director in Topeka in 1989. During those years my life was <u>24/7 ZOO</u>. I miss it. The excitement of zoobiz will always be in my blood.

After zoobiz I devoted my full time to sharing Africa with people on a succession of safaris, completing safari number 140 in 2006. In that time my life was non-stop <u>AFRICA</u>. I miss it, too. The adventure of safari will always be a part of my spirit.

And yet, as I move into the third phase of my life during my 70th year, I am blessed with a sense of fulfillment and contentment. There is great satisfaction in living the cycle of each day—and each season—in Kansas, my birthplace. There is such joy in being with my ten bright, energetic grandchildren as they discover life's many facets and emerge from childhood into young adulthood.

The time is now to once more rejoice in the majesty of the Flint Hills, to savor my privileged role of grandfather, to listen again to the classics of music for their own sake, to read the finest literary works for the joy of reading . . . and, who knows—maybe to do a little more writing as well . . .